The author and his work

Francis Parkman (1823-1893), Boston born and Harvard educated, was a historian whose love of the wilderness and training in the classics found their most complete expression in his great life work: the ambitious, multi-volumed *France and England in North America.*

Best known and still most widely read today for *The Oregon Trail,* the stirring account of his Western adventures which appeared in 1849, Parkman projected *The Conspiracy of Pontiac* as his first work. He began to gather material for it in the summer of 1845 during an extensive field trip, and then postponed the book to participate in a hunting expedition in the Far West. Two years after *The Oregon Trail* was published, the story of Pontiac's rebellion was finished, inaugurating the series that was to occupy him for the next forty years.

Other volumes in what Parkman described as his "history of the American forest" include *Pioneers of France in the New World* (1865), *The Jesuits in North America in the Seventeenth Century* (1867), *The Discovery of the Great West* (1869), *The Old Regime in Canada* (1874), and *Count Frontenac and New France under Louis XIV* (1877).

The final two sections were *Montcalm and Wolfe* (1884) and *A Half-Century of Conflict* (1892). As with *The Conspiracy of Pontiac,* each was published in two volumes. All three of these works are now being made available by Collier Books in uniform, unabridged, one-volume paperback editions.

FRANCIS PARKMAN

A

OF

HALF-CENTURY CONFLICT

With a New Introduction by
SAMUEL ELIOT MORISON

COLLIER BOOKS
NEW YORK, N.Y.

Collier Books is a division of The Crowell-Collier Publishing
Company

First Collier Books Edition 1962

Introduction

THIS BOOK concluded Francis Parkman's series, *France and England in North America,* the volumes of which were not printed in chronological order. *The Conspiracy of Pontiac,* eighth in historical order, came out first, in 1851; *Pioneers of France in the New World,* which is Volume I, appeared in 1865. The next four were published in chronological order— *The Jesuits in North America in the Seventeenth Century* (1867); *The Discovery of the Great West* (1869—renamed *La Salle and the Discovery of the Great West* in the tenth edition of 1878); *The Old Régime in Canada* (1874); and *Count Frontenac and New France under Louis XIV* (1877). The author then skipped one and published *Montcalm and Wolfe* in 1884. It took him eight years to fill the one remaining gap with *A Half-Century of Conflict,* in 1892.

This title, one suspects, was a deliberate pun. The book did cover a fifty-year conflict between France and England, but it also ended the author's half-century of conflict with ill health, and marked the triumphant conclusion of his resolve, made at the age of eighteen in 1842, to write the story of France in North America.

Parkman, born in Boston in 1823, graduated from Harvard College in 1844, and in his sophomore year decided upon his life work. His first and still most famous book, *The Oregon Trail* (1849), was written after an expedition to the Far West in search of health, adventure, and firsthand knowledge of the American Indians. He had plenty of adventure shooting buffalo with a party of Sioux, and obtained an intimate knowledge of Indian psychology. But he sacrificed his already precarious health. During the rest of his life Parkman spent long months in semi-blindness, and suffered from arthritis and splitting headaches. But he refused to give up his youthful dream, and persisted through healthy intervals in the completion of his destined work. From the time *Montcalm and Wolfe* was finished, in 1884, he got only two or three hours sleep on an average during every twenty-four; and although he could still row a boat and work in his rose garden from a wheeled chair, he could walk but painfully, with two sticks. Nevertheless, he still managed to make an annual visit to the places he wrote about. June of 1886 he spent camping and fishing on the Batiscan River in Canada, then returned to Cambridge to take part in Harvard Commencement (as he was now a fellow of the Harvard corporation), and spent the latter half of the summer on the Rangeley Lakes. His last visit to France in search of documents and of expert medical treatment took place in 1887.

From that time on, Parkman followed a very careful regimen. Spring and fall were spent at his house on Jamaica Pond, which had been rebuilt in 1874. After his death this property was taken by the Commonwealth as part of the metropolitan park system, which (as official bodies love to do), pulled down the house and bulldozed the garden. Parkman's friends then erected a monument on the site, with an imaginary portrait of Pontiac in relief. Winters he spent at 50 Chestnut Street, Boston, with his sister Eliza or his niece Mrs. Cordner as housekeeper. There he chose for his study a small room with a northern exposure on the top floor, and had it connected by elevator with the ground floor. For sixty years after his death this room remained unchanged; and there, in the desk drawer, Mason Wade found Parkman's journals, for which other historians had searched high and low. The house, still standing, is marked by a tablet, but changed hands after Mrs. Cordner's death in 1955. The contents of Parkman's study were then removed to a room of the same shape and outlook at 87 Mount Vernon Street, the house of the Colonial Society of Massachusetts, to which Parkman was elected at its first meeting. There one may still see the same desk where he worked, the sofa where he reclined when being read to aloud, the wheeled chair he used when unable to walk, the wire frame which enabled him to write with closed eyes, and faded photographs and Indian trophies of the Oregon trail. Most of his working library went to Harvard, and the abundant transcripts of documents from foreign archives to the Massachusetts Historical Society.

During midsummer Parkman stayed with his married daughter, Mrs. J. Templeman Coolidge, in the old Governor Wentworth house at Little Harbor, New Hampshire, of which he has written a charming description in Chapter 18 of *A Half-Century of Conflict.*

In spite of his almost over-eager ambition to complete the series before being overtaken by senility, Parkman, between the ages of sixty and seventy, led the normal social life of a

Boston gentleman. He dined out and had friends to dinner, attended the monthly luncheons of the Saturday Club where Holmes the "Autocrat" held forth, and over which the aging Emerson shed his benign smile; attended meetings of his college classmates and of the Historical Society; helped to organize the convivial St. Botolph Club in 1880, and, as its first president, presided with relish over its Twelfth Night festivals, when the "brethren," dressed as monks, drank deep and roared out bawdy ballads. Barrett Wendell, who knew Parkman well, wrote that "there was always about his eyes and mouth an expression of kindly, alert interest in what was doing, which did away with the notion of severity," and another friend, Edward Wheelwright, mentions the "peculiar charm" of his smile. "It was not merely external: it seemed to arise in an inner consciousness, as it were, first stealing into his eyes, and spreading at last to the sensitive, flexible mouth. . . ." He was essentially an uncomplicated gentleman of simple rather than luxurious tastes, kindly, with a whimsical sense of humor, and naturally sociable. But he had dedicated his life to a great literary task, and that always came first.

In appearance, even in old age, Francis Parkman was a handsome man—well set up, alert in his movements, and with a soldier's rather than a scholar's carriage. In an age of luxurious whiskers, Parkman retained the clean-shaven fashion of his youth, Wheelwright wrote, "no beard disguised the high-bred refinement of his face, or hid the varying expressions of his sensitive mouth, where gentleness was joined to strength." Another friend, the Abbé Casgrain, said: "The fashion of his youth, Wheelwright wrote. "no beard disguised that Leonardo da Vinci loved to paint: a harmonious combination of intelligence, *finesse* and energy; large forehead, finely sculptured nose, strong and prominent chin." Friends visiting Venice were struck by the resemblance of Verrochio's head of Bartolomeo Colleoni to Parkman's, and a photograph of the famous equestrian statue in the historian's study indicates that the comparison pleased him. For Parkman would have enjoyed being a man of action, such as a cavalry officer in the Civil War; and it was his ambition in that direction, thwarted by ill health, which gave him complete understanding of men of action in history such as Champlain, La Salle, Montclam, Wolfe and Sir William Pepperell. This trait attracted Theodore Roosevelt to Parkman; *The Winning of the West* is dedicated to him.

In religion, Parkman was brought up a Unitarian, his father having been a Unitarian minister; and, while he never broke with that denomination, and occasionally attended divine service, he described himself as a "reverent agnostic." He made an earnest effort to understand and appreciate the Catholic point of view, even though he was unable to share that faith. Although a descendant, on his mother's side, of the Reverend John Cotton, one of the Puritan founders of New England, Parkman detested the Puritan pastors as much as he did Jesuit politicians; he is always on the side of the layman against the cleric. Note the relish with which he describes the brawl between Carheil and Cadillac in Chapter 2 of the present work; one feels that Parkman wished that Cadillac had given the fist-brandishing cleric that sock in the jaw, as he was tempted to do.

A Half-Century of Conflict was published, in two volumes, in 1892, when Parkman was in his seventieth year. It shows all the vigor of his style forty years earlier, with a maturer wisdom and judgment of men and sources. It contains four of the finest historical narratives by his, or any other, pen: the founding of Detroit by Cadillac (Chapter 2), the assault on Deerfield in 1704 (Chapter 4), the founding of Louisiana (Chapter 13) and the first Siege of Louisbourg (Chapters 18-20). Others have written on these themes, but never so well. Several Canadians, both English and French, somewhat jealous of the fame of this New England Yankee, have promised to write histories that would supersede his, but they never have. And I doubt whether they, or anyone else, ever will. Parkman's histories, as John Fiske predicted, are "for all mankind and for all time," like those of Gibbon, Macaulay and Prescott.

After the publication of *A Half-Century of Conflict* Parkman had only one more year of life. That year he improved to write fifty additional pages, on "The Feudal Chiefs of Acadia," for the twenty-ninth edition of *The Old Régime in Canada*. This appeared at the time of his seventieth birthday, September 16, 1893, which friends celebrated with him at his home on Jamaica Pond. In November he suffered a severe attack of peritonitis, and on the eighth day of that month he died.

Shortly after, Robert Beverley Hale, a minor poet of the time, published this touching sonnet to a major historian:

With youth's blue sky and streaming sunlight blest,
    And flushed with hope, he set himself to trace
    The fading footprints of a banished race,
Unmindful of the storm-clouds in the west.
In silent pain and torments unconfessed,
    Determination written on his face,
    He struggled on, nor faltered in his pace
Until his work was done and he could rest.

He was no frightened paleface stumbling through
    An unknown forest, wandering round and round,
Like his own Indians, with instinct fine
He knew his trail, though none saw how he knew
    Reckoned his time, and reached his camping-ground
Just as the first white stars began to shine.

SAMUEL ELIOT MORISON

References

Van Wyck Brooks, *New England: Indian Summer* (New York: Dutton, 1940), chap. viii. A notable description and appreciation.

Henri-Raymond Casgrain, *Francis Parkman* (Quebec: 1872); reprinted in his *Oeuvres complètes* (Quebec: 1885), II 294-335. A hitherto unprinted account of his visit to Parkman in 1871 is translated in S. E. Morison, *The Parkman Reader*, 4-7. Parkman's letters to Casgrain are printed serially in *Le Canada français* XXIX (1942), as well as in the Jacobs edition, below.

Francis Doughty, *Francis Parkman* (New York: The Macmillan Company, 1962). Chapter xv contains the comments on this volume.

Charles H. Farnham, *A Life of Francis Parkman* (Boston: Little, Brown, 1900) and included in several sets of Parkman's Works. Farnham was Parkman's secretary during the period when he wrote *Half-Century*. A sensitive appreciation.

Wilbur R. Jacobs (ed.), *Letters of Francis Parkman*, 2 vols. (Norman: University of Oklahoma Press, 1960). Volume II contains his letters of the period when he was writing *Half-Century*.

Henry D. Sedgwick, *Francis Parkman* (Boston: Houghton Mifflin Co., 1904). Includes in an appendix a brief autobiography.

Richard Sonderegger, *Francis Parkman* (Mexico, D. F.: Instituto Panamericano de Geografia e Historia, 1951). Also in Spanish translation. A charming sketch by a young Western historian, with analysis of Parkman's style.

Mason Wade, *Francis Parkman, Heroic Historian* (New York: Viking Press, 1942). The best biography.

Barrett Wendell, "Francis Parkman" in *Proceedings*, American Academy of Arts and Sciences XXIX (1894) 435-77. Excellent analysis of his style, and firsthand impressions of his personality.

Edward Wheelwright, "Memoir of Francis Parkman" in *Publications*, Colonial Society of Massachusetts I (1895) 305-50. By a close friend and classmate.

Preface

THIS BOOK, forming Part VI. of the series called France and England in North America, fills the gap between Part V., "Count Frontenac," and Part VII., "Montcalm and Wolfe"; so that the series now forms a continuous history of the efforts of France to occupy and control this continent.

In the present volumes the nature of the subject does not permit an unbroken thread of narrative, and the unity of the book lies in its being throughout, in one form or another, an illustration of the singularly contrasted characters and methods of the rival claimants to North America.

Like the rest of the series, this work is founded on original documents. The statements of secondary writers have been accepted only when found to conform to the evidence of contemporaries, whose writings have been sifted and collated with the greatest care. As extremists on each side have charged me with favoring the other, I hope I have been unfair to neither.

The manuscript material collected for the preparation of the series now complete forms about seventy volumes, most of them folios. These have been given by me from time to time to the Massachusetts Historical Society, in whose library they now are, open to the examination of those interested in the subjects of which they treat. The collection was begun forty-five years ago, and its formation has been exceedingly slow, having been retarded by difficulties which seemed insurmountable, and for years were so in fact. Hence the completion of the series has required twice the time that would have sufficed under less unfavorable conditions.

BOSTON, March 26, 1892.

Contents

Chapter 1

1700–1713
Eve of War

THE WAR which in the British colonies was called Queen Anne's War, and in England the War of the Spanish Succession, was the second of a series of four conflicts which ended in giving to Great Britain a maritime and colonial preponderance over France and Spain. So far as concerns the colonies and the sea, these several wars may be regarded as a single protracted one, broken by intervals of truce. The three earlier of them, it is true, were European contests, begun and waged on European disputes. Their American part was incidental and apparently subordinate, yet it involved questions of prime importance in the history of the world.

The War of the Spanish Succession sprang from the ambition of Louis XIV. We are apt to regard the story of that gorgeous monarch as a tale that is told; but his influence shapes the life of nations to this day. At the beginning of his reign two roads lay before him, and it was a momentous question for posterity, as for his own age, which one of them he would choose,—whether he would follow the wholesome policy of his great minister Colbert, or obey his own vanity and arrogance, and plunge France into exhausting wars; whether he would hold to the principle of tolerance embodied in the Edict of Nantes, or do the work of fanaticism and priestly ambition. The one course meant prosperity, progress, and the rise of a middle class; the other meant bankruptcy and the Dragonades,—and this was the King's choice. Crushing taxation, misery, and ruin followed, till France burst out at last in a frenzy, drunk with the wild dreams of Rousseau. Then came the Terror and the Napoleonic wars, and reaction on reaction, revolution on revolution, down to our own day.

Louis placed his grandson on the throne of Spain, and insulted England by acknowledging as her rightful King the son of James II., whom she had deposed. Then England declared war. Canada and the northern British colonies had had but a short breathing time since the Peace of Ryswick; both were tired of slaughtering each other, and both needed rest. Yet before the declaration of war, the Canadian officers of the Crown prepared, with their usual energy, to meet the expected crisis. One of them wrote: "If war be declared, it is certain that the King can very easily conquer and ruin New England." The French of Canada often use the name "New England" as applying to the British colonies in general. They are twice as populous as Canada, he goes on to say; but the people are great cowards, totally undisciplined, and ignorant of war, while the Canadians are brave, hardy, and well trained. We have, besides, twenty-eight companies of regulars, and could raise six thousand warriors from our Indian allies. Four thousand men could easily lay waste all the northern English colonies, to which end we must have five ships of war, with one thousand troops on board, who must land at Penobscot, where they must be joined by two thousand regulars, militia, and Indians, sent from Canada by way of the Chaudière and the Kennebec. Then the whole force must go to Portsmouth, take it by assault, leave a garrison there, and march to Boston, laying waste all the towns and villages by the way; after destroying Boston, the army must march for New York, while the fleet follows along the coast. "Nothing could be easier," says the writer, "for the road is good, and there is plenty of horses and carriages. The troops would ruin everything as they advanced, and New York would quickly be destroyed and burned."[1]

Another plan, scarcely less absurd, was proposed about the same time by the celebrated Le Moyne d'Iberville. The essential point, he says, is to get possession of Boston; but there are difficulties and risks in the way. Nothing, he adds, referring to the other plan, seems difficult to persons without experience; but unless we are prepared to raise a great and costly armament, our only hope is in surprise. We should make it in winter, when the seafaring population, which is the chief strength of the place, is absent on long voyages. A thousand Canadians, four hundred regulars, and as many Indians should leave Quebec in November, ascend the Chaudière, then descend the Kennebec, approach Boston under cover of the forest, and carry it by a night attack. Apparently he did not know that but for its lean neck—then but a few yards wide —Boston was an island, and that all around for many leagues

[1] *Premier Projet pour L'Expédition contre la Nouvelle Angleterre*, 1701. *Second Projet*, etc. Compare *N. Y. Col. Docs.*, ix. 725.

the forest that was to have covered his approach had already
been devoured by numerous busy settlements. He offers to
lead the expedition, and declares that if he is honored with
the command, he will warrant that the New England capital
will be forced to submit to King Louis, after which New
York can be seized in its turn.[2]

In contrast to these incisive proposals, another French
officer breathed nothing but peace. Brouillan, governor of
Acadia, wrote to the governor of Massachusetts to suggest
that, with the consent of their masters, they should make a
treaty of neutrality. The English governor being dead, the
letter came before the council, who received it coldly. Canada,
and not Acadia, was the enemy they had to fear. Moreover,
Boston merchants made good profit by supplying the Acadians
with necessaries which they could get in no other way; and
in time of war these profits, though lawless, were greater than
in time of peace. But what chiefly influenced the council
against the overtures of Brouillan was a passage in his letter
reminding them that, by the Treaty of Ryswick, the New
England people had no right to fish within sight of the
Acadian coast. This they flatly denied, saying that the New
England people had fished there time out of mind, and that
if Brouillan should molest them, they would treat it as an
act of war.[3]

While the New England colonies, and especially Massachusetts and New Hampshire, had most cause to deprecate a
war, the prospect of one was also extremely unwelcome to
the people of New York. The conflict lately closed had
borne hard upon them through the attacks of the enemy, and
still more through the derangement of their industries. They
were distracted, too, with the factions rising out of the recent
revolution under Jacob Leisler. New York had been the bul-
wark of the colonies farther south, who, feeling themselves

[2] *Mémoire du Sieur d'Iberville sur Boston et ses Dépendances,*
1700 (1701?). Baron de Saint-Castin also drew up a plan for
attacking Boston in 1702 with lists of necessary munitions and
other supplies.

[3] *Brouillan à Bellomont,* 10 *Août,* 1701. *Conseil de Baston
à Brouillan,* 22 *Août,* 1701. Brouillan acted under royal orders,
having been told, in case of war being declared, to propose a treaty
with New England, unless he should find that he can "se garantir
des insultes des Anglais" and do considerable harm to their trade,
in which case he is to make no treaty. *Mémoire du Roy au Sieur
de Brouillan,* 23 *Mars,* 1700.

safe, had given their protector little help, and that little grudg-
ingly, seeming to regard the war as no concern of theirs. Three
thousand and fifty-one pounds, provincial currency, was the
joint contribution of Virginia, Maryland, East Jersey, and
Connecticut to the aid of New York during five years of the
later war.[4] Massachusetts could give nothing, even if she
would, her hands being full with the defence of her own
borders. Colonel Quary wrote to the Board of Trade that New
York could not bear alone the cost of defending herself; that
the other colonies were "stuffed with commonwealth notions,"
and were "of a sour temper in opposition to government," so
that Parliament ought to take them in hand and compel each
to do its part in the common cause.[5] To this Lord Cornbury
adds that Rhode Island and Connecticut are even more stubborn than the rest, hate all true subjects of the Queen, and
will not give a farthing to the war so long as they can help
it.[6] Each province lived in selfish isolation, recking little of its
neighbor's woes.

New York, left to fight her own battles, was in a wretched
condition for defence. It is true that, unlike the other colonies,
the King had sent her a few soldiers, counting at this time
about one hundred and eighty, all told;[7] but they had been left
so long without pay that they were in a state of scandalous
destitution. They would have been left without rations had
not three private gentlemen—Schuyler, Livingston, and Cort-
landt—advanced money for their supplies, which seems never
to have been repaid.[8] They are reported to have been "without shirts, breeches, shoes, or stockings," and "in such a
shameful condition that the women when passing them are
obliged to cover their eyes." "The Indians ask," says the
governor, " 'Do you think us such fools as to believe that a
king who cannot clothe his soldiers can protect us from the
French, with their fourteen hundred men all well equipped?' "[9]

The forts were no better than their garrisons. The governor
complains that those of Albany and Schenectady "are so
weak and ridiculous that they look more like pounds for cattle

[4] Schuyler, *Colonial New York,* i. 431, 432.
[5] *Colonel Quary to the Lords of Trade,* 16 *June,* 1703.
[6] *Cornbury to the Lords of Trade,* 9 *September,* 1703.
[7] *Bellomont to the Lords of Trade,* 28 *February,* 1700.
[8] *Ibid.*
[9] Schuyler, *Colonial New York,* i. 488.

than forts." At Albany the rotten stockades were falling from their own weight.

If New York had cause to complain of those whom she sheltered, she herself gave cause of complaint to those who sheltered her. The Five Nations of the Iroquois had always been her allies against the French, had guarded her borders and fought her battles. What they wanted in return were gifts, attentions, just dealings, and active aid in war; but they got them in scant measure. Their treatment by the province was short-sighted, if not ungrateful. New York was a mixture of races and religions not yet fused into a harmonious body politic, divided in interests and torn with intestine disputes. Its Assembly was made up in large part of men unfitted to pursue a consistent scheme of policy, or spend the little money at their disposal on any objects but those of present and visible interest. The royal governors, even when personally competent, were hampered by want of means and by factious opposition. The Five Nations were robbed by land-speculators, cheated by traders, and feebly supported in their constant wars with the French. Spasmodically, as it were, on occasions of crisis, they were summoned to Albany, soothed with such presents as could be got from unwilling legislators, or now and then from the Crown, and exhorted to fight vigorously in the common cause. The case would have been far worse but for a few patriotic men, with Peter Schuyler at their head, who understood the character of these Indians, and labored strenuously to keep them in what was called their allegiance.

The proud and fierce confederates had suffered greatly in the late war. Their numbers had been reduced about one half, and they now counted little more than twelve hundred warriors. They had learned a bitter and humiliating lesson, and their arrogance had changed to distrust and alarm. Though hating the French, they had learned to respect their military activity and prowess, and to look askance on the Dutch and English, who rarely struck a blow in their defence, and suffered their hereditary enemy to waste their fields and burn their towns. The English called the Five Nations British subjects, on which the French taunted them with being British slaves, and told them that the King of England had ordered the governor of New York to poison them. This invention had great effect. The Iroquois capital, Onondaga, was filled with wild rumors. The credulous savages were tossed among doubts, suspicions, and fears. Some were in terror of poison, and some of witchcraft. They believed that the rival European nations had leagued to destroy them and divide their lands, and that they were bewitched by sorcerers, both French and English.[10]

After the Peace of Ryswick, and even before it, the French governor kept agents among them. Some of these were soldiers, like Joncaire, Maricourt, or Longueuil, and some were Jesuits, like Bruyas, Lamberville, or Vaillant. The Jesuits showed their usual ability and skill in their difficult and perilous task. The Indians derived various advantages from their presence, which they regarded also as a flattering attention; while the English, jealous of their influence, made feeble attempts to counteract it by sending Protestant clergymen to Onondaga. "But," writes Lord Bellomont, "it is next to impossible to prevail with the ministers to live among the Indians. They [the Indians] are so nasty as never to wash their hands, or the utensils they dress their victuals with."[11] Even had their zeal been proof to these afflictions, the ministers would have been no match for their astute opponents. In vain Bellomont assured the Indians that the Jesuits were "the greatest lyars and impostors in the world."[12] In vain he offered a hundred dollars for every one of them whom they should deliver into his hands. They would promise to expel them; but their minds were divided, and they stood in fear of one another. While one party distrusted and disliked the priests, another was begging the governor of Canada to send more. Others took a practical view of the question. "If the English sell goods cheaper than the French, we will have ministers; if the French sell them cheaper than the English, we will have priests." Others, again, wanted neither Jesuits nor ministers, "because both of you [English and French] have made us drunk with the noise of your praying."[13]

The aims of the propagandists on both sides were secular. The French wished to keep the Five Nations neutral in the event of another war; the English wished to spur them to active hostility; but while the former pursued their purpose with energy and skill, the efforts of the latter were intermittent and generally feeble.

[10] *N. Y. Col. Docs.*, iv. 658.
[11] *Bellomont to the Lords of Trade*, 17 *October*, 1700.
[12] *Conference of Bellomont with the Indians*, 26 *August*, 1700.
[13] *Journal of Bleeker and Schuyler on their visit to Onondaga*, *August, September*, 1701.

"The Nations," writes Schuyler, "are full of factions." There was a French party and an English party in every town, especially in Onondaga, the centre of intrigue. French influence was strongest at the western end of the confederacy, among the Senecas, where the French officer Joncaire, an Iroquois by adoption, had won many to France; and it was weakest at the eastern end, among the Mohawks, who were nearest to the English settlements. Here the Jesuits had labored long and strenuously in the work of conversion, and from time to time they had led their numerous proselytes to remove to Canada, where they settled at St. Louis, or Caughnawaga, on the right bank of the St. Lawrence, a little above Montreal, where their descendants still remain. It is said that at the beginning of the eighteenth century two-thirds of the Mohawks had thus been persuaded to cast their lot with the French, and from enemies to become friends and allies. Some of the Oneidas and a few of the other Iroquois nations joined them and strengthened the new mission settlement; and the Caughnawagas afterwards played an important part between the rival European colonies.

The "Far Indians," or "Upper Nations," as the French called them, consisted of the tribes of the Great Lakes and adjacent regions, Ottawas, Pottawattamies, Sacs, Foxes, Sioux, and many more. It was from these that Canada drew the furs by which she lived. Most of them were nominal friends and allies of the French, who in the interest of trade strove to keep these wild-cats from tearing one another's throats, and who were in constant alarm lest they should again come to blows with their old enemies, the Five Nations, in which case they would call on Canada for help, thus imperilling those pacific relations with the Iroquois confederacy which the French were laboring constantly to secure.

In regard to the "Far Indians," the French, the English, and the Five Iroquois Nations all had distinct and opposing interests. The French wished to engross their furs, either by inducing the Indians to bring them down to Montreal, or by sending traders into their country to buy them. The English, with a similar object, wished to divert the "Far Indians" from Montreal and draw them to Albany; but this did not suit the purpose of the Five Nations, who, being sharp politicians and keen traders, as well as bold and enterprising warriors, wished to act as middle-men between the beaver-hunting tribes and the Albany merchants, well knowing that good profit might

thus accrue. In this state of affairs the converted Iroquois
settled at Caughnawaga played a peculiar part. In the province of New York, goods for the Indian trade were of excellent quality and comparatively abundant and cheap; while
among the French, especially in time of war, they were often
scarce and dear. The Caughnawagas accordingly, whom neither the English nor the French dared offend, used their position to carry on a contraband trade between New York and
Canada. By way of Lake Champlain and the Hudson they
brought to Albany furs from the country of the "Far Indians,"
and exchanged them for guns, blankets, cloths, knives, beads,
and the like. These they carried to Canada and sold to the
French traders, who in this way, and often in this alone, supplied themselves with the goods necessary for bartering furs
from the "Far Indians." This lawless trade of the Caughnawagas went on even in time of war; and opposed as it was
to every principle of Canadian policy, it was generally con-
nived at by the French authorities as the only means of obtaining the goods necessary for keeping their Indian allies in
good humor.

It was injurious to English interests; but the fur-traders of
Albany and also the commissioners charged with Indian
affairs, being Dutchmen converted by force into British subjects, were, with a few eminent exceptions, cool in their devotion to the British Crown; while the merchants of the port of
New York, from whom the fur-traders drew their supplies,
thought more of their own profits than of the public good. The
trade with Canada through the Caughnawagas not only gave
aid and comfort to the enemy, but continually admitted spies
into the colony, from whom the governor of Canada gained
information touching English movements and designs.

The Dutch traders of Albany and the importing merchants
who supplied them with Indian goods had a strong interest in
preventing active hostilities with Canada, which would have
spoiled their trade. So, too, and for similar reasons, had influ-
ential persons in Canada. The French authorities, moreover,
thought it impolitic to harass the frontiers of New York by
war parties, since the Five Nations might come to the aid of
their Dutch and English allies, and so break the peaceful relations which the French were anxious to maintain with them.
Thus it happened that, during the first six or seven years of the
eighteenth century, there was a virtual truce between Canada
and New York, and the whole burden of the war fell upon

New England, or rather upon Massachusetts, with its outlying district of Maine and its small and weak neighbor, New
Hampshire.[14]

[14] The foregoing chapter rests on numerous documents in the
Public Record Office, Archives de la Marine, Archives Nationales,
N. Y. Colonial Documents, vols. iv. v. ix., and the *Second and
Third Series of the Correspondance Officielle* at Ottawa.

Chapter 2

1694–1704
Detroit

IN THE FEW YEARS of doubtful peace that preceded Queen Anne's War, an enterprise was begun, which, nowise in accord with the wishes and expectations of those engaged in it, was destined to produce as its last result an American city.

Antoine de La Mothe-Cadillac commanded at Michilimackinac, whither Frontenac had sent him in 1694. This old mission of the Jesuits, where they had gathered the remnants of the lake tribes dispersed by the Iroquois at the middle of the seventeenth century, now savored little of its apostolic beginnings. It was the centre of the western fur-trade and the favorite haunt of the *coureurs de bois*. Brandy and squaws abounded, and according to the Jesuit Carheil, the spot where Marquette had labored was now a witness of scenes the most unedifying.

At Michilimackinac was seen a curious survival of Huron-Iroquois customs. The villages of the Hurons and Ottawas, which were side by side, separated only by a fence, were surrounded by a common enclosure of triple palisades, which, with the addition of loop-holes for musketry, were precisely like those seen by Cartier at Hochelaga, and by Champlain in the Onondaga country. The dwellings which these defences enclosed were also after the old Huron-Iroquois pattern,—those long arched structures covered with bark which Brébeuf found by the shores of Matchedash Bay, and Jogues on the banks of the Mohawk. Besides the Indians, there was a French colony at the place, chiefly of fur-traders, lodged in log-cabins, roofed with cedar bark, and forming a street along the shore close to the palisaded villages of the Hurons and Ottawas. The fort, known as Fort Buade, stood at the head of the little bay.[1]

The Hurons and Ottawas were thorough savages, though the Hurons retained the forms of Roman Catholic Christianity. This tribe, writes Cadillac, "are reduced to a very small

[1] *Relation de La Mothe-Cadillac,* in Margry, v. 75.

number; and it is well for us that they are, for they are ill-disposed and mischievous, with a turn for intrigue and a capacity for large undertakings. Luckily, their power is not great; but as they cannot play the lion, they play the fox, and do their best to make trouble between us and our allies."

La Mothe-Cadillac[2] was a captain in the colony troops, and an admirer of the late governor, Frontenac, to whose policy he adhered, and whose prejudices he shared. He was amply gifted with the kind of intelligence that consists in quick observation, sharpened by an inveterate spirit of sarcasm, was energetic, enterprising, well instructed, and a bold and some-times a visionary schemer, with a restless spirit, a nimble and biting wit, a Gascon impetuosity of temperament, and as much devotion as an officer of the King was forced to profess, coupled with small love of priests and an aversion to Jesuits.[3] Carheil and Marest, missionaries of that order at Michili-mackinac, were objects of his especial antipathy, which they fully returned. The two priests were impatient of a military commandant to whose authority they were in some small measure subjected; and they imputed to him the disorders which he did not, and perhaps could not, prevent. They were opposed also to the traffic in brandy, which was favored by Cadillac on the usual ground that it attracted the Indians, and so prevented the English from getting control of the fur-trade, —an argument which he reinforced by sanitary considera-tions based on the supposed unwholesomeness of the fish and smoked meat which formed the chief diet of Michilimackinac.

[2] He wrote his name as above. It is often written La Motte, which has the advantage of conveying the pronunciation unequivo-cally to an unaccustomed English ear. La Mothe-Cadillac came of a good family of Languedoc. His father, Jean de La Mothe, seigneur de Cadillac et de Launay, or Laumet, was a counsellor in the Parliament of Toulouse. The date of young Cadillac's birth is uncertain. The register of his marriage places it in 1661, and that of his death in 1657. Another record, cited by Farmer in his *History of Detroit*, makes it 1658. In 1703 he himself declared that he was forty-seven years old. After serving as lieutenant in the regiment of Clairembault, he went to Canada about the year 1683. He became skilled in managing Indians, made himself well ac-quainted with the coasts of New England, and strongly urged an attack by sea on New York and Boston, as the only sure means of securing French ascendency. He was always in opposition to the clerical party.

[3] See *La Mothe-Cadillac à* ——, 3 *Août*, 1695.

"A little brandy after the meal," he says, with the solemnity of the learned Purgon, "seems necessary to cook the bilious meats and the crudities they leave in the stomach."[4]

Cadillac calls Carheil, superior of the mission, the most passionate and domineering man he ever knew, and further declares that the Jesuit tried to provoke him to acts of violence, in order to make matter of accusation against him. If this was Carheil's aim, he was near succeeding. Once, in a dispute with the commandant on the brandy-trade, he upbraided him sharply for permitting it; to which Cadillac replied that he only obeyed the orders of the Court. The Jesuit rejoined that he ought to obey God, and not man,—"on which," says the commandant, "I told him that his talk smelt of sedition a hundred yards off, and begged that he would amend it. He told me that I gave myself airs that did not belong to me, holding his fist before my nose at the same time. I confess I almost forgot that he was a priest, and felt for a moment like knocking his jaw out of joint; but, thank God, I contented myself with taking him by the arm, pushing him out, and ordering him not to come back."[5]

Such being the relations of the commandant and the Father Superior, it is not surprising to find the one complaining that he cannot get absolved from his sins, and the other painting the morals and manners of Michilimackinac in the blackest colors.

I have spoken elsewhere of the two opposing policies that divided Canada,—the policies of concentration and of expansion, on the one hand leaving the west to the keeping of the Jesuits, and confining the population to the borders of the St. Lawrence; on the other, the occupation of the interior of the continent by posts of war and trade. Through the force of events the latter view had prevailed; yet while the military chiefs of Canada could not but favor it, the Jesuits were unwilling to accept it, and various interests in the colony still

[4] *La Mothe-Cadillac à* ——, 3 *Août,* 1695.

[5] "Il me dit que je me donnois des airs qui ne m'appartenoient pas, en me portant le poing au nez. Je vous avoue, Monsieur, que je pensai oublier qu'il étoit prêtre, et que je vis le moment où j'allois luy démonter la mâchoire; mais, Dieu merci, je me contentai de le prendre par le bras et de le pousser dehors, avec ordre de n'y plus rentrer." Margry, v. (author's edition), Introduction, civ. This introduction, with other editorial matter, is omitted in the edition of M. Margry's valuable collection, printed under a vote of the American Congress.

opposed it openly or secretly. Frontenac had been its strongest champion, and Cadillac followed in his steps. It seemed to him that the time had come for securing the west for France.

The strait—*détroit*—which connects Lake Huron with Lake Erie was the most important of all the western passes. It was the key of the three upper lakes, with the vast countries watered by their tributaries, and it gave Canada her readiest access to the valley of the Mississippi. If the French held it, the English would be shut out from the northwest; if, as seemed likely, the English should seize it, the Canadian fur-trade would be ruined.[6] The possession of it by the French would be a constant curb and menace to the Five Nations, as well as a barrier between those still formidable tribes and the western Indians, allies of Canada; and when the intended French establishment at the mouth of the Mississippi should be made, Detroit would be an indispensable link of communication between Canada and Louisiana.

Denonville had recognized the importance of the position, and it was by his orders that Greysolon Du Lhut, in 1686, had occupied it for a time, and built a picket fort near the site of Fort Gratiot.[7]

It would be idle to imagine that the motives of Cadillac were wholly patriotic. Fur-trading interests were deeply involved in his plans, and bitter opposition was certain. The fur-trade, in its nature, was a constant breeder of discord. The people of Montreal would have the tribes come down every summer from the west and northwest and hold a fair under the palisades of their town. It is said that more than four hundred French families lived wholly or in part by this home trade, and therefore regarded with deep jealousy the establishment of interior posts, which would forestall it. Again, every new western post would draw away trade from those already established, and every trading license granted to a company or an individual would rouse the animosity of those who had been licensed before. The prosperity of Detroit would be the ruin of Michilimackinac, and those whose interests centred at the latter post angrily opposed the scheme of Cadillac.

He laid his plans before Count de Maurepas by a characteristic memorial, apparently written in 1699. In this he proposed to gather all the tribes of the lakes at Detroit, civi-

[6] Robert Livingston urged the occupation of Detroit as early as 1700. *N. Y. Col. Docs.*, iv. 650.

[7] *Denonville à Du Lhut*, 6 *Juin*, 1686. Count Frontenac, 133.

lize them and teach them French, "insomuch that from pagans they would become children of the Church, and therefore good subjects of the King." They will form, he continues, a considerable settlement, "strong enough to bring the English and the Iroquois to reason, or, with help from Montreal, to destroy both of them." Detroit, he adds, should be the seat of trade, which should not be permitted in the countries beyond it. By this regulation the intolerable glut of beaver-skins, which spoils the market, may be prevented. This proposed restriction of the beaver-trade to Detroit was enough in itself to raise a tempest against the whole scheme. "Cadillac well knows that he has enemies," pursues the memorial, "but he keeps on his way without turning or stopping for the noise of the puppies who bark after him."[8]

Among the essential features of his plan was a well-garrisoned fort, and a church, served not by Jesuits alone, but also by Récollet friars and priests of the Missions Étrangères. The idea of this ecclesiastical partnership was odious to the Jesuits, who felt that the west was their proper field, and that only they had a right there. Another part of Cadillac's proposal pleased them no better. This was his plan of civilizing the Indians and teaching them to speak French; for it was the reproach of the Jesuit missions that they left the savage a savage still, and asked little of him but the practice of certain rites and the passive acceptance of dogmas to him incomprehensible.

"It is essential," says the memorial, "that in this matter of teaching the Indians our language the missionaries should act in good faith, and that his Majesty should have the goodness to impose his strictest orders upon them; for which there are several good reasons. The first and most stringent is that when members of religious orders or other ecclesiastics undertake anything, they never let it go. The second is that by not teaching French to the Indians they make themselves necessary [as interpreters] to the King and the governor. The third is that if all Indians spoke French, all kinds of ecclesiastics would be able to instruct them. This might cause them [the Jesuits] to lose some of the presents they get; for though these Reverend Fathers come here only for the glory of God, yet the one thing does not prevent the other,"—meaning that God and

[8] "Sans se destourner et sans s'arrester au bruit des jappereaux qui crient après luy."—*Mémoir ede La Mothe-Cadillac adressé au Comte de Maurepas.*

Mammon may be served at once. "Nobody can deny that the priests own three quarters of Canada. From St. Paul's Bay to Quebec, there is nothing but the seigniory of Beauport that belongs to a private person. All the rest, which is the best part, belongs to the Jesuits or other ecclesiastics. The Upper Town of Quebec is composed of six or seven superb palaces belonging to Hospital Nuns, Ursulines, Jesuits, Récollets, Seminary priests, and the bishop. There may be some forty private houses, and even these pay rent to the ecclesiastics, which shows that *the one thing does not prevent the other*." From this it will be seen that, in the words of one of his enemies, Cadillac "was not quite in the odor of sanctity."

"One may as well knock one's head against a wall," concludes the memorial, "as hope to convert the Indians in any other way [than that of civilizing them]; for thus far all the fruits of the missions consist in the baptism of infants who die before reaching the age of reason."[9] This was not literally true, though the results of the Jesuit missions in the west had been meagre and transient to a surprising degree.

Cadillac's plan of a settlement at Detroit was not at first received with favor by Callières, the governor; while the intendant Champigny, a fast friend of the Jesuits, strongly opposed it. By their order the chief inhabitants of Quebec met at the Château St. Louis,—Callières, Champigny, and Cadillac himself being present. There was a heated debate on the beaver-trade, after which the intendant commanded silence, explained the projects of Cadillac, and proceeded to oppose them. His first point was that the natives should not be taught French, because the Indian girls brought up at the Ursuline Convent led looser lives than the young squaws who had received no instruction, while it was much the same with the boys brought up at the Seminary.

"M. de Champigny," returned the sarcastic Cadillac, "does great honor to the Ursulines and the Seminary. It is true that some Indian women who have learned our language have lived viciously; but that is because their teachers were too stiff with them, and tried to make them nuns."[10]

Champigny's position, as stated by his adversary, was that "all intimacy of the Indians with the French is dangerous and corrupting to their morals," and that their only safety lies in

[9] *Mémoire adressé au Comte de Maurepas*, in Margry, v. 138.
[10] La Mothe-Cadillac, *Rapport au Ministre*, 1700, in Margry, v. 157.

keeping them at a distance from the settlements. This was the view of the Jesuits, and there is much to be said in its favor; but it remains not the less true that conversion must go hand in hand with civilization, or it is a failure and a fraud.

Cadillac was not satisfied with the results of the meeting at the Château St. Louis, and he wrote to the minister: "You can never hope that this business will succeed if it is discussed here on the spot. Canada is a country of cabals and intrigues, and it is impossible to reconcile so many different interests."[11] He sailed for France, apparently in the autumn of 1699, to urge his scheme at court. Here he had an interview with the colonial minister, Ponchartrain, to whom he represented the military and political expediency of his proposed establishment;[12] and in a letter which seems to be addressed to La Touche, chief clerk in the Department of Marine and Colonies, he promised that the execution of his plan would insure the safety of Canada and the ruin of the British colonies.[13] He asked for fifty soldiers and fifty Canadians to begin the work, to be followed in the next year by twenty or thirty families and by two hundred picked men of various trades, sent out at the King's charge, along with priests of several communities, and nuns to attend the sick and teach the Indian girls. "I cannot tell you," continues Cadillac, "the efforts my enemies have made to deprive me of the honor of executing my project; but so soon as M. de Ponchartrain decides in its favor, the whole country will applaud it."

Ponchartrain accepted the plan, and Cadillac returned to Canada commissioned to execute it. Early in June, 1701, he left La Chine with a hundred men in twenty-five canoes loaded with provisions, goods, munitions, and tools. He was accompanied by Alphonse de Tonty, brother of Henri de Tonty, the companion of La Salle, and by two half-pay lieutenants, Dugué and Chacornacle, together with a Jesuit and a Récollet.[14] Following the difficult route of the Ottawa and Lake Huron, they reached their destination on the twenty-fourth of July, and built a picket fort sixty yards square,

[11] *Rapport au Ministre*, 1700.

[12] Cadillac's report of this interview is given in Sheldon, *Early History of Michigan*, 85–91.

[13] *La Mothe-Cadillac à un premier commis*, 18 *Octobre*, 1700, in Margry, v. 166.

[14] *Callières au Ministre*, 4 *Octobre*, 1701. *Autre lettre du même, sans date*, in Margry, v. 187, 190.

which by order of the governor they named Fort Ponchartrain.[15] It stood near the west bank of the strait, about forty
paces from the water.[16] Thus was planted the germ of the city
of Detroit.

Cadillac sent back Chacornacle with the report of what he
had done, and a description of the country written in a strain
of swelling and gushing rhetoric in singular contrast with his
usual sarcastic utterances. "None but enemies of the truth,"
his letter concludes, "are enemies of this establishment, so
necessary to the glory of the King, the progress of religion,
and the destruction of the throne of Baal."[17]

What he had, perhaps, still more at heart was making
money out of it by the fur-trade. By command of the King a
radical change had lately been made in this chief commerce
of Canada, and the entire control of it had been placed in
the hands of a company in which all Canadians might take
shares. But as the risks were great and the conditions ill-
defined, the number of subscribers was not much above one
hundred and fifty; and the rest of the colony found themselves shut out from the trade,—to the ruin of some, and the
injury of all.[18]

All trade in furs was restricted to Detroit and Fort Frontenac, both of which were granted to the company, subject
to be resumed by the King at his pleasure.[19] The company was
to repay the eighty thousand francs which the expedition to
Detroit had cost; and to this were added various other burdens. The King, however, was to maintain the garrison.

All the affairs of the company were placed in the hands of
seven directors, who began immediately to complain that
their burdens were too heavy, and to beg for more privileges;
while an outcry against the privileges already granted rose
from those who had not taken shares in the enterprise. Both
in the company and out of it there was nothing but discontent.
None were worse pleased than the two Jesuits Carheil and
Marest, who saw their flocks at Michilimackinac, both Hurons

[15] *Callières et Champigny au Ministre, sans date.*

[16] *Relation du Destroit* (by the Jesuit who accompanied the
expedition).

[17] *Description de la Rivière du Détroit, jointe à la lettre de MM.
de Callières et de Champigny, 8 Octobre, 1701.*

[18] *Callières au Ministre, 9 Novembre, 1700.*

[19] *Traité fait avec la Compagnie de la Colonie de Canada, 31
Octobre, 1701.*

and Ottawas, lured away to a new home at Detroit. Cadillac took a peculiar satisfaction in depriving Carheil of his converts, and in 1703 we find him writing to the minister Ponchartrain, that only twenty-five Hurons are left at Michilimackinac; and "I hope," he adds, "that in the autumn I shall pluck this last feather from his wing; and I am convinced that this obstinate priest will die in his parish without one parishioner to bury him."[20]

If the Indians came to Detroit, the French would not come. Cadillac had asked for five or six families as the modest beginning of a settlement; but not one had appeared. The Indians, too, were angry because the company asked too much for its goods; while the company complained that a forbidden trade, fatal to its interests, went on through all the region of the upper lakes. It was easy to ordain a monopoly, but impossible to enforce it. The prospects of the new establishment were deplorable; and Cadillac lost no time in presenting his views of the situation to the court. "Detroit is good, or it is bad," he writes to Ponchartrain. "If it is good, it ought to be sustained, without allowing the people of Canada to deliberate any more about it. If it is bad, the court ought to make up its mind concerning it as soon as may be. I have said what I think. I have explained the situation. You have felt the need of Detroit, and its utility for the glory of God, the progress of religion, and the good of the colony. Nothing is left me to do but to imitate the governor of the Holy City,——take water, and wash my hands of it." His aim now appears. He says that if Detroit were made a separate government, and he were put at the head of it, its prospects would improve. "You may well believe that the company cares for nothing but to make a profit out of it. It only wants to have a storehouse and clerks; no officers, no troops, no inhabitants. Take this business in hand, Monseigneur, and I promise that in two years your Detroit shall be established of itself." He then informs the minister that as the company complain of losing money, he has told

[20] *Lamothe-Cadillac à Ponchartrain*, 31 *Aoust*, 1703 (Margry, v. 301). On Cadillac's relations with the Jesuits, see *Conseils tenus par Lamothe-Cadillac avec les Sauvages* (Margry, v. 253–300); also a curious collection of Jesuit letters sent by Cadillac to the minister, with copious annotations of his own. He excepts from his strictures Father Engelran, who, he says, incurred the ill-will of the other Jesuits by favoring the establishment of Detroit, and he also has a word of commendation for Father Germain.

them that if they will make over their rights to him, he will pay them back all their past outlays. "I promise you," he informs Ponchartrain, "that if they accept my proposal and you approve it, I will make our Detroit flourish. Judge if it is agreeable to me to have to answer for my actions to five or six merchants [the directors of the company], who not long ago were blacking their masters' boots." He is scarcely more reserved as to the Jesuits. "I do what I can to make them my friends, but, impiety apart, one had better sin against God than against them; for in that case one gets one's pardon, whereas in the other the offence is never forgiven in this world, and perhaps never would be in the other, if their credit were as great there as it is here."[21]

The letters of Cadillac to the court are unique. No governor of New France, not even the audacious Frontenac, ever wrote to a minister of Louis XIV with such off-hand freedom of language as this singular personage,—a mere captain in the colony troops; and to a more stable and balanced character it would have been impossible.

Cadillac's proposal was accepted. The company was required to abandon Detroit to him on his paying them the expenses they had incurred. Their monopoly was transferred to him; but as far as concerned beaver-skins, his trade was limited to twenty thousand francs a year. The governor was ordered to give him as many soldiers as he might want, permit as many persons to settle at Detroit as might choose to do so, and provide missionaries.[22] The minister exhorted him to quarrel no more with the Jesuits, or anybody else, to banish blasphemy and bad morals from the post, and not to offend the Five Nations.

The promised era of prosperity did not come. Detroit lingered on in a weak and troubled infancy, disturbed, as we shall see, by startling incidents. Its occupation by the French produced a noteworthy result. The Five Nations, filled with jealously and alarm, appealed to the King of England for protection, and the better to insure it, conveyed the whole

[21] *La Mothe-Cadillac à Ponchartrain*, 31 *Août*, 1703. "Toute impiété à part, il vaudroit mieux pescher contre Dieu que contre eux, parce que d'un costé on en reçoit son pardon, et de l'autre, l'offense, mesme prétendue, n'est jamais remise dans ce monde, et ne le seroit peut-estre jamais dans l'autre, si leur crédit y estoit aussi grand qu'il est dans ce pays."

[22] *Ponchartrain à La Mothe-Cadillac*, 14 *Juin*, 1704.

country from Lake Ontario northward to Lake Superior, and westward as far as Chicago, "unto our souveraigne Lord King William the Third" and his heirs and successors forever. This territory is described in the deed as being about eight hundred miles long and four hundred wide, and was claimed by the Five Nations as theirs by right of conquest.[23] It of course included Detroit itself. The conveyance was drawn by the English authorities at Albany in a form to suit their purposes, and included terms of subjection and sovereignty which the signers could understand but imperfectly, if at all. The Five Nations gave away their land to no purpose. The French remained in undisturbed possession of Detroit. The English made no attempt to enforce their title, but they put the deed on file, and used it long after as the base of their claim to the region of the Lakes.

[23] *Deed from the Five Nations to the King of their Beaver Hunting Ground,* in *N. Y. Col. Docs.,* iv. 908. It is signed by the totems of sachems of all the Nations.

Chapter 3

1703–1713
Queen Anne's War

FOR UNTOLD AGES Maine had been one unbroken forest, and
it was so still. Only along the rocky seaboard or on the lower
waters of one or two great rivers a few rough settlements had
gnawed slight indentations into this wilderness of woods; and
a little farther inland some dismal clearing around a blockhouse or stockade let in the sunlight to a soil that had lain in
shadow time out of mind. This waste of savage vegetation survives, in some part, to this day, with the same prodigality of
vital force, the same struggle for existence and mutual havoc
that mark all organized beings from men to mushrooms.
Young seedlings in millions spring every summer from the
black mould, rich with the decay of those that had preceded
them, crowding, choking, and killing one another, perishing by
their very abundance,—all but a scattered few, stronger than
the rest, or more fortunate in position, which survive by
blighting those about them. They in turn, as they grow, inter-
lock their boughs, and repeat in a season or two the same
process of mutual suffocation. The forest is full of lean sap-
lings dead or dying with vainly stretching towards the light.
Not one infant tree in a thousand lives to maturity; yet these
survivors form an innumerable host, pressed together in struggling confusion, squeezed out of symmetry and robbed of
normal development, as men are said to be in the level same-
ness of democratic society. Seen from above, their mingled
tops spread in a sea of verdure basking in light; seen from
below, all is shadow, through which spots of timid sunshine
steal down among legions of lank, mossy trunks, toadstools
and rank ferns, protruding roots, matted bushes, and rotting
carcasses of fallen trees. A generation ago one might find here
and there the rugged trunk of some great pine lifting its
verdant spire above the undistinguished myriads of the forest.
The woods of Maine had their aristocracy; but the axe of the
woodman has laid them low, and these lords of the wilderness
are seen no more.

The life and light of this grim solitude were in its countless streams and lakes, from little brooks stealing clear and cold under the alders, full of the small fry of trout, to the mighty arteries of the Penobscot and the Kennebec; from the great reservoir of Moosehead to a thousand nameless ponds shining in the hollow places of the forest.

It had and still has its beast of prey,—wolves, savage, cowardly, and mean; bears, gentle and mild compared to their grisly relatives of the Far West, vegetarians when they can do no better, and not without something grotesque and quaint in manners and behavior; sometimes, though, rarely, the strong and sullen wolverine; frequently the lynx; and now and then the fierce and agile cougar.

The human denizens of this wilderness were no less fierce, and far more dangerous. These were the various tribes and sub-tribes of the Abenakis, whose villages were on the Saco, the Kennebec, the Penobscot, and the other great water-courses. Most of them had been converted by the Jesuits, and, as we have seen already, some had been persuaded to remove to Canada, like the converted Iroquois of Caughnawaga. The rest remained in their native haunts, where, under the direction of their missionaries, they could be used to keep the English settlements in check.

We know how busily they plied their tomahawks in William and Mary's War, and what havoc they made among the scattered settlements of the border. Another war with France was declared on the fourth of May, 1702, on which the Abenakis again assumed a threatening attitude. In June of the next year Dudley, governor of Massachusetts, called the chiefs of the various bands to a council at Casco. Here presently appeared the Norridgewocks from the Kennebec, the Penobscots and Androscoggins from the rivers that bear their names, the Penacooks from the Merrimac, and the Pequawkets from the Saco, all well armed, and daubed with ceremonial paint. The principal among them, gathered under a large tent, were addressed by Dudley in a conciliatory speech. Their orator replied that they wanted nothing but peace, and that their thoughts were as far from war as the sun was from the earth, —words which they duly confirmed by a belt of wampum.[1]

[1] Penhallow, *History of the Wars of New England with the Eastern Indians,* 16 (ed. 1859). Penhallow was present at the council. In Judge Sewall's clumsy abstract of the proceedings (*Diary of Sewall,* ii. 85) the Indians are represented as professing neutrality. The governor and intendant of Canada write that the Abenakis had

Presents were distributed among them and received with apparent satisfaction, while two of their principal chiefs, known as Captain Samuel and Captain Bomazeen, declared that several French missionaries had lately come among them to excite them against the English, but that they were "firm as mountains," and would remain so "as long as the sun and moon endured." They ended the meeting with dancing, singing, and whoops of joy, followed by a volley of musketry, answered by another from the English. It was discovered, however, that the Indians had loaded their guns with ball, intending, as the English believed, to murder Dudley and his attendants if they could have done so without danger to their chiefs, whom the governor had prudently kept about him. It was afterwards found, if we may believe a highly respectable member of the party, that two hundred French and Indians were on their way, "resolved to seize the governor, council, and gentlemen, and then to sacrifice the inhabitants at pleasure;" but when they arrived, the English officials had been gone three days.[2]

The French governor, Vaudreuil, says that about this time some of the Abenakis were killed or maltreated by Englishmen. It may have been so: desperadoes, drunk or sober, were not rare along the frontier; but Vaudreuil gives no particulars, and the only English outrage that appears on record at the time was the act of a gang of vagabonds who plundered the house of the younger Saint-Castin, where the town of Castine now stands. He was Abenaki by his mother; but he was absent when the attack took place, and the marauders seem to have shed no blood. Nevertheless, within six weeks after the Treaty of Casco, every unprotected farmhouse in Maine was in a blaze.

---

begun a treaty of neutrality with the English, but that as "les Jésuites observoient les sauvages, le traité ne fut pas conclu." They add that Rale, Jesuit missionary at Norridgewock, informs them that his Indians were ready to lift the hatchet against the English. *Vaudreuil et Beauharnois au Ministre,* 1703.

[2] Penhallow, 17, 18 (ed. 1859). There was a previous meeting of conciliation between the English and the Abenakis in 1702. The Jesuit Bigot says that the Indians assured him that they had scornfully repelled the overtures of the English, and told them that they would always stand fast by the French. (*Relation des Abenakis,* 1702.) This is not likely. The Indians probably lied both to the Jesuit and to the English, telling to each what they knew would be most acceptable.

The settlements of Maine, confined to the southwestern corner of what is now the State of Maine, extended along the coast in a feeble and broken line from Kittery to Casco. Ten years of murderous warfare had almost ruined them. East of the village of Wells little was left except one or two forts and the so-called "garrisons," which were private houses pierced with loopholes and having an upper story projecting over the lower, so that the defenders could fire down on assailants battering the door or piling fagots against the walls. A few were fenced with palisades, as was the case with the house of Joseph Storer at the east end of Wells, where an overwhelming force of French and Indians had been gallantly repulsed in the summer of 1692. These fortified houses were, however, very rarely attacked, except by surprise and treachery. In case of alarm such of the inhabitants as found time took refuge in them with their families, and left their dwellings to the flames; for the first thought of the settler was to put his women and children beyond reach of the scalping-knife. There were several of these asylums in different parts of Wells; and without them the place must have been abandoned. In the little settlement of York, farther westward, there were five of them, which had saved a part of the inhabitants when the rest were surprised and massacred.

Wells was a long, straggling settlement, consisting at the beginning of William and Mary's War of about eighty houses and log-cabins,[3] strung at intervals along the north side of the rough track, known as the King's Road, which ran parallel to the sea. Behind the houses were rude, half-cleared pastures, and behind these again, the primeval forest. The cultivated land was on the south side of the road; in front of the houses, and beyond it, spread great salt-marshes, bordering the sea and haunted by innumerable game-birds.

The settlements of Maine were a dependency of Massachusetts,—a position that did not please their inhabitants, but which they accepted because they needed the help of their Puritan neighbors, from whom they differed widely both in their qualities and in their faults. The Indian wars that checked their growth had kept them in a condition more than half barbarous. They were a hard-working and hard-drinking race; for though tea and coffee were scarcely known, the land flowed with New England rum, which was ranked among the

---

[3] Bourne, *History of Wells and Kennebunk.*

necessaries of life. The better sort could read and write in a bungling way; but many were wholly illiterate, and it was not till long after Queen Anne's War that the remoter settlements established schools, taught by poor students from Harvard or less competent instructors, and held at first in private houses or under sheds. The church at Wells had been burned by the Indians; and though the settlers were beggared by the war, they voted in town-meeting to build another. The new temple, begun in 1699, was a plain wooden structure thirty feet square. For want of money the windows long remained unglazed, the walls without plaster, and the floor without seats; yet services were duly held here under direction of the minister, Samuel Emery, to whom they paid £45 a year, half in provincial currency, and half in farm-produce and fire-wood.

In spite of these efforts to maintain public worship, they were far from being a religious community; nor were they a peaceful one. Gossip and scandal ran riot; social jealousies abounded; and under what seemed entire democratic equality, the lazy, drunken, and shiftless envied the industrious and thrifty. Wells was infested, moreover, by several "frightfully turbulent women," as the chronicle styles them, from whose rabid tongues the minister himself did not always escape; and once, in its earlier days, the town had been indicted for not providing a ducking-stool to correct these breeders of discord.

Judicial officers were sometimes informally chosen by popular vote, and sometimes appointed by the governor of Massachusetts from among the inhabitants. As they knew no law, they gave judgment according to their own ideas of justice, and their sentences were oftener wanting in wisdom than in severity. Until after 1700 the county courts met by beat of drum at some of the primitive inns or taverns with which the frontier abounded.

At Wells and other outlying and endangered hamlets life was still exceedingly rude. The log-cabins of the least thrifty were no better furnished than Indian wigwams. The house of Edmond Littlefield, reputed the richest man in Wells, consisted of two bedrooms and a kitchen, which last served a great variety of uses, and was supplied with a table, a pewter pot, a frying-pan, and a skillet; but no chairs, cups, saucers, knives, forks, or spoons. In each of the two bedrooms there was a bed, a blanket, and a chest. Another village notable—Ensign John Barrett—was better provided, being the possessor of two beds, two chests and a box, four pewter dishes, four earthen pots, two iron pots, seven trays, two buckets, some pieces of wooden-ware, a skillet, and a frying-pan. In the inventory of the patriarchal Francis Littlefield, who died in 1712, we find the exceptional items of one looking-glass, two old chairs, and two old books. Such of the family as had no bed slept on hay or straw, and no provision for the toilet is recorded.[4]

On the tenth of August, 1703, these rugged borderers were about their usual callings, unconscious of danger,—the women at their household work, the men in the fields or on the more distant salt-marshes. The wife of Thomas Wells had reached the time of her confinement, and her husband had gone for a nurse. Some miles east of Well's cabin lived Stephen Harding,—hunter, blacksmith, and tavernkeeper, a sturdy, good-natured man, who loved the woods, and whose frequent hunting trips sometimes led him nearly to the White Mountains. Distant gunshots were heard from the westward, and his quick eye presently discovered Indians approaching, on which he told his frightened wife to go with their infant to a certain oak-tree beyond the creek while he waited to learn whether the strangers were friends or foes.

That morning several parties of Indians had stolen out of the dismal woods behind the houses and farms of Wells, and approached different dwellings of the far-extended settlement at about the same time. They entered the cabin of Thomas Wells, where his wife lay in the pains of childbirth, and murdered her and her two small children. At the same time they killed Joseph Saver, a neighbor of Wells, with all his family.

Meanwhile Stephen Harding, having sent his wife and child to a safe distance, returned to his blacksmith's shop, and, seeing nobody, gave a defiant whoop; on which four Indians sprang at him from the bushes. He escaped through a back-door of the shop, eluded his pursuers, and found his wife and child in a cornfield, where the woman had fainted with fright. They spent the night in the woods, and on the next day, after a circuit of nine miles, reached the palisaded house of Joseph Storer.

They found the inmates in distress and agitation. Storer's

[4] The above particulars are drawn from the *History of Wells and Kennebunk*, by the late Edward E. Borne, of Wells,—a work of admirable thoroughness, fidelity, and candor.

daughter Mary, a girl of eighteen, was missing. The Indians had caught her, and afterwards carried her prisoner to Canada. Samuel Hill and his family were captured, and the younger children butchered. But it is useless to record the names and fate of the sufferers. Thirty-nine in all, chiefly women and children, were killed or carried off, and then the Indians disappeared as quickly and silently as they had come, leaving many of the houses in flames.

This raid upon Wells was only part of a combined attack on all the settlements from that place to Casco. Those eastward of Wells had been, as we have seen, abandoned in the last war, excepting the forts and fortified houses; but the inhabitants, reassured, no doubt, by the Treaty of Casco, had begun to return. On this same day, the tenth of August, they were startled from their security. A band of Indians mixed with Frenchmen fell upon the settlements about the stone fort near the Falls of the Saco, killed eleven persons, captured twenty-four, and vainly attacked the fort itself. Others surprised the settlers at a place called Spurwing, and killed or captured twenty-two. Others, again, destroyed the huts of the fishermen at Cape Porpoise, and attacked the fortified house at Winter Harbor, the inmates of which, after a brave resistance, were forced to capitulate. The settlers at Scarborough were also in a fortified house, where they made a long and obstinate defence till help at last arrived. Nine families were settled at Purpooduck Point, near the present city of Portland. They had no place of refuge, and the men being, no doubt, fishermen, were all absent, when the Indians burst into the hamlet, butchered twenty-five women and children, and carried off eight.

The fort at Casco, or Falmouth, was held by Major March, with thirty-six men. He had no thought of danger, when three well-known chiefs from Norridgewock appeared with a white flag, and asked for an interview. As they seemed to be alone and unarmed, he went to meet them, followed by two or three soldiers and accompanied by two old men named Phippeny and Kent, inhabitants of the place. They had hardly reached the spot when the three chiefs drew hatchets from under a kind of mantle which they wore and sprang upon them, while other Indians, ambushed near by, leaped up and joined in the attack. The two old men were killed at once; but March, who was noted for strength and agility, wrenched a hatchet from one of his assailants, and kept them all at bay till Sergeant Hook came to his aid with a file of men and drove them off.

They soon reappeared, burned the deserted cabins in the neighborhood, and beset the garrison in numbers that continually increased, till in a few days the entire force that had been busied in ravaging the scattered settlements was gathered around the place. It consisted of about five hundred Indians of several tribes, and a few Frenchmen under an officer named Beaubassin. Being elated with past successes, they laid siege to the fort, sheltering themselves under a steep bank by the water-side and burrowing their way towards the rampart. March could not dislodge them, and they continued their approaches till the third day, when Captain Southack, with the Massachusetts armed vessel known as the "Province Galley," sailed into the harbor, recaptured three small vessels that the Indians had taken along the coast, and destroyed a great number of their canoes, on which they gave up their enterprise and disappeared.[5]

Such was the beginning of Queen Anne's War. These attacks were due less to the Abenakis than to the French who set them on. "Monsieur de Vaudreuil," writes the Jesuit historian Charlevoix, "formed a party of these savages, to whom he joined some Frenchmen under the direction of the Sieur de Beaubassin, when they effected some ravages of no great consequence; they killed, however, about three hundred men." This last statement is doubly incorrect. The whole number of persons killed and carried off during the August attacks did not much exceed one hundred and sixty;[6] and these were of both sexes and all ages, from octogenarians to newborn infants. The able-bodied men among them were few, as most of the attacks were made upon unprotected houses in the absence of the head of the family; and the only fortified place

[5] On these attacks on the frontier of Maine, Penhallow, who well knew the country and the people, is the best authority. Niles, in his *Indian and French Wars*, copies him without acknowledgment, but not without blunders. As regards the attack on Wells, what particulars we have are mainly due to the research of the indefatigable Bourne. Compare Belknap, i. 330; Folsom, *History of Saco and Biddeford*, 198; *Coll. Maine Hist. Soc.*, iii. 140, 348; Williamson, *History of Maine*, ii. 42. Beaubassin is called "Bobasser" in most of the English accounts.

[6] The careful and well-informed Belknap puts it at only 130. *History of New Hampshire*, i. 331.

captured was the garrison-house at Winter Harbor, which surrendered on terms of capitulation. The instruments of this ignoble warfare and the revolting atrocities that accompanied it were all, or nearly all, converted Indians of the missions. Charlevoix has no word of disapproval for it, and seems to regard its partial success as a gratifying one so far as it went.

One of the objects was, no doubt, to check the progress of the English settlements; but, pursues Charlevoix, "the essential point was to commit the Abenakis in such a manner that they could not draw back."[7] This object was constantly kept in view. The French claimed at this time that the territory of Acadia reached as far westward as the Kennebec, which therefore formed, in their view, the boundary between the rival nations, and they trusted in the Abenakis to defend this assumed line of demarcation. But the Abenakis sorely needed English guns, knives, hatchets, and kettles, and nothing but the utmost vigilance could prevent them from coming to terms with those who could supply their necessities. Hence the policy of the French authorities on the frontier of New England was the opposite of their policy on the frontier of New York. They left the latter undisturbed, lest by attacking the Dutch and English settlers they should stir up the Five Nations to attack Canada; while, on the other hand, they constantly spurred the Abenakis against New England, in order to avert the dreaded event of their making peace with her.

The attack on Wells, Casco, and the intervening settlements was followed by murders and depredations that lasted through the autumn and extended along two hundred miles of frontier. Thirty Indians attacked the village of Hampton, killed the Widow Mussey, a famous Quakeress, and then fled to escape pursuit. At Black Point nineteen men going to their work in the meadows were ambushed by two hundred Indians, and all but one were shot or captured. The fort was next attacked. It was garrisoned by eight men under Lieutenant Wyatt, who stood their ground for some time, and then escaped by means of a sloop in the harbor. At York the wife and children of Arthur Brandon were killed, and the Widow Parsons and her daughter carried off. At Berwick the Indians attacked the fotrified house of Andrew Neal, but were repulsed with the loss of nine killed and many wounded, for which they revenged themselves by burning alive Joseph Ring, a prisoner whom they had taken. Early in February a small

[7] Charlevoix, ii. 289, 290 (quarto edition).

party of them hovered about the fortified house of Joseph Bradley at Haverhill, till seeing the gate open and nobody on the watch, they rushed in. The woman of the house was boiling soap, and in her desperation she snatched up the kettle and threw the contents over them with such effect that one of them, it is said, was scalded to death. The man who should have been on the watch was killed, and several persons were captured, including the woman. It was the second time that she had been a prisoner in Indian hands. Half starved and bearing a heavy load, she followed her captors in their hasty retreat towards Canada. After a time she was safely delivered of an infant in the midst of the winter forest; but the child pined for want of sustenance, and the Indians hastened its death by throwing hot coals into its mouth when it cried. The astonishing vitality of the woman carried her to the end of the frightful journey. A Frenchman bought her from the Indians, and she was finally ransomed by her husband.

By far the most dangerous and harassing attacks were those of small parties skulking under the edge of the forest, or lying hidden for days together, watching the opportunity to murder unawares, and vanishing when they had done so. Against such an enemy there was no defence. The Massachusetts government sent a troop of horse to Portsmouth, and another to Wells. These had the advantage of rapid movement in case of alarm along the roads and forest-paths from settlement to settlement; but once in the woods, their horses were worse than useless, and they could only fight on foot. Fighting, however, was rarely possible; for on reaching the scene of action they found nothing but mangled corpses and burning houses.

The best defence was to take the offensive. In September Governor Dudley sent three hundred and sixty men to the upper Saco, the haunt of the Pequawket tribe; but the place was deserted. Major, now Colonel, March soon after repeated the attempt, killing six Indians, and capturing as many more. The General Court offered £40 for every Indian scalp, and one Captin Tyng, in consequence, surprised an Indian village in midwinter and brought back five of these disgusting trophies. In the spring of 1704 word came from Albany that a band of French Indians had built a fort and planted corn at Coos meadows, high up the river Connecticut. On this, one Caleb Lyman with five friendly Indians, probably Mohegans, set out from Northampton, and after a long march through the forest, surprised, under cover of a thunderstorm, a wigwam containing nine warriors,—bound, no doubt, against the frontier. They killed seven of them; and this was all that was done at present in the way of reprisal or prevention.[8]

The murders and burnings along the borders were destined to continue with little variety and little interruption during ten years. It was a repetition of what the pedantic Cotton Mather calls *Deccennium luctuosum*, or the "woful decade" of William and Mary's War. The wonder is that the outlying settlements were not abandoned. These ghastly, insidious, and ever-present dangers demanded a more obstinate courage than the hottest battle in the open field.

One curious frontier incident may be mentioned here, though it did not happen till towards the end of the war. In spite of poverty, danger, and tribulation, marrying and giving in marriage did not cease among the sturdy borderers; and on a day in September there was a notable wedding feast at the palisaded house of John Wheelwright, one of the chief men of Wells. Elisha Plaisted was to espouse Wheelwright's daughter Hannah, and many guests were assembled, some from Portsmouth, and even beyond it. Probably most of them came in sailboats; for the way by land was full of peril, especially on the road from York, which ran through dense woods, where Indians often waylaid the traveller. The bridegroom's father was present with the rest. It was a concourse of men in homespun, and women and girls in such improvised finery as their poor resources could supply; possibly, in default of better, some wore nightgowns, more or less disguised, over their daily dress, as happened on similar occasions half a century later among the frontiersmen of West Virginia.[9] After an evening of rough merriment and gymnastic dancing, the guests lay down to sleep under the roof of their host or in adjacent barns and sheds. When morning came, and they were preparing to depart, it was found that two horses were missing; and not doubting that they had strayed away, three young men—Sergeant Tucker, Joshua Downing, and Isaac Cole— went to find them. In a few minutes several gunshots were heard. The three young men did not return. Downing and Cole were killed, and Tucker was wounded and made prisoner.

Believing that, as usual, the attack came from some small

[8] Penhallow, *Wars of New England with the Eastern Indians.*
[9] Doddridge, *Notes on Western Virginia and Pennsylvania.*

scalping-party, Elisha Plaisted and eight or ten more threw themselves on the horses that stood saddled before the house, and galloped across the fields in the direction of the firing; while others ran to cut off the enemy's retreat. A volley was presently heard, and several of the party were seen running back towards the house. Elisha Plaisted and his companions had fallen into an ambuscade of two hundred Indians. One or more of them were shot, and the unfortunate bridegroom was captured. The distress of his young wife, who was but eighteen, may be imagined.

Two companies of armed men in the pay of Massachusetts were then in Wells, and some of them had come to the wedding. Seventy marksmen went to meet the Indians, who ensconced themselves in the edge of the forest, whence they could not be dislodged. There was some desultory firing, and one of the combatants was killed on each side, after which the whites gave up the attack, and Lieutenant Banks went forward with a flag of truce, in the hope of ransoming the prisoners. He was met by six chiefs, among whom were two noted Indians of his acquaintance, Bomazeen and Captain Nathaniel. They well knew that the living Plaisted was worth more than his scalp; and though they would not come to terms at once, they promised to meet the English at Richmond's Island in a few days and give up both him and Tucker on payment of a sufficient ransom. The flag of truce was respected, and Banks came back safe, bringing a hasty note to the elder Plaisted from his captive son. This note now lies before me, and it runs thus, in the dutiful formality of the olden time:—

SIR,—I am in the hands of a great many Indians, with which there is six captains. They say that what they will have for me is 50 pounds, and thirty pounds for Tucker, my fellow prisoner, in good goods, as broadcloth, some provisions, some tobacco pipes, Pomisstone [pumice-stone], stockings, and a little of all things. If you will, come to Richmond's Island in 5 days at farthest, for here is 200 Indians, and they belong to Canada.

If you do not come in 5 days, you will not see me, for Captain Nathaniel the Indian will not stay no longer, for the Canada Indians is not willing for to sell me. Pray, Sir, don't fail, for they have given me one day, for the days were but

4 at first. Give my kind love to my dear wife. This from your dutiful son till death,

ELISHA PLAISTED.

The alarm being spread and a sufficient number of men mustered, they set out to attack the enemy and recover the prisoners by force; but not an Indian could be found.

Bomazeen and Captain Nathaniel were true to the rendezvous; in due time Elisha Plaisted was ransomed and restored to his bride.[10]

[10] On this affair, see the note of Elisha Plaisted in Massachusetts Archives; *Richard Waldron to Governor Dudley, Portsmouth,* 19 *September,* 1712; Bourne, *Wells and Kennebunk,* 278.

Chapter 4

1704–1740
Deerfield

ABOUT MIDWINTER the governor of Canada sent another large war-party against the New England border. The object of attack was an unoffending hamlet, that from its position could never be a menace to the French, and the destruction of which could profit them nothing. The aim of the enterprise was not military, but political. "I have sent no war-party towards Albany," writes Vaudreuil, "because we must do nothing that might cause a rupture between us and the Iroquois; but we must keep things astir in the direction of Boston, or else the Abenakis will declare for the English." In short, the object was fully to commit these savages to hostility against New England, and convince them at the same time that the French would back their quarrel.[1]

The party consisted, according to French accounts, of fifty Canadians and two hundred Abenakis and Caughnawagas,— the latter of whom, while trading constantly with Albany, were rarely averse to a raid against Massachusetts or New Hampshire.[2] The command was given to the younger Hertel de Rouville, who was accompanied by four of his brothers. They began their march in the depth of winter, journeyed nearly three hundred miles on snow-shoes through the forest, and approached their destination on the afternoon of the twenty-eighth of February, 1704. It was the village of Deerfield, which then formed the extreme northwestern frontier of Massachusetts,—its feeble neighbor, the infant settlement of Northfield, a little higher up the Connecticut, having been abandoned during the last war. Rouville halted his followers

---

[1] *Vaudreuil au Ministre, 14 Novembre,* 1703; *Ibid., 3 Avril,* 1704; *Vaudreuil et Beauharnois au Ministre, 17 Novembre,* 1704. French writers say that the English surprised and killed some of the Abenakis, who thereupon asked help from Canada. This perhaps refers to the expeditions of Colonel March and Captain Tyng, who, after the bloody attacks upon the settlements of Maine, made reprisal upon Abenaki camps.

[2] English accounts make the whole number 342.

at a place now called Petty's Plain, two miles from the village; and here, under the shelter of a pine forest, they all lay hidden, shivering with cold,—for they dared not make fires,—and hungry as wolves, for their provisions were spent. Though their numbers, by the lowest account, were nearly equal to the whole population of Deerfield,—men, women, and children,—they had no thought of an open attack, but trusted to darkness for an easy victory.

Deerfield stood on a plateau above the river meadows, and the houses—forty-one in all—were chiefly along the road towards the villages of Hadley and Hatfield, a few miles distant. In the middle of the place, on a rising ground called Meeting-house Hill, was a small square wooden meeting-house. This, with about fifteen private houses, besides barns and sheds, was enclosed by a fence of palisades eight feet high, flanked by "mounts," or blockhouses, at two or more of the corners. The four sides of this palisaded enclosure, which was called the fort, measured in all no less than two hundred and two rods, and within it lived some of the principal inhabitants of the village, of which it formed the centre or citadel. Chief among its inmates was John Williams, the minister, a man of character and education, who, after graduating at Harvard, had come to Deerfield when it was still suffering under the ruinous effects of King Philip's War, and entered on his ministry with a salary of sixty pounds in depreciated New England currency, payable, not in money, but in wheat, Indian-corn, and pork.[3] His parishioners built him a house, he married, and had now eight children, one of whom was absent with friends at Hadley.[4] His next neighbor was Benoni Stebbins, sergeant in the county militia, who lived a few rods from the meeting-house. About fifty yards distant, and near the northwest angle of the enclosure, stood the house of Ensign John Sheldon, a framed building, one of the largest in the village, and, like that of Stebbins, made bullet-proof by a layer of bricks between the outer and inner sheathing, while its small windows and its projecting upper story also helped to make it defensible.

The space enclosed by the palisade, though much too large for effective defence, served in time of alarm as an asylum for the inhabitants outside, whose houses were scattered,—some

[3] Stephen W. Williams, *Biographical Memoir of Rev. John Williams*.

[4] *Account of y° destruction at Deref*, February 29, 1703/4.

on the north towards the hidden enemy, and some on the south towards Hadley and Hatfield. Among those on the south side was that of the militia captain, Jonathan Wells, which had a palisade of its own, and, like the so-called fort, served as an asylum for the neighbors.

These private fortified houses were sometimes built by the owners alone, though more often they were the joint work of the owners and of the inhabitants, to whose safety they contributed. The palisade fence that enclosed the central part of the village was made under a vote of the town, each inhabitant being required to do his share; and as they were greatly impoverished by the last war, the General Court of the province remitted for a time a part of their taxes in consideration of a work which aided the general defence.[5]

Down to the Peace of Ryswick the neighborhood had been constantly infested by scalping-parties, and once the village had been attacked by a considerable force of French and Indians, who were beaten off. Of late there had been warnings of fresh disturbance. Lord Cornbury, governor of New York, wrote that he had heard through spies that Deerfield was again to be attacked, and a message to the same effect came from Peter Schuyler, who had received intimations of the danger from Mohawks lately on a visit to their Caughnawaga relatives. During the autumn the alarm was so great that the people took refuge within the palisades, and the houses of the enclosure were crowded with them; but the panic had now subsided, and many, though not all, had returned to their homes. They were reassured by the presence of twenty volunteers from the villages below, whom, on application from the minister, Williams, the General Court had sent as a garrison to Deerfield, where they were lodged in the houses of the villagers. On the night when Hertel de Rouville and his band lay hidden among the pines there were in all the settlement a little less than three hundred souls, of whom two hundred and sixty-eight were inhabitants, twenty were yeomen soldiers of the garrison, two were visitors from Hatfield, and three were negro slaves. They were of all ages,—from the Widow Allison, in her eighty-fifth year, to the infant son of Deacon French, aged four weeks.[6]

[5] Papers in the Archives of Massachusetts. Among these a letter of Rev. John Williams to the governor, 21 October, 1703, states that the palisade is rotten, and must be rebuilt.

[6] The names of nearly all the inhabitants are preserved, and even

Heavy snows had lately fallen and buried the clearings, the meadow, and the frozen river to the depth of full three feet. On the northwestern side the drifts were piled nearly to the top of the palisade fence, so that it was no longer an obstruction to an active enemy.

As the afternoon waned, the sights and sounds of the little border hamlet were, no doubt, like those of any other rustic New England village at the end of a winter day,—an ox-sledge creaking on the frosty snow as it brought in the last load of firewood, boys in homespun snowballing one another in the village street, farmers feeding their horses and cattle in the barns, a matron drawing a pail of water with the help of one of those long well-sweeps still used in some remote districts, or a girl bringing a pail of milk from the cow-shed. In the houses, where one room served as kitchen, dining-room, and parlor, the housewife cooked the evening meal, children sat at their bowls of mush and milk, and the men of the family, their day's work over, gathered about the fire, while perhaps some village coquette sat in the corner with fingers busy at the spinning-wheel, and ears intent on the stammered wooings of her rustic lover. Deerfield kept early hours, and it is likely that by nine o'clock all were in their beds. There was a patrol inside the palisade, but there was little discipline among these extemporized soldiers; the watchers grew careless as the frosty night went on; and it is said that towards morning they, like the villagers, betook themselves to their beds.

Rouville and his men, savage with hunger, lay shivering under the pines till about two hours before dawn, then, leaving their packs and their snow-shoes behind, they moved cautiously towards their prey. There was a crust on the snow strong enough to bear their weight, though not to prevent a rustling noise as it crunched under the feet of so many men. It is said that from time to time Rouville commanded a halt, in order that the sentinels, if such there were, might mistake the distant sound for rising and falling gusts of wind. In any case, no alarm was given till they had mounted the palisade and dropped silently into the unconscious village. Then with one accord they screeched the war-whoop, and assailed the doors of the houses with axes and hatchets.

---

the ages of most of them have been ascertained, through the indefatigable research of Mr. George Sheldon, of Deerfield, among contemporary records. The house of Thomas French, the town clerk, was not destroyed, and his papers were saved.

The hideous din startled the minister, Williams, from his sleep. Half-wakened, he sprang out of bed, and saw dimly a crowd of savages bursting through the shattered door. He shouted to two soldiers who were lodged in the house; and then, with more valor than discretion, snatched a pistol that hung at the head of the bed, cocked it, and snapped it at the breast of the foremost Indian, who proved to be a Caughnawaga chief. It missed fire, or Williams would, no doubt, have been killed on the spot. Amid the screams of his terrified children, three of the party seized him and bound him fast; for they came well provided with cords, since prisoners had a market value. Nevertheless, in the first fury of their attack they dragged to the door and murdered two of the children and a negro woman called Parthena, who was probably their nurse. In an upper room lodged a young man named Stoddard, who had time to snatch a cloak, throw himself out of the window, climb the palisade, and escape in the darkness. Half-naked as he was, he made his way over the snow to Hatfield, binding his bare feet with strips torn from the cloak.

They kept Williams shivering in his shirt for an hour while a frightful uproar of yells, shrieks, and gunshots sounded from without. At length they permitted him, his wife, and five remaining children to dress themselves. Meanwhile the Indians and their allies burst into most of the houses, killed such of the men as resisted, butchered some of the women and children, and seized and bound the rest. Some of the villagers escaped in the confusion, like Stoddard, and either fled half dead with cold towards Hatfield, or sought refuge in the fortified house of Jonthan Wells.

The house of Stebbins, the minister's next neighbor, had not been attacked so soon as the rest, and the inmates had a little time for preparation. They consisted of Stebbins himself, with his wife and five children, David Hoyt, Joseph Catlin, Benjamin Church, a namesake of the old Indian fighter of Philip's War, and three other men,—probably refugees who had brought their wives and families within the palisaded enclosure for safety. Thus the house contained seven men, four or five women, and a considerable number of children. Though the walls were bullet-proof, it was not built for defence. The men, however, were well supplied with guns, powder, and lead, and they seem to have found some means of barricading the windows. When the enemy tried to break in, they drove them back with loss. On this, the French and Indians gathered in great numbers before the house, showered

bullets upon it, and tried to set it on fire. They were again repulsed, with the loss of several killed and wounded; among
the former a Caughnawaga chief, and among the latter a
French officer. Still the firing continued. If the assailants had
made a resolute assault, the defenders must have been overpowered; but to risk lives in open attack was contrary to
every maxim of forest warfare. The women in the house behaved with great courage, and moulded bullets, which the
men shot at the enemy. Stebbins was killed outright, and
Church was wounded, as was also the wife of David Hoyt. At
length most of the French and Indians, disgusted with the ob-
stinacy of the defence, turned their attention to other quarters; though some kept up their fire under cover of the meeting-house and another building within easy range of gunshot.

This building was the house of Ensign John Sheldon, already mentioned. The Indians had had some difficulty in mastering it; for the door being of thick oak plank, studded with
nails of wrought iron and well barred, they could not break it
open. After a time, however, they hacked a hole in it, through
which they fired and killed Mrs. Sheldon as she sat on the
edge of a bed in a lower room. Her husband, a man of great
resolution, seems to have been absent. Their son John, with
Hannah his wife, jumped from an upper chamber window.
The young woman sprained her ankle in the fall, and lay helpless, but begged her husband to run to Hatfield for aid, which
he did, while she remained a prisoner. The Indians soon got
in at a back door, seized Mercy Sheldon, a little girl of two
years, and dashed out her brains on the door-stone. Her two
brothers and her sister Mary, a girl of sixteen, were captured.
The house was used for a short time as a depot for prisoners,
and here also was brought the French officer wounded in the
attack on the Stebbins house. A family tradition relates that as
he lay in great torment he begged for water, and that it was
brought him by one of the prisoners, Mrs. John Catlin, whose
husband, son, and infant grandson had been killed, and who,
nevertheless, did all in her power to relieve the sufferings of
the wounded man. Probably it was in recognition of this
charity that when the other prisoners were led away, Mrs.
Catlin was left behind. She died of grief a few weeks later.

The sun was scarcely an hour high when the miserable
drove of captives was conducted across the river to the foot
of a mountain or high hill. Williams and his family were soon
compelled to follow, and his house was set on fire. As they
led him off he saw that other houses within the palisade were

burning, and that all were in the power of the enemy except that of his neighbor Stebbins, where the gallant defenders still kept their assailants at bay. Having collected all their prisoners, the main body of the French and Indians began to withdraw towards the pine forest, where they had left their packs and snow-shoes, and to prepare for a retreat before the country should be roused, first murdering in cold blood Marah Carter, a little girl of five years, whom they probably thought unequal to the march. Several parties, however, still lingered in the village, firing on the Stebbins house, killing cattle, hogs, and sheep, and gathering such plunder as the place afforded.

Early in the attack, and while it was yet dark, the light of burning houses, reflected from the fields of snow, had been seen at Hatfield, Hadley, and Northampton. The alarm was sounded through the slumbering hamlets, and parties of men mounted on farm-horses, with saddles or without, hastened to the rescue, not doubting that the fires were kindled by Indians. When the sun was about two hours high, between thirty and forty of them were gathered at the fortified house of Jonathan Wells, at the southern end of the village. The houses of this neighborhood were still standing, and seem not to have been attacked,—the stubborn defence of the Stebbins house having apparently prevented the enemy from pushing much beyond the palisaded enclosure. The house of Wells was full of refugee families. A few Deerfield men here joined the horsemen from the lower towns, as also did four or five of the yeoman soldiers who had escaped the fate of most of their comrades. The horsemen left their horses within Wells's fence; he himself took the lead, and the whole party rushed in together at the southern gate of the palisaded enclosure, drove out the plunderers, and retook a part of their plunder. The assailants of the Stebbins house, after firing at it for three hours, were put to flight, and those of its male occupants who were still alive joined their countrymen, while the women and children ran back for harborage to the house of Wells.

Wells and his men, now upwards of fifty, drove the flying enemy more than a mile acros the river meadows, and ran in headlong pursuit over the crusted snow, killing a considerable number. In the eagerness of the chase many threw off their overcoats, and even their jackets. Wells saw the danger, and vainly called on them to stop. Their blood was up, and most of them were young and inexperienced.

Meanwhile the firing at the village had been heard by

Rouville's main body, who had already begun their retreat northward. They turned back to support their comrades, and hid themselves under the bank of the river till the pursuers drew near, when they gave them a close volley and rushed upon them with the war-whoop. Some of the English were shot down, and the rest driven back. There was no panic. "We retreated," says Wells, "facing about and firing." When they reached the palisade they made a final stand, covering by their fire such of their comrades as had fallen within range of musket-shot, and thus saving them from the scalping-knife. The French did not try to dislodge them. Nine of them had been killed, several were wounded, and one was captured.[7]

The number of English carried off prisoners was one hundred and eleven, and the number killed was according to one list forty-seven, and according to another fifty-three, the latter including some who were smothered in the cellars of their burning houses. The names, and in most cases the ages, of both captives and slain are preserved. Those who escaped with life and freedom were, by the best account, one hundred and thirty-seven. An official tabular statement, drawn up on the spot, sets the number of houses burned at seventeen. The house of the town clerk, Thomas French, escaped, as before mentioned, and the town records, with other papers in his charge, were saved. The meeting-house also was left standing. The house of Sheldon was hastily set on fire by the French and Indians when their rear was driven out of the village by Wells and his men; but the fire was extinguished, and "the Old Indian House," as it was called, stood till the year 1849. Its door, deeply scarred with hatchets, and with a hole cut

[7] On the thirty-first of May, 1704, Jonathan Wells and Ebenezer Wright petitioned the General Court for compensation for the losses of those who drove the enemy out of Deerfield and chased them into the meadow. The petition, which was granted, gives an account of the affair, followed by a list of all the men engaged. They number fifty-seven, including the nine who were killed. A list of the plunder retaken from the enemy, consisting of guns, blankets, hatchets, etc., is also added. Several other petitions for the relief of men wounded at the same time are preserved in the archives of Massachusetts. In 1736 the survivors of the party, with the representatives of those who had died, petitioned the General Court for allotments of land, in recognition of their services. This petition also was granted. It is accompanied by a narrative written by Wells. These and other papers on the same subject have been recently printed by Mr. George Sheldon, of Deerfield.

near the middle, is still preserved in the Memorial Hall at Deerfield.[8]

Vaudreuil wrote to the minister, Ponchartrain, that the French lost two or three killed, and twenty or twenty-one wounded, Rouville himself being among the latter. This cannot include the Indians, since there is proof that the enemy left behind a considerable number of their dead. Wherever resistance was possible it had been of the most prompt and determined character.[9]

Long before noon the French and Indians were on their northward march with their train of captives. More armed men came up from the settlements below, and by midnight about eighty were gathered at the ruined village. Couriers had been sent to rouse the country, and before evening of the next day (the first of March) the force at Deerfield was increased to two hundred and fifty; but a thaw and a warm rain had set in, and as few of the men had snow-shoes, pursuit was out of the question. Even could the agile savages and their allies have been overtaken, the probable consequence would have been the murdering of the captives to prevent their escape.

In spite of the foul blow dealt upon it, Deerfield was not abandoned. Such of its men as were left were taken as soldiers into the pay of the province, while the women and children were sent to the villages below. A small garrison was also stationed at the spot, under command of Captain Jonathan Wells, and thus the village held its ground till the storm of war should pass over.[10]

[8] After the old house was demolished, this door was purchased by my friend Dr. Daniel Denison Slade, and given by him to the town of Deerfield, on condition that it should be carefully preserved. For an engraving of "the Old Indian House," see Hoyt, *Indian Wars* (ed. 1824).

[9] Governor Dudley, writing to Lord —— on 21 April, 1704, says that thirty dead bodies of the enemy were found in the village and on the meadow. Williams, the minister, says that they did not seem inclined to rejoice over their success, and continued for several days to bury members of their party who died of wounds on the return march. He adds that he learned in Canada that they lost more than forty, though Vaudreuil assured him that they lost but eleven.

[10] On the attack of Deerfield, see Williams, *The Redeemed Captive Returning to Zion*. This is the narrative of the minister, John Williams. *Account of the Captivity of Stephen Williams, written by*

We have seen that the minister, Williams, with his wife and family, were led from their burning house across the river to the foot of the mountain, where the crowd of terrified and disconsolate captives—friends, neighbors, and relatives—were already gathered. Here they presently saw the fight in the meadow, and were told that if their countrymen attempted a rescue, they should all be put to death. "After this," writes

himself. This is the narrative of one of the minister's sons, eleven years old when captured. It is printed in the Appendix to the *Biographical Memoir of Rev. John Williams* (Hartford, 1837); *An account of yᵉ destruction at Derefd. febʳ. 29, 1703/4,* in *Proceedings of the Mass. Hist. Soc.,* 1867, p. 478. This valuable document was found among the papers of Fitz-John Winthrop, governor of Connecticut. The authorities of that province, on hearing of the catastrophe at Deerfield, promptly sent an armed force to its relief, which, however, could not arrive till long after the enemy were gone. The paper in question seems to be the official report of one of the Connecticut officers. After recounting what had taken place, he gives a tabular list of the captives, the slain, and those who escaped, with the estimated losses in property of each inhabitant. The list of captives is not quite complete. Compare the lists given by Stephen Williams at the end of his narrative. The town records of Hatfield give various particulars concerning the attack on its unfortunate neighbor, as do the letters of Colonel Samuel Partridge, commanding the militia of the county. Hoyt, *Antiquarian Researches,* gives a valuable account of it. The careful and unwearied research of Mr. George Sheldon, the lineal descendant of Ensign John Sheldon, among all sources, public or private, manuscript or in print, that could throw light on the subject cannot be too strongly commended, and I am indebted to him for much valued information.

Penhallow's short account is inexact, and many of the more recent narratives are not only exaggerated, but sometimes absurdly incorrect.

The French notices of the affair are short, and give few particulars. Vaudreuil in one letter sets the number of prisoners at one hundred and fifty, and increases it in another to two hundred and fifty. Ramesay, governor of Montreal, who hated Hertel de Rouville, and bore no love to Vaudreuil, says that fifty-six women and children were murdered on the way to Canada,—which is a gross exaggeration. (*Ramesay au Ministre,* 14 *Novembre,* 1704.) The account by Dr. Ethier in the *Revue Canadienne* of 1874 is drawn entirely from the *Redeemed Captive* of Williams, with running comments by the Canadian writer, but no new information. The comments chiefly consist in praise of Williams for truth when he speaks favorably of the Canadians, and charges of lying when he speaks otherwise.

Williams, "we went up the mountain, and saw the smoke of the fires in town, and beheld the awful desolation of Deerfield; and before we marched any farther they killed a suckling child of the English."

The French and Indians marched that afternoon only four or five miles,—to Greenfield meadows,—where they stopped to encamp, dug away the snow, laid spruce-boughs on the ground for beds, and bound fast such of the prisoners as seemed able to escape. The Indians then held a carousal on some liquor they had found in the village, and in their drunken rage murdered a negro man belonging to Williams. In spite of their precautions, Joseph Alexander, one of the prisoners, escaped during the night, at which they were greatly incensed; and Rouville ordered Williams to tell his companions in misfortune that if any more of them ran off, the rest should be burned alive.[11]

The prisoners were the property of those who had taken them. Williams had two masters, one of the three who had seized him having been shot in the attack on the house of Stebbins. His principal owner was a surly fellow who would not let him speak to the other prisoners; but as he was presently chosen to guard the rear, the minister was left in the hands of his other master, who allowed him to walk beside his wife and help her on the way. Having borne a child a few weeks before, she was in no condition for such a march, and felt that her hour was near. Williams speaks of her in the strongest terms of affection. She made no complaint, and accepted her fate with resignation. "We discoursed," he says, "of the happiness of those who had God for a father and friend, as also that it was our reasonable duty quietly to submit to his will." Her thoughts were for her remaining children, whom she commended to her husband's care. Their intercourse was short. The Indian who had gone to the rear of the train soon returned, separated them, ordered Williams to the front, "and so made me take a last farewell of my dear wife, the desire of my eyes and companion in many mercies and afflictions." They came soon after to Green River, a stream then about knee-deep, and so swift that the water had not frozen. After wading it with difficulty, they climbed a snow-covered hill beyond. The minister, with strength almost spent, was permitted to rest a few moments at the top; and as

[11] John Williams, *The Redeemed Captive.* Compare Stephen Williams, *Account of the Captivity,* etc.

the other prisoners passed by in turn, he questioned each for news of his wife. He was not left long in suspense. She had fallen from weakness in fording the stream, but gained her feet again, and, drenched in the icy current, struggled to the farther bank, when the savage who owned her, finding that she could not climb the hill, killed her with one stroke of his hatchet. Her body was left on the snow till a few of her townsmen, who had followed the trail, found it a day or two after, carried it back to Deerfield, and buried it in the church-yard.

On the next day the Indians killed an infant and a little girl of eleven years; on the day following, Friday, they toma-hawked a woman, and on Saturday four others. This apparent cruelty was in fact a kind of mercy. The victims could not keep up with the party, and the death-blow saved them from a lonely and lingering death from cold and starvation. Some of the children, when spent with the march, were carried on the backs of their owners,—partly, perhaps, through kindness, and partly because every child had its price.

On the fourth day of the march they came to the mouth of West River, which enters the Connecticut a little above the present town of Brattleboro'. Some of the Indians were dis-contented with the distribution of the captives, alleging that others had got more than their share; on which the whole troop were mustered together, and some changes of ownership were agreed upon. At this place dog-trains and sledges had been left, and these served to carry their wounded, as well as some of the captive children. Williams was stripped of the better part of his clothes, and others given him instead, so full of vermin that they were a torment to him through all the journey. The march now continued with pitiless speed up the frozen Connecticut, where the recent thaw had covered the ice with slush and water ankle-deep.

On Sunday they made a halt, and the minister was per-mitted to preach a sermon from the text, "Hear, all people, and behold my sorrow: my virgins and my young men are gone into captivity." Then amid the ice, the snow, the forest, and the savages, his forlorn flock joined their voices in a psalm.[12] On Monday guns were heard from the rear, and the Indians and their allies, in great alarm, bound their prisoners fast, and prepared for battle. It proved, however, that the

[12] The small stream at the mouth of which Williams is supposed to have preached is still called Williams River.

guns had been fired at wild geese by some of their own number; on which they recovered their spirits, fired a volley for joy, and boasted that the English could not overtake them.[13] More women fainted by the way and died under the hatchet, —some with pious resignation, some with despairing apathy, some with a desperate joy.

Two hundred miles of wilderness still lay between them and the Canadian settlements. It was a waste without a house or even a wigwam, except here and there the bark shed of some savage hunter. At the mouth of White River, the party divided into small bands,—no doubt in order to subsist by hunting, for provisions were fast failing. The Williams family were separated. Stephen was carried up the Connecticut; Samuel and Eunice, with two younger children, were carried off in various directions; while the wretched father, along with two small children of one of his parishioners, was compelled to follow his Indian masters up the valley of White River. One of the children—a little girl—was killed on the next morning by her Caughnawaga owner, who was unable to carry her.[14] On the next Sunday the minister was left in camp with one Indian and the surviving child,—a boy of nine,— while the rest of the party were hunting. "My spirit," he says, "was almost overwhelmed within me." But he found comfort in the text, "Leave thy fatherless children, I will preserve them alive." Nor was his hope deceived. His youngest surviving child,—a boy of four,—though harshly treated by his owners, was carried on their shoulders or dragged on a sledge to the end of the journey. His youngest daughter—seven years old —was treated with great kindness thoughout. Samuel and Eunice suffered much from hunger, but were dragged on sledges when too faint to walk. Stephen nearly starved to death; but after eight months in the forest, he safely reached Chambly with his Indian masters.

Of the whole band of captives, only about half ever again saw friends and home. Seventeen broke down on the way and were killed; while David Hoyt and Jacob Hix died of starvation at Coos Meadows, on the upper Connecticut. During the entire march, no woman seems to have been subjected to violence; and this holds true, with rare exceptions, in all the

[13] Stephen Williams, *Account of the Captivity*, etc. His father also notices the incident.

[14] The name Macquas (Mohawks) is always given to the Caughnawagas by the elder Williams.

Indian wars of New England. Their remarkable forbearance towards female prisoners, so different from the practice of many western tribes, was probably due to a form of super-stition, aided perhaps by the influence of the missionaries.[15] It is to be observed, however, that the heathen savages of King Philip's War, who had never a Jesuit, were no less for-bearing in this respect.

The hunters of Williams's party killed five moose, the flesh of which, smoked and dried, was carried on their backs and that of the prisoner whom they had provided with snow-shoes. Thus burdened, the minister toiled on, following his masters along the frozen current of White River till, crossing the snowy backs of the Green Mountains, they struck the head-waters of the stream then called French River, now the Winooski, or Onion. Being in great fear of a thaw, they pushed on with double speed. Williams was not used to snow-shoes, and they gave him those painful cramps of the legs and ankles called in Canada *mal à la raquette*. One morning at dawn he was waked by his chief master and or-dered to get up, say his prayers, and eat his breakfast, for they must make a long march that day. The minister was in de-spair. "After prayer," he says, "I arose from my knees; but my feet were so tender, swollen, bruised, and full of pain that I could scarce stand upon them without holding on the wig-wam. And when the Indians said, 'You must run to-day,' I answered I could not run. My master, pointing to his hatchet, said to me, 'Then I must dash out your brains and take your scalp.'" The Indian proved better than his word, and Williams was suffered to struggle on as he could. "God wonderfully supported me," he writes, "and my strength was restored and renewed to admiration." He thinks that he walked that day forty miles on the snow. Following the Winooski to its mouth, the party reached Lake Champlain a little north of the pres-ent city of Burlington. Here the swollen feet of the prisoner were tortured by the rough ice, till snow began to fall and cover it with a soft carpet. Bending under his load, and powdered by the falling flakes, he toiled on till, at noon of a Saturday, lean, tired, and ragged, he and his masters reached the French outpost of Chambly, twelve or fifteen miles from Montreal.

Here the unhappy wayfarer was treated with great kindness

[15] The Iroquois are well known to have had superstitions in connection with sexual abstinence.

both by the officers of the fort and by the inhabitants, one of the chief among whom lodged him in his house and welcomed him to his table. After a short stay at Chambly, Williams and his masters set out in a canoe for Sorel. On the way a French-woman came down to the bank of the river and invited the party to her house, telling the minister that she herself had once been a prisoner among the Indians, and knew how to feel for him. She seated him a table, spread a table-cloth, and placed food before him, while the Indians, to their great in-dignation, were supplied with a meal in the chimney-corner. Similar kindness was shown by the inhabitants along the way till the party reached their destination, the Abenaki village of St. Francis, to which his masters belonged. Here there was a fort, in which lived two Jesuits, directors of the mission, and here Williams found several English children, captured the summer before during the raid on the settlements of Maine, and already transformed into little Indians both in dress and behavior. At the gate of the fort one of the Jesuits met him, and asked him to go into the church and give thanks to God for sparing his life, to which he replied that he would give thanks in some other place. The priest then commanded him to go, which he refused to do. When on the next day the bell rang for mass, one of his Indian masters seized him and dragged him into the church, where he got behind the door, and watched service from his retreat with extreme disapproba-tion. One of the Jesuits telling him that he would go to hell for not accepting the apostolic traditions, and trusting only in the Bible, he replied that he was glad to know that Christ was to be his judge, and not they. His chief master, who was a zealot in his way, and as much bound to the rites and forms of the Church as he had been before his conversion to his "medicines," or practices of heathen superstition, one day ordered him to make the sign of the cross, and on his refusal, tried to force him. But as the minister was tough and mus-cular, the Indian could not guide his hand. Then, pulling out a crucifix that hung at his neck, he told Williams in broken English to kiss it; and being again refused, he brandished his hatchet over him and threatened to knock out his brains. This failing of the desired effect, he threw down the hatchet and said he would first bite out the minister's finger-nails,—a form of torture then in vogue among the northern Indians, both converts and heathen. Williams offered him a hand and in-vited him to begin; on which he gave the thumb-nail a gripe with his teeth, and then let it go, saying, "No good minister, bad as the devil." The failure seems to have discouraged him, for he made no further attempt to convert the intractable heretic.

The direct and simple narrative of Williams is plainly the work of an honest and courageous man. He was the most important capture of the year; and the governor, hearing that he was at St. Francis, despatched a canoe to request the Jesuits of the mission to send him to Montreal. Thither, therefore, his masters carried him, expecting, no doubt, a good price for their prisoner. Vaudreuil, in fact, bought him, exchanged his tattered clothes for good ones, lodged him in his house, and, in the words of Williams, "was in all respects relating to my outward man courteous and charitable to admiration." He sent for two of the minister's children who were in the town, bought his eldest daughter from the Indians, and promised to do what he could to get the others out of their hands. His youngest son was bought by a lady of the place, and his eldest by a merchant. His youngest daughter, Eunice, then seven or eight years old, was at the mission of St. Louis, or Caughnawaga. Vaudreuil sent a priest to conduct Williams thither and try to ransom the child. But the Jesuits of the mission flatly refused to let him speak to or see her. Williams says that Vaudreuil was very angry at hearing of this; and a few days after, he went himself to Caughnawaga with the minister. This time the Jesuits, whose authority within their mission seemed almost to override that of the governor himself, yielded so far as to permit the father to see his child, on condition that he spoke to no other English prisoner. He talked with her for an hour, exhorting her never to forget her catechism, which she had learned by rote. Vaudreuil and his wife afterwards did all in their power to procure her ransom; but the Indians, or the missionaries in their name, would not let her go. "She is there still," writes Williams two years later, "and has forgotten to speak English." What grieved him still more, Eunice had forgotten her catechism.

While he was at Montreal, his movements were continually watched, lest he should speak to other prisoners and prevent their conversion. He thinks these precautions were due to the priests, whose constant endeavor it was to turn the captives, or at least the younger and more manageable among them, into Catholics and Canadians. The governor's kindness towards him never failed, though he told him that he should not be set free till the English gave up one Captain Baptiste, a noted sea-rover whom they had captured some time before.

He was soon after sent down the river to Quebec along with the superior of the Jesuits. Here he lodged seven weeks with a member of the council, who treated him kindly, but told him that if he did not avoid intercourse with the other English prisoners he would be sent farther away. He saw much of the Jesuits, who courteously asked him to dine; though he says that one of them afterwards made some Latin verses about him, in which he was likened to a captive wolf. Another Jesuit told him that when the mission Indians set out on their raid against Deerfield, he charged them to baptize all children before killing them,—such, he said, was his desire for the salvation even of his enemies. To murdering the children after they were baptized, he appears to have made no objection. Williams says that in their dread lest he should prevent the conversion of the other prisoners, the missionaries promised him a pension from the King and free intercourse with his children and neighbors if he would embrace the Catholic faith and remain in Canada; to which he answered that he would do so without reward if he thought their religion was true, but as he believed the contrary, "the offer of the whole world would tempt him no more than a blackberry."

To prevent him more effectually from perverting the minds of his captive countrymen, and fortifying them in their heresy, he was sent to Château Richer, a little below Quebec, and lodged with the parish priest, who was very kind to him. "I am persuaded," he writes, "that he abhorred their sending down the heathen to commit outrages against the English, saying it is more like committing murders than carrying on war."

He was sorely tried by the incessant efforts to convert the prisoners. "Sometimes they would tell me my children, sometimes my neighbors, were turned to be of their religion. Some made it their work to allure poor souls by flatteries and great promises; some threatened, some offered abuse to such as refused to go to church and be present at mass; and some they industriously contrived to get married among them. I understood they would tell the English that I was turned, that they might gain them to change their religion. These their endeavors to seduce to popery were very exercising to me."

After a time he was permitted to return to Quebec, where he met an English Franciscan, who, he says, had been sent from France to aid in converting the prisoners. Lest the minister should counteract the efforts of the friar, the priests had him sent back to Château Richer; "but," he observes, "God showed his dislike of such a persecuting spirit; for the very next day the Seminary, a very famous building, was most of it burnt down, by a joiner letting a coal of fire drop among the shavings."[16]

The heaviest of all his tribulations now fell upon him. His son Samuel, about sixteen years old, had been kept at Montreal under the tutelage of Father Meriel, a priest of St. Sulpice. The boy afterwards declared that he was promised great rewards if he would make the sign of the cross, and severe punishment if he would not. Proving obstinate, he was whipped till at last he made the sign; after which he was told to go to mass and on his refusal, four stout boys of the school were ordered to drag him in. Williams presently received a letter in Samuel's handwriting, though dictated, as the father believed, by his priestly tutors. In this was recounted, with many edifying particulars, the deathbed conversion of two New England women; and to the minister's unspeakable grief and horror, the messenger who brought the letter told him that the boy himself had turned Catholic. "I have heard the news," he wrote to his recreant son, "with the most distressing, afflicting, sorrowful spirit. Oh, I pity you, I mourn over you day and night. Oh, I pity your weakness that, through the craftiness of man, you are turned from the simplicity of the gospel." Though his correspondence was strictly watched, he managed to convey to the boy a long exposition, from his own pen, of the infallible truth of Calvinistic orthodoxy, and the damnable errors of Rome. This, or something else, had its effect. Samuel returned to the creed of his fathers; and being at last exchanged, went home to Deerfield, where he was chosen town-clerk in 1713, and where he soon after died.[17]

Williams gives many particulars of the efforts of the priests to convert the prisoners, and his account, like the rest of his story, bears the marks of truth. There was a treble motive for conversion: it recruited the Church, weakened the enemy, and strengthened Canada, since few of the converts would peril their souls by returning to their heretic relatives. The means of conversion varied. They were gentle when gentleness seemed likely to answer the purpose. Little girls and young women were placed in convents, where it is safe to assume that they were treated with the most tender kindness by the

[16] Williams remarks that the Seminary had also been burned three years before. This was the fire of November, 1701.
[17] Note of Mr. George Sheldon.

sisterhood, who fully believed that to gain them to the faith was to snatch them from perdition. But when they or their brothers proved obdurate, different means were used. Threats of hell were varied by threats of a whipping, which, according to Williams, were often put into execution. Parents were rigorously severed from their families; though one Lalande, who had been sent to watch the elder prisoners, reported that they would persist in trying to see their children, till some of them were killed in the attempt. "Here," writes Williams, "might be a history in itself of the trials and sufferings of many of our children, who, after separation from grown persons, have been made to do as they would have them. I mourned when I thought with myself that I had one child with the Maquas [Caughnawagas], a second turned papist, and a little child of six years of age in danger to be instructed in popery, and knew full well that all endeavors would be used to prevent my seeing or speaking with them." He also says that he and others were told that if they would turn Catholic their children should be restored to them; and among other devices, some of his parisoners were assured that their pastor himself had seen the error of his ways and bowed in submission to Holy Church.

In midwinter, not quite a year after their capture, the prisoners were visited by a gleam of hope. John Sheldon, accompanied by young John Wells, of Deerfield, and Captain Livingston, of Albany, came to Montreal with letters from Governor Dudley, proposing an exchange. Sheldon's wife and infant child, his brother-in-law, and his son-in-law had been killed. Four of his children, with his daughter-in-law, Hannah, —the same who had sprained her ankle in leaping from her chamber window,—besides others of his near relatives and connections, were prisoners in Canada; and so also was the mother of young Wells. In the last December, Sheldon and Wells had gone to Boston and begged to be sent as envoys to the French governor. The petition was readily granted, and Livingston, who chanced to be in the town, was engaged to accompany them. After a snow-shoe journey of extreme hardship they reached their destination, and were received with courtesy by Vaudreuil. But difficulties arose. The French, and above all the clergy, were unwilling to part with captives, many of whom they hoped to transform into Canadians by conversion and adoption. Many also were in the hands of the Indians, who demanded payment for them,—which Dudley had always refused, declaring that he would not "set up an Algiers trade" by buying them from their pretended owners; and he wrote to Vaudreuil that for his own part he "would never permit a savage to tell him that any Christian prisoner was at his disposal." Vaudreuil had insisted that his Indians could not be compelled to give up their captives, since they were not subjects of France, but only allies,—which, so far as concerned the mission Indians within the colony, was but a pretext. It is true, however, that the French authorities were in such fear of offending even these that they rarely ventured to cross their interests or their passions. Other difficulties were raised, and though the envoys remained in Canada till late in spring, they accomplished little. At last, probably to get rid of their importunities, five prisoners were given up to them,— Sheldon's daughter-in-law, Hannah; Esther Williams, eldest daughter of the minister; a certain Ebeneezer Carter; and two others unknown. With these, Sheldon and his companions set out in May on their return; and soon after they were gone, four young men,—Baker, Nims, Kellogg, and Petty,—desperate at being left in captivity, made their escape from Montreal, and reached Deerfield before the end of June, half dead with hunger.

Sheldon and his party were escorted homeward by eight soldiers under Courtemanche, an officer of distinction, whose orders were to "make himself acquainted with the country." He fell ill at Boston, where he was treated with much kindness, and on his recovery was sent home by sea, along with Captain Vetch and Samuel Hill, charged to open a fresh negotiation. With these, at the request of Courtemanche, went young William Dudley, son of the governor.[18]

They were received at Quebec with a courtesy qualified by extreme caution, lest they should spy out the secrets of the land. The mission was not very successful, though the elder Dudley had now a good number of French prisoners in his hands, captured in Acadia or on the adjacent seas. A few only of the English were released, including the boy, Stephen Williams, whom Vaudreuil had bought for forty crowns from his Indian master.

[18] The elder Dudley speaks wtih great warmth of Courtemanche, who, on his part, seems equally pleased with his entertainers. Young Dudley was a boy of eighteen. "Il a du mérite," says Vaudreuil. *Dudley to Vaudreuil, 4 July, 1705; Vaudreuil au Ministre, 19 Octobre, 1705.*

In the following winter John Sheldon made another journey on foot to Canada, with larger powers than before. He arrived in March, 1706, and returned with forty-four of his released countrymen, who, says Williams, were chiefly adults permitted to go because there was no hope of converting them. The English governor had by this time seen the necessity of greater concessions, and had even consented to release the noted Captain Baptiste, whom the Boston merchants regarded as a pirate. In the same summer Samuel Appleton and John Bonner, in the brigantine "Hope," brought a considerable number of French prisoners to Quebec, and returned to Boston at the end of October with fifty-seven English, of all ages. For three, at least, of this number money was paid by the English, probably on account of prisoners bought by Frenchmen from the Indians. The minister, Williams, was exchanged for Baptiste, the so-called pirate, and two of his children were also redeemed, though the Caughnawagas, or their missionaries, refused to part with his daughter Eunice. Williams says that the priests made great efforts to induce the prisoners to remain in Canada, tempting some with the prospect of pensions from the King, and frightening others with promises of damnation, joined with predictions of shipwreck on the way home. He thinks that about one hundred were left in Canada, many of whom were children in the hands of the Indians, who could easily hide them in the woods, and who were known in some cases to have done so. Seven more were redeemed in the following year by the indefatigable Sheldon, on a third visit to Canada.[19]

The exchanged prisoners had been captured at various times and places. Those from Deerfield amounted in all to about sixty, or a little more than half the whole number carried off. Most of the others were dead or converted. Some married Canadians, and others their fellow-captives. The history of some of them can be traced with certainty. Thus, Thomas French, blacksmith and town clerk of Deerfield, and

[19] In 1878 Miss C. Alice Baker, of Cambridge, Mass., a descendant of Abigail Stebbins, read a paper on John Sheldon before the Memorial Association at Deerfield. It is the result of great research, and contains much original matter, including correspondence between Sheldon and the captives when in Canada, as well as a full and authentic account of his several missions. Mr. George Sheldon has also traced out with great minuteness the history of his ancestor's negotiations.

deacon of the church, was captured, with his wife and six children. His wife and infant child were killed on the way to Canada. He and his two eldest children were exchanged and brought home. His daughter Freedom was converted, baptized under the name of Marie Françoise, and married to Jean Daulnay, a Canadian. His daughter Martha was baptized as Marguerite, and married to Jacques Roy, on whose death she married Jean Louis Ménard, by whom she became ancestress of Joseph Plessis, eleventh bishop of Quebec. Elizabeth Corse, eight years old when captured, was baptized under her own name, and married to Jean Dumontel. Abigail Stebbins, baptized as Marguerite, lived many years at Boucherville, wife of Jacques de Noyon, a sergeant in the colony troops. The widow, Sarah Hurst, whose youngest child, Benjamin, had been murdered on the Deerfield meadows, was baptized as Marie Jeanne.[20] Joanna Kellogg, eleven years old when taken, married a Caughnawaga chief, and became, at all points, an Indian squaw.

She was not alone in this strange transformation. Eunice Williams, the namesake of her slaughtered mother, remained in the wigwams of the Caughnawagas, forgot, as we have seen, her English and her catechism, was baptized, and in due time married to an Indian of the tribe, who thenceforward called himself Williams. Thus her hybrid children bore her family name. Her father, who returned to his parish at Deerfield, and her brother Stephen, who became a minister like his parent, never ceased to pray for her return to her country and her faith. Many years after, in 1740, she came with her husband to visit her relatives in Deerfield, dressed as a squaw and wrapped in an Indian blanket. Nothing would induce her to stay, though she was persuaded on one occasion to put on a civilized dress and go to church; after which she impatiently discarded her gown and resumed her blanket. As she was

[20] The above is drawn mainly from extracts made by Miss Baker from the registers of the Church of Notre Dame at Montreal. Many of the acts of baptism bear the signature of Father Meriel, so often mentioned in the narrative of Williams. Apparently, Meriel spoke English. At least there is a letter in English from him, relating to Eunice Williams, in the Massachusetts Archives, vol. 51. Some of the correspondence between Dudley and Vaudreuil concerning exchange of prisoners will be found among the Paris documents in the State House at Boston. Copies of these papers were printed at Quebec in 1883–1885, though with many inaccuracies.

kindly treated by her relatives, and as no attempt was made to detain her against her will, she came again in the next year, bringing two of her half-breed children, and twice afterwards repeated the visit. She and her husband were offered a tract of land if they would settle in New England; but she positively refused, saying that it would endanger her soul. She lived to a great age, a squaw to the last.[21]

One of her grandsons, Eleazer Williams, turned Protestant, was educated at Dartmouth College at the charge of friends in New England, and was for a time missionary to the Indians of Green Bay, in Wisconsin. His character for veracity was not of the best. He deceived the excellent antiquarian, Hoyt, by various inventions touching the attack on Deerfield, and in the latter part of his life tried to pass himself off as the lost Dauphin, son of Louis XVI.[22]

Here it may be observed that the descendants of young captives brought into Canada by the mission Indians during the various wars with the English colonies became a considerable element in the Canadian population. Perhaps the most prominent example is that of the Gill family. In June, 1697, a boy named Samuel Gill, then in his tenth year, was captured by the Abenakis at Salisbury in Massachusetts, car-

[21] Stephen W. Williams, *Memoir of the Rev. John Williams*, 53. *Sermon preached at Mansfield, August 4, 1741, on behalf of Mrs. Eunice, the daughter of Rev. John Williams; by Solomon Williams, A.M. Letter of Mrs. Colton, great granddaughter of John Williams* (in appendix to the *Memoir of Rev. John Williams*).

[22] I remember to have seen Eleazer Williams at my father's house in Boston, when a boy. My impression of him is that of a good-looking and somewhat portly man, showing little trace of Indian blood, and whose features, I was told, resembled those of the Bourbons. Probably this likeness, real or imagined, suggested the imposition he was practising at the time. The story of the "Bell of St. Regis" is probably another of his inventions. It is to the effect that the bell of the church at Deerfield was carried by the Indians to the mission of St. Regis, and that it is there still. But there is reason to believe that there was no church bell at Deerfield, and it is certain that St. Regis did not exist till more than a half-century after Deerfield was attacked. It has been said that the story is true, except that the name of Caughnawaga should be substituted for that of St. Regis; but the evidence for this conjecture is weak. On the legend of the bell, see Le Moine, *Maple Leaves, New Series* (1873), 29; *Proceedings of the Mass. Hist. Soc.*, 1869, 1870, 311; *Hist. Mag. 2d Series*, ix. 401. Hough, *Hist. St. Lawrence and Franklin Counties*, 116, gives the story without criticism.

ried to St. Francis, and converted. Some years later he married a young English girl, said to have been named James, and to have been captured at Kennebunk.[23] In 1866 the late Abbé Maurault, missionary at St. Francis, computed their descendants at nine hundred and fifty-two, in whose veins French, English, and Abenaki blood were mixed in every conceivable proportion. He gives the tables of genealogy in full, and says that two hundred and thirteen of this prolific race still bear the surname of Gill. "If," concludes the worthy priest, "one should trace out all the English families brought into Canada by the Abenakis, one would be astonished at the number of persons who to-day are indebted to these savages for the blessing of being Catholics and the advantage of being Canadians,"[24]—an advantage for which French-Canadians are so ungrateful that they migrate to the United States by myriads.

[23] The earlier editions of this book follow, in regard to Samuel Gill, the statements of Maurault, which are erroneous, as has been proved by the careful and untiring research of Miss C. Alice Baker, to whose kindness I owe the means of correcting them. Papers in the archives of Massachusetts leave no doubt as to the time and place of Samuel Gill's capture.

[24] Maurault, *Hist. des Abenakis*, 377. I am indebted to R. A. Ramsay, Esq., of Montreal, for a paper on the Gill family, by Mr. Charles Gill, who confirms the statements of Maurault so far as relates to the genealogies.

John and Zechariah Tarbell, captured when boys at Groton, became Caughnawaga chiefs; and one of them, about 1760, founded the mission of St. Regis. Green, *Groton during the Indian Wars,* 116, 117–120.

Chapter 5

1704–1713
The Tormented Frontier

I HAVE TOLD the fate of Deerfield in full, as an example of the desolating raids which for years swept the borders of Massachusetts and New Hampshire. The rest of the miserable story may be passed more briefly. It is in the main a weary detail of the murder of one, two, three, or more men, women, or children waylaid in fields, woods, and lonely roads, or surprised in solitary cabins. Sometimes the attacks were on a larger scale. Thus, not long after the capture of Deerfield, a band of fifty or more Indians fell at dawn of day on a hamlet of five houses near Northampton. The alarm was sounded, and they were pursued. Eight of the prisoners were rescued, and three escaped; most of the others being knocked in the head by their captors. At Oyster River the Indians attacked a loopholed house, in which the women of the neighboring farms had taken refuge while the men were at work in the fields. The women disguised themselves in hats and jackets, fired from the loopholes, and drove off the assailants. In 1709 a hundred and eighty French and Indians again attacked Deerfield, but failed to surprise it, and were put to flight. At Dover, on a Sunday, while the people were at church, a scalping-party approached a fortified house, the garrison of which consisted of one woman,—Esther Jones, who, on seeing them, called out to an imaginary force within, "Here they are! come on! come on!" on which the Indians disappeared.

Soon after the capture of Deerfield, the French authorities, being, according to the prisoner Williams, "wonderfully lifted up with pride," formed a grand war-party, and assured the minister that they would catch so many prisoners that they should not know what to do with them. Beaucour, an officer of great repute, had chief command, and his force consisted of between seven and eight hundred men, of whom about a hundred and twenty were French, and the rest mission Indians.[1] They declared that they would lay waste all the settlements on the Connecticut,—meaning, it seems, to begin with Hatfield. "This army," says Williams, "went away in such a

[1] *Vaudreuil et Beauharnois au Ministre,* 17 *Novembre,* 1704.

78

boasting, triumphant manner that I had great hopes God would discover and disappoint their designs." In fact, their plans came to nought, owing, according to French accounts, to the fright of the Indians; for a soldier having deserted within a day's march of the English settlements, most of them turned back, despairing of a surprise, and the rest broke up into small parties to gather scalps on the outlying farms.[2]

In the summer of 1708 there was a more successful attempt. The converts of all the Canadian missions were mustered at Montreal, where Vaudreuil, by exercising, as he says, "the patience of an angel," soothed their mutual jealousies and persuaded them to go upon a war-party against Newbury, Portsmouth, and other New England villages. Fortunately for the English, the Caughnawagas were only half-hearted towards the enterprise; and through them the watchful Peter Schuyler got hints of it which enabled him, at the eleventh hour, to set the intended victims on their guard. The party consisted of about four hundred, of whom one hundred were French, under twelve young officers and cadets; the whole commanded by Saint-Ours des Chaillons and Hertel de Rouville. For the sake of speed and secrecy, they set out in three bodies, by different routes. The rendezvous was at Lake Winnepesaukee, where they were to be joined by the Norridgewocks, Penobscots, and other eastern Abenakis. The Caughnawagas and Hurons turned back by reason of evil omens and a disease which broke out among them. The rest met on the shores of the lake,—probably at Alton Bay,— where, after waiting in vain for their eastern allies, they resolved to make no attempt on Portsmouth or Newbury, but to turn all their strength upon the smaller village of Haverhill, on the Merrimac. Advancing quickly under cover of night, they made their onslaught at half an hour before dawn, on Sunday, the twenty-ninth of August.

Haverhill consisted of between twenty and thirty dwelling-houses, a meeting-house, and a small picket fort. A body of militia from the lower Massachusetts towns had been hastily distributed along the frontier, on the vague reports of danger sent by Schuyler from Albany; and as the intended point of attack was unknown, the men were of necessity widely scattered. French accounts say that there were thirty of them in

[2] *Vaudreuil et Beauharnois au Ministre,* 17 *Novembre,* 1704; *Vaudreuil au Ministre,* 16 *Novembre,* 1704; *Ramesay au Ministre,* 14 *Novembre,* 1704. Compare Penhallow.

the fort at Haverhill, and more in the houses of the villagers; while others still were posted among the distant farms and hamlets.

In spite of darkness and surprise, the assailants met a stiff resistance and a hot and persistent fusillade. Vaudreuil says that they could dislodge the defenders only by setting fire to both houses and fort. In this they were not very successful, as but few of the dwellings were burned. A fire was kindled against the meeting-house, which was saved by one Davis and a few others, who made a dash from behind the adjacent parsonage, drove the Indians off, and put out the flames. Rolfe, the minister, had already been killed while defending his house. His wife and one of his children were butchered; but two others—little girls of six and eight years—were saved by the self-devotion of his maid-servant, Hagar, apparently a negress, who dragged them into the cellar and hid them under two inverted tubs, where they crouched, dumb with terror, while the Indians ransacked the place without finding them. English accounts say that the number of persons killed—men, women, and children—was forty-eight; which the French increase to a hundred.

The distant roll of drums was presently heard, warning the people on the scattered farms; on which the assailants made a hasty retreat. Posted near Haverhill were three militia officers,—Turner, Price, and Gardner,—lately arrived from Salem. With such men as they had with them, or could hastily get together, they ambushed themselves at the edge of a piece of woods, in the path of the retiring enemy, to the number, as the French say, of sixty or seventy, which it is safe to diminish by a half. The French and Indians, approaching rapidly, were met by a volley which stopped them for the moment; then, throwing down their packs, they rushed on, and after a sharp skirmish broke through the ambuscade and continued their retreat. Vaudreuil sets their total loss at eight killed and eighteen wounded,—the former including two officers. Verchères and Chambly. He further declares that in the skirmish all the English, except ten or twelve, were killed outright; while the English accounts say that the French and Indians took to the woods, leaving nine of their number dead on the spot, along with their medicine chest and all their packs.[3]

[3] *Vaudreuil au Ministre,* 5 *Novembre,* 1708; *Vaudreuil et Raudot au Ministre,* 14 *Novembre,* 1708; Hutchinson, ii. 156; *Mass. Hist. Coll. 2d Series,* iv. 129; Sewall, *Diary,* ii. 234. Penhallow.

Scarcely a hamlet of the Massachusetts and New Hampshire borders escaped a visit from the nimble enemy. Groton, Lancaster, Exeter, Dover, Kittery, Casco, Kingston, York, Berwick, Wells, Winter Harbor, Brookfield, Amesbury, Marlborough, were all more or less infested, usually by small scalping-parties, hiding in the outskirts, waylaying stragglers, or shooting men at work in the fields, and disappearing as soon as their blow was struck. These swift and intangible persecutors were found a far surer and more effectual means of annoyance than larger bodies. As all the warriors were converts of the Canadian missions, and as prisoners were an article of value, cases of torture were not very common; though now and then, as at Exeter, they would roast some poor wretch alive, or bite off his fingers and sear the stumps with red-hot tobacco pipes.

This system of petty, secret, and transient attack put the impoverished colonies to an immense charge in maintaining a cordon of militia along their northern frontier,—a precaution often as vain as it was costly; for the wily savages, covered by the forest, found little difficulty in dodging the scouting-parties, pouncing on their victims, and escaping. Rewards were offered for scalps; but one writer calculates that, all things considered, it cost Massachusetts a thousand pounds of her currency to kill an Indian.[4]

In 1703-1704 six hundred men were kept ranging the woods all winter without finding a single Indian, the enemy having deserted their usual haunts and sought refuge with the French, to emerge in February for the destruction of Deerfield. In the next summer nineteen hundred men were posted along two hundred miles of frontier.[5] This attitude of passive defence exasperated the young men of Massachusetts, and it is said that five hundred of them begged Dudley for leave to make a raid into Canada, on the characteristic condition of

[4] The rewards for scalps were confined to male Indians thought old enough to bear arms,—that is to say, above twelve years. *Act of General Court,* 19 *August,* 1706.

[5] *Dudley to Lord* ——, 21 *April,* 1704. *Address of Council and Assembly to the Queen,* 12 *July,* 1704. The burden on the people was so severe that one writer—not remarkable, however, for exactness of statement—declares that he "is credibly informed that some have been forced to cut open their beds and sell the feathers to pay their taxes." The general poverty did not prevent a contribution in New England for the suffering inhabitants of the Island of St. Christopher.

choosing their own officers. The governor consented; but on a message from Peter Schuyler that he had at last got a promise from the Caughnawagas and other mission Indians to attack the New England borders no more, the raid was countermanded, lest it should waken the tempest anew.[6]

What was the object of these murderous attacks, which stung the enemy without disabling him, confirmed the Indians in their native savagery, and taught the French to emulate it? In the time of Frontenac there was a palliating motive for such barbarous warfare. Canada was then prostrate and stunned under the blows of the Iroquois war. Successful war-parties were needed as a tonic and a stimulant to rouse the dashed spirits of French and Indians alike; but the remedy was a dangerous one, and it drew upon the colony the attack under Sir William Phips, which was near proving its ruin. At present there was no such pressing call for butchering women, children, and peaceful farmers. The motive, such as it was, lay in the fear that the Indian allies of France might pass over to the English, or at least stand neutral. These allies were the Christian savages of the missions, who, all told, from the Caughnawagas to the Micmacs, could hardly have mustered a thousand warriors. The danger was that the Caughnawagas, always open to influence from Albany, might be induced to lay down the hatchet and persuade the rest to follow their example. Therefore, as there was for the time a virtual truce with New York, no pains were spared to commit them irrevocably to war against New England. With the Abenaki tribes of Maine and New Hampshire the need was still more urgent, for they were continually drawn to New England by the cheapness and excellence of English goods; and the only sure means to prevent their trading with the enemy was to incite them to kill him. Some of these savages had been settled in Canada, to keep them under influence and out of temptation; but the rest were still in their native haunts, where it was thought best to keep them well watched by their missionaries, as sentinels and outposts to the colony.

There were those among the French to whom this barba-rous warfare was repugnant. The minister, Ponchartrain, by no means a person of tender scruples, also condemned it for a time. After the attack on Wells and other places under Beaubassin in 1703, he wrote: "It would have been well if this

---

[6] *Vaudreuil au Ministre,* 12 *Novembre,* 1708. Vaudreuil says that he got his information from prisoners.

expedition had not taken place. I have certain knowledge that the English want only peace, knowing that war is contrary to the interests of all the colonies. Hostilities in Canada have always been begun by the French."[7] Afterwards, when these bloody raids had produced their natural effect and spurred the sufferers to attempt the ending of their woes once for all by the conquest of Canada, Ponchartrain changed his mind and encouraged the sending out of war-parties, to keep the English busy at home.

The schemes of a radical cure date from the attack on Deerfield and the murders of the following summer. In the autumn we find Governor Dudley urging the capture of Quebec. "In the last two years," he says, "the Assembly of Massachusetts has spent about £ 50,000 in defending the Province, whereas three or four of the Queen's ships and fifteen hundred New England men would rid us of the French and make further outlay needless,"—a view, it must be admitted, sufficiently sanguine.[8]

But before seeking peace with the sword, Dudley tried less strenuous methods. It may be remembered that in 1705 Captain Vetch and Samuel Hill, together with the governor's young son William, went to Quebec to procure an exchange of prisoners. Their mission had also another object. Vetch carried a letter from Dudley to Vaudreuil, proposing a treaty of neutrality between their respective colonies, and Vaudreuil seems to have welcomed the proposal. Notwithstanding the pacific relations between Canada and New York, he was in constant fear that Dutch and English influence might turn the Five Nations into open enemies of the French; and he therefore declared himself ready to accept the proposals of Dudley, on condition that New York and the other English colonies

[7] *Resumé d'une Lettre de MM. de Vaudreuil et de Beauharnois du 15 Novembre,* 1703, *avec les Observations du Ministre.* Subercase, governor of Acadia, writes on 25 December, 1708, that he hears that a party of Canadians and Indians have attacked a place on the *Maramet* (Merrimac), "et qu'ils y ont égorgé 4 à 500 personnes sans faire quartier aux femmes ni aux enfans." This is an exaggerated report of the affair of Haverhill. M. de Chevry writes in the margin of the letter: "Ces actions de cruauté devroient être modérées:" to which Ponchartrain adds: "Bon; les déendre." His attitude, however, was uncertain; for as early as 1707 we find him approving Vaudreuil for directing the missionaries to prompt the Abenakis to war. *N. Y. Col. Docs.,* ix. 805.

[8] *Dudley to* ——, *26 November,* 1704.

should be included in the treaty, and that the English should be excluded from fishing in the Gulf of St. Lawrence and the Acadian seas. The first condition was difficult, and the second impracticable; for nothing could have induced the people of New England to accept it. Vaudreuil, moreover, would not promise to give up prisoners in the hands of the Indians, but only to do what he could to persuade their owners to give them up. The negotiations dragged on for several years. For the first three or four months Vaudreuil stopped his war-parties; but he let them loose again in the spring, and the New England boarders were tormented as before.

The French governor thought that the New England country people, who had to bear the brunt of the war, were ready to accept his terms. The French court approved the plan, though not without distrust; for some enemy of the governor told Ponchartrain that under pretence of negotiations he and Dudley were carrying on trading speculations,—which is certainly a baseless slander.[9] Vaudreuil on his part had strongly suspected Dudley's emissary, Vetch, of illicit trade during his visit to Quebec; and perhaps there was ground for the suspicion. It is certain that Vetch, who had visited the St. Lawrence before, lost no opportunity of studying the river, and looked forward to a time when he could turn his knowledge to practical account.[10]

Joseph Dudley, governor of Massachusetts and New Hampshire, was the son of a former governor of Massachusetts,— that upright, sturdy, narrow, bigoted old Puritan, Thomas Dudley, in whose pocket was found after his death the notable couplet,—

"Let men of God in courts and churches watch
O'er such as do a toleration hatch."

Such a son of such a father was the marvel of New England. Those who clung to the old traditions and mourned for the old theocracy under the old charter, hated Joseph Dudley as a renegade; and the worshippers of the Puritans have not forgiven him to this day. He had been president of the council

[9] *Abrégé d'une lettre de M. de Vaudreuil, avec les notes du Ministre,* 19 *Octobre,* 1705.

[10] On the negotiations for neutrality, see the correspondence and other papers in the *Paris Documents* in the Boston State House; also *N. Y. Col. Docs.,* ix. 770, 776, 779, 809; Hutchinson, ii. 141.

under the detested Andros, and when that representative of
the Stuarts was overthrown by a popular revolution, both he
and Dudley were sent prisoners to England. Here they found
a reception different from the expectations and wishes of those
who sent them. Dudley became a member of Parliament and
lieutenant-governor of the Isle of Wight, and was at length, in
the beginning of the reign of Queen Anne, sent back to
govern those who had cast him out. Any governor imposed
on them by England would have been an offence; but Joseph
Dudley was more than they could bear.

He found bitter opposition from the old Puritan party. The
two Mathers, father and son, who through policy had at first
favored him, soon denounced him with insolent malignity, and
the honest and conscientious Samuel Sewall regarded him
with as much asperity as his kindly nature would permit. To
the party of religious and political independency he was an
abomination, and great efforts were made to get him recalled.
Two pamphlets of the time, one printed in 1707 and the other
in the next year, reflect the bitter animosity he excited.[11] Both
seem to be the work of several persons, one of whom, there
can be little doubt, was Cotton Mather; for it is not easy to
mistake the mingled flippancy and pedantry of his style. He
bore the governor a grudge, for Dudley had chafed him in his
inordinate vanity and love of power.

If Dudley loved himself first, he loved his native New England next, and was glad to serve her if he could do so in his
own way and without too much sacrifice of his own interests.
He was possessed by a restless ambition, apparently of the
cheap kind that prefers the first place in a small community
to the second in a large one. He was skilled in the arts of the
politician, and knew how, by attentions, dinners, or commissions in the militia, to influence his Council and Assembly
to do his will. His abilities were beyond question, and his
manners easy and graceful; but his instincts were arbitrary.
He stood fast for prerogative, and even his hereditary Calvinism had strong Episcopal leanings. He was a man of the
world in the better as well as the worse sense of the term; was

[11] *A Memorial of the Present Deplorable State of New England*,
Boston, 1707. *The Deplorable State of New England, by Reason of
a Covetous and Treacherous Governour and Pusillanimous Consel-
lors*, London, 1708. The first of the above is answered by a pamphlet called a *Modest Inquiry*. All three are reprinted in *Mass.
Hist. Coll., 5th Series*, vi.

loved and admired by some as much as he was hated by others; and in the words of one of his successors, "had as many virtues as can consist with so great a thirst for honor and power."[12]

His enemies, however, set no bounds to their denunciation. "All the people here are bought and sold betwixt the governour and his son Paul," says one. "It is my belief," says another, probably Cotton Mather, "that he means to help the French and Indians to destroy all they can." And again, "He is a criminal governour. . . . His God is Mammon, his aim is the ruin of his country." The meagreness and uncertainty of his salary, which was granted by yearly votes of the Assembly, gave color to the charge that he abused his official position to improve his income. The worst accusation against him was that of conniving in trade with the French and Indians under pretence of exchanging prisoners. Six prominent men of the colony—Borland, Vetch, Lawson, Rous, Phillips, and Coffin, only three of whom were of New England origin— were brought to trial before the Assembly for trading at Port Royal; and it was said that Dudley, though he had no direct share in the business, found means to make profit from it. All the accused were convicted and fined. The more strenuous of their judges were for sending them to jail, and Rous was to have been sentenced to "sit an hour upon the gallows with a rope about his neck;" but the governor and council objected to these severities, and the assembly forbore to impose them. The popular indignation against the accused was extreme, and probably not without cause.[13] There was no doubt an illicit trade between Boston and the French of Acadia, who during the war often depended on their enemies for the necessaries of life, since supplies from France, precarious at the best, were made doubly so by New England cruisers. Thus the Acadians and their Indian allies were but too happy to exchange their furs for very modest supplies of tools, utensils, and perhaps, at times, of arms, powder, and lead.[14] What with privateering

[12] Hutchinson, ii. 194.

[13] The agent of Massachusetts at London, speaking of the three chief offenders, says that they were neither "of English extraction, nor natives of the place, and two of them were very new comers." Jeremiah Dummer, *Letter to a Noble Lord concerning the late Expedition to Canada.*

[14] The French naval captain Bonaventure says that the Acadians were forced to depend on Boston traders, who sometimes plundered

and illicit trade, it was clear that the war was a source of profit to some of the chief persons in Boston. That place, moreover, felt itself tolerably safe from attack, while the borders were stung from end to end as by a swarm of wasps; and thus the country conceived the idea that the town was fattening at its expense. Vaudreuil reports to the minister that the people of New England want to avenge themselves by an attack on Canada, but that their chief men are for a policy of defence. This was far from being wholly true; but the notion that the rural population bore a grudge against Boston had taken strong hold of the French, who even believed that if the town were attacked, the country would not move hand or foot to help it. Perhaps it was well for them that they did not act on the belief, which, as afterwards appeared, was one of their many mistakes touching the character and disposition of their English neighbors.

The sentences on Borland and his five companions were annulled by the Queen and Council, on the ground that the Assembly was not competent to try the case.[15] The passionate charges against Dudley and a petition to the Queen for his removal were equally unavailing. The Assemblies of Massachusetts and New Hampshire, the chief merchants, the officers of militia, and many of the ministers sent addresses to the Queen in praise of the governor's administration;[16] and though his enemies declared that the votes and signatures were obtained by the arts familiar to him, his recall was prevented, and he held his office seven years longer.

---

them, and sometimes sold them supplies. (*Bonaventure au Ministre,* 30 *Novembre,* 1705.) Colonel Quary, Judge of Admiralty at New York, writes: "There hath been and still is, as I am informed, a Trade carried on with Port Royal by some of the topping men of that government [Boston], under colour of sending and receiving Flaggs of truce."—*Quary to the Lords of Trade,* 10 *January,* 1708.

[15] *Council Record,* in Hutchinson, ii. 144.

[16] These addresses are appended to *A Modest Inquiry into the Grounds and Occasions of a late Pamphlet intituled a Memorial of the present Deplorable State of New England. London,* 1707.

Chapter 6

1700–1710
The Old Régime in Acadia

THE FRENCH PROVINCE of Acadia, answering to the present
Nova Scotia and New Brunswick, was a government separate
from Canada and subordinate to it. Jacques François de
Brouillan, appointed to command it, landed at Chibucto, the
site of Halifax, in 1702, and crossed by hills and forests to
the Basin of Mines, where he found a small but prosperous
settlement. "It seems to me," he wrote to the minister, "that
these people live like true republicans, acknowledging neither
royal authority nor courts of law."[1] It was merely that their
remoteness and isolation made them independent, of necessity,
so far as concerned temporal government. When Brouillan
reached Port Royal he found a different state of things. The
fort and garrison were in bad condition; but the adjacent
settlement, primitive as it was, appeared on the whole duly
submissive.

Possibly it would have been less so if it had been more
prosperous; but the inhabitants had lately been deprived of
fishing, their best resource, by a New England privateer which
had driven their craft from the neighboring seas; and when
the governor sent Lieutenant Neuvillette in an armed vessel
to seize the interloping stranger, a fight ensued, in which
the lieutenant was killed, and his vessel captured. New
England is said to have had no less than three hundred vessels every year in these waters.[2] Before the war a French
officer proposed that New England sailors should be hired
to teach the Acadians how to fish, and the King seems
to have approved the plan.[3] Whether it was adopted or not,
New England in peace or war had a lion's share of the
Acadian fisheries. "It grieves me to the heart," writes Subercase, Brouillan's successor, "to see Messieurs les Bastonnais

[1] *Brouillan au Ministre,* 6 *Octobre,* 1702.
[2] *Mémoire de Subercase.*
[3] *Mémoire du Roy au Sieur de Brouillan,* 23 *Mars,* 1700; *Le
Ministre à Villebon,* 9 *Avril,* 1700.

enrich themselves in our domain; for the base of their commerce is the fish which they catch off our coasts, and send to all parts of the world."

When the war broke out, Brouillan's fighting resources were so small that he was forced to depend largely for help on searovers of more than doubtful character. They came chiefly from the West Indies,—the old haunt of buccaneers,—and were sometimes mere pirates, and sometimes semi-piratical privateers commissioned by French West Indian governors. Brouillan's successor writes that their opportunities are good, since at least a thousand vessels enter Boston every year.[4] Besides these irregular allies, the governor usually had at his disposal two French frigates of thirty and sixty guns, to which was opposed the Massachusetts navy, consisting of a ship of fifty-six guns, and the "province galley," of twenty-two. In 1710 one of these Massachusetts vessels appeared off the coast escorting a fishing-fleet of no less than two hundred and fifty sail, some of which were afterwards captured by French corsairs. A good number of these last, however, were taken from time to time by Boston sea-rovers, who, like their enemies, sometimes bore a close likeness to pirates. They seized French fishing and trading vessels, attacked French corsairs, sometimes traded with the Acadians, and sometimes plundered them. What with West India rum brought by the French freebooters, and New England rum brought by the English, it is reported that one could get drunk in Acadia for two sous.

Port Royal, now Annapolis, was the seat of government, and the only place of any strength in the colony. The fort, a sodded earthwork, lately put into tolerable repair by the joint labor of the soldiers and inhabitants, stood on the point of land between the mouth of the river Annapolis and that of the small stream now called Allen's River, whence it looked down the long basin, or land-locked bay, which, framed in hills and forests, had so won the heart of the Baron de Poutrincourt a century before. The garrison was small, counting in 1704 only a hundred and eighty-five soldiers and eight commissioned officers. At the right of the fort, between it and the mouth of the Annapolis, was the Acadian village, consisting of seventy or eighty small houses of one story and an attic, built of planks, boards, or logs, simple and rude, but tolerably comfortable. It had also a small, new wooden

4 *Subercase au Ministre*, 3 *Janvier*, 1710.

church, to the building of which the inhabitants had contributed eight hundred francs, while the King paid the rest. The inhabitants had no voice whatever in public affairs, though the colonial minister had granted them the privilege of travelling in time of peace without passports. The ruling class, civil and military, formed a group apart, living in or near the fort, in complete independence of public opinion, supposing such to have existed. They looked only to their masters at Versailles; and hence a state of things as curious as it was lamentable. The little settlement was a hot-bed of gossip, backbiting, and slander. Officials of every degree were continually trying to undermine and supplant one another, besieging the minister with mutual charges. Brouillan, the governor, was a frequent object of attack. He seems to have been of an irritable temper, aggravated perhaps by an old unhealed wound in the cheek, which gave him constant annoyance. One writer declares that Acadia languishes under selfish greed and petty tyranny; that everything was hoped from Brouillan when he first came, but that hope has changed to despair; that he abuses the King's authority to make money, sells wine and brandy at retail, quarrels with officers who are not punctilious enough in saluting him, forces the inhabitants to catch seal and cod for the King, and then cheats them of their pay, and countenances an obnoxious churchwarden whose daughter is his mistress. "The country groans, but dares not utter a word," concludes the accuser, as he closes his indictment.[5]

Brouillan died in the autumn of 1705, on which M. de Goutin, a magistrate who acted as intendant, and was therefore at once the colleague of the late governor and a spy upon him, writes to the minister that "the divine justice has at last taken pity on the good people of this country," but that as it is base to accuse a dead man, he will not say that the public could not help showing their joy at the late governor's departure; and he adds that the deceased was charged with a scandalous connection with the Widow de Freneuse. Nor will he reply, he says, to the governor's complaint to the court about a pretended cabal, of which he, De Goutin, was the head, and which was in reality only three or four honest men, incapable of any kind of deviation, who used to meet in

[5] La Touche, *Mémoire sur l'Acadie,* 1702 (adressé à Ponchartrain).

a friendly way, and had given offence by not bowing down before the beast.[6]

Then he changes the subject, and goes on to say that on a certain festal occasion he was invited by Bonaventure, who acted as governor after the death of Brouillan, to share with him the honor of touching off a bonfire before the fort gate; and that this excited such envy, jealousy, and discord that he begs the minister, once for all, to settle the question whether a first magistrate has not the right to the honor of touching off a bonfire jointly with a governor.

De Goutin sometimes discourses of more serious matters. He tells the minister that the inhabitants have plenty of cattle, and more hemp than they can use, but neither pots, scythes, sickles, knives, hatchets, kettles for the Indians, nor salt for themselves. "We should be fortunate if our enemies would continue to supply our necessities and take the beaver-skins with which the colony is gorged;" adding, however, that the Acadians hate the English, and will not trade with them if they can help it.[7]

In the next year the "Bastonnais" were again bringing supplies, and the Acadians again receiving them. The new governor, Subercase, far from being pleased at this, was much annoyed, or professed to be so, and wrote to Ponchartrain, "Nobody could suffer more than I do at seeing the English so coolly carry on their trade under our very noses." Then he proceeds to the inevitable personalities. "You wish me to write without reserve of the officers here; I have little good to tell you;" and he names two who to the best of his belief have lost their wits, a third who is incorrigibly lazy, and a fourth who is eccentric; adding that he is tolerably well satisfied with the rest, except M. de la Ronde. "You see, Monseigneur, that I am as much in need of a madhouse as of barracks; and what is worse, I am afraid that the *mauvais esprit* of this country will drive me crazy too."[8] "You write to me," he continues,

---

[6] "Que trois ou quatre amis, honnêtes gens, incapables de gauchir en quoique ce soit, pour n'avoir pas fléché devant la bête, aient été qualifiés de cabalistes."—*De Goutin au Ministre, 4 Décembre,* 1705.

[7] *De Goutin au Ministre,* 22 *Décembre,* 1707. In 1705 Bonaventure, in a time of scarcity, sent a vessel to Boston to buy provisions, on pretence of exchanging prisoners. *Bonaventure au Ministre,* 30 *Novembre,* 1705.

[8] "Ne me fasse à mon tour tourner la cervelle."—*Subercase au Ministre,* 20 *Décembre,* 1708.

"that you are informed that M. Labat has killed some cattle belonging to the inhabitants. If so, he has expiated his fault by blowing off his thumb by the bursting of his gun while he was firing at a sheep. I am sure that the moon has a good deal to do with his behavior; he always acts very strangely when she is on the wane."

The charge brought against Brouillan in regard to Madame de Freneuse was brought also against Bonaventure in connection with the same lady. "The story," says Subercase, "was pushed as far as hell could desire;"[9] and he partially defends the accused, declaring that at least his fidelity to the King is beyond question.

De Goutin had a quarrel with Subercase, and writes: "I do all that is possible to live on good terms with him, and to that end I walk as if in the chamber of a sick prince whose sleep is of the lightest." As Subercase defends Bonaventure, De Goutin attacks him, and gives particulars concerning him and Madame de Freneuse which need not be recounted here. Then comes a story about a quarrel caused by some cows belonging to Madame de Freneuse which got into the garden of Madame de Saint-Vincent, and were driven out by a soldier who presumed to strike one of them with a long stick. "The facts," gravely adds De Goutin, "have been certified to me as I have the honor to relate them to your Grandeur."[10] Then the minister is treated to a story of one Allein. "He insulted Madame de Belleisle at the church door after high mass, and when her son, a boy of fourteen, interposed, Allein gave him such a box on the ear that it drew blood; and I am assured that M. Petit, the priest, ran to the rescue in his sacerdotal robes." Subercase, on his side, after complaining that the price of a certain canoe had been unjustly deducted from his pay, though he never had the said canoe at all, protests to Ponchartrain, "there is no country on earth where I would not rather live than in this, by reason of the ill-disposed persons who inhabit it."[11]

There was the usual friction between the temporal and the spiritual powers. "The Church," writes Subercase, "has long claimed the right of commanding here, or at least of sharing

[9] "On a poussé la chose aussi que loin l'enfer le pouvait désirer." —*Subercase au Ministre*, 20 *Décembre*, 1708.

[10] *De Goutin au Ministre*, 20 *Décembre*, 1708.

[11] *Subercase au Ministre*, 20 *Décembre*, 1708.

authority with the civil rulers."[12] The Church had formerly been represented by the Capuchin friars, and afterwards by the Récollets. Every complaint was of course carried to the minister. In 1700 we find M. de Villieu, who then held a provisional command in the colony, accusing the ecclesiastics of illicit trade with the English.[13] Bonaventure reports to Ponchartrain that Père Félix, chaplain of the fort, asked that the gate might be opened, in order that he might carry the sacraments to a sick man, his real object being to marry Captain Duvivier to a young woman named Marie Muis de Poubomcoup,—contrary, as the governor thought, to the good of the service. He therefore forbade the match; on which the priests told him that when they had made up their minds to do anything, nobody had power to turn them from it; and the chaplain presently added that he cared no more for the governor than for the mud on his shoes.[14] He carried his point, and married Duvivier in spite of the commander.

Every king's ship from Acadia brought to Ponchartrain letters full of matters like these. In one year, 1703, he got at least fourteen such. If half of what Saint-Simon tells us of him is true, it is not to be supposed that he gave himself much trouble concerning them. This does not make it less astonishing that in the midst of a great and disastrous war a minister of State should be expected to waste time on matters worthy of a knot of old gossips babbling round a teatable. That pompous spectre which calls itself the Dignity of History would scorn to take note of them; yet they are highly instructive, for the morbid anatomy of this little colony has a scientific value as exhibiting, all the more vividly for the narrowness of the field, the workings of an unmitigated paternalism acting from across the Atlantic. The King's servants in Acadia pestered his minister at Versailles with their pettiest squabbles, while Marlborough and Eugene were threatening his throne with destruction.[15] The same system prevailed in Canada; but as there the field was broader and the men often

[12] *Ibid.*

[13] *Villieu au Ministre,* 20 *Octobre,* 1700.

[14] "Il répondit qu'il se soucioit de moi comme de la boue de ses souliers."—*Bonaventure au Ministre,* 30 *Novembre,* 1705.

[15] These letters of Acadian officials are in the Archives du Ministère de la Marine et des Colonies at Paris. Copies of some of them will be found in the 3d series of the *Correspondance Officielle* at Ottawa.

larger, the effects are less whimsically vivid than they appear under the Acadian microscope. The two provinces, however, were ruled alike; and about this time the Canadian Intendant Raudot was writing to Ponchartrain in a strain worthy of De Goutin, Subercase, or Bonaventure.[16]

[16] *Raudot au Ministre, 20 Septembre,* 1709. The copy before me covers 108 folio pages, filled with gossiping personalities.

Chapter 7

1704–1710
Acadia Changes Hands

WHEN WAR-PARTIES from Canada struck the English borders, reprisal was difficult against those who had provoked it. Canada was made almost inaccessible by a hundred leagues of pathless forest, prowled by her Indian allies, who were sure to give the alarm of an approaching foe; while, on the other hand, the New Englanders could easily reach Acadia by their familiar element, the sea; and hence that unfortunate colony often made vicarious atonement for the sins of her northern sister. It was from French privateers and fishing-vessels on the Acadian seas that Massachusetts drew most of the prisoners whom she exchanged for her own people held captive in Canada.

Major Benjamin Church, the noted Indian fighter of King Philip's War, was at Tiverton in Rhode Island when he heard of Hertel de Rouville's attack on Deerfield. Boiling with rage, he mounted his horse and rode to Boston to propose a stroke of retaliation. Church was energetic, impetuous, and bull-headed, sixty-five years old, and grown so fat that when pushing through the woods on the trail of Indians, he kept a stout sergeant by him to hoist him over fallen trees. Governor Dudley approved his scheme, and appointed him to command the expedition, with the rank of colonel. Church repaired to his native Duxbury; and here, as well as in Plymouth and other neighboring settlements, the militia were called out, and the veteran readily persuaded a sufficient number to volunteer under him. With the Indians of Cape Cod he found more difficulty, they being, as his son observes, "a people that need much treating, especially with drink." At last, however, some of them were induced to join him. Church now returned to Boston, and begged that an attack on Port Royal might be included in his instructions,—which was refused, on the ground that a plan to that effect had been laid before the Queen, and that nothing could be done till her answer was received. The governor's enemies seized the occasion to say that he wished Port Royal to remain French, in order to make money by trading with it.

The whole force, including Indians and sailors, amounted to about seven hundred men; they sailed to Matinicus in brigs and sloops, the province galley, and two British frigates. From Matinicus most of the sailing-vessels were sent to Mount Desert to wait orders, while the main body rowed eastward in whale-boats. Touching at Saint-Castin's fort, where the town of Castine now stands, they killed or captured everybody they found there. Receiving false information that there was a large war-party on the west side of Passamaquoddy Bay, they hastened to the place, reached it in the night, and pushed into the woods in hope of surprising the enemy. The movement was difficult; and Church's men, being little better than a mob, disregarded his commands, and fell into disorder. He raged and stormed; and presently, in the darkness and confusion, descrying a hut or cabin on the farther side of a small brook, with a crowd gathered about it, he demanded what was the matter, and was told that there were Frenchmen inside who would not come out. "Then knock them in the head," shouted the choleric old man; and he was obeyed. It was said that the victims belonged to a party of Canadians captured just before, under a promise of life. Afterwards, when Church returned to Boston, there was an outcry of indignation against him for this butchery. In any case, however, he could have known nothing of the alleged promise of quarter.

To hunt Indians with an endless forest behind them was like chasing shadows. The Acadians were surer game. Church sailed with a part of his force up the Bay of Fundy, and landed at Grand Pré,—a place destined to a dismal notoriety half a century later. The inhabitants of this and the neighboring settlements made some slight resistance, and killed a lieutenant named Baker, and one soldier, after which they fled; when Church, first causing the houses to be examined, to make sure that nobody was left in them, ordered them to be set on fire. The dikes were then broken, and the tide let in upon the growing crops.[1] In spite of these harsh proceedings, he fell far short in his retaliation for the barbarities at Deerfield, since he restrained his Indians and permitted no woman

[1] Church, *Entertaining Passages.* "Un habitant des Mines a dit que les ennemis avaient été dans toutes les rivières, qu'il n'y restait plus que quatre habitations en entier, le restant ayant été brulé." —*Expéditions faites par les Anglois,* 1704. "Qu'ils avaient . . . brulé toutes les maisons à la reserve du haut des rivières."—Labat, *Invasion des Anglois,* 1704.

or child to be hurt,—at the same time telling his prisoners that if any other New England village were treated as Deerfield had been, he would come back with a thousand Indians and leave them free to do what they pleased. With this bluster, he left the unfortunate peasants in the extremity of terror, after carrying off as many of them as were needed for purpose of exchange. A small detachement was sent to Beaubassin, where it committed similar havoc.

Church now steered for Port Royal, which he had been forbidden to attack. The two frigates and the transports had by this time rejoined him, and in spite of Dudley's orders to make no attempt on the French fort, the British and provincial officers met in council to consider whether to do so. With one voice they decided in the negative, since they had only four hundred men available for landing, while the French garrison was no doubt much stronger, having had ample time to call the inhabitants to its aid. Church, therefore, after trying the virtue of a bombastic summons to surrender, and destroying a few houses, sailed back to Boston. It was a miserable retaliation for a barbarous outrage; as the guilty were out of reach, the invaders turned their ire on the innocent.[2]

If Port Royal in French hands was a source of illicit gain to some persons in Boston, it was also an occasion of loss by the privateers and corsairs it sent out to pray on trading and fishing vessels, while at the same time it was a standing menace as the possible naval base for one of those armaments against the New England capital which were often threatened, though never carried into effect. Hence, in 1707 the New England colonists made, in their bungling way, a serious attempt to get possession of it.

Dudley's enemies raised the old cry that at heart he wished Port Royal to remain French, and was only forced by popular clamor to countenance an attack upon it. The charge seems a malicious slander. Early in March he proposed the enterprise to the General Court; and the question being referred to a committee, they reported that a thousand soldiers should be raised, vessels impressed, and her Majesty's frigate "Dept-

---

[2] On this affair, Thomas Church, *Entertaining Passages* (1716). The writer was the son of Benjamin Church. Penhallow; Belknap, i. 266; *Dudley to* ——, 21 *April*, 1704; Hutchinson, ii. 132; *Deplorable State of New England; Entreprise des Anglais sur l'Acadie*, 1704; *Expéditions faites par les Anglais de la Nouvelle Angleterre*, 1704; Labat, *Invasion des Anglois de Baston*, 1704.

ford," with the province galley, employed to convoy them. An Act was passed accordingly.[3] Two regiments were soon afoot, one uniformed in red, and the other in blue; one commanded by Colonel Francis Wainwright, and the other by Colonel Winthrop Hilton. Rhode Island sent eighty more men, and New Hampshire sixty, while Connecticut would do nothing. The expedition sailed on the thirteenth of May, and included one thousand and seventy-six soldiers, with about four hundred and fifty sailors.

The soldiers were nearly all volunteers from the rural militia, and their training and discipline were such as they had acquired in the uncouth frolics and plentiful New England rum of the periodical "muster days." There chanced to be one officer who knew more or less of the work in hand. This was the English engineer Rednap, sent out to look after the fortifications of New York and New England. The commander-in-chief was Colonel John March, of Newbury, who had popular qualities, had seen frontier service, and was personally brave, but totally unfit for his present position. Most of the officers were civilians from country towns,—Ipswich, Topsfield, Lynn, Salem, Dorchester, Taunton, or Weymouth.[4] In the province galley went, as secretary of the expedition, that intelligent youth, William Dudley, son of the governor.

New England has been blamed for not employing trained officers to command her levies; but with the exception of Rednap, and possibly of Captain Samuel Vetch, there were none in the country, nor were they wanted. In their stubborn and jealous independence, the sons of the Puritans would have resented their presence. The provincial officers were, without exception, civilians. British regular officers, good, bad or indifferent, were apt to put on airs of superiority which galled the democratic susceptibilites of the natives, who, rather than endure a standing military force imposed by the mother-country, preferred to suffer if they must, and fight their own battles in their own crude way. Even for irregular warfare they were at a disadvantage; Canadian feudalism developed good partisan leaders, which was rarely the case with New England democracy. Colonel John March was a tyro set over

[3] *Report of a Committee to consider his Excellency's Speech,* 12 *March* 1707. *Resolve for an Expedition against Port Royal* (Massachusetts Archives).

[4] *Autobiography of Rev. John Barnard,* one of the five chaplains of the expedition.

a crowd of ploughboys, fishermen, and mechanics, officered by tradesmen, farmers, blacksmiths, village magnates, and deacons of the church,—for the characters of deacon and militia officer were often joined in one. These improvised soldiers commonly did well in small numbers, and very ill in large ones.

Early in June the expedition sailed into Port Royal Basin, and Lieutenant-Colonel Appleton, with three hundred and fifty men, landed on the north shore, four or five miles below the fort, marched up to the mouth of the Annapolis, and was there met by an ambushed body of French, who, being outnumbered, presently took to their boats and retreated to the fort. Meanwhile, March, with seven hundred and fifty men, landed on the south shore and pushed on to the meadows of Allen's River, which they were crossing in battle array when a fire blazed out upon them from a bushy hill on the farther bank, where about two hundred French lay in ambush under Subercase, the governor. March and his men crossed the stream, and after a skirmish that did little harm to either side, the French gave way. The English then advanced to a hill known as the Lion Rampart, within cannon-shot of the fort, and here began to intrench themselves, stretching their lines right and left towards the Annapolis on the one hand, and Allen's River on the other, so as to form a semicircle before the fort, where all the inhabitants had by this time taken refuge.

Soon all was confusion in the New England camp,—the consequence of March's incapacity for a large command, and the greenness and ignorance of both himself and his subordinates. There were conflicting opinions, wranglings, and disputes. The men, losing all confidence in their officers, became unmanageable. "The devil was at work among us," writes one of those present. The engineer, Rednap, the only one of them who knew anything of the work in hand, began to mark out the batteries; but he soon lost temper, and declared that "it was not for him to venture his reputation with such ungovernable and undisciplined men and inconstant officers."[5] He refused to bring up the cannon, saying that it could not be done under the fire of the fort; and the naval captains were of the same opinion.

One of the chaplains, Rev. John Barnard, being of a martial

[5] *A Boston Gentleman to his Friend*, 13 *June*, 1707 (Mass. Archives).

turn and full of zeal, took it upon himself to make a plan of the fort; and to that end, after providing himself with pen, ink, paper, and a horse-pistol, took his seat at a convenient spot; but his task was scarcely begun when it was ended by a cannon-ball that struck the ground beside him, peppered him with gravel, and caused his prompt retreat.[6]

French deserters reported that there were five hundred men in the fort, with forty-two heavy cannon, and that four or five hundred more were expected every day. This increased the general bewilderment of the besiegers. There was a council of war. Rednap declared that it would be useless to persist; and after hot debate and contradiction, it was resolved to decamp. Three days after, there was another council, which voted to bring up the cannon and open fire, in spite of Rednap and the naval captains; but in the next evening a third council resolved again to raise the siege as hopeless. This disgusted the rank and file, who were a little soothed by an order to destroy the storehouse and other buildings outside the fort; and, ill led as they were, they did the work thoroughly. "Never did men act more boldly," says the witness before quoted; "they threatened the enemy to his nose, and would have taken the fort if the officers had shown any spirit. They found it hard to bring them off. At the end we broke up with the confusion of Babel, and went about our business like fools."[7]

The baffled invaders sailed crestfallen to Casco Bay, and a vessel was sent to carry news of the miscarriage to Dudley, who, vexed and incensed, ordered another attempt. March was in a state of helpless indecision, increased by a bad cold; but the governor would not recall him, and chose instead the lamentable expedient of sending three members of the provincial council to advise and direct him. Two of them had commissions in the militia; the third, John Leverett, was a learned bachelor of divinity, formerly a tutor in Harvard College, and soon after its president,—capable, no doubt, of preaching Calvinistic sermons to the students, but totally unfit to command men or conduct a siege.

Young William Dudley was writing meanwhile to his father how jealousies and quarrels were rife among the officers, how their conduct bred disorder and desertion among the soldiers,

[6] *Autobiography of Rev. John Barnard.*

[7] *A Boston Gentleman to his Friend,* 13 June (old style), 1707. The final attack here alluded to took place on the night of the sixteenth of June (new style).

and how Colonel March and others behaved as if they had nothing to do but make themselves popular.[8] Many of the officers seem, in fact, to have been small politicians in search of notoriety, with an eye to votes or appointments. Captain Stuckley, of the British frigate, wrote to the governor in great discontent about the "nonsensical malice" of Lieutenant-Colonel Appleton, and adds, "I don't see what good I can do by lying here, where I am almost murdered by mosquitoes."[9]

The three commissioners came at last, with a reinforcement of another frigate and a hundred recruits, which did not supply losses, as the soldiers had deserted by scores. In great ill-humor, the expedition sailed back to Port Royal, where it was found that reinforcements had also reached the French, including a strongly manned privateer from Martinique. The New England men landed, and there was some sharp skirmishing in an orchard. Chaplain Barnard took part in the fray. "A shot brushed my wig," he says, "but I was mercifully preserved. We soon drove them out of the orchard, killed a few of them, desperately wounded the privateer captain, and after that we all embarked and returned to Boston as fast as we could." This summary statement is imperfect, for there was a good deal of skirmishing from the thirteenth August to the twentieth, when the invaders sailed for home. March was hooted as he walked Boston streets, and children ran after him crying, "Wooden sword!" There was an attempt at a court-martial, but so many officers were accused, on one ground or another, that hardly enough were left to try them, and the matter was dropped. With one remarkable exception, the New England militia reaped scant laurels on their various expeditions eastward; but of all their shortcomings, this was the most discreditable.[10]

[8] *William Dudley to Governor Dudley, 24 June, 1707.*

[9] *Stuckley to Dudley, 28 June, 1707.*

[10] A considerable number of letters and official papers on this expedition will be found in the 51st and 71st volumes of the Massachusetts Archives. See also Hutchinson, ii. 151, and Belknap, i. 273. The curious narrative of the chaplain, Barnard, is in *Mass. Hist. Coll.,* 3d *Series,* v. 189–196. The account in the *Deplorable State of New England* is meant solely to injure Dudley. The chief French accounts are *Enterprise des Anglois contre l'Acadie, 26 Juin,* 1707; *Subercase au Ministre, même date; Labat au Ministre, 6 Juillet,* 1707; *Relation* appended to Dièreville, *Voyage de l'Acadie.* The last is extremely loose and fanciful. Subercase puts the English force at three thousand men, whereas the official re-

Meanwhile events worthy of note were passing in New-foundland. That island was divided between the two conflict-ing powers,—the chief station of the French being at Pla-centia, and that of the English at St. John. In January, 1705, Subercase, who soon after became governor of Acadia, marched with four hundred and fifty soldiers, Canadians, and buccaneers, aided by a band of Indians, against St. John,—a fishing-village defended by two forts, the smaller, known as the castle, held by twelve men, and the larger, called Fort William, by forty men under Captain Moody. The latter was attacked by the French who were beaten off; on which they burned the unprotected houses and fishing-huts with a brutal-ity equal to that of Church in Acadia, and followed up the exploit by destroying the hamlet at Ferryland and all the de-fenceless hovels and fish-stages along the shore towards Trinity Bay and Bonavista.[11]

Four years later, the Sieur de Saint-Ovide, a nephew of Brouillan, late governor at Port Royal, struck a more credit-able blow. He set out from Placentia on the thirteenth of December, 1708, with one hundred and sixty-four men, and on the first of January approached Fort William two hours be-fore day, found the gate leading to the covered way open, entered with a band of volunteers, rapidly crossed the ditch, planted ladders against the wall, and leaped into the fort, then, as he declares, garrisoned by a hundred men. His main body followed close. The English were taken unawares; their commander, who showed great courage, was struck down by three shots, and after some sharp fighting the place was in the hands of the assailants. The small fort at the mouth of the harbor capitulated on the second day, and the palisaded village of the inhabitants, which, if we are to believe Saint-Ovide, contained nearly six hundred men, made little resistance. St. John became for the moment a French possession; but Coste-belle, governor at Placentia, despaired of holding it, and it was abandoned in the following summer.[12]

---

turns show it to have been, soldiers and sailors, about half this number.

[11] Penhallow puts the French force at five hundred and fifty. Jeremiah Dummer, *Letter to a Noble Lord concerning the late Expedition to Canada*, says that the havoc committed occasioned a total loss of £80,000.

[12] *Saint-Ovide au Ministre*, 20 *Janvier*, 1709; *Ibid.*, 6 *Septembre*, 1709; *Rapport de Costebelle*, 26 *Février*, 1709. Costebelle makes the French force one hundred and seventy-five.

About this time a scheme was formed for the permanent riddance of New England from war-parties by the conquest of Canada.[13] The prime mover in it was Samuel Vetch, whom we have seen as an emissary to Quebec for the exchange of prisoners, and also as one of the notables fined for illicit trade with the French. He came of a respectable Scotch family. His grandfather, his father, three of his uncles, and one of his brothers were Covenanting ministers, who had suffered some persecution under Charles II. He himself was destined for the ministry; but his inclinations being in no way clerical, he and his brother William got commissions in the army, and took an active part in the war that ended with the Peace of Ryswick.

In the next year the two brothers sailed for the Isthmus of Panama as captains in the band of adventurers embarked in the disastrous enterprise known as the Darien Scheme. William Vetch died at sea, and Samuel repaired to New York, where he married a daughter of Robert Livingston, one of the chief men of the colony, and engaged largely in the Canadian trade. From New York he went to Boston, where we find him when the War of the Spanish Succession began. During his several visits to Canada he had carefully studied the St. Lawrence and its shores, and boasted that he knew them better than the Canadians themselves.[14] He was impetuous, sanguine, energetic, and headstrong, astute withal, and full of ambition. A more vigorous agent for the execution of the proposed plan of conquest could not have been desired. The General Court of Massachusetts, contrary to its instinct and its past practice, resolved, in view of the greatness of the stake, to ask this time for help from the mother-country, and Vetch sailed for England, bearing an address to the Queen, begging for an armament to aid in the reduction of Canada and Acadia. The scheme waxed broader yet in the ardent brain of the agent; he proposed to add Newfoundland to the other conquests, and when all was done in the North to sail to the Gulf of Mexico

[13] Some of the French officials in Acadia foresaw aggressive action on the part of the English in consequence of the massacre at Haverhill. "Le coup que les Canadiens viennent de faire, où Mars, plus féroce qu'en Europe, a donné carrière à sa rage, me fait appréhender une représaille."—*De Goutin au Ministre*, 29 *Décembre*, 1708.

[14] Patterson, *Memoir of Hon. Samuel Vetch*, in *Collections of the Nova Scotia Historical Society*, iv. Compare a paper by General James Grant Wilson in *International Review*, November, 1881.

and wrest Pensacola from the Spaniards; by which means, he writes, "Her Majesty shall be sole empress of the vast North American continent." The idea was less visionary than it seems. Energy, helped by reasonable good luck, might easily have made it a reality, so far as concerned the possessions of France.

The court granted all that Vetch asked. On the eleventh of March he sailed for America, fully empowered to carry his plans into execution, and with the assurance that when Canada was conquered, he should be its governor. A squadron bearing five regiments of regular troops was promised. The colonies were to muster their forces in all haste. New York was directed to furnish eight hundred men; New Jersey, two hundred; Pennsylvania, one hundred and fifty; and Connecticut, three hundred and fifty,—the whole to be at Albany by the middle of May, and to advance on Montreal by way of Wood Creek and Lake Champlain, as soon as they should hear that the squadron had reached Boston. Massachusetts, New Hampshire, and Rhode Island were to furnish twelve hundred men, to join the regulars in attacking Quebec by way of the St. Lawrence.[15]

Vetch sailed from Portsmouth in the ship "Dragon," accompanied by Colonel Francis Nicholson, late lieutenant-governor of New York, who was to take an important part in the enterprise. The squadron with the five regiments was to follow without delay. The weather was bad, and the "Dragon," beating for five weeks against headwinds, did not enter Boston harbor till the evening of the twenty-eighth of April. Vetch, chafing with impatience, for every moment was precious, sent off expresses that same night to carry the Queen's letters to the governors of Rhode Island, Connecticut, New Jersey, and Pennsylvania. Dudley and his council met the next morning, and to them Vetch delivered the royal message, which was received he says, "with the dutiful obedience becoming good subjects, and all the marks of joy and thankfulness."[16] Vetch, Nicholson, and the Massachusetts authorities

[15] *Instructions to Colonel Vetch*, 1 *March*, 1709; *The Earl of Sunderland to Dudley*, 28 *April*, 1709; *The Queen to Lord Lovelace*, 1 *March*, 1709; *The Earl of Sunderland to Lord Lovelace*, 28 *April*, 1709.

[16] *Journal of Vetch and Nicholson* (Public Record Office). This is in the form of a letter, signed by both, and dated at New York, 29 June, 1709.

quickly arranged their plans. An embargo was laid on the shipping; provision was made for raising men and supplies and providing transportation. When all was in train, the two emissaries hired a sloop for New York, and touching by the way at Rhode Island, found it in the throes of the annual election of governor. Yet every war-like preparation was already made, and Vetch and his companion sailed at once for New Haven to meet Saltonstall, the newly elected governor of Connecticut. Here too, all was ready, and the envoys, well pleased, continued their voyage to New York, which they reached on the eighteenth of May. The governor, Lord Lovelace, had lately died, and Colonel Ingoldsby, the lieutenant-governor, acted in his place. The Assembly was in session, and being summoned to the council-chamber, the members were addressed by Vetch and Nicholson with excellent effect.

In accepting the plan of conquest, New York completely changed front. She had thus far stood neutral, leaving her neighbors to defend themselves, and carrying on an active trade with the French and their red allies. Still, it was her interest that Canada should become English, thus throwing open to her the trade of the Western tribes; and the promises of aid from England made the prospects of the campaign so flattering that she threw herself into the enterprise, though not without voices of protest,—for while the frontier farmers and some prominent citizens like Peter Schuyler thought that the time for action had come, the Albany traders and their allies, who fattened on Canadian beaver, were still for peace at any price.[17]

With Pennsylvania and New Jersey the case was different. The one, controlled by non-combatant Quakers and safe from French war-parties, refused all aid; while the other, in less degree under the same military blight, would give no men, though granting a slow and reluctant contribution of £3,000, taking care to suppress on the record every indication that the money was meant for military uses. New York, on the other hand, raised her full contingent, and Massachusetts and New Hampshire something more, being warm in the faith that their borders would be plagued with war-parties no longer.

It remained for New York to gain the help of the Five Nations of the Iroquois, to which end Abraham Schuyler went

[17] *Thomas Cockerill to Mr. Popple, 2 July,* 1709.

to Onondaga, well supplied with presents. The Iroquois capital was now, as it had been for years, divided between France and England. French interests were represented by the two Jesuits, Mareuil and Jacques Lamberville. The skilful management of Schuyler, joined to his gifts and his rum, presently won over so many to the English party, and raised such excitement in the town that Lamberville thought it best to set out for Montreal with news of what was going on. The intrepid Joncaire, agent of France among the Senecas, was scandalized at what he calls the Jesuit's flight, and wrote to the commandant of Fort Frontenac that its effect on the Indians was such that he, Joncaire, was in peril of his life.[18] Yet he stood his ground, and managed so well that he held the Senecas firm in their neutrality. Lamberville's colleague, Mareuil, whose position was still more critical, was persuaded by Schuyler that his only safety was in going with him to Albany, which he did; and on this the Onondagas, excited by rum, plundered and burned the Jesuit mission-house and chapel.[19] Clearly, the two priests at Onondaga were less hungry for martyrdom than their murdered brethren Jogues, Brébeuf, Lalemant, and Charles Garnier; but it is to be remembered that the Canadian Jesuit of the first half of the seventeenth century was before all things an apostle, and his successor of a century later was before all things a political agent.

As for the Five Nations, that once haughty confederacy, in spite of divisions and waverings, had conceived the idea that its true policy lay, not in siding with either of the European rivals, but in making itself important to both, and courted and caressed by both. While some of the warriors sang the war-song at the prompting of Schuyler, they had been but half-hearted in doing so; and even the Mohawks, nearest neighbors and best friends of the English, sent word to their Canadian kindred, the Caughnawagas, that they took up the hatchet only because they could not help it.

The attack on Canada by way of the Hudson and Lake Champlain was to have been commanded by Lord Lovelace or some officer of his choice; but as he was dead, Ingoldsby, his successor in the government of the province, jointly with the governors of several adjacent colonies who had met at New

[18] Joncaire in *N. Y. Col. Docs.,* ix. 838.

[19] Mareuil in *N. Y. Col. Docs.,* ix. 836, text and note. *Vaudreuil au Ministre,* 14 *Novembre,* 1709.

York, appointed Colonel Nicholson in his stead.[20] Nicholson went to Albany, whence, with about fifteen hundred men, he moved up the Hudson, built a stockade fort opposite Saratoga, and another at the spot known as the Great Carrying Place. This latter he called Fort Nicholson,—a name which it afterwards exchanged for that of Fort Lydius, and later still for that of Fort Edward, which the town that occupies the site owns to this day.[21] Thence he cut a rough roadway through the woods to where Wood Creek, choked with beaver dams, writhed through flat green meadows, walled in by rock and forest. Here he built another fort, which was afterwards rebuilt and named Fort Anne. Wood Creek led to Lake Champlain, and Lake Champlain to Chambly and Montreal,—the objective points of the expedition. All was astir at the camp. Flat-boats and canoes were made, and stores brought up from Albany, till everything was ready for an advance the moment word should come that the British fleet had reached Boston. Vetch, all impatience, went thither to meet it, as if his presence could hasten its arrival.

Reports of Nicholson's march to Wood Creek had reached Canada, and Vaudreuil sent Ramesay, governor of Montreal, with fifteen hundred troops, Canadians, and Indians, to surprise his camp. Ramesay's fleet of canoes had reached Lake Champlain, and was halfway to the mouth of Wood Creek, when his advance party was discovered by English scouts, and the French commander began to fear that he should be surprised in his turn; in fact, some of his Indians were fired upon from an ambuscade. All was now doubt, perplexity, and confusion. Ramesay landed at the narrows of the lake, a little south of the place now called Crown Point. Here, in the dense woods, his Indians fired on some Canadians whom they took for English. This was near producing a panic. "Every tree seemed an enemy," writes an officer present. Ramesay lost himself in the woods, and could not find his army. One Deruisseau, who had gone out as a scout, came back with the report that nine hundred Englishmen were close at hand. Seven English canoes did in fact appear, supported, as the French in their excitement imagined, by a numerous though

---

[20] "If I had not accepted the command, there would have been insuperable difficulties" (arising from provincial jealousies).— *Nicholson to Sunderland, 8 July,* 1709.

[21] Forts Nicholson, Lydius, and Edward were not the same, but succeeded each other on the same ground.

invisible army in the forest; but being fired upon, and seeing that they were entering a hornet's nest, the English sheered off. Ramesay having at last found his army, and order being gradually restored, a council of war was held, after which the whole force fell back to Chambly, having accomplished nothing.[22]

Great was the alarm in Canada when it became known that the enemy aimed at nothing less than the conquest of the colony. One La Plaine spread a panic at Quebec by reporting that, forty-five leagues below, he had seen eight or ten ships under sail and heard the sound of cannon. It was afterwards surmised that the supposed ships were points of rocks seen through the mist at low tide, and the cannon the floundering of whales at play.[23] Quebec, however, was all excitement, in expectation of attack. The people of the Lower Town took refuge on the rock above; the men of the neighboring parishes were ordered within the walls; and the women and children, with the cattle and horses, were sent to hiding-places in the forest. There had been no less consternation at Montreal, caused by exaggerated reports of Iroquois hostility and the movements of Nicholson. It was even proposed to abandon Chambly and Fort Frontenac, and concentrate all available force to defend the heart of the colony. "A most bloody war is imminent," wrote Vaudreuil to the minister, Ponchartrain.

Meanwhile, for weeks and months Nicholson's little army lay in the sultry valley of Wood Creek, waiting those tidings of the arrival of the British squadron at Boston which were to be its signal of advance. At length a pestilence broke out. It is

[22] *Mémoire sur le Canada, Année* 1709. This paper, which has been ascribed to the engineer De Léry, is printed in *Collection de Manuscrits relatifs à la Nouvelle France,* i. 615 (Quebec, 1883), printed from the MS. *Paris Documents* in the Boston State House. The writer of the *Mémoire* was with Ramesay's expedition. Also *Ramesay à Vaudreuil, 19 Octobre,* 1709, and *Vaudreuil au Ministre, 14 Novembre,* 1709. Charlevoix says that Ramesay turned back because he believed that there were five thousand English at Wood Creek; but Ramesay himself makes their number only one thousand whites and two hundred Indians. He got his information from two Dutchmen caught just after the alarm near Pointe à la Chevelure (Crown Point). He turned back because he had failed to surprise the English, and also, it seems, because there were disagreements among his officers.

[23] *Monseigneur de Saint-Vallier et l'Hôpital Général de Québec,* 203.

said to have been the work of the Iroquois allies, who thought that the French were menaced with ruin, and who, true to their policy of balancing one European power against the other, poisoned the waters of the creek by throwing into it, above the camp, the skins and offal of the animals they had killed in their hunting. The story may have some foundation, though it rests only on the authority of Charlevoix. No contemporary writer mentions it; and Vaudreuil says that the malady was caused by the long confinement of the English in their fort. Indeed, a crowd of men, penned up through the heats of midsummer in a palisaded camp, ill-ordered and unclean as the camps of the raw provincials usually were, and infested with pestiferous swarms of flies and mosquitoes, could hardly have remained in health. Whatever its cause, the disease, which seems to have been a malignant dysentery, made more havoc than the musket and the sword. A party of French who came to the spot late in the autumn, found it filled with innumerable graves.

The British squadron, with the five regiments on board, was to have reached Boston at the middle of May. On the twentieth of that month the whole contingent of Massachusetts, New Hampshire, and Rhode Island was encamped by Boston harbor, with transports and stores, ready to embark for Quebec at ten hours' notice.[24] When Vetch, after seeing everything in readiness at New York, returned to Boston on the third of July, he found the New England levies encamped there still, drilled diligently every day by officers whom he had brought from England for the purpose. "The bodies of the men," he writes to Lord Sunderland, "are in general better than in Europe, and I hope their courage will prove so too; so that nothing in human probability can prevent the success of this glorious enterprise but the too late arrival of the fleet."[25] But of the fleet there was no sign. "The government here is put to vast expense," pursues Vetch, "but they cheerfully pay it, in hopes of being freed from it forever hereafter. All that they can do now is to fast and pray for the safe and speedy arrival of the fleet, for which they have already had two public fast-days kept."

If it should not come in time, he continues, "it would be the

[24] *Dudley to Sunderland,* 14 *August,* 1709.

[25] *Vetch to Sunderland,* 2 *August,* 1709. The pay of the men was nine shillings a week, with eightpence a day for provisions; and most of them had received an enlistment bounty of £12.

last disappointment to her Majesty's colonies, who have so heartily complied with her royal order, and would render them much more miserable than if such a thing had never been undertaken." Time passed, and no ships appeared. Vetch wrote again: "I shall only presume to acquaint your Lordship how vastly uneasy all her Majesty's loyall subjects here on this continent are. Pray God hasten the fleet."[26] Dudley, scarcely less impatient, wrote to the same effect. It was all in vain, and the soldiers remained in their camp, monotonously drilling day after day through all the summer and half the autumn. At length, on the eleventh of October, Dudley received a letter from Lord Sunderland, informing him that the promised forces had been sent to Portugal to meet an exigency of the European war. They were to have reached Boston, as we have seen, by the middle of May. Sunderland's notice of the change of destination was not written till the twenty-seventh of July, and was eleven weeks on its way, thus imposing on the colonists a heavy and needless tax in time, money, temper, and, in the case of the expedition against Montreal, health and life.[27] What was left of Nicholson's force had fallen back before Sunderland's letter came, making a scapegoat of the innocent Vetch, cursing him, and wishing him hanged.

In New England the disappointment and vexation were extreme; but, not to lose all the fruits of their efforts, the governors of Massachusetts, Connecticut, New Hampshire, and Rhode Island met and resolved to attack Port Royal if the captains of several British frigates then at New York and Boston would take part in the enterprise. To the disgust of the provincials, the captains, with one exception, refused, on the score of the late season and the want of orders.

A tenacious energy has always been a characteristic of New England, and the hopes of the colonists had been raised too high to be readily abandoned. Port Royal was in their eyes a pestilent nest of privateers and pirates that preyed on the New England fisheries; and on the refusal of the naval commanders to join in an immediate attack, they offered to the court to besiege the place themselves next year, if they could count on the help of four frigates and five hundred soldiers, to be at

[26] *Vetch to Sunderland,* 12 *August,* 1709. Dudley writes with equal urgency two days later.

[27] *Letters of Nicholson, Dudley, and Vetch,* 20 *June* to 24 *October,* 1709.

Boston by the end of March.[28] The Assembly of Massachusetts requested Nicholson, who was on the point of sailing for Europe, to beg her Majesty to help them in an enterprise which would be so advantageous to the Crown, "and which, by the long and expensive war, we are so impoverished and enfeebled as not to be in a capacity to effect."[29]

Nicholson sailed in December, and Peter Schuyler soon followed. New York, having once entered on the path of war, saw that she must continue in it; and to impress the Five Nations with the might and majesty of the Queen, and so dispose them to hold fast to the British cause, Schuyler took five Mohawk chiefs with him to England. One died on the voyage; the rest arrived safe, and their appearance was the sensation of the hour. They were clad, at the Queen's expense, in strange and gay attire, invented by the costumer of one of the theatres; were lodged and feasted as the guests of the nation, driven about London in coaches with liveried servants, conducted to dockyards, arsenals, and reviews, and saluted with cannon by ships of war. The Duke of Shrewsbury presented them to Queen Anne,—one as emperor of the Mohawks, and the other three as kings,—and the Archbishop of Canterbury solemnly gave each of them a Bible. Steele and Addison wrote essays about them, and the Dutch artist Verelst painted their portraits, which were engraved in mezzotint.[30] Their presence and the speech made in their name before the

[28] *Joint Letter of Nicholson, Dudley, Vetch, and Moody to Sunderland, 24 October, 1709;* also *Joint Letter of Dudley, Vetch, and Moody to Sunderland, 25 October, 1709; Abstracts of Letters and Papers relating to the Attack of Port Royal,* 1709 (Public Record Office); *Address of ye Inhabitants of Boston and Parts adjacent,* 1709. Moody, named above, was the British naval captain who had consented to attack Port Royal.

[29] *Order of Assembly, 27 October,* 1709. Massachusetts had spent about £22,000 on her futile expedition of 1707, and, with New Hampshire and Rhode Island, a little more than £46,000 on that of 1709, besides continual outlay in guarding her two hundred miles of frontier,—a heavy expense for the place and time.

[30] See J. R. Bartlett, in *Magazine of American History,* March, 1878, and Schuyler, *Colonial New York,* ii. 34–39. The chiefs returned to America in May on board the "Dragon." An elaborate pamphlet appeared in London, giving an account of them and their people. A set of the mezzotint portraits, which are large and well executed, is in the John Carter Brown collection at Providence. For photographic reproductions, see Winsor, *Nar. and Crit. Hist.,* v. 107. Compare Smith, *Hist. N. Y.,* i. 204 (1830).

court seem to have had no small effect in drawing attention to the war in America and inclining the ministry towards the proposals of Nicholson. These were accepted, and he sailed for America commissioned to command the enterprise against Port Royal, with Vetch as adjutant-general.[31]

Colonel Francis Nicholson had held some modest military positions, but never, it is said, seen active service. In colonial affairs he had played an important part, and in the course of his life governed, at different times, Virginia, New York, Maryland, and Carolina. He had a robust, practical brain, capable of broad views and large schemes. One of his plans was a confederacy of the provinces to resist the French, which, to his great indignation, Virginia rejected. He had Jacobite leanings, and had been an adherent of James II.; but being no idealist, and little apt to let his political principles block the path of his interests, he turned his back on the fallen cause and offered his services to the Revolution. Though no pattern of domestic morals, he seems to have been officially upright, and he wished well to the colonies, saving always the dominant interests of England. He was bold, ambitious, vehement, and sometimes headstrong and perverse.

Though the English ministry had promised aid, it was long in coming. The Massachusetts Assembly had asked that the ships should be at Boston before the end of March; but it was past the middle of May before they sailed from Plymouth. Then, towards midsummer, a strange spasm of martial energy seems to have seized the ministry, for Viscount Shannon was ordered to Boston with an additional force, commissioned to take the chief command and attack, not Port Royal, but Quebec.[32] This ill-advised change of plan seems to have been reconsidered; at least, it came to nothing.[33]

Meanwhile, the New England people waited impatiently for the retarded ships. No order had come from England for

[31] Commission of Colonel Francis Nicholson, 18 May, 1710. Instructions to Colonel Nicholson, same date.

[32] Instructions to Richard Viscount Shannon, July, 1710. A report of the scheme reached Boston. Hutchinson, ii. 164.

[33] The troops, however, were actually embarked. True State of the Forces commanded by the Right Honble The Lord Viscount Shannon, as they were Embark'd the 14th of October, 1710. The total was three thousand two hundred and sixty-five officers and men. Also, Shannon to Sunderland, 16 October, 1710. The absurdity of the attempt at so late a season is obvious. Yet the fleet lay some weeks more at Portsmouth, waiting for a fair wind.

raising men, and the colonists resolved this time to risk nothing till assured that their labor and money would not be wasted. At last, not in March, but in July, the ships appeared. Then all was astir with preparation. First, the House of Representatives voted thanks to the Queen for her "royal aid." Next, it was proclaimed that no vessel should be permitted to leave the harbor "till the service is provided"; and a committee of the House proceeded to impress fourteen vessels to serve as transports. Then a vote was passed that nine hundred men be raised as the quota of Massachusetts, and a month's pay in advance, together with a coat worth thirty shillings, was promised to volunteers; a committee of three being at the same time appointed to provide the coats. On the next day appeared a proclamation from the governor announcing the aforesaid "encouragements," calling on last year's soldiers to enlist again, promising that all should return home as soon as Port Royal was taken, and that each might keep as his own forever the Queen's musket that would be furnished him. Now came an order to colonels of militia to muster their regiments on a day named, read the proclamation at the head of each company, and if volunteers did not come forward in sufficient number, to draft as many men as might be wanted, appointing, at the same time, officers to conduct them to the rendezvous at Dorchester or Cambridge; and, by a stringent and unusual enactment, the House ordered that they should be quartered in private houses, with or without the consent of the owners, "any law or usage to the contrary notwithstanding." Sailors were impressed without ceremony to man the transports; and, finally, it was voted that a pipe of wine, twenty sheep, five pigs, and one hundred fowls be presented to the Honorable General Nicholson for his table during the expedition.[34] The above, with slight variation, may serve as an example of the manner in which, for several generations, men were raised in Massachusetts to serve against the French.

Autumn had begun before all was ready. Connecticut, New Hampshire, and Rhode Island sent their contingents; there was a dinner at the Green Dragon Tavern in honor of Nicholson, Vetch, and Sir Charles Hobby, the chief officers of the expedition; and on the eighteenth of September the whole put to sea.

[34] *Archives of Massachusetts,* vol. lxxi., where the original papers are preserved.

On the twenty-fourth the squadron sailed into the narrow entrance of Port Royal, where the tide runs like a mill-stream. One vessel was driven upon the rocks, and twenty-six men were drowned. The others got in safely, and anchored above Goat Island, in sight of the French fort. They consisted of three fourth-rates,—the "Dragon," the "Chester," and the "Falmouth;" two fifth-rates,—the "Lowestoffe" and the "Feversham;" the province galley, one bomb-ketch, twenty-four small transports, two or three hospital ships, a tender, and several sloops carrying timber to make beds for cannon and mortars. The landing force consisted of four hundred British marines, and about fifteen hundred provincials, divided into four battalions.[35] Its unnecessary numbers were due to the belief of Nicholson that the fort had been reinforced and strengthened.

In the afternoon of the twenty-fifth they were all on shore, —Vetch with his two battalions on the north side, and Nicholson with the other two on the south. Vetch marched to his camping-ground, on which, in the words of Nicholson's journal, "the French began to fire pretty thick." On the next morning Nicholson's men moved towards the fort, hacking their way through the woods and crossing the marshes of Allen's River, while the French fired briskly with cannon from the ramparts, and small-arms from the woods, houses, and fences. They were driven back, and the English advance guard intrenched itself within four hundred yards of the works. Several days passed in landing artillery and stores, cannonading from the fort and shelling from the English bomb-ketch, when on the twenty-ninth, Ensign Perelle, with a drummer and a flag of truce, came to Nicholson's tent, bringing a letter from Subercase, who begged him to receive into his camp and under his protection certain ladies of the fort who were distressed by the bursting of the English shells. The conduct of Perelle was irregular, as he had not given notice of his approach by beat of drum and got himself and attendants blindfolded before entering the camp. Therefore Nicholson detained him, sending back an officer of his own with a letter to the effect that he would receive the ladies and

[35] *Nicholson and Vetch to the Secretary of State,* 16 *September,* 1710; Hutchinson, ii. 164; Penhallow. Massachusetts sent two battalions of four hundred and fifty men each, and Connecticut one battalion of three hundred men, while New Hampshire and Rhode Island united their contingents to form a fourth battalion.

lodge them in the same house with the French ensign, "for the queen, my royal mistress, hath not sent me hither to make war against women." Subercase on his part detained the English officer, and wrote to Nicholson,—

> SIR,—You have one of my officers, and I have one of yours; so that now we are equal. However, that hinders me not from believing that once you have given me your word, you will keep it very exactly. On that ground I now write to tell you, sir, that to prevent the spilling of both English and French blood, I am ready to hold up both hands for a capitulation that will be honorable to both of us.[36]

In view of which agreement, he adds that he defers sending the ladies to the English camp.

Another day passed, during which the captive officers on both sides were treated with much courtesy. On the next morning, Sunday, October 1, the siege-guns, mortars, and coehorns were in position; and after some firing on both sides, Nicholson sent Colonel Tailor and Captain Abercrombie with a summons to surrender the fort. Subercase replied that he was ready to listen to proposals; the firing stopped, and within twenty-four hours the terms were settled. The garrison were to march out with the honors of war, and to be carried in English ships to Rochelle or Rochefort. The inhabitants within three miles of the fort were to be permitted to remain, if they chose to do so, unmolested, in their homes during two years, on taking an oath of allegiance and fidelity to the Queen.

Two hundred provincials marched to the fort gate and formed in two lines on the right and left. Nicholson advanced between the ranks, with Vetch on one hand and Hobby on the other, followed by all the field-officers. Subercase came to meet them, and gave up the keys, with a few words of compliment. The French officers and men marched out with shouldered arms, drums beating, and colors flying, saluting the English commander as they passed; then the English troops marched in, raised the union flag, and drank the Queen's health amid a general firing of cannon from the fort and ships. Nicholson changed the name of Port Royal to An-

[36] The contemporary English translation of this letter is printed among the papers appended to *Nicholson's Journal* in *Collections of the Nova Scotia Historical Society,* i.

napolis Royal; and Vetch, already commissioned as governor, took command of the new garrison, which consisted of two hundred British marines, and two hundred and fifty provincials who had offered themselves for the service.

The English officers gave a breakfast to the French ladies in the fort. Sir Charles Hobby took in Madame de Bonaventure, and the rest followed in due order of precedence; but as few of the hosts could speak French, and few of the guests could speak English, the entertainment could hardly have been a lively one.

The French officers and men in the fort when it was taken were but two hundred and fifty-eight. Some of the soldiers and many of the armed inhabitants deserted during the siege, which, no doubt, hastened the surrender; for Subercase, a veteran of more than thirty years' service, had borne fair repute as a soldier.

Port Royal had twice before been taken by New England men,—once under Major Sedgwick in 1654, and again under Sir William Phips in the last war; and in each case it had been restored to France by treaty. This time England kept what she had got; and as there was no other place of strength in the province, the capture of Port Royal meant the conquest of Acadia.[37]

[37] In a letter to Ponchartrain, 1 *October,* 1710 (new style), Subercase declares that he has not a sou left, nor any credit. "I have managed to borrow enough to maintain the garrison for the last two years, and have paid what I could by selling all my furniture." Charlevoix's account of the siege has been followed by most writers, both French and English; but it is extremely incorrect. It was answered by one De Gannes, apparently an officer under Subercase, in a paper called *Observations sur les Erreurs de la Relation du Siège du Port Royal . . . faittes sur de faux mémoires par le révérend Pére Charlevoix,* whom De Gannes often contradicts flatly. Thus Charlevoix puts the besieging force at thirty-four hundred men, besides officers and sailors, while De Gannes puts it at fourteen hundred; and while Charlevoix says that the garrison were famishing, his critic says that they were provisioned for three months. See the valuable notes to Shea's *Charlevoix,* v. 227–232.

The journal of Nicholson was published "by authority" in the *Boston News Letter, November,* 1710, and has been reprinted, with numerous accompanying documents, including the French and English correspondence during the siege, in the *Collections of the Nova Scotia Historical Society,* i.

Vaudreuil, before the siege, sent a reinforcement to Subercase, who, by a strange infatuation, refused it. *N. Y. Col. Docs.,* ix. 853.

Chapter 8

1710, 1711
Walker's Expedition

MILITARY AID from Old England to New, promised in one year and actually given in the next, was a fact too novel and surprising to escape the notice either of friends or of foes.

The latter drew strange conclusions from it. Two Irish deserters from an English station in Newfoundland appeared at the French post of Placentia full of stories of British and provincial armaments against Canada. On this, an idea seized the French commandant, Costebelle, and he hastened to make it known to the colonial minister. It was to the effect that the aim of England was not so much to conquer the French colonies as to reduce her own to submission, especially Massachusetts,—a kind of republic which has never willingly accepted a governor from its king.[1] In sending ships and soldiers to the "Bastionnais" under pretence of helping them to conquer their French neighbors, Costebelle is sure that England only means to bring them to a dutiful subjection. "I do not think," he writes on another occasion, "that they are so blind as not to see that they will insensibly be brought under the yoke of the Parliament of Old England; but by the cruelties that the Canadians and Indians exercise in continual incursions upon their lands, I judge that they would rather be delivered from the inhumanity of such neighbors than preserve all the former powers of their little republic."[2] He thinks,

[1] *Rapport de Costebelle*, 14 *Octobre*, 1709. *Ibid.*, 3 *Décembre*, 1709.

[2] "Je ne les crois pas assez aveugles pour ne point s'apercevoir qu'insensiblement ils vont subir le joug du parlement de la vieille Angleterre, mais par les cruautés que les Canadiens et sauvages exercent sur leurs terres par des courses continuelles de juge qu'ils aiment encore mieux se délivrer de l'inhumanité de semblables voisins que de conserver toute l'ancienne autorité de leur petite république."—*Costebelle au Ministre*, 3 *Décembre*, 1710. He clung tenaciously to this idea, and wrote again in 1712 that "les cruautés de nos sauvages, qui font horreur à rapporter," would always incline the New England people to peace. They had, however, an opposite effect.

however, that the design of England ought to be strongly represented to the Council at Boston, and that M. de la Ronde Denys will be a good man to do it, as he speaks English, has lived in Boston, and has many acquaintances there.[3]

The minister, Ponchartrain, was struck by Costebelle's suggestion, and wrote both to him and to Vaudreuil in high approval of it. To Vaudreuil he says: "Monsieur de Costebelle has informed me that the chief object of the armament made by the English last year was to establish their sovereignty at Boston and New York, the people of these provinces having always maintained a sort of republic, governed by their council, and having been unwilling to receive absolute governors from the kings of England. This destination of the armament seems to me probable, and it is much to be wished that the Council at Boston could be informed of the designs of the English court, and shown how important it is for that province to remain in the state of a republic. The King would even approve our helping it to do so. If you see any prospect of success, no means should be spared to secure it. The matter is of the greatest importance, but care is essential to employ persons who have the talents necessary for conducting it, besides great secrecy and prudence, as well as tried probity and fidelity. This affair demands your best attention, and must be conducted with great care and precaution, in order that no false step may be taken."[4]

Ponchartrain could not be supposed to know that while under her old charter Massachusetts, called by him and other Frenchmen the government of Boston, had chosen her own governor, New York had always received hers from the court. What is most curious in this affair is the attitude of Louis XIV, who abhorred republics, and yet was prepared to bolster up one or more of them beyond the Atlantic,—thinking, no doubt, that they would be too small and remote to be dangerous.

Costebelle, who had suggested the plan of warning the Council at Boston, proceeded to unfold his scheme for executing it. This was to send La Ronde Denys to Boston in the spring, under the pretext of treating for an exchange of prisoners, which would given him an opportunity of insinu-

[3] It is more than probable that La Ronde Denys, who had studied the "Bastonnais" with care, first gave the idea to Costebelle.

[4] *Ponchartrain à Vaudreuil, 10 Août, 1710. Ponchartrain à Costebelle, même date.* These letters are in answer to the reports of Costebelle, before cited.

ating to the colonists that the forces which the Queen of England sends to join their own for the conquest of Acadia and Canada have no object whatever but that of ravishing from them the liberties they have kept so firmly and so long, but which would be near ruin if the Queen should become mistress of New France by the fortune of war; and that either they must have sadly fallen from their ancient spirit, or their chiefs have been corrupted by the Court of London, if they do not see that they are using their own weapons for the destruction of their republic.[5]

La Ronde Denys accordingly received his instructions, which authorized him to negotiate with the "Bastonnais" as with an independent people, and offer them complete exemption from French hostility if they would promise to give no more aid to Old England either in ships or men. He was told at the same time to approach the subject with great caution, and unless he found willing listeners, to pass off the whole as a pleasantry.[6] He went to Boston, where he was detained in consequence of preparations then on foot for attacking Canada. He tried to escape; but his vessel was seized and moored under the guns of the town, and it is needless to say that his mission was a failure.

The idea of Costebelle, or rather of La Ronde,—for it probably originated with him,—was not without foundation; for though there is no reason to believe that in sending ships and soldiers against the French, England meant to use them against the liberties of her own colonies, there can be no doubt that she thought those liberties excessive and troublesome; and, on the other side, while the people of Massachusetts were still fondly attached to the land of their fathers, and still called it "Home," they were at the same time enamoured of their autonomy, and jealously watchful against any abridgment of it.

While La Ronde Denys was warning Massachusetts of the danger of helping England to conquer Canada, another

[5] *Costebelle à Ponchartrain,* 3 *Décembre,* 1710.

[6] *Instruction pour Monsieur de la Ronde, Capitaine d'Infanterie des Détachments de la Marine,* 1711. "Le dit sieur de la Ronde pourroit entrer en négociation et se promettre de faire cesser toutes sortes d'hostilités du côté du Canada, supposé que les Bastonnais promissent d'en faire de même de leur côté, et qu'ils ne donassent aucun secours à l'avenir, d'hommes ni de vaisseaux, aux puissances de la vieille Angleterre et d'Ecosse."

Frenchman, in a more prophetic spirit, declared that England would make a grave mistake if she helped her colonies to the same end. "There is an antipathy," this writer affirms, "between the English of Europe and those of America, who will not endure troops from England even to guard their forts;" and he goes on to say that if the French colonies should fall, those of England would control the continent from Newfoundland to Florida. "Old England"—such are his words— "will not imagine that these various provinces will then unite, shake off the yoke of the English monarchy, and erect themselves into a democracy."[7] Forty or fifty years later, several Frenchmen made the same prediction; but at this early day, when the British provinces were so feeble and divided, it is truly a remarkable one.

The anonymous prophet regards the colonies of England, Massachusetts above all, as a standing menace to those of France; and he proposes a drastic remedy against the danger. This is a powerful attack on Boston by land and sea, for which he hopes that God will prepare the way. "When Boston is reduced, we would call together all the chief men of the other towns of New England, who would pay heavy sums to be spared from the flames. As for Boston, it should be pillaged, its workshops, manufactures, shipyards, all its fine establishments ruined, and its ships sunk." If these gentle means are used thoroughly, he thinks that New England will cease to be a dangerous rival for some time, especially if "Rhodelene" (Rhode Island) is treated like Boston.[8]

While the correspondent of the French court was thus consigning New England to destruction, an attack was preparing against Canada less truculent but quite as formidable as that

[7] "La vieille Angleterre ne s'imaginera pas que ces diverses Provinces se réuniront, et, secouant le joug de la monarchie Anglaise, s'érigeront en démocratie."—*Mémoire sur la Nouvelle Angleterre*, 1710, 1711. (Archives de la Marine.)

[8] "Pour Baston, il faudrait la piller, ruiner ses ateliers, ses manufactures, tous ses beaux établissements, couler bas ses navires, . . . ruiner les ateliers de construction de navires."—*Mémoire sur la Nouvelle Angleterre*, 1710, 1711. The writer was familiar with Boston and its neighborhood, and had certainly spent some time there. Possibly he was no other than La Ronde Denys himself, after the failure of his mission to excite the "Bastonnais" to refuse co-operation with British armaments. He enlarges with bitterness on the extent of the fisheries, foreign trade, and ship-building of New England.

which he urged against Boston. The French colony was threatened by an armament stronger in proportion to her present means of defence than that which brought her under British rule half a century later. But here all comparison ceases; for there was no Pitt to direct and inspire, and no Wolfe to lead.

The letters of Dudley, the proposals of Vetch, the representations of Nicholson, the promptings of Jeremiah Dummer, agent of Massachusetts in England, and the speech made to the Queen by the four Indians who had been the London sensation of the last year, had all helped to draw the attention of the ministry to the New World, and the expediency of driving the French out of it. Other influences conspired to the same end, or in all likelihood little or nothing would have been done. England was tiring of the Continental war, the costs of which threatened ruin. Marlborough was rancorously attacked, and his most stanch supporters the Whigs had given place to the Tories, led by the Lord Treasurer Harley, and the Secretary of State St. John, soon afterwards Lord Bolingbroke. Never was party spirit more bitter; and the new ministry found a congenial ally in the coarse and savage but powerful genius of Swift, who, incensed by real or imagined slights from the late minister, Godolphin, gave all his strength to the winning side.

The prestige of Marlborough's victories was still immense. Harley and St. John dreaded it as their chief danger, and looked eagerly for some means of counteracting it. Such means would be supplied by the conquest of New France. To make America a British continent would be an achievement almost worth Blenheim or Ramillies, and one, too, in which Britain alone would be the gainer; whereas the enemies of Marlborough, with Swift at their head, contended that his greatest triumphs turned more to the profit of Holland or Germany than of England.[9] Moreover, to send a part of his army across the Atlantic would tend to cripple his movements and diminish his fame.

St. John entered with ardor into the scheme. Seven veteran regiments, five of which were from the army in Flanders, were ordered to embark. But in the choice of commanders the judgment of the ministers was not left free; there were influences that they could not disregard. The famous Sarah, Duchess of Marlborough, lately the favorite of the feeble but wilful queen, had lost her good graces and given place to Mrs.

[9] See Swift, *Conduct of the Allies.*

Masham, one of the women of her bedchamber. The new favorite had a brother, John Hill, known about the court as Jack Hill, whom Marlborough had pronounced good for nothing, but who had been advanced to the rank of colonel, and then of brigadier, through the influence of Mrs. Masham; and though his agreeable social qualities were his best recommendation, he was now appointed to command the troops on the Canada expedition. It is not so clear why the naval command was given to Admiral Sir Hovenden Walker, a man whose incompetence was soon to become notorious.

Extreme care was taken to hide the destination of the fleet. Even the Lords of the Admirality were kept ignorant of it. Some thought the ships bound for the West Indies; some for the South Sea. Nicholson was sent to America with orders to the several colonies to make ready men and supplies. He landed at Boston on the eighth of June. The people of the town, who were nearly all Whigs, were taken by surprise, expecting no such enterprise on the part of the Tory ministry; and their perplexity was not diminished when they were told that the fleet was at hand, and that they were to supply it forthwith with provisions for ten weeks.[10] There was no time to lose. The governors of New York, Connecticut, and Rhode Island were summoned to meet at New London, and Dudley and Nicholson went thither to join them. Here plans were made for the double attack; for while Walker and Hill were to sail up the St. Lawrence against Quebec, Nicholson, as in the former attempt, was to move against Montreal by way of Lake Champlain. In a few days the arrangements were made, and the governors hastened back to their respective posts.[11]

When Dudley reached Boston, he saw Nantasket Roads crowded with transports and ships of war, and the pastures of Noddle's Island studded with tents. The fleet had come on the twenty-fourth, having had what the Admiral calls "by the blessing of God a favorable and extraordinary passage,

[10] Boston, devoted to fishing, shipbuilding, and foreign trade, drew most of its provisions from neighboring colonies. (Dummer, *Letter to a Noble Lord.*) The people only half believed that the Tory ministry were sincere in attacking Canada, and suspected that the sudden demand for provisions, so difficult to meet at once, was meant to furnish a pretext for throwing the blame of failure upon Massachusetts. Hutchinson, ii. 173.

[11] *Minutes of Proceedings of the Congress of Governors, June,* 1711.

being but seven weeks and two days between Plymouth and Nantasket."[12]

The Admiral and the General had been welcomed with all honor. The provincial Secretary, with two members of the Council, conducted them to town amid salutes from the batteries of Copp's Hill and Fort Hill, and the Boston militia regiment received them under arms; after which they were feasted at the principal tavern, and accompanied in ceremony to the lodgings provided for them.[13] When the troops were disembarked and the tents pitched curious townspeople and staring rustics crossed to Noddle's Island, now East Boston, to gaze with wonder on a military pageant the like of which New England had never seen before. Yet their joy at this unlooked-for succor was dashed with deep distrust and jealousy. They dreaded these new and formidable friends, with their imperious demeanor and exacting demands. The British officers, on their part, were no better pleased with the colonists, and one of them, Colonel King of the artillery, thus gives vent to his feelings: "You'll find in my Journal what Difficultyes we mett with through the Misfortune that the Coloneys were not inform'd of our Coming two Months sooner, and through the Interestedness, ill Nature, and Sowerness of those People, whose Government, Doctrine, and Manners, whose Hypocracy and canting, are insupportable; and no man living but one of Gen'l Hill's good Sense and good Nature could have managed them. But if such a Man mett with nothing he could depend on, altho' vested with the Queen's Royal Power and Authority, and Supported by a Number of Troops sufficient to reduce by force all the Coloneys, 't is easy to determine the Respect and Obedience her Majesty may reasonably expect from them." And he gives it as his conviction that till all the colonies are deprived of their charters and brought under one government, "they will grow more stiff and disobedient every Day."[14]

It will be seen that some coolness on the part of the Bostonians was not unnatural. But whatever may have been the popular feeling, the provincial authorities did their full part towards supplying the needs of the new-comers; for Dudley,

[12] *Walker to Burchett, Secretary of the Admiralty,* 14 *August,* 1711.

[13] *Abstract of the Journal of the Governor, Council, and Assembly of the Province of the Massachusetts Bay.*

[14] *King to Secretary St. John,* 25 *July,* 1711.

with his strong Tory leanings, did not share the prevailing jealousy, and the country members of the Assembly were anxious before all things to be delivered from war-parties. The problem was how to raise the men and furnish the supplies in the least possible time. The action of the Assembly, far from betraying any slackness, was worthy of a military dictatorship. All ordinary business was set aside. Bills of credit for £40,000 were issued to meet the needs of the expedition. It was ordered that the prices of provisions and other necessaries of the service should stand fixed at the point where they stood before the approach of the fleet was known. Sheriffs and constables, jointly with the Queen's officers, were ordered to search all the town for provisions and liquors, and if the owners refused to part with them at the prescribed prices, to break open the doors and seize them. Stringent and much-needed Acts were passed against harboring deserters. Provincial troops, in greater number than the ministry had demanded, were ordered to be raised at once, and quartered upon the citizens, with or without their consent, at the rate of eightpence a day for each man.[15] Warrants were issued for impressing pilots, and also mechanics and laborers, who, in spite of Puritan scruples, were required to work on Sundays.

Such measures, if imposed by England, would have roused the most bitter resentment. Even when ordered by their own representatives, they caused a sullen discontent among the colonists, and greatly increased the popular dislike of their military visitors. It was certain that when the expedition sailed and the operation of the new enactments ceased, prices would rise; and hence the compulsion to part with goods at low fixed rates was singularly trying to the commercial temper. It was a busy season, too, with the farmers, and they showed no haste to bring their produce to the camp. Though many of the principal inhabitants bound themselves by mutual agreement to live on their family stores of salt provisions, in order that the troops might be better supplied with fresh, this failed to soothe the irritation of the British officers, aggravated by frequent desertions, which the colonists favored, and by the impossibility of finding pilots familiar with the St. Lawrence.

[15] The number demanded from Massachusetts was one thousand, and that raised by her was eleven hundred and sixty. *Dudley to Walker*, 27 *July,* 1711.

Some when forced into the service made their escape, to the great indignation of Walker, who wrote to the governor: "Her Majesty will resent such actions in a very signal manner; and when it shall be represented that the people live here as if there were no king in Israel, but every one does what seems right in his own eyes, measures will be taken to put things upon a better foot for the future."[16] At length, however, every preparation was made, the supplies were all on board, and after a grand review of the troops on the fields of Noddle's Island, the whole force set sail on the thirtieth of July, the provincials wishing them success, and heartily rejoicing that they were gone.

The fleet consisted of nine ships of war and two bomb-ketches, with about sixty transports, store-ships, hospital-ships, and other vessels, British and provincial. They carried the seven British regiments, numbering, with the artillery train, about fifty-five hundred men, besides six hundred marines and fifteen hundred provincials; counting, with the sailors, nearly twelve thousand in all.[17]

Vetch commanded the provincials, having been brought from Annapolis for that purpose. The great need was of pilots. Every sailor in New England who had seen the St. Lawrence had been pressed into the service, though each and all declared themselves incapable of conducting the fleet to Quebec. Several had no better knowledge of the river than they had picked up when serving as soldiers under Phips twenty-one years before. The best among them was the veteran Captain Bonner, who afterwards amused his old age by making a plan of Boston, greatly prized by connoisseurs in such matters. Vetch had studied the St. Lawrence in his several visits to Quebec, but, like Bonner, he had gone up the river only in sloops or other small craft, and was, moreover, no sailor. One of Walker's ships, the "Chester," sent in advance

[16] Walker prints this letter in his Journal. Colonel King writes in his own Journal: "The conquest of Canada will naturally lead the Queen into changing their present disorderly government;" and he thinks that the conviction of this made the New Englanders indifferent to the success of the expedition.

[17] The above is drawn from the various lists and tables in Walker, *Journal of the Canada Expedition*. The armed ships that entered Boston in June were fifteen in all; but several had been detached for cruising. The number of British transports, store-ships, etc., was forty, the rest being provincial.

to cruise in the Gulf, had captured a French vessel commanded by one Paradis, an experienced old voyager, who knew the river well. He took a bribe of five hundred pistoles to act as pilot; but the fleet would perhaps have fared better if he had refused the money. He gave such dismal accounts of the Canadian winter that the Admiral could see nothing but ruin ahead, even if he should safely reach his destination. His tribulation is recorded in his Journal. "That which now chiefly took up my thoughts, was contriving how to secure the ships if we got up to Quebec; for *the ice in the river freezing to the bottom* would have utterly destroyed and bilged them as much as if they had been squeezed between rocks."[18] These misgivings may serve to give the measure of his professional judgment. Afterwards, reflecting on the situation, he sees cause for gratitude in his own mishaps; "because, had we arrived safe at Quebec, our provisions would have been reduced to a very small proportion, not exceeding eight or nine weeks at short allowance, so that between ten and twelve thousand men must have been left to perish with the extremity of cold and hunger. I must confess the melancholy contemplation of this (had it happened) strikes me with horror; for how dismal must it have been to have beheld the seas and earth locked up by adamantine frosts, and swoln with high mountains of snow, in a barren and uncultivated region; great numbers of brave men famishing with hunger, and drawing lots who should die first to feed the rest."[19]

All went well till the eighteenth of August, when there was a strong head-wind, and the ships ran into the Bay of Gaspé. Two days after, the wind shifted to the southeast, and they set sail again, Walker in his flagship, the "Edgar," being at or near the head of the fleet. On the evening of the twenty-second they were at some distance above the great Island of Anticosti. The river is here about seventy miles wide, and no land had been seen since noon of the day before. There was a strong east wind, with fog. Walker thought that he was not far from the south shore, when in fact he was at least fifty miles from it, and more than half that distance north of his true course. At eight in the evening the Admiral signalled the fleet to bring to, under mizzen and maintopsails, with heads turned southward. At half-past ten, Paddon, the captain of

18 Walker, *Journal: Introduction.*
19 *Ibid.,* 25.

the "Edgar," came to tell him that he saw land which he supposed must be the south shore; on which Walker, in a fatal moment, signalled for the ships to wear and bring to, with heads northward. He then turned into his berth, and was falling asleep, when a military officer, Captain Goddard, of Seymour's regiment, hastily entered, and begged him to come on deck, saying that there were breakers on all sides. Walker, scornful of a landsman, and annoyed at being disturbed, answered impatiently and would not stir. Soon after, Goddard appeared again, and implored him for Heaven's sake to come up and see for himself, or all would be lost. At the same time the Admiral heard a great noise and trampling, on which he turned out of his berth, put on his dressing-gown and slippers, and going in this attire on deck, found a scene of fright and confusion. At first he could see nothing, and shouted to the men to reassure them; but just then the fog opened, the moon shone out, and the breaking surf was plainly visible to leeward. The French pilot, who at first could not be found, now appeared on deck, and declared, to the astonishment of both the Admiral and Captain Paddon, that they were off the north shore. Paddon, in his perplexity, had ordered an anchor to be let go; Walker directed the cable to be cut, and, making all sail, succeeded in beating to windward and gaining an offing.[20]

The ship that carried Colonel King, of the artillery, had a narrow escape. King says that she anchored in a driving rain, "with a shoal of rocks on each quarter within a cable's length of us, which we plainly perceived by the waves breaking over them in a very violent manner." They were saved by a lull in the gale; for if it had continued with the same violence, he pursues, "our anchors could not have held, and the wind and the vast seas which ran, would have broken our ship into ten thousand pieces against the rocks. All night we heard nothing but ships firing and showing lights, as in the utmost distress."[21]

Vetch, who was on board the little frigate "Despatch," says that he was extremely uneasy at the course taken by Walker on the night of the storm. "I told Colonel Dudley and Captain Perkins, commander of the 'Despatch,' that I wondered what the Wag meant by that course, and why he did not

[20] Walker, *Journal*, 124, 125.
[21] King, *Journal*.

steer west and west-by-south."[22] The "Despatch" kept well astern, and so escaped the danger. Vetch heard through the fog guns firing signals of distress; but three days passed before he knew how serious the disaster was. The ships of war had all escaped; but eight British transports, one store-ship, and one sutler's sloop were dashed to pieces.[23] "It was lamentable to hear the shrieks of the sinking, drowning, departing souls," writes the New England commissary, Sheaf, who was very near sharing their fate.

The disaster took place at and near a rocky island, with adjacent reefs, lying off the north shore and called Isle aux Œufs. On the second day after it happened, Walker was told by the master of one of the wrecked transports that eight hundred and eighty-four soldiers had been lost, and he gives this hasty estimate in his published Journal; though he says in his Introduction to it that the total loss of officers, soldiers, and sailors was scarcely nine hundred.[24] According to a later and more trustworthy statement, the loss of the troops was twenty-nine officers, six hundred and seventy-six sergeants, corporals, drummers, and private soldiers, and thirty-five women attached to the regiments; that is, a total of seven hundred and forty lives.[25] The loss of the sailors is not given; but it could scarcely have exceeded two hundred.

The fleet spent the next two days in standing to and fro between the northern and southern shores, with the exception of some of the smaller vessels employed in bringing off the survivors from the rocks of Isle aux Œufs. The number thus saved was, according to Walker, four hundred and ninety-nine. On the twenty-fifth he went on board the General's ship, the "Windsor," and Hill and he resolved to call a council of war. In fact, Hill had already got his colonels together. Signals were made for the captains of the men-of-war to join them, and the council began.

"Jack Hill," the man about town, placed in high command by the influence of his sister, the Queen's tire-woman, had now

[22] Vetch, Journal.

[23] King, Journal.

[24] Compare Walker, Journal, 45, and Ibid., 127, 128. He elsewhere intimates that his first statement needed correction.

[25] Report of yᵉ Soldiers, etc., Lost. (Public Record Office.) This is a tabular statement, giving the names of the commissioned officers and the positions of their subordinates, regiment by regiment. All the French accounts of the losses are exaggerations.

an opportunity to justify his appointment and prove his mettle. Many a man of pleasure and fashion, when put to the proof, has revealed the latent hero within him; but Hill was not one of them. Both he and Walker seemed to look for nothing but a pretext for retreat; and when manhood is conspicuously wanting in the leaders, a council of war is rarely disposed to supply it. The pilots were called in and examined, and they all declared themselves imperfectly acquainted with the St. Lawrence, which, as some of the captains observed, they had done from the first. Sir William Phips, with pilots still more ignorant, had safely carried his fleet to Quebec in 1690, as Walker must have known, for he had with him Phips's Journal of the voyage. The expedition had lost about a twelfth part of its soldiers and sailors, besides the transports that carried them; with this exception there was no reason for retreat which might not as well have been put forward when the fleet left Boston. All the war-ships were safe, and the loss of men was not greater than might have happened in a single battle. Hill says that Vetch, when asked if he would pilot the fleet to Quebec, refused to undertake it;[26] but Vetch himself gives his answer as follows: "I told him [the Admiral] I never was bred to sea, nor was it any part of my province; but I would do my best by going ahead and showing them where the difficulty of the river was, which I knew pretty well."[27] The naval captains, however, resolved that by reason of the ignorance of the pilots and the dangerous currents it was impossible to go up to Quebec.[28] So discreditable a backing out from a great enterprise will hardly be found elsewhere in English annals. On the next day Vetch, disappointed and indignant, gave his mind freely to the Admiral. "The late disaster cannot, in my humble opinion, be anyways imputed to the difficulty of the navigation, but to the wrong course we steered, which most unavoidably carried us upon the north shore. Who directed that course you best know; and as our return without any further attempt would be a vast reflection upon the conduct of this affair, so it would be of very fatal consequence to the interest of the Crown and all the British colonies upon this conti-

[26] *Hill to Dudley,* 25 *August,* 1711.

[27] Vetch, *Journal.* His statement is confirmed by the report of the council.

[28] *Report of a Consultation of Sea Officers belonging to the Squadron under Command of Sir Hovenden Walker, Kt.,* 25 *August,* 1711. Signed by Walker and eight others.

nent."[29] His protest was fruitless. The fleet retraced its course to the gulf, and then steered for Spanish River, — now the harbor of Sydney, — in the Island of Cape Breton; the Admiral consoling himself with the reflection that the wreck was a blessing in disguise and a merciful intervention of Providence to save the expedition from the freezing, starvation, and cannibalism which his imagination had conjured up.[30]

The frigate "Sapphire" was sent to Boston with news of the wreck and the retreat, which was at once despatched to Nicholson, who, if he continued his movement on Montreal, would now be left to conquer Canada alone. His force consisted of about twenty-three hundred men, white and red, and when the fatal news reached him he was encamped on Wood Creek, ready to pass Lake Champlain. Captain Butler, a New York officer at the camp, afterwards told Kalm, the Swedish naturalist, that when Nicholson heard what had happened, he was beside himself with rage, tore off his wig, threw it on the ground and stamped upon it, crying out, "Roguery! Treachery!"[31] When his fit was over, he did all that was now left for him to do,—burned the wooden forts he had built, marched back to Albany, and disbanded his army, after leaving one hundred and fifty men to protect the frontier against scalping-parties.[32]

Canada had been warned of the storm gathering against her. Early in August, Vaudreuil received letters from Costebelle, at Placentia, telling him that English prisoners had reported mighty preparations at Boston against Quebec, and that Montreal was also to be attacked.[33] The colony was ill prepared for the emergency, but no effort was spared to give the enemy a warm reception. The militia were mustered, Indians called together, troops held in readiness, and defences strengthened. The saints were invoked, and the aid of Heaven was implored by masses, processions, and penances, as in New England by a dismal succession of fasts. Mother Juchereau de Saint-Denis tells us how devout Canadians prayed for help from God and the most holy Virgin; "since their glory was involved, seeing that the true religion would quickly perish if the English should prevail." The general alarm produced

29 *Vetch to Walker,* 26 *August,* 1711.
30 Walker, *Journal, Introduction,* 25.
31 Kalm, *Travels,* ii. 135.
32 Schuyler, *Colonial New York,* ii. 48.
33 *Vaudreuil au Ministre,* 25 *Octobre,* 1711.

effects which, though transient, were thought highly commendable while they lasted. The ladies, according to Mother Juchereau, gave up their ornaments, and became more modest and more pious. "Those of Montreal," pursues the worthy nun, "even outdid those of Quebec; for they bound themselves by oath to wear neither ribbons nor lace, to keep their throats covered, and to observe various holy practices for the space of a year." The recluse of Montreal, Mademoiselle Le Ber, who, by reason of her morbid seclusion and ascetic life, was accounted almost a saint, made a flag embroidered with a prayer to the Virgin, to be borne against the heretical bands of Nicholson.

When that commander withdrew, his retreat, though not the cause of it, was quickly known at Montreal, and the forces gathered there went down to Quebec to aid in repelling the more formidable attack by sea. Here all was suspense and expectancy till the middle of October, when the report came that two large ships had been seen in the river below. There was great excitement, for they were supposed to be the van of the British fleet; but alarm was soon turned to joy by the arrival of the ships, which proved to be French. On the nineteenth, the Sieur de la Valterie, who had come from Labrador in September, and had been sent down the river again by Vaudreuil to watch for the English fleet, appeared at Quebec with tidings of joy. He had descended the St. Lawrence in a canoe, with two Frenchmen and an Indian, till, landing at Isle aux Œufs on the first of October, they met two French sailors or fishermen loaded with plunder, and presently discovered the wrecks of seven English ships, with, as they declared, fifteen or sixteen hundred dead bodies on the strand hard by, besides dead horses, sheep, dogs, and hens, three or four hundred large iron-hooped casks, a barrel of wine and a barrel and a keg of brandy, cables, anchors, chains, planks, boards, shovels, picks, mattocks, and piles of old iron three feet high.[34]

"The least devout," writes Mother Juchereau, "were touched by the grandeur of the miracle wrought in our behalf,—a marvellous effect of God's love for Canada, which, of all these countries, is the only one that professes the true religion."

[34] *Déposition de François de Marganne, Sieur de la Valterie; par devant Nous, Paul Dupuy, Ecuyer, Conseiller du Roy, etc., 19 Octobre, 1711.*

Quebec was not ungrateful. A solemn mass was ordered every month during a year, to be followed by the song of Moses after the destruction of Pharaoh and his host.[35] Amazing reports were spread concerning the losses of the English. About three thousand of "these wretches"—so the story ran—died after reaching land, without counting the multitudes drowned in the attempt; and even this did not satisfy divine justice, for God blew up one of the ships by lightning during the storm. Vessels were sent to gather up the spoils of the wreck, and they came back, it was reported, laden with marvellous treasures, including rich clothing, magnificent saddles, plate, silver-hilted swords, and the like; bringing also the gratifying announcement that though the autumn tides had swept away many corpses, more than two thousand still lay on the rocks, naked and in attitudes of despair.[36] These stories, repeated by later writers, find believers to this day.[37]

When Walker and his ships reached Spanish River, he called another council of war. The question was whether, having failed to take Quebec, they should try to take Placentia; and it was resolved that the short supply of provisions, the impossibility of getting more from Boston before the first of November, and the risks of the autumnal storms, made the attempt impracticable. Accordingly, the New England transports sailed homeward, and the British fleet steered for the Thames.

Swift writes on the sixth of October in his Journal to Stella: "The news of Mr. Hill's miscarriage in his expedition came to-day, and I went to visit Mrs. Masham and Mrs. Hill, his two sisters, to condole with them." A week after, he mentions the arrival of the general himself; and again on the sixteenth writes thus: "I was to see Jack Hill this morning, who

[35] *Monseigneur de Saint-Vallier et l'Histoire de l'Hôpital Général de Québec,* 209.

[36] Juchereau, *Histoire de l'Hôtel-Dieu de Québec,* 473-491. La Ronde Denys says that nearly one thousand men were drowned, and that about two thousand died of injuries received. *La Ronde au Ministre,* 30 *Décembre,* 1711.

[37] Some exaggeration was natural enough. Colonel Lee, of the Rhode Island contingent, says that a day or two after the wreck he saw "the bodies of twelve or thirteen hundred brave men, with women and children, lying in heaps." *Lee to Governor Cranston,* 12 *September,* 1711.

made that unfortunate expedition; and there is still more misfortune, for that ship which was admiral of his fleet [the "Edgar"] is blown up in the Thames by an accident and carelessness of some rogue, who was going, as they think, to steal some gunpowder: five hundred men are lost."

A report of this crowning disaster reached Quebec, and Mother Juchereau does not fail to improve it. According to her, the Admiral, stricken with divine justice, and wrought to desperation, blew up the ship himself, and perished with all on board, except only two men.

There was talk of an examination into the causes of the failure, but nothing was done. Hill, strong in the influence of Mrs. Masham, reaped new honor and offices. Walker, more answerable for the result, and less fortunate in court influence, was removed from command, and his name was stricken from the half-pay list. He did not, however, blow himself up, but left England and emigrated to South Carolina, whence, thinking himself ill-treated by the authorities, he removed to Barbadoes, and died some years later.[38]

---

[38] Walker's Journal was published in 1720, with an Introduction of forty-eight pages, written in bad temper and bad taste. The Journal contains many documents, printed in full. In the Public Record Office are preserved the Journals of Hill, Vetch, and King. Copies of these, with many other papers on the same subject, from the same source, are before me. Vetch's Journal and his letter to Walker after the wreck are printed in the *Collections of the Nova Scotia Historical Society*, vol. ix.

It appears by the muster-rolls of Massachusetts that what with manning the coast-guard vessels, defending the frontier against Indians, and furnishing her contingent to the Canada expedition, more than one in five of her able-bodied men were in active service in the summer of 1711. Years passed before she recovered from the effects of her financial exhaustion.

Chapter 9

1712–1749
Louisbourg and Acadia

THE GREAT EUROPEAN WAR was drawing to an end, and with it the American war, which was but its echo. An avalanche of defeat and disaster had fallen upon the old age of Louis XIV., and France was burdened with an insupportable load of debt. The political changes in England came to her relief. Fifty years later, when the elder Pitt went out of office and Bute came in, France had cause to be grateful; for the peace of 1763 was far more favorable to her than it would have been under the imperious war minister. It was the same in 1712. The Whigs who had fallen from power would have wrung every advantage from France; the triumphant Tories were eager to close with her on any terms not so easy as to excite popular indignation. The result was the Treaty of Utrecht, which satisfied none of the allies of England, and gave to France conditions more favorable than she had herself proposed two years before. The fall of Godolphin and the disgrace of Marlborough were a godsend to her.

Yet in America Louis XIV. made important concessions. The Five Nations of the Iroquois were acknowledged to be British subjects; and this became in future the preposterous foundation for vast territorial claims of England. Hudson Bay, Newfoundland, and Acadia, "according to its ancient limits," were also given over by France to her successful rival; though the King parted from Acadia with a reluctance shown by the great offers he made for permission to retain it.[1]

But while the Treaty of Utrecht seemed to yield so much, and yielded so much in fact, it staved off the settlement of questions absolutely necessary for future peace. The limits of Acadia, the boundary line between Canada and the British colonies, and the boundary between those colonies and the

[1] *Offres de la France; Demandes de l'Angleterre et Réponses de la France,* in *Memorials of the English and French Commissaries concerning the Limits of Acadia.*

great western wilderness claimed by France, were all left unsettled, since the attempt to settle them would have rekindled
the war. The peace left the embers of war still smouldering,
sure, when the time should come, to burst into flame. The
next thirty years were years of chronic, smothered war,
disguised, but never quite at rest. The standing subjects of
dispute were three, very different in importance. First, the
question of Acadia: whether the treaty gave England a vast
country, or only a strip of seacoast. Next, that of northern
New England and the Abenaki Indians, many of whom
French policy still left within the borders of Maine, and
whom both powers claimed as subjects or allies. Last and
greatest was the question whether France or England should
hold the valleys of the Mississippi and the Great Lakes, and
with them the virtual control of the continent. This was the
triple problem that tormented the northern English colonies
for more than a generation, till it found a solution at last
in the Seven Years' War.

Louis XIV. had deeply at heart the recovery of Acadia. Yet
the old and infirm King, whose sun was setting in clouds
after half a century of unrivalled splendor, felt that peace
was a controlling necessity, and he wrote as follows to his
plenipotentiaries at Utrecht: "It is so important to prevent
the breaking off of the negotiations that the King will give
up both Acadia and Cape Breton, if necessary for peace;
but the plenipotentiaries will yield this point only in the
last extremity, for by this double cession Canada will become
useless, the access to it will be closed, the fisheries will come
to an end, and the French marine be utterly destroyed."[2]
And he adds that if the English will restore Acadia, he, the
King, will give them, not only St. Christopher, but also the
islands of St. Martin and St. Bartholomew.

The plenipotentiaries replied that the offer was refused,
and that the best they could do without endangering the
peace was to bargain that Cape Breton should belong to
France.[3] On this, the King bid higher still for the coveted
province, and promised that if Acadia were returned to him,
the fortifications of Placentia should be given up untouched,
the cannon in the forts of Hudson Bay abandoned to the

[2] *Mémoire de Roy à ses Plénipotentiaires,* 20 *Mars,* 1712.

[3] *Précis de ce qui s'est passé pendant la Négotiation de la Paix
d'Utrecht au Sujet de l'Acadie; Juillet,* 1711–*Mai,* 1712.

English, and the Newfoundland fisheries debarred to French-men,[4]—a remarkable concession; for France had fished on the banks of Newfoundland for two centuries, and they were invaluable to her as a nursery of sailors. Even these offers were rejected, and England would not resign Acadia.

Cape Breton was left to the French. This large island, henceforth called by its owners Isle Royale, lies east of Acadia, and is separated from it only by the narrow Strait of Canseau. From its position, it commands the chief entrance of the gulf and river of St. Lawrence. Some years before, the intendant Raudot had sent to the court an able paper, in which he urged its occupation and settlement, chiefly on commercial and industrial grounds. The war was then at its height; the plan was not carried into effect, and Isle Royale was still a wilderness. It was now proposed to occupy it for military and political reasons. One of its many harbors, well fortified and garrisoned, would guard the approaches of Canada, and in the next war furnish a base for attacking New England and recovering Acadia.

After some hesitation the harbor called Port à l'Anglois was chosen for the proposed establishment, to which the name of Louisbourg was given, in honor of the King. It lies near the southeastern point of the island, where an opening in the iron-bound coast, at once easily accessible and easily defended, gives entrance to a deep and sheltered basin, where a fleet of war-ships may find good anchorage. The proposed fortress was to be placed on the tongue of land that lies between this basin and the sea. The place, well chosen from the point of view of the soldier or the fisher-man, was unfit for an agricultural colony, its surroundings being barren hills studded with spruce and fir, and broad marshes buried in moss.

In spite of the losses and humiliations of the war, great expectations were formed from the new scheme. Several years earlier, when the proposals of Raudot were before the Marine Council, it was confidently declared that a strong fortress on Cape Breton would make the King master of North America. The details of the establishment were settled in advance. The King was to build the fortifications, supply

4 *Mémoire du Roy*, 20 *Avril*, 1712.

them with cannon, send out eight companies of soldiers, besides all the usual officers of government, establish a well-endowed hospital, conducted by nuns, as at Quebec, provide Jesuits and Récollets as chaplains, besides Filles de la Congrégation to teach girls, send families to the spot, support them for two years, and furnish a good number of young women to marry the soldiers.[5]

This plan, or something much like it, was carried into effect. Louisbourg was purely and solely the offspring of the Crown and its ally, the Church. In time it grew into a compact fishing town of about four thousand inhabitants, with a strong garrison and a circuit of formidable ramparts and batteries. It became by far the strongest fortress on the Atlantic coast, and so famous as a resort of privateers that it was known as the Dunquerque of America.

What concerns us now is its weak and troubled infancy. It was to be peopled in good part from the two lost provinces of Acadia and Newfoundland, whose inhabitants were to be transported to Louisbourg or other parts of Isle Royale, which would thus be made at once and at the least possible cost a dangerous neighbor to the newly acquired possessions of England. The Micmacs of Acadia, and even some of the Abenakis, were to be included in this scheme of immigration.

In the autumn, the commandant of Plaisance, or Placentia, —the French stronghold in Newfoundland,—received the following mandate from the King:—

MONSIEUR DE COSTEBELLE,—I have caused my orders to be given you to evacuate the town and forts of Plaisance and the other places of your government of Newfoundland, ceded to my dear sister the Queen of Great Britain. I have given my orders for the equipment of the vessels necessary to make the evacuation and transport you, with the officers, garrison, and inhabitants of Plaisance and other places of Newfoundland, to my Isle Royale, vulgarly called Cape Breton; but as the season is so far advanced that this cannot be done without exposing my troops and my subjects to perishing from cold and misery, and placing

[5] *Mémoire sur l'Isle du Cap Breton,* 1709.

my vessels in evident peril of wreck, I have judged it proper to defer the transportation till the next spring.[6]

The inhabitants of Placentia consisted only of twenty-five or thirty poor fishermen, with their families,[7] and some of them would gladly have become English subjects and stayed where they were; but no choice was given them. "Nothing," writes Costebelle, "can cure them of the error, to which they obstinately cling, that they are free to stay or go, as best suits their interest."[8] They and their fishing-boats were in due time transported to Isle Royale, where for a while their sufferings were extreme.

Attempts were made to induce the Indians of Acadia to move to the new colony; but they refused, and to compel them was out of the question. But by far the most desirable accession to the establishment of Isle Royale would be that of the Acadian French, who were too numerous to be transported in the summary manner practised in the case of the fishermen of Placentia. It was necessary to persuade rather than compel them to migrate, and to this end great reliance was placed on their priests, especially Fathers Pain and Dominique. Ponchartrain himself wrote to the former on the subject. The priest declares that he read the letter to his flock, who answered that they wished to stay in Acadia; and he adds that the other Acadians were of the same mind, being unwilling to leave their rich farms and risk starvation on a wild and barren island.[9] "Nevertheless," he concludes, "we shall fulfill the intentions of his Majesty by often holding before their eyes that religion for which they ought to make every sacrifice." He and his brother priests kept their word. Freedom of worship was pledged on certain conditions to the Acadians by the Treaty of Utrecht, and no attempt was ever made to deprive them of it; yet the continual declaration of their missionaries that their souls were in danger under English rule was the strongest spur to impel them to migrate.

[6] *Le Roy à Costebelle, 29 Septembre, 1713.*

[7] *Recensement des Habitans de Plaisance et Iles de St. Pierre, rendus à Louisbourg avec leurs Femmes et Enfans, 5 Novembre, 1714.*

[8] *Costebelle au Ministre, 19 Juillet, 1713.*

[9] *Félix Pain à Costebelle, 23 Septembre, 1713.*

The condition of the English in Acadia since it fell into their hands had been a critical one. Port Royal, thenceforth called Annapolis Royal, or simply Annapolis, had been left, as before mentioned, in charge of Colonel Vetch, with a heterogeneous garrison of four hundred and fifty men.[10] The Acadians of the *banlieue*—a term defined as covering a space of three miles round the fort—had been included in the capitulation, and had taken an oath of allegiance to Queen Anne, binding so long as they remained in the province. Some of them worked for the garrison and helped to repair the fort, which was in a ruinous condition. Meanwhile the Micmac Indians remained fiercely hostile to the English; and in June, 1711, aided by a band of Penobscots, they ambuscaded and killed or captured nearly seventy of them. This completely changed the attitude of the Acadians. They broke their oath, rose against their new masters, and with their Indian friends, invested the fort to the number of five or six hundred. Disease, desertion, and the ambuscade had reduced the garrison to about two hundred effective men, and the defences of the place were still in bad condition.[11] The assailants, on the other hand, had no better leader than the priest, Gaulin, missionary of the Micmacs and prime mover in the rising. He presently sailed for Placentia to beg for munitions and a commander; but his errand failed, the siege came to nought, and the besiegers dispersed. Vaudreuil, from whom the Acadians had begged help, was about to send it when news of the approach of Walker's fleet forced him to keep all his strength for his own defence.

From this time to the end of the war, the chief difficulties of the governor of Acadia rose, not from the enemy, but from the British authorities at home. For more than two years

[10] Vetch was styled "General and Commander-in-chief of all his Majesty's troops in these parts, and Governor of the fort of Annapolis Royal, country of l'Accady and Nova Scotia." Hence he was the first English governor of Nova Scotia after its conquest in 1710. He was appointed a second time in 1715, Nicholson having served in the interim.

[11] *Narrative of Paul Mascarene*, addressed to Nicholson. According to French accounts, a pestilence at Annapolis had carried off three fourths of the garrison. *Gaulin à* ——, 5 *Septembre*, 1711; *Cahouet au Ministre*, 20 *Juillet*, 1711. In reality a little more than one hundred had died.

he, with his starved and tattered garrison, were treated with absolute neglect. He received no orders, instructions, or money.[12] Acadia seemed forgotten by the ministry, till Vetch heard at last that Nicholson was appointed to succeed him.

Now followed the Treaty of Utrecht, the cession of Acadia to England, and the attempt on the part of France to induce the Acadians to remove to Isle Royale. Some of the English officials had once been of opinion that this French Catholic population should be transported to Martinique or some other distant French colony, and its place supplied by Protestant families sent from England or Ireland.[13] Since the English Revolution, Protestantism was bound up with the new political order, and Catholicism with the old. No Catholic could favor the Protestant succession, and hence politics were inseparable from creed. Vetch, who came of a race of hot and stubborn Covenanters, had been one of the most earnest for replacing the Catholic Acadians by Protestants; but after the peace he and others changed their minds. No Protestant colonists appeared, nor was there the smallest sign that the government would give itself the trouble to attract any. It was certain that if the Acadians removed at all, they would go, not to Martinique or any other distant colony, but to the new military establishment of Isle Royale, which would thus become a strong and dangerous neighbor to the feeble British post of Annapolis. Moreover, the labor of the French inhabitants was useful and sometimes necessary to the English garrison, which depended mainly on them for provisions; and if they left the province, they would leave it a desert, with the prospect of long remaining so.

Hence it happened that the English were for a time almost as anxious to keep the Acadians in Acadia as they were forty years later to get them out of it; nor had the Acadians themselves any inclination to leave their homes. But the French authorities needed them at Isle Royale, and made every effort to draw them thither. By the fourteenth article of the Treaty of Utrecht such of them as might choose to leave Acadia were free to do so within the space of a year, carrying with them their personal effects; while a letter of Queen

---

[12] Passages from Vetch's letters, in Patterson, *Memoir of Vetch.*
[13] *Vetch to the Earl of Dartmouth,* 22 *January,* 1711; *Memorial of Council of War at Annapolis,* 14 *October,* 1710.

Anne, addressed to Nicholson, then governor of Acadia, permitted the emigrants to sell their lands and houses.

The missionary Félix Pain had reported, as we have seen, that they were, in general, disposed to remain where they were; on which Costebelle, who now commanded at Louisbourg, sent two officers, La Ronde Denys and Pensens, with instructions to set the priests at work to persuade their flocks to move.[14] La Ronde Denys and his colleague repaired to Annapolis, where they promised the inhabitants vessels for their removal, provisions for a year, and freedom from all taxation for ten years. Then, having been well prepared in advance, the heads of families were formed in a circle, and in presence of the English governor, the two French officers, and the priests Justinien, Bonaventure, and Gaulin, they all signed, chiefly with crosses, a paper to the effect that they would live and die subjects of the King of France.[15] A few embarked at once for Isle Royale in the vessel "Marie-Joseph," and the rest were to follow within the year.

This result was due partly to the promises of La Ronde Denys, and still more to a pastoral letter from the Bishop of Quebec, supporting the assurances of the missionaries that the heretics would rob them of the ministrations of the Church. This was not all. The Acadians about Annapolis had been alienated by the conduct of the English authorities, which was not conciliating, and on the part of the governor was sometimes outrageous.[16] Yet those of the *banlieue* had no right to complain, since they had made themselves liable to the penalties of treason by first taking an oath of allegiance to Queen Anne, and then breaking it by trying to seize her fort.[17]

Governor Nicholson, like his predecessor, was resolved to keep the Acadians in the province if he could. This personage,

[14] Costebelle, *Instruction au Capitaine de la Ronde,* 1714.

[15] *Écrit des Habitants d'Annapolis Royale,* 25 *Aoust,* 1714; *Mémoire de La Ronde Denys,* 30 *Aoust,* 1714.

[16] In 1711, however, the missionary Félix Pain says, "The English have treated the Acadians with much humanity."—*Père Félix à* ———, 8 *Septembre,* 1711.

[17] This was the oath taken after the capitulation, which bound those who took it to allegiance so long as they remained in the province.

able, energetic, perverse, headstrong, and unscrupulous, conducted himself, even towards the English officers and soldiers, in a manner that seems unaccountable, and that kindled their utmost indignation.[18] Towards the Acadians his behavior was still worse. As Costebelle did not keep his promise to send vessels to bring them to Isle Royale, they built small ones for themselves, and the French authorities at Louisbourg sent them the necessary rigging. Nicholson ordered it back, forbade the sale of their lands and houses,—a needless stretch of power, as there was nobody to buy,—and would not let them sell even their personal effects, coolly setting at nought both the Treaty of Utrecht and the letter of the Queen.[19]

Nicholson was but a short time at Annapolis, leaving the government, during most of his term, to his deputies, Caulfield and afterwards Doucette, both of whom roundly denounce their principal for his general conduct; while both, in one degree or another, followed his example in preventing so far as they could the emigration of the Acadians. Some of them, however, got away, and twelve or fifteen families who settled at Port Toulouse, on Isle Royale, were near perishing from cold and hunger.[20]

From Annapolis the French agents, La Ronde Denys and Pensens, proceeded to the settlements about Chignecto and the Basin of Mines,—the most populous and prosperous parts of Acadia. Here they were less successful than before. The people were doubtful and vacillating,—ready enough to promise, but slow to perform. While declaring with perfect sincerity their devotion to "our invincible monarch," as they called King Louis, who had just been compelled to surrender their country, they clung tenaciously to the abodes of their fathers. If they had wished to emigrate, the English governor had no power to stop them. From Baye Verte, on the isthmus, they had frequent and easy communication with the French at Louisbourg, which the English did not and could not interrupt. They were armed, and they far outnumbered the English garrison; while at a word they could bring to their

[18] "As he used to curse and Damm Governor Vetch and all his friends, he is now served himself in the same manner."—*Adams to Steele*, 24 January, 1715.

[19] For a great number of extracts from documents on this subject see a paper by Abbé Casgrain in *Canada Français*, i. 411–414; also the documentary supplement of the same publication.

[20] *La Ronde Denys au Ministre*, 3 Décembre, 1715.

aid the Micmac warriors, who had been taught to detest the English heretics as foes of God and man. To say that they wished to leave Acadia, but were prevented from doing so by a petty garrison at the other end of the province, so feeble that it could hardly hold Annapolis itself, is an unjust reproach upon a people who, though ignorant and weak of purpose, were not wanting in physical courage. The truth is that from this time to their forced expatriation in 1755, all the Acadians, except those of Annapolis and its immediate neighborhood, were free to go or stay at will. Those of the eastern parts of the province especially, who formed the greater part of the population, were completely their own masters. This was well known to the French authorities. The governor of Louisbourg complains of the apathy of the Acadians.[21] Saint-Ovide declares that they do not want to fulfil the intentions of the King and remove to Isle Royale. Costebelle makes the same complaint; and again, after three years of vain attempts to overcome their reluctance, he writes that every effort has failed to induce them to migrate.

From this time forward the state of affairs in Acadia was a peculiar one. By the Treaty of Utrecht it was a British province, and the nominal sovereignty resided at Annapolis, in the keeping of the miserable little fort and the puny garrison, which as late as 1743 consisted of but five companies, counting, when the ranks were full, thirty-one men each.[22] More troops were often asked for, and once or twice were promised; but they were never sent. "This has been hitherto no more than a mock government, its authority never yet having extended beyond cannon-shot of the fort," wrote Governor Philipps in 1720. "It would be more for the honour of the Crown, and profit also, to give back the country to the French, than to be contented with the name only of government."[23] Philipps repaired the fort, which, as the engineer Mascarene says, "had lain tumbling down" before

[21] *Costebelle au Ministre, 15 Janvier,* 1715.
[22] *Governor Mascarene to the Secretary of State, 1 December,* 1743. At this time there was also a blockhouse at Canseau, where a few soldiers were stationed. These were then the only British posts in the province. In May, 1727, Philipps wrote to the Lords of Trade: "Everything there [at Annapolis] is wearing the face of ruin and decay," and the ramparts are "lying level with the ground in breaches sufficiently wide for fifty men to enter abreast."
[23] *Philipps to Secretary Craggs, 26 September,* 1720.

his arrival; but Annapolis and the whole province remained totally neglected and almost forgotten by England till the middle of the century. At one time the soldiers were in so ragged a plight that Lieutenant-Colonel Armstrong was forced to clothe them at his own expense.[24]

While this seat of British sovereignty remained in unchanging feebleness for more than forty years, the French Acadians were multiplying apace. Before 1749 they were the only white inhabitants of the province, except ten or twelve English families who, about the year 1720, lived under the guns of Annapolis. At the time of the cession the French population seems not to have exceeded two thousand souls, about five hundred of whom lived within the *banlieue* of Annapolis, and were therefore more or less under English control. They were all alike a simple and ignorant peasantry, prosperous in their humble way, and happy when rival masters ceased from troubling, though vexed with incessant quarrels among themselves, arising from the unsettled boundaries of their lands, which had never been properly surveyed. Their mental horizon was of the narrowest, their wants were few, no military service was asked of them by the English authorities, and they paid no taxes to the government. They could even indulge their strong appetite for litigation free of cost; for when, as often happened, they brought their land disputes before the Council at Annapolis, the cases were settled and the litigants paid no fees. Their communication with the English officials was carried on through deputies chosen by themselves, and often as ignorant as their constituents, for a remarkable equality prevailed through this primitive little society.

Except the standing garrison at Annapolis, Acadia was as completely let alone by the British government as Rhode Island or Connecticut. Unfortunately, the traditional British policy of inaction towards her colonies was not applicable in the case of a newly conquered province with a disaffected population and active, enterprising, and martial neighbors bent on recovering what they had lost. Yet it might be supposed that a neglect so invigorating in other cases might have developed among the Acadians habits of self-reliance

[24] *Selections from the Public Documents of Nova Scotia*, 18, note.

and faculties of self-care. The reverse took place; for if England neglected Acadia, France did not; and though she had renounced her title to it, she still did her best to master it and make it hers again. The chief instrument of her aggressive policy was the governor of Isle Royale, whose station was the fortress of Louisbourg, and who was charged with the management of Acadian affairs. At all the Acadian settlements he had zealous and efficient agents in the missionary priests, who were sent into the province by the Bishop of Quebec, or in a few cases by their immediate ecclesiastical superiors in Isle Royale.

The Treaty of Utrecht secured freedom of worship to the Acadians under certain conditions. These were that they should accept the sovereignty of the British Crown, and that they and their pastors should keep within the limits of British law.[25] Even supposing that by swearing allegiance to Queen Anne the Acadians had acquired the freedom of worship which the treaty gave them on condition of their becoming British subjects, it would have been an abuse of this freedom to use it for subverting the power that had granted it. Yet this is what the missionaries did. They were not only priests of the Roman Church, they were also agents of the King of France; and from first to last they labored against the British government in the country that France had ceded to the British Crown. So confident were they, and with so much reason, of the weakness of their opponents that they openly avowed that their object was to keep the Acadians faithful to King Louis. When two of their number Saint-Poncy and Chevereaux, were summoned before the Council at Annapolis, they answered, with great contempt, "We are here on the business of the King of France." They were ordered to leave Acadia. One of them stopped among the Indians at Cape Sable; the other, in defiance of the Council, was sent back to Annapolis by the Governor of Isle Royale.[26] Apparently he was again ordered away; for four years later the

[25] "Those who are willing to remain there [in Acadia] and to be subject to the kingdom of Great Britain, are to enjoy the free exercise of their religion according to the usage of the Church of Rome, as far as the laws of Great Britain do allow the same."— *Treaty of Utrecht*, 14th article.

[26] *Minutes of Council*, 18 *May*, 1736. *Governor Armstrong to the Secretary of State*, 22 *November*, 1736.

French governor, in expectation of speedy war, sent him to Chignecto with orders secretly to prepare the Acadians for an attack on Annapolis.[27]

The political work of the missionaries began with the cession of the colony, and continued with increasing activity till 1755, kindling the impotent wrath of the British officials, and drawing forth the bitter complaints of every successive governor. For this world and the next, the priests were fathers of their flocks, generally commanding their attachment, and always their obedience. Except in questions of disputed boundaries, where the Council alone could settle the title, the ecclesiastics took the place of judges and courts of justice, enforcing their decisions by refusal of the sacraments.[28] They often treated the British officials with open scorn. Governor Armstrong writes to the Lords of Trade: "Without some particular directions as to the insolent behavior of those priests, the people will never be brought to obedience, being by them incited to daily acts of rebellion." Another governor complains that they tell the Acadians of the destitution of the soldiers and the ruinous state of the fort, and assure them that the Pretender will soon be King of England, and that Acadia will then return to France.[29] "The bearer, Captain Bennett," writes Armstrong, "can further tell your Grace of the disposition of the French inhabitants of this province, and of the conduct of their missionary priests, who instil hatred into both Indians and French against the English."[30] As to the Indians, Governor Philipps declares that their priests hear a general confession from them twice a year, and give them absolution on condition of always being enemies to the English.[31] The condition was easy, thanks to the neglect of the British government, which took no pains to conciliate the Micmacs, while the French governor of Isle Royale corresponded secretly with them and made them yearly presents.

In 1720 Philipps advised the recall of the French priests, and the sending of others in their place, as the only means

[27] *Minutes of Council*, 18 *September*, 1740, in *Nova Scotia Archives*.

[28] *Governor Mascarene to Père des Enclaves, 29 June*, 1741.

[29] *Deputy-Governor Doucette to the Secretary of State, 5 November*, 1717.

[30] *Governor Armstrong to the Secretary of State, 30 April*, 1727.

[31] *Governor Philipps to Secretary Craggs, 26 September*, 1720.

of making British subjects of the Acadians,[32] who at that
time, having constantly refused the oath of allegiance, were
not entitled, under the treaty, to the exercise of their religion.
Governor Armstrong wrote sixteen years after: "By some of
the above papers your Grace will be informed how high the
French government carries its pretensions over its priests'
obedience; and how to prevent the evil consequences I know
not, unless we could have missionaries from places independent of that Crown."[33] He expresses a well-grounded
doubt whether the home government will be at the trouble
and expense of such a change, though he adds that there is
not a missionary among either Acadians or Indians who is
not in the pay of France.[34] Gaulin, missionary of the Micmacs, received a "gratification" of fifteen hundred livres, besides an annual allowance of five hundred, and is described
in the order granting it as a "brave man, capable even of
leading these savages on an expedition."[35] In 1726 he was
brought before the Council at Annapolis charged with incendiary conduct among both Indians and Acadians; but on asking pardon and promising nevermore to busy himself with
affairs of government, he was allowed to remain in the
province, and even to act as curé of the Mines.[36] No evidence appears that the British authorities ever molested a
priest, except when detected in practices alien to his proper
functions and injurious to the government. On one occasion
when two cures were vacant, one through sedition and the
other apparently through illness or death, Lieutenant-Gover-

[32] *Ibid.*, 26 May, 1720.

[33] *Armstrong to the Secretray of State*, 22 November, 1736. The
dismissal of French priests and the substitution of others was
again recommended some time after.

[34] The motives for paying priests for instructing the people of a
province ceded to England are given in a report of the French
Marine Council. The Acadians "ne pourront jamais conserver un
véritable attachment à la religion et *à leur légitime souverain* sans
le secours d'un missionnaire" (*Délibérations du Conseil de Marine,*
23 *Mai*, 1719, in *Le Canada-Français*). The Intendant Bégon
highly commends the efforts of the missionaries to keep the
Acadians in the French interest (*Bégon au Ministre*, 25 *Septembre*,
1715), and Vaudreuil praises their zeal in the same cause
(*Vaudreuil au Ministre*, 31 *Octobre*, 1717).

[35] *Délibérations du Conseil de Marine*, 3 *Mai*, 1718.

[36] *Record of Council at Annapolis*, 11 *and* 24 *October*, 1726.

nor Armstrong requested the governor of Isle Royale to send two priests "of known probity" to fill them.[37]

Who were answerable for the anomalous state of affairs in the province,—the *imperium in imperio* where the inner power waxed and strengthened every day, and the outer relatively pined and dwindled? It was not mainly the Crown of France nor its agents, secular or clerical. Their action under the circumstances, though sometimes inexcusable, was natural, and might have been foreseen. Nor was it the Council at Annapolis, who had little power either for good or evil. It was mainly the neglect and apathy of the British ministers, who seemed careless as to whether they kept Acadia or lost it, apparently thinking it not worth their notice.

About the middle of the century they wakened from their lethargy, and warned by the signs of the times, sent troops and settlers into the province at the eleventh hour. France and her agents took alarm, and redoubled their efforts to keep their hold on a country which they had begun to regard as theirs already. The settlement of the English at Halifax startled the French into those courses of intrigue and violence which were the immediate cause of the removal of the Acadians in 1755.

At the earlier period which we are now considering, the storm was still remote. The English made no attempt either to settle the province or to secure it by sufficient garrisons; they merely tried to bind the inhabitants by an oath of allegiance which the weakness of the government would constantly tempt them to break. When George I. came to the throne, Deputy-Governor Caulfield tried to induce the inhabitants to swear allegiance to the new monarch. The Acadians asked advice of Saint-Ovide, governor at Louisbourg, who sent them elaborate directions how to answer the English demand and remain at the same time faithful children of France. Neither Caulfield nor his successor could carry their point. The Treaty of Utrecht, as we have seen, gave the Acadians a year in which to choose between remaining in the province and becoming British subjects, or leaving it as subjects of the King of France. This year had long ago expired, and most of them were still in Acadia, unwilling to leave it, yet refusing to own King George. In 1720 Gen-

[37] *Armstrong to Saint-Ovide,* 17 *June,* 1732.

eral Richard Philipps, the governor of the province, set himself to the task of getting the oath taken, while the missionaries and the French officers at Isle Royale strenuously opposed his efforts. He issued a proclamation ordering the Acadians to swear allegiance to the King of England or leave the country, without their property, within four months. In great alarm, they appealed to their priests, and begged the Récollet, Père Justinien, curé of Mines, to ask advice and help from Saint-Ovide, successor of Costebelle at Louisbourg, protesting that they would abandon all rather than renounce their religion and their King.[38] At the same time they prepared for a general emigration by way of the isthmus and Baye Verte, where it would have been impossible to stop them.[39]

Without the influence of their spiritual and temporal advisers, to whom they turned in all their troubles, it is clear that the Acadians would have taken the oath and remained in tranquil enjoyment of their homes; but it was then thought important to French interests that they should remove either to Isle Royale or to Isle St. Jean, now Prince Edward's Island. Hence no means were spared to prevent them from becoming British subjects, if only in name; even the Micmacs were enlisted in the good work, and induced to threaten them with their enmity if they should fail in allegiance to King Louis. Philipps feared that the Acadians would rise in arms if he insisted on the harsh requirements of his proclamation; in which case his position would have been difficult, as they now outnumbered his garrison about five to one. Therefore he extended indefinitely the term of four months, that he had fixed for their final choice, and continued to urge and persuade, without gaining a step towards the desired result. In vain he begged for aid from the British authorities. They would do nothing for him, but merely observed that while the French officers and priests had such influence over the Acadians, they would never be good subjects, and

[38] *The Acadians to Saint-Ovide*, 6 *May*, 1720, in *Public Documents of Nova Scotia*, 25. This letter was evidently written for them,—no doubt by a missionary.

[39] "They can march off at their leisure, by way of the Baye Verte, with their effects, without danger of being molested by this garrison, which scarce suffices to secure the Fort."—*Philipps to Secretary Craggs*, 26 *May*, 1720.

so had better be put out of the country.[40] This was easier said than done; for at this very time there were signs that the Acadians and the Micmacs would unite to put out the English garrison.[41]

Philipps was succeeded by a deputy-governor, Lieutenant-Colonel Armstrong,—a person of ardent impulses and unstable disposition. He applied himself with great zeal and apparent confidence to accomplishing the task in which his principal had failed. In fact, he succeeded in 1726 in persuading the inhabitants about Annapolis to take the oath, with a proviso that they should not be called upon for military service; but the main body of the Acadians stiffly refused. In the next year he sent Ensign Wroth to Mines, Chignecto, and neighboring settlements to renew the attempt on occasion of the accession of George II. The envoy's instructions left much to his discretion or his indiscretion, and he came back with the signatures, or crosses, of the inhabitants attached to an oath so clogged with conditions that it left them free to return to their French allegiance whenever they chose.

Philipps now came back to Acadia to resume his difficult task. And here a surprise meets us. He reported a complete success. The Acadians, as he declared, swore allegiance without reserve to King George; but he does not tell us how they were brought to do so. Compulsion was out of the question. They could have cut to pieces any part of the paltry English garrison that might venture outside the ditches of Annapolis, or they might have left Acadia, with all their goods and chattels, with no possibility of stopping them. The taking of the oath was therefore a voluntary act.

But what was the oath? The words reported by Philipps were as follows: "I promise and swear sincerely, on the faith of a Christian, that I will be entirely faithful, and will truly obey his Majesty King George the Second, whom I recognize as sovereign lord of Acadia or Nova Scotia. So help me God." To this the Acadians affixed their crosses, or, in exceptional cases, their names. Recently, however, evidence has appeared

[40] *The Board of Trade to Philipps*, 28 *December*, 1720.

[41] *Délibérations du Conseil de Marine, Aoust*, 1720. The attempt against the garrison was probably opposed by the priests, who must have seen the danger that it would rouse the ministry into sending troops to the province, which would have been disastrous to their plans.

that, so far at least as regards the Acadians on and near
Mines Basin, the effect of the oath was qualified by a promise
on the part of Philipps that they should not be required to
take up arms against either French or Indians,—they on their
part promising never to take up arms against the English.
This statement is made by Gaudalie, curé of the parish of
Mines, and Noiville, priest at Pigiquid, or Pisiquid, now
Windsor.[42] In fact, the English never had the folly to call
on the Acadians to fight for them; and the greater part of
this peace-loving people were true to their promise not to
take arms against the English, though a considerable number
of them did so, especially at the beginning of the Seven Years'
War. It was to this promise, whether kept or broken, that
they owed their name of Neutral French.

From first to last, the Acadians remained in a child-like
dependence on their spiritual and temporal guides. Not one
of their number stands out prominently from among the
rest. They seem to have been totally devoid of natural leaders, and, unhappily for themselves, left their fate in the hands
of others. Yet they were fully aware of their numerical
strength, and had repeatedly declared, in a manner that the
English officers called insolent, that they would neither leave
the country nor swear allegiance to King George. The truth
probably is that those who governed them had become convinced that this simple population, which increased rapidly,
and could always be kept French at heart, might be made
more useful to France in Acadia than out of it, and that it
was needless further to oppose the taking of an oath which
would leave them in quiet possession of their farms without
making any change in their feelings, and probably none in
their actions. By force of natural increase Acadia would in
time become the seat of a large population ardently French
and ardently Catholic; and while officials in France sometimes complained of the reluctance of the Acadians to move
to Isle Royale, those who directed them in their own country
seem to have become willing that they should stay where they
were, and place themselves in such relations with the English
as should leave them free to increase and multiply undis-

[42] Certificat de Charles de la Gaudalie, prêtre, curé missionnaire
de la paroisse des Mines, et Noël-Alexandre Noiville, . . . curé de
l'Assomption et de la Sainte Famille de Pigiguit; printed in
Rameau, Une Colonie Féodale en Amérique (ed. 1889), ii. 53.

turbed. Deceived by the long apathy of the British government, French officials did not foresee that a time would come when it would bestir itself to make Acadia English in fact as well as in name.[43]

[43] The preceding chapter is based largely on two collections of documents relating to Acadia,—the *Nova Scotia Archives*, or *Selections from the Public Documents of Nova Scotia*, printed in 1869 by the government of that province, and the mass of papers collected by Rev. H. R. Casgrain and printed in the documentary department of *Le Canada-Français*, a review published under direction of Laval University at Quebec. Abbé Casgrain, with passionate industry, has labored to gather everything in Europe or America that could tell in the favor of the French and against the English. Mr. Akins, the editor of the *Nova Scotia Archives*, leans to the other side, so that the two collections supplement each other. Both are copious and valuable. Besides these, I have made use of various documents from the archives of Paris not to be found in either of the above-named collections.

Chapter 10

1713–1724
Sebastien Rale

BEFORE THE Treaty of Utrecht, the present Nova Scotia, New Brunswick, and a part of Maine were collectively called Acadia by the French; but after the treaty gave Acadia to England, they insisted that the name meant only Nova Scotia. The English on their part claimed that the cession of Acadia made them owners, not only of the Nova Scotian peninsula, but of all the country north of it to the St. Lawrence, or at least to the dividing ridge or height of land.

This and other disputed questions of boundary were to be settled by commissioners of the two powers; but their meeting was put off for forty years, and then their discussions ended in the Seven Years' War. The claims of the rival nations were in fact so discordant that any attempt to reconcile them must needs produce a fresh quarrel. The treaty had left a choice of evils. To discuss the boundary question meant to renew the war; to leave it unsettled was a source of constant irritation; and while delay staved off a great war, it quickly produced a small one.

The river Kennebec, which was generally admitted by the French to be the dividing line between their possessions and New England,[1] was regarded by them with the most watchful jealousy. Its headwaters approached those of the Canadian river Chaudière, the mouth of which is near Quebec; and by ascending the former stream and crossing to the headwaters of the latter, through an intricacy of forests, hills, ponds, and marshes, it was possible for a small band of hardy men, unencumbered by cannon, to reach the Canadian capital,—as was done long after by the followers of Benedict

---

[1] In 1700, however, there was an agreement, under the treaty of Ryswick, which extended the English limits as far as the river St. George, a little west of the Penobscot.

Arnold. Hence it was thought a matter of the last importance to close the Kennebec against such an attempt. The Norridgewock band of the Abenakis, who lived on the banks of that river, were used to serve this purpose and to form a sort of advance-guard to the French colony, while other kindred bands on the Penobscot, the St. Croix, and the St. John were expected to aid in opposing a living barrier to English intrusion. Missionaries were stationed among all these Indians to keep them true to Church and King. The most important station, that of the Norridgewocks, was in charge of Father Sebastien Rale, the most conspicuous and interesting figure among the later French-American Jesuits.

Since the middle of the seventeenth century a change had come over the Jesuit missions of New France. Nothing is more striking or more admirable than the self-devoted apostleship of the earlier period. The movement in Western Europe known as the Renaissance was far more than a revival of arts and letters,—it was an awakening of intellectual, moral, and religious life; the offspring of causes long in action, and the parent of other movements in action to this day. The Protestant Reformation was a part of it. That revolt against Rome produced a counter Renaissance in the bosom of the ancient Church herself. In presence of that peril she woke from sloth and corruption, and girded herself to beat back the invading heresies, by force or by craft, by inquisitorial fires, by the arms of princely and imperial allies, and by the self-sacrificing enthusiasm of her saints and martyrs. That time of danger produced the exalted zeal of Xavier and the intense, thoughtful, organizing zeal of Loyola. After a century had passed, the flame still burned, and it never shone with a purer or brighter radiance than in the early missions of New France.

Such ardors cannot be permanent; they must subside, from the law of their nature. If the great Western mission had been a success, the enthusiasm of its founders might have maintained itself for some time longer; but that mission was extinguished in blood. Its martyrs died in vain, and the burning faith that had created it was rudely tried. Canada ceased to be a mission. The civil and military powers grew strong, and the Church no longer ruled with undivided sway. The times changed, and the men changed with them. It is a characteristic of the Jesuit Order, and one of the sources of its strength, that it chooses the workman for his work,

studies the qualities of its members, and gives to each the
task for which he is fitted best. When its aim was to convert
savage hordes and build up another Paraguay in the Northern
wilderness, it sent a Jogues, a Brébeuf, a Charles Garnier,
and a Gabriel Lalemant, like a forlorn hope, to storm the
stronghold of heathendom. In later times it sent other men
to meet other needs and accomplish other purposes.

Before the end of the seventeenth century the functions of
the Canadian Jesuit had become as much political as religious; but if the fires of his apostolic zeal burned less high,
his devotion to the Order in which he had merged his personality was as intense as before. While in constant friction
with the civil and military powers, he tried to make himself
necessary to them, and in good measure he succeeded. Nobody was so able to manage the Indian tribes and keep them
in the interest of France. "Religion," say Charlevoix, "is the
chief bond by which the savages are attached to us;" and it
was the Jesuit above all others who was charged to keep
this bond firm.

The Christianity that was made to serve this useful end did
not strike a deep root. While humanity is in the savage state,
it can only be Christianized on the surface; and the convert of
the Jesuits remained a savage still. They did not even try to
civilize him. They taught him to repeat a catechism which
he could not understand, and practise rites of which the
spiritual significance was incomprehensible to him. He saw
the symbols of his new faith in much the same light as the
superstitions that had once enchained him. To his eyes the
crucifix was a fetich of surpassing power, and the mass a
beneficent "medicine," or occult influence, of supreme efficacy.
Yet he would not forget his old rooted beliefs, and it needed
the constant presence of the missionary to prevent him
from returning to them.

Since the Iroquois had ceased to be a danger to Canada,
the active alliance of the Western Indians had become less
important to the colony. Hence the missions among them
had received less attention, and most of these tribes had re-
lapsed into heathenism. The chief danger had shifted eastward, and was, or was supposed to be, in the direction of
New England. Therefore the Eastern missions were cultivated with diligence,—whether those within or adjoining the
settled limits of Canada, like the Iroquois mission of Caughnawaga, the Abenaki missions of St. Francis and Becancour,

and the Huron mission of Lorette, or those that served as outposts and advance-guards of the colony, like the Norridge-wock Abenakis of the Kennebec, or the Penobscot Abenakis of the Penobscot. The priests at all these stations were in close correspondence with the government, to which their influence over their converts was invaluable. In the wilderness dens of the Hurons or the Iroquois, the early Jesuit was a marvel of self-sacrificing zeal; his successor, half missionary and half agent of the King, had thought for this world as well as the next.

Sebastien Rale,[2] born in Franche-Comté in 1657, was sent to the American missions in 1689 at the age of thirty-two. After spending two years among the Abenakis of Canada, then settled near the mouth of the Chaudière, he was sent for two years more to the Illinois, and thence to the Abenakis of the Kennebec, where he was to end his days.

Near where the town of Norridgewock now stands, the Kennebec curved round a broad tongue of meadow land, in the midst of a picturesque wilderness of hills and forests. On this tongue of land, on ground a few feet above the general level, stood the village of the Norridgewocks, fenced with a stockade of round logs nine feet high. The enclosure was square; each of its four sides measured one hundred and sixty feet, and each had its gate. From the four gates ran two streets, or lanes, which crossed each other in the middle of the village. There were twenty-six Indian houses, or cabins, within the stockade, described as "built much after the English manner," though probably of logs. The church was outside the enclosure, about twenty paces from the east gate.[3]

Such was the mission village of Norridgewock in 1716. It had risen from its ashes since Colonel Hilton destroyed it in 1705, and the church had been rebuilt by New England workmen hired for the purpose.[4] A small bell, which is still

[2] So written by himself in an autograph letter of 18 November, 1712. It is also spelled Rasle, Rasles, Ralle, and, very incorrectly, Rallé, or Rallee.

[3] The above particulars are taken from an inscription on a manuscript map in the library of the Maine Historical Society, made in 1716 by Joseph Heath, one of the principal English settlers on the Kennebec, and for a time commandant of the fort at Brunswick.

[4] When Colonel Westbrook and his men came to Norridgewock in 1722, they found a paper pinned to the church door, containing, among others, the following words, in the handwriting of Rale,

preserved at Brunswick, rang for mass at early morning, and
for vespers at sunset. Rale's leisure hours were few. He
preached, exhorted, catechised the young converts, counselled
their seniors for this world and the next, nursed them in
sickness, composed their quarrels, tilled his own garden, cut
his own firewood, cooked his own food, which was of Indian
corn, or, at a pinch, of roots and acorns, worked at his
Abenaki vocabulary, and, being expert at handicraft, made
ornaments for the church, or moulded candles from the fruit
of the bayberry, or wax-myrtle.[5] Twice a year, summer and
winter, he followed his flock to the sea-shore and the islands,
where they lived at their ease on fish and seals, clams, oysters,
and seafowl.

This Kennebec mission had been begun more than half a
century before; yet the conjurers, or "medicine men,"—natural enemies of the missionary,—still remained obdurate and
looked on the father askance, though the body of the tribe
were constant at mass and confession, and regarded him
with loving reverence. He always attended their councils, and,
as he tells us, his advice always prevailed; but he was less
fortunate when he told them to practise no needless cruelty
in their wars, on which point they were often disobedient
children.[6]

Rale was of a strong, enduring frame, and a keen, vehement, caustic spirit. He had the gift of tongues, and was as
familiar with the Abenaki and several other Indian languages
as he was with Latin.[7] Of the genuineness of his zeal there

---

meant as a fling at the English invaders: "It [the church] is ill
built, because the English don't work well. It is not finished, although five or six Englishmen have wrought here during four
years, and the Undertaker [contractor], who is a great Cheat,
hath been paid in advance for to finish it." The money came
from the Canadian government.

[5] *Myrica cerifera.*

[6] The site of the Indian village is still called Indian Old Point.
Norridgewock is the Naurantsouak, or Narantsouak, of the French.
For Rale's mission life, see two letters of his, 15 October, 1722,
and 12 October, 1722, and a letter of Père La Chasse, Superior of
the Missions, 29 October, 1724, These are printed in the *Lettres
Édifiantes,* xvii. xxiii.

[7] Père La Chasse, in his eulogy of Rale, says that there was not
a language on the continent with which he had not some acquaintance. This is of course absurd. Besides a full knowledge of

is no doubt, nor of his earnest and lively interest in the fortunes of the wilderness flock of which he was the shepherd for half his life. The situation was critical for them and for him. The English settlements were but a short distance below, while those of the French could be reached only by a hard journey of twelve or fourteen days.

With two intervals of uneasy peace, the borders of Maine had been harried by war-parties for thirty-eight years; and since 1689 these raids had been prompted and aided by the French. Thus it happened that extensive tracts, which before Philip's War were dotted with farmhouses and fishing hamlets, had been abandoned, and cultivated fields were turning again to forests. The village of Wells had become the eastern frontier. But now the Treaty of Utrecht gave promise of lasting tranquillity. The Abenakis, hearing that they were to be backed no longer by the French, became alarmed, sent messengers to Casco, and asked for peace. In July there was a convention at Portsmouth, when delegates of the Norridgewocks, Penobscots, Malicites, and other Abenaki bands met Governor Dudley and the councillors of Massachusetts and New Hampshire. A paper was read to them by sworn interpreters, in which they confessed that they had broken former treaties, begged pardon for "past rebellions, hostilities, and violations of promises," declared themselves subjects of Queen Anne, pledged firm friendship with the English, and promised them that they might re-enter without molestation on all their former possessions. Eight of the principal Abenaki chiefs signed this document with their totemic marks, and the rest did so, after similar interpretation, at another convention in the next year.[8] Indians when in trouble can waive

---

the Norridgewock Abenaki, he had more or less acquaintance with two other Algonquin languages,—the Ottawa and the Illinois,— and also with the Huron; which is enough for one man.

[8] This treaty is given in full by Penhallow. It is also printed from the original draft by Mr. Frederic Kidder, in his *Abenaki Indians: their Treaties of 1713 and 1717.* The two impressions are substantially the same, but with verbal variations. The version of Kidder is the more complete, in giving not only the Indian totemic marks, but also the autographs in facsimile of all the English officials. Rale gives a dramatic account of the treaty, which he may have got from the Indians, and which omits their submission and their promises.

their pride, and lavish professions and promises; but when they called themselves subjects of Queen Anne, it is safe to say that they did not know what the words meant.

Peace with the Indians was no sooner concluded than a stream of settlers began to move eastward to reoccupy the lands that they owned or claimed in the region of the lower Kennebec. Much of this country was held in extensive tracts, under old grants of the last century, and the proprietors offered great inducements to attract emigrants. The government of Massachusetts, though impoverished by three wars, of which it had borne the chief burden, added what encouragements it could. The hamlets of Saco, Scarborough, Falmouth, and Georgetown rose from their ashes; mills were built on the streams, old farms were retilled, and new ones cleared. A certain Dr. Noyes, who had established a sturgeon fishery on the Kennebec, built at his own charge a stone fort at Cushnoc, or Augusta; and it is said that as early as 1714 a blockhouse was built many miles above, near the mouth of the Sebasticook.[9] In the next year Fort George was built at the lower falls of the Androscoggin, and some years later Fort Richmond, on the Kennebec, at the site of the present town of Richmond.[10]

Some of the claims to these Kennebec lands were based on old Crown patents, some on mere prescription, some on Indian titles, good or bad. Rale says that an Englishman would give an Indian a bottle of rum, and get from him in return a large tract of land.[11] Something like this may have happened; though in other cases the titles were as good as Indian titles usually are, the deeds being in regular form and signed by the principal chiefs for a consideration which they thought sufficient. The lands of Indians, however, are owned, so far as owned at all, by the whole community; and in the case of the Algonquin tribes the chiefs had no real authority to alienate them without the consent of the tribesmen. Even supposing this consent to have been given, the Norridgewocks would not have been satisfied; for Rale taught them

[9] It was standing in 1852, and a sketch of it is given by Winsor, *Narrative and Critical History*, v. 185. I have some doubts as to the date of erection.

[10] Williamson, *History of Maine*, ii. 88, 97. Compare Penhallow.

[11] *Remarks out of the Fryar Sebastian Rale's Letter from Norridgewock*, 7 *February*, 1720, in the *Common Place Book* of Rev. Henry Flynt.

that they could not part with their lands, because they held them in trust for their children, to whom their country belonged as much as to themselves.

Long years of war and mutual wrong had embittered the Norridgewocks against their English neighbors, with whom, nevertheless, they wished to be at peace, because they feared them, and because their trade was necessary to them.

The English borderers, on their part, regarded the Indians less as men than as vicious and dangerous wild animals. In fact, the benevolent and philanthropic view of the American savage is for those who are beyond his reach: it has never yet been held by any whose wives and children have lived in danger of his scalping-knife. In Boston and other of the older and safer settlements, the Indians had found devoted friends before Philip's War; and even now they had apologists and defenders, prominent among whom was the relic of antique Puritanism, old Samuel Sewall, who was as conscientious and humane as he was prosy, narrow, and sometimes absurd, and whose benevolence towards the former owners of the soil was trebly reinforced by his notion that they were descendants of the ten lost tribes of Israel.[12]

The intrusion of settlers, and the building of forts and blockhouses on lands which they still called their own, irritated and alarmed the Norridgewocks, and their growing resentment was fomented by Rale, both because he shared it himself, and because he was prompted by Vaudreuil. Yet, dreading another war with the English, the Indians kept quiet for a year or two, till at length the more reckless among them began to threaten and pilfer the settlers.

In 1716 Colonel Samuel Shute came out to succeed Dudley as governor; and in the next summer he called the Indians to a council at Georgetown, a settlement on Arrowsick Island, at the mouth of the Kennebec. Thither he went in the frigate "Squirrel," with the councillors of Massachusetts and New Hampshire; while the deputies of the Norridgewocks, Penobscots, Pequawkets, or Abenakis of the Saco, and Assagunticooks, or Abenakis of the Androscoggin, came in canoes to meet him, and set up their wigwams on a neighboring island. The council opened on the ninth of August, under

---

[12] Sewall's *Memorial relating to the Kennebec Indians* is an argument against war with them.

a large tent, over which waved the British flag. The oath was administered to the interpreters by the aged Judge Sewall, and Shute then made the Indians a speech in which he told them that the English and they were subjects of the great, good, and wise King George; that as both peoples were under the same King, he would gladly see them also of the same religion, since it was the only true one; and to this end he gave them a Bible and a minister to teach them,—pointing to Rev. Joseph Baxter, who stood near by. And he further assured them that if any wrong should be done them, he would set it right. He then condescended to give his hand to the chiefs, telling them, through the interpreter, that it was to show his affection.

The Indians, after their usual custom, deferred their answer to the next day, when the council again met, and the Norridgewock chief, Wiwurna, addressed the governor as spokesman for his people. In defiance of every Indian idea of propriety, Shute soon began to interrupt him with questions and remarks. Wiwurna remonstrated civilly; but Shute continued his interruptions, and the speech turned to a dialogue, which may be abridged thus, Shute always addressing himself, not to the Indian orator, but to the interpreter.

The orator expressed satisfaction at the arrival of the governor, and hoped that peace and friendship would now prevail.

GOVERNOR (*to the interpreter*). Tell them that if they behave themselves, I shall use them kindly.

ORATOR (*as rendered by the interpreter*). Your Excellency was pleased to say that we must obey King George. We will if we like his way of treating us.

GOVERNOR. They must obey him.

ORATOR. We will if we are not disturbed on our lands.

GOVERNOR. Nor must they disturb the English on theirs.

ORATOR. We are pleased that your Excellency is ready to hear our complaints when wrong is done us.

GOVERNOR. They must not pretend to lands that belong to the English.

ORATOR. We beg leave to go on in order with our answer.

GOVERNOR. Tell him to go on.

ORATOR. If there should be any quarrel and bloodshed, we will not avenge ourselves, but apply to your Excellency.

We will embrace in our bosoms the English that have come to settle on our land.

GOVERNOR. They must not call it their land, for the English have bought it of them and their ancestors.

ORATOR. We pray leave to proceed with our answer, and talk about the land afterwards.

Wiwurna, then, with much civility, begged to be excused from receiving the Bible and the minister, and ended by wishing the governor good wind and weather for his home-ward voyage.

There was another meeting in the afternoon, in which the orator declared that his people were willing that the English should settle on the west side of the Kennebec as far up the river as a certain mill; on which the governor said to the interpreter: "Tell them we want nothing but our own, and that that we will have;" and he ordered an old deed of sale, signed by six of their chiefs, to be shown and explained to them. Wiwurna returned that though his tribe were un-easy about their lands, they were willing that the English should keep what they had got, excepting the forts. On this point there was a sharp dialogue, and Shute said bluntly that if he saw fit, he should build a fort at every new settlement. At this all the Indians rose abruptly and went back to their camp, leaving behind an English flag that had been given them.

Rale was at the Indian camp, and some of them came back in the evening with a letter from him, in which he told Shute that the governor of Canada had asked the King of France whether he had even given the Indians' land to the English, to which the King replied that he had not, and would help the Indians to repel any encroachment upon them. This cool assumption on the part of France of paramount right to the Abenaki country incensed Shute, who rejected the letter with contempt.

As between the governor and the Indian orator, the savage had shown himself by far the more mannerly; yet so unwill-ing were the Indians to break with the English that on the next morning, seeing Shute about to re-embark, they sent messengers to him to apologize for what they called their rudeness, beg that the English flag might be returned to them, and ask for another interview, saying that they would ap-

point another spokesman instead of Wiwurna, who had given
so much offence. Shute consented, and the meeting was held.
The new orator presented a wampum belt, expressed a wish
for peace, and said that his people wished the English to
extend their settlements as far as they had formerly done.
Shute, on his part, promised that trading-houses should be
established for supplying their needs, and that they should
have a smith to mend their guns, and an interpreter of their
own choice. Twenty chiefs and elders then affixed their totemic
marks to a paper, renewing the pledges made four years
before at Portsmouth, and the meeting closed with a dance
in honor of the governor.[13]

The Indians, as we have seen, had shown no eagerness to
accept the ministrations of Rev. Joseph Baxter. The Massachusetts Assembly had absurdly tried to counteract the influence of Rale by offering £150 a year in their depreciated
currency to any one of their ministers who would teach
Calvinism to the Indians. Baxter, whom Rale, with characteristic exaggeration, calls the ablest of the Boston ministers, but who was far from being so, as he was the pastor
of the small country village of Medfield, took up the task,
and, with no experience of Indian life or knowledge of any
Indian language, entered the lists against an adversary who
had spent half his days among savages, had gained the love
and admiration of the Norridgewocks, and spoke their language fluently. Baxter, with the confidence of a novice, got
an interpreter and began to preach, exhort, and launch sarcasms against the doctrines and practices of the Roman
Church. Rale excommunicated such of his flock as listened
to him;[14] yet some persisted in doing so, and three of these
petitioned the English governor to order "a small praying-
house" to be built for their use.[15]

Rale, greatly exasperated, opened a correspondence with

[13] A full report of this conference was printed at the time in
Boston. It is reprinted in *N. H. Historical Collections,* ii. 242, and
N. H. Provincial Papers, iii. 693. Penhallow was present at the
meeting, but his account of it is short. The accounts of Williamson and Hutchinson are drawn from the above-mentioned report.

[14] *Shute to Rale,* 21 *February,* 1718.

[15] This petition is still in the Massachusetts Archives, and is
printed by Dr. Francis in *Spark's American Biography,* New
Series, xvii. 259.

Baxter, and wrote a treatise for his benefit, in which, through a hundred pages of polemical Latin, he proved that the Church of Rome was founded on a rock. This he sent to Baxter, and challenged him to overthrow his reasons. Baxter sent an answer for which Rale expresses great scorn as to both manner and matter. He made a rejoinder, directed not only against his opponent's arguments, but against his Latin, in which he picked flaws with great apparent satisfaction. He says that he heard no more from Baxter for a long time, but at last got another letter, in which there was nothing to the purpose, the minister merely charging him with an irascible and censorious spirit. This letter is still preserved, and it does not answer to Rale's account of it. Baxter replies to his correspondent vigorously, defends his own Latin, attacks that of Rale, and charges him with losing temper.[16]

Rale's correspondence with the New England ministers seems not to have been confined to Baxter. A paper is preserved, translated apparently from a Latin original, and entitled, "Remarks out of the Fryar Sebastian Rale's Letter from Norridgewock, February 7, 1720." This letter appears to have been addressed to some Boston minister, and is of a scornful and defiant character, using language ill fitted to conciliate, as thus: "You must know that a missionary is not a cipher, like a minister;" or thus: "A Jesuit is not a Baxter or a Boston minister." The tone is one of exasperation dashed with contempt, and the chief theme is English encroachment and the inalienability of Indian lands.[17] Rale says that Baxter gave up his mission after receiving the treatise on the infallible supremacy of the true Church; but this is a mistake, as the minister made three successive visits to the Eastern country before he tired of his hopeless mission.

In the letter just quoted, Rale seems to have done his best to rasp the temper of his New England correspondent. He boasts of his power over the Indians, who, as he declares,

[16] This letter was given by Mr. Adams, of Medfield, a connection of the Baxter family, to the Massachusetts Historical Society, in whose possession it now is, in a worn condition. It was either captured with the rest of Rale's papers and returned to the writer, or else is a duplicate kept by Baxter.

[17] This curious paper is in the *Common Place Book* of Rev. Henry Flynt, of which the original is in the library of the Massachusetts Historical Society.

always do as he advises them. "Any treaty with the governor," he goes on to say, "and especially that of Arrowsick, is null and void if I do not approve it, for I give them so many reasons against it that they absolutely condemn what they have done." He says further that if they do not drive the English from the Kennebec, he will leave them, and that they will then lose both their lands and their souls; and he adds that, if necessary, he will tell them that they may make war.[18] Rale wrote also to Shute; and though the letter is lost, the governor's answer shows that it was sufficiently aggressive.

The wild Indian is unstable as water. At Arrowsick, the Norridgewocks were all for peace; but when they returned to their village their mood changed, and, on the representations of Rale, they began to kill the cattle of the English settlers on the river below, burn their haystacks, and otherwise annoy them.[19] The English suspected that the Jesuit was the source of their trouble; and as they had always regarded the lands in question as theirs, by virtue of the charter of the Plymouth Company in 1620, and the various grants under it, as well as by purchase from the Indians, their ire against him burned high. Yet afraid as the Indians were of another war, even Rale could scarcely have stirred them to violence but for the indignities put upon them by Indian-hating ruffians of the border, vicious rum-selling traders, and hungry land-thieves. They had still another cause of complaint. Shute had promised to build trading-houses where their wants should be supplied without fraud and extortion; but he had not kept his word, and could not keep it, for reasons that will soon appear.

In spite of such provocations, Norridgewock was divided

[18] See Francis, *Life of Rale,* where the entire passage is given.
[19] Rale wrote to the governor of Canada that it was "sur Les Représentations qu'Il Avoit fait aux Sauvages de Sa Mission" that they had killed "un grand nombre de Bestiaux apartenant aux Anglois," and threatened them with attack if they did not retire. (*Réponse fait par MM. Vaudreuil et Bégon au Mémoire du Roy du 8 Juin,* 1721.) Rale told the governor of Massachusetts, on another occasion, that his character as a priest permitted him to give the Indians nothing but counsels of peace. Yet as early as 1703 he wrote to Vaudreuil that the Abenakis were ready, at a word from him, to lift the hatchet against the English. *Beauharnois et Vaudreuil au Ministre,* 15 Novembre, 1703.

in opinion. Not only were the Indians in great dread of war, but they had received English presents to a considerable amount, chiefly from private persons interested in keeping them quiet. Hence, to Rale's great chagrin, there was an English party in the village so strong that when the English authorities demanded reparation for the mischief done to the settlers, the Norridgewocks promised two hundred beaver-skins as damages, and gave four hostages as security that they would pay for misdeeds in the past, and commit no more in the future.[20]

Rale now feared that his Indians would all go over to the English and tamely do their bidding; for though most of them, when he was present, would denounce the heretics and boast of the brave deeds they would do against them, yet after a meeting with English officials, they would change their minds and accuse their spiritual father of lying. It was clear that something must be done to end these waverings, lest the lands in dispute should be lost to France forever.

The Norridgewocks had been invited to another interview with the English at Georgetown; and Rale resolved, in modern American phrase, to "capture the meeting." Vaudreuil and the Jesuit La Chasse, superior of the mission, lent their aid. Messengers were sent to the converted Indians of Canada, whose attachment to France and the Church was past all doubt, and who had been taught to abhor the English as children of the Devil. The object of the message was to induce them to go to the meeting at Georgetown armed and equipped for any contingency.

They went accordingly,—Abenakis from Becancour and St. Francis, Hurons from Lorette, and Iroquois from Caughnawaga, besides others, all stanch foes of heresy and England. Rale and La Chasse directed their movements and led them first to Norridgewock, where their arrival made a revolution. The peace party changed color like a chameleon, and was all for war. The united bands, two hundred and fifty

---

[20] *Joseph Heath and John Minot to Shute,* 1 *May,* 1710. Rale says that these hostages were seized by surprise and violence; but Vaudreuil complains bitterly of the faintness of heart which caused the Indians to give them (*Vaudreuil à Rale,* 15 *Juin,* 1721), and both he and the intendant lay the blame on the English party at Norridgewock, who, "with the consent of all the Indians of that mission, had the weakness to give four hostages." *Réponse de Vaudreuil et Bégon au Mémoire du Roy du* 8 *Juin,* 1721.

warriors in all, paddled down the Kennebec along with the two Jesuits and two French officers, Saint-Castin and Croisil. In a few days the English at Georgetown saw them parading before the fort, well armed, displaying French flags,—feathers dangling from their scalp-locks, and faces fantastically patterned in vermilion, ochre, white clay, soot, and such other pigments as they could find or buy.

They were met by Captain Penhallow and other militia officers of the fort, to whom they gave the promised two hundred beaver-skins, and demanded the four hostages in return; but the hostages had been given as security, not only for the beaver-skins, but also for the future good behavior of the Indians, and Penhallow replied that he had no authority to surrender them. On this they gave him a letter to the governor, written for them by Père de la Chasse, and signed by their totems. It summoned the English to leave the country at once, and threatened to rob and burn their houses in case of rufusal.[21] The threat was not executed, and they presently disappeared, but returned in September in increased numbers, burned twenty-six houses and attacked the fort, in which the inhabitants had sought refuge. The garrison consisted of forty men, who being reinforced by the timely arrival of several whale-boats bringing thirty more, made a sortie. A skirmish followed; but being outnumbered and ouflanked, the English fell back behind their defences.[22]

[21] *Eastern Indians' Letter to the Governour,* 27 July, 1721, in *Mass., Hist. Coll., Second* viii. 259. This is the original French. It is signed with totems of all the Abenaki bands, and also of the Caughnawagas, Iroquois of the Mountain, Hurons, Micmacs, Montagnais, and several other tribes. On this interview, Penhallow; Belknap, ii. 51; *Shute to Vaudreuil,* 21 July, 1721 (O. S.); *Ibid.,* 23 *April,* 1722; Rale in *Lettres Édifiantes,* xvii. 285. Rale blames Shute for not being present at the meeting, but a letter of the governor shows that he had never undertaken to be there. He could not have come in any case, from the effects of a fall, which disabled him for some months even from going to Portsmouth to meet the Legislature. *Provincial Papers of New Hampshire,* iii. 822.

[22] Williamson, *Hist. of Maine,* ii. 119; Penhallow. Rale's account of the affair, found among his papers at Norridgewock, is curiously exaggerated. He says that he himself was with the Indians, and "to pleasure the English" showed himself to them several times,—a point which the English writers do not mention, though it is one which they would be most likely to seize upon. He says that fifty houses were burned, and that there were five

The French authorities were in a difficult position. They thought it necessary to stop the progress of English settlement along the Kennebec; and yet, as there was peace between the two Crowns, they could not use open force. There was nothing for it but to set on the Abenakis to fight for them. "I am well pleased," wrote Vaudreuil to Rale, "that you and Père de la Chasse have prompted the Indians to treat the English as they have done. My orders are to let them want for nothing, and I send them plenty of ammunition." Rale says that the King allowed him a pension of six thousand livres a year, and that he spent it all "in good works." As his statements are not remarkable for precision, this may mean that he was charged with distributing the six thousand livres which the King gave every year in equal shares to the three Abenaki missions of Medoctec, Norridgewock, and Panawamské, or Penobscot, and which generally took the form of presents of arms, gunpowder, bullets, and other munitions of war, or of food and clothing to support the squaws and children while the warriors were making raids on the English.[23]

Vaudreuil had long felt the delicacy of his position, and even before the crisis seemed near he tried to provide against it, and wrote to the minister that he had never called the Abenakis subjects of France, but only allies, in order to avoid responsibility for anything they might do.[24] "The English," he says elsewhere, "must be prevented from settling on Abenaki lands; and to this end we must let the Indians act for us (*laisser agir les sauvages*)."[25]

Yet while urging the need of precaution, he was too zealous to be always prudent; and once, at least, he went so far as to suggest that French soldiers should be sent to help the Abenakis,—which, he thought, would frighten the English into retreating from their settlements; whereas if such help

---

forts, two of which were of stone, and that in one of these six hundred armed men, besides women and children, had sought refuge, though there was not such a number of men in the whole region of the Kennebec.

[23] Vaudreuil, *Mémoire adressé au Roy, 5 Juin,* 1723.
[24] *Vaudreuil au Ministre,* 6 *Septembre,* 1716.
[25] *Extrait d'une Liasse de Papiers concernant le Canada,* 1720. (Archives du Ministère des Affaires Étrangères.)

were refused, the Indians would go over to the enemy.[26] The court was too anxious to avoid a rupture to permit the use of open force, and would only promise plenty of ammunition to Indians who would fight the English, directing at the same time that neither favors nor attentions should be given to those who would not.[27]

The half-breed officer, Saint-Castin, son of Baron Vincent de Saint-Castin by his wife, a Penobscot squaw, bore the double character of a French lieutenant and an Abenaki chief, and had joined with the Indians in their hostile demonstration at Arrowsick Island. Therefore, as chief of a tribe styled subjects of King George, the English seized him, charged him with rebellion, and brought him to Boston, where he was examined by a legislative committee. He showed both tact and temper, parried the charges against him, and was at last set at liberty. His arrest, however, exasperated his tribesmen, who soon began to burn houses, kill settlers, and commit various acts of violence, for all of which Rale was believed to be mainly answerable. There was great indignation against him. He himself says that a reward of a thousand pounds sterling was offered for his head, but that the English should not get it for all their sterling money. It does not appear that such a reward was offered, though it is true that the Massachusetts House of Representatives once voted five hundred pounds in their currency—then equal to about a hundred and eighty pounds sterling—for the same purpose; but as the governor and Council refused their concurrence, the Act was of no effect.

All the branches of the government, however, presently joined in sending three hundred men to Norridgewock, with a demand that the Indians should give up Rale "and the other heads and fomenters of their rebellion." In case of refusal they were to seize the Jesuit and the principal chiefs and bring them prisoners to Boston. Colonel Westbrook was put in command of the party. Rale, being warned of their approach by some of his Indians, swallowed the consecrated wafers, hid the sacred vessels, and made for the woods, where, as he thinks, he was saved from discovery by a special intervention of Providence. His papers fell into the hands of Westbrook, including letters that proved beyond all doubt that

[26] *Réponse de Vaudreuil et Bégon au Mémoire du Roy,* 8 Juin, 1721.
[27] *Bégon à Rale,* 14 Juin, 1721.

he had acted as agent of the Canadian authorities in exciting his flock against the English.[28]

Incensed by Westbrook's invasion, the Indians came down the Kennebec in large numbers, burned the village of Brunswick, and captured nine families at Merry-meeting Bay; though they soon set them free, except five men whom they kept to exchange for the four hostages still detained at Boston.[29] At the same time they seized several small vessels in the harbors along the coast. On this the governor and Council declared war against the Eastern Indians, meaning the Abenakis and their allies, whom they styled traitors and robbers.

In Massachusetts many persons thought that war could not be justified, and were little disposed to push it with vigor. The direction of it belonged to the governor in his capacity of Captain-General of the Province. Shute was an old soldier who had served with credit as lieutenant-colonel under Marlborough; but he was hampered by one of those disputes which in times of crisis were sure to occur in every British province whose governor was appointed by the Crown. The Assembly, jealous of the representative of royalty, and looking back mournfully to their virtual independence under the lamented old charter, had from the first let slip no opportunity to increase its own powers and abridge those of the governor, refused him the means of establishing the promised trading-houses in the Indian country, and would grant no money for presents to conciliate the Norridgewocks. The House now wanted, not only to control supplies for the war, but to direct the war itself and conduct operations by committees of its own. Shute made his plans of campaign, and proceeded to appoint officers from among the frontier inhabitants, who had at least the qualification of being accustomed to the woods. One of them, Colonel Walton, was obnoxious to some of the representatives, who brought charges against him, and the House demanded that he should be recalled from the

[28] Some of the papers found in Rale's "strong box" are still preserved in the Archives of Massachusetts, including a letter to him from Vaudreuil, dated at Quebec, 25 September, 1721, in which the French governor expresses great satisfaction at the missionary's success in uniting the Indians against the English, and promises military aid, if necessary.

[29] Wheeler, *History of Brunswick, Topsham, and Harpswell,* 54.

field to answer to them for his conduct. The governor objected to this as an encroachment on his province as commander-in-chief. Walton was now accused of obeying orders of the governor in contravention of those of the representatives, who thereupon passed a vote requiring him to lay his journal before them. This was more than Shute could bear. He had the character of a good-natured man; but the difficulties and mortifications of his position had long galled him, and he had got leave to return to England and lay his case before the King and Council. The crisis had now come. The Assembly were for usurping all authority, civil and military. Accordingly, on the first of January, 1723, the governor sailed in a merchant ship, for London, without giving notice of his intention to anybody except two or three servants.[30]

The burden of his difficult and vexatious office fell upon the lieutenant-governor, William Dummer. When he first met the Council in his new capacity, a whimsical scene took place. Here, among the rest, was the aged, matronly countenance of the worthy Samuel Sewall, deeply impressed with the dignity and importance of his position as senior member of the Board. At his best he never had the faintest sense of humor or perception of the ludicrous, and being now perhaps touched with dotage, he thought it incumbent upon him to address a few words of exhortation and encouragement to the incoming chief magistrate. He rose from his seat with long locks, limp and white, drooping from under his black skull-cap,—for he abhorred a wig as a sign of backsliding, —and in a voice of quavering solemnity spoke thus:—

"If your Honour and this Honourable Board please to give me leave, I would speak a Word or two upon this solemn Occasion. Altho the unerring Providence of God has brought you to the Chair of Government in a cloudy and tempestuous season, yet you have this for your Encouragement, that the people you Have to do with are a part of the Israel of God, and you may expect to have of the Prudence and Patience of Moses communicated to you for your Conduct. It is evident that our Almighty Saviour counselled the first planters to remove hither and

[30] Hutchinson, ii. 261. On these dissensions compare Palfrey, *Hist. of New England,* ix. 406–428.

Settle here, and they dutifully followed his Advice, and therefore He will never leave nor forsake them nor Theirs; so that your Honour must needs be happy in sincerely seeking their Interest and Welfare, which your Birth and Education will incline you to do. *Difficilia quæ pulchra.* I promise myself that they who sit at this Board will yield their Faithful Advice to your Honour according to the Duty of their Place."

Having thus delivered himself to an audience not much more susceptible of the ludicrous than he was, the old man went home well pleased, and recorded in his diary that the lieutenant-governor and councillors rose and remained standing while he was speaking, "and they expressed a handsom Acceptance of what I had said; *Laus Deo.*"[31]

Dummer was born in New England, and might, therefore, expect to find more favor than had fallen to his predecessor; but he was the representative of royalty, and could not escape the consequences of being so. In earnest of what was in store for him, the Assembly would not pay his salary, because he had sided with the governor in the late quarrel. The House voted to dismiss Colonel Walton and Major Moody, the chief officers appointed by Shute; and when Dummer reminded it that this was a matter belonging to him as commander-in-chief, it withheld the pay of the obnoxious officers and refused all supplies for the war till they should be removed. Dummer was forced to yield.[32] The House would probably have pushed him still farther, if the members had not dreaded the effect of Shute's representations at court, and feared lest persistent encroachment on the functions of the governor might cost them their charter, to which, insufficient as they thought it, and far inferior to the one they had lost, they clung tenaciously as the palladium of their liberties. Yet Dummer needed the patience of Job; for his Assembly seemed more bent on victories over him than over the Indians.

There was another election, which did not improve the situation. The new House was worse than the old, being made up largely of narrow-minded rustics, who tried to

[31] *Sewall Papers,* iii. 317, 318.
[32] Palfrey, iv. 432, 433.

relieve the governor of all conduct of the war by assigning it to a committee chosen from among themselves; but the Council would not concur with them.

Meanwhile the usual ravages went on. Farmhouses were burned, and the inmates waylaid and killed, while the Indians generally avoided encounters with armed bodies of whites. Near the village of Oxford four of them climbed upon the roof of a house, cut a hole in it with their hatchets, and tried to enter. A woman who was alone in the building, and who had two loaded guns and two pistols, seeing the first savage struggling to shove himself through the hole, ran to him in desperation and shot him; on which the others dragged the body back and disappeared.[33]

There were several attempts of a more serious kind. The small wooden fort at the river St. George, the most easterly English outpost, was attacked, but the assailants were driven off. A few weeks later it was attacked again by the Penobscots under their missionary, Father Lauverjat. Other means failing, they tried to undermine the stockade; but their sap caved in from the effect of rains, and they retreated, with severe loss. The warlike contagion spread to the Indians of Nova Scotia. In July the Micmacs seized sixteen or seventeen fishing-smacks at Canseau; on which John Eliot, of Boston, and John Robinson, of Cape Ann, chased the marauders in two sloops, retook most of the vessels, and killed a good number of the Indians. In the autumn a war-party, under the noted chief Grey Lock, prowled about the village of Rutland, met the minister, Joseph Willard, and attacked him. He killed one savage and wounded another, but was at last shot and scalped.[34]

The representatives had long been bent on destroying the mission village of the Penobscots on the river of that name; and one cause of their grudge against Colonel Walton was that, by order of the governor, he had deferred a projected attack upon it. His successor, Colonel Westbrook, now took the work in hand, went up the Penobscot in February with two hundred and thirty men in sloops and whaleboats, left these at the head of navigation, and pushed through the forest to the Indian town called Panawamské by the French.

[33] Penhallow. Hutchinson, ii. 279.
[34] Penhallow. Temple and Sheldon, *History of Northfield*, 195.

It stood apparently above Bangor, at or near Passadumkeag. Here the party found a stockade enclosure fourteen feet high, seventy yards long, and fifty yards wide, containing twenty-three houses, which Westbrook, a better woodsman than grammarian, reports to have been "built regular." Outside the stockade stood the chapel, "well and handsomely furnished within and without, and on the south side of that the Fryer's dwelling-house."[35] This "Fryer" was Father Lauverjat, who had led his flock to the attack of the fort at the St. George. Both Indians and Missionary were gone. Westbrook's men burned the village and chapel, and sailed back to the St. George. In the next year, 1724, there was a more noteworthy stroke; for Dummer, more pliant than Shute, had so far soothed his Assembly that it no longer refused money for the war. It was resolved to strike at the root of the evil, seize Rale, and destroy Norridgewock. Two hundred and eight men in four companies, under Captains Harmon, Moulton, and Brown, and Lieutenant Bean, set out from Fort Richmond in seventeen whaleboats on the eighth of August. They left the boats at Taconic Falls in charge of a lieutenant and forty men, and on the morning of the tenth the main body, accompanied by three Mohawk Indians, marched through the forest for Norridgewock. Towards evening they saw two squaws, one of whom they brutally shot, and captured the other, who proved to be the wife of the noted chief Bomazeen. She gave them a full account of the state of the village, which they approached early in the afternoon of the twelfth. In the belief that some of the Indians would be in their cornfields on the river above, Harmon, who was in command, divided the force, and moved up the river with about eighty men, while Moulton, with as many more, made for the village, advancing through the forest with all possible silence. About three o'clock he and his men emerged from a tangle of trees and bushes, and saw the Norridgewock cabins before them, no longer enclosed with a stockade, but open and unprotected. Not an Indian was stirring, till at length a warrior came out from one of the huts, saw the English, gave a startled war-whoop, and ran back for his gun. Then all was dismay and confusion. Squaws and children ran screaming for the river, while the warriors, fifty or sixty in number, came to meet the enemy. Moulton order his men to reserve their fire till the Indians had emptied their guns. As he had foreseen, the excited savages fired wildly, and did little or no harm. The English, still keeping their ranks, returned a volley with deadly effect. The Indians gave one more fire, and then ran for the river. Some tried to wade to the farther side, the water being low; others swam across, while many jumped into their canoes, but could not use them, having left the paddles in their houses. Moulton's men followed close, shooting the fugitives in the water or as they climbed the farther bank.

When they returned to the village they found Rale in one of the houses, firing upon some of their comrades who had not joined in the pursuit. He presently wounded one of them, on which a lieutenant named Benjamin Jaques burst open the door of the house, and, as he declared, found the priest loading his gun for another shot. The lieutenant said further that he called on him to surrender, and that Rale replied that he would neither give quarter nor take it; on which Jaques shot him through the head.[36] Moulton, who had given orders that Rale should not be killed, doubted this report of his subordinate so far as concerned the language used by Rale, though believing that he had exasperated the lieutenant by provoking expressions of some kind. The old chief Mogg had shut himself up in another house, from which he fired and killed one of Moulton's three Mohawks, whose brother then beat in the door and shot the chief dead. Several of the English followed, and brutally murdered Mogg's squaw and his two children. Such plunder as the village afforded, consisting of three barrels of gunpowder, with a few guns, blankets, and kettles, was then seized; and the Puritan militia thought it a meritorious act to break what they called the "idols" in the church, and carry off the sacred vessels.

Harmon and his party returned towards night from their useless excursion to the cornfields, where they found nobody. In the morning a search was made for the dead, and twenty-six Indians were found and scalped, including the principal

[36] Hutchinson, ii. 283 (ed. 1795). Hutchinson had the story from Moulton. Compare the tradition in the family of Jaques, as told by his great-grandson, in *Historical Magazine*, viii. 177.

chiefs and warriors of the place. Then, being anxious for the safety of their boats, the party marched for Taconic Falls. They had scarcely left the village when one of the two surviving Mohawks, named Christian, secretly turned back, set fire to the church and the houses, and then rejoined the party. The boats were found safe, and embarking, they rowed down to Richmond with their trophies.[37]

The news of the fate of the Jesuit and his mission spread joy among the border settlers, who saw in it the end of their troubles. In their eyes Rale was an incendiary, setting on a horde of bloody savages to pillage and murder. While they thought him a devil, he passed in Canada for a martyred saint. He was neither the one nor the other, but a man with the qualities and faults of a man,—fearless, resolute, enduring; boastful, sarcastic, often bitter and irritating; a vehement partisan; apt to see things, not as they were, but as he wished them to be; given to inaccuracy and exaggeration, yet no doubt sincere in opinions and genuine in zeal; hating the English more than he loved the Indians; calling himself their friend, yet using them as instruments of worldly policy, to their danger and final ruin. In considering the ascription of martyrdom, it is to be remembered that he did not die because he was an apostle of the faith, but because he was the active agent of the Canadian government.

There is reason to believe that he sometimes exercised a humanizing influence over his flock. The war which he helped

[37] The above rests on the account of Hutchinson, which was taken from the official Journal of Harmon, the commander of the expedition, and from the oral statements of Moulton, whom Hutchinson examined on the subject. Charlevoix, following a letter of La Chasse in the Jesuit *Lettres Édifiantes,* gives a widely different story. According to him, Norridgewock was surprised by eleven hundred men, who first announced their presence by a general volley, riddling all the house with bullets. Rale, says La Chasse, ran out to save his flock by drawing the rage of the enemy on himself; on which they raised a great shout and shot him dead at the foot of the cross in the middle of the village. La Chasse does not tell us where he got the story; but as there were no French witnesses, the story must have come from the Indians, who are notorious liars where their interest and self-love are concerned. Nobody competent to judge of evidence can doubt which of the two statements is the more trustworthy.

to kindle was marked by fewer barbarities—fewer tortures, mutilations of the dead, and butcheries of women and infants —than either of the preceding wars. It is fair to assume that this was due in part to him, though it was chiefly the result of an order given, at the outset, by Shute that non-combatants in exposed positions should be sent to places of safety in the older settlements.[38]

[38] It is also said that Rale taught some of his Indians to read and write,—which was unusual in the Jesuit mission. On his character, compare the judicial and candid *Life of Rale,* by Dr. Convers Francis, in Sparks's *American Biography, New Series,* vii.

Chapter 11

1724, 1725
Lovewell's Fight

THE DEATH of Rale and the destruction of Norridgewock did not at once end the war. Vaudreuil turned all the savages of the Canadian missions against the borders, not only of Maine, but of western Massachusetts, whose peaceful settlers had given no offence. Soon after the Norridgewock expedition, Dummer wrote to the French governor, who had lately proclaimed the Abenakis his allies: "As they are subjects of his Britannic Majesty, they cannot be your allies, except through me, his representative. You have instigated them to fall on our people in the most outrageous manner. I have seen your commission to Sebastien Rale. But for your protection and incitement they would have made peace long ago."[1]

In reply, Vaudreuil admitted that he had given a safe-conduct and a commission to Rale, which he could not deny, as the Jesuit's papers were in the hands of the English governor. "You will have to answer to your king for his murder," he tells Dummer. "It would have been strange if I had abandoned our Indians to please you. I cannot help taking the part of our allies. You have brought your troubles upon yourself. I advise you to pull down all the forts you have built on the Abenaki lands since the Peace of Utrecht. If you do so, I will be your mediator with the Norridgewocks. As to the murder of Rale, I leave that to be settled between the two Crowns."[2]

Apparently the French court thought it wise to let the question rest, and make no complaint. Dummer, however, gave his views on the subject to Vaudreuil. "Instead of preaching peace, love, and friendship, agreeably to the Christian religion, Rale was an incendiary, as appears by many letters I have by me. He was once and again appeared at the head of a great many Indians, threatening and insulting us. If such a disturber of

[1] *Dummer to Vaudreuil*, 15 *September*, 1724.
[2] *Vaudreuil à Dummer*, 29 *Octobre*, 1724.

the peace has been killed in the heat of action, nobody is to blame but himself. I have much more cause to complain that Mr. Willard, minister of Rutland, who is innocent of all that is charged against Rale, and always confined himself to preaching the Gospel, was slain and scalped by your Indians, and his scalp carried in triumph to Quebec."

Dummer then denies that France has any claim to the Abenakis, and declares that the war between them and the English is due to the instigations of Rale and the encouragements given them by Vaudreuil. But he adds that in his wish to promote peace he sends two prominent gentlement, Colonel Samuel Thaxter and Colonel William Dudley, as bearers of his letter.[3]

Mr. Atkinson, envoy on the part of New Hampshire, joined Thaxter and Dudley, and the three set out for Montreal, over the ice of Lake Champlain. Vaudreuil received them with courtesy. As required by their instructions, they demanded the release of the English prisoners in Canada, and protested against the action of the French governor in setting on the Indians to attack English settlements when there was peace between the two Crowns. Vaudreuil denied that he had done so, till they showed him his own letters to Rale, captured at Norridgewock. These were unanswerable; but Vaudreuil insisted that the supplies sent to the Indians were only the presents which they received every year from the King. As to the English prisoners, he said that those in the hands of the Indians were beyond his power; but that the envoys could have those whom the French had bought from their captors, on paying back the price they had cost. The demands were exorbitant, but sixteen prisoners were ransomed, and bargains were made for ten more. Vaudreuil proposed to Thaxter and his colleagues to have an interview with the Indians, which they at first declined, saying that they had no powers to treat with them, though, if the Indians wished to ask for peace, they were ready to hear them. At length a meeting was arranged. The French governor writes: "Being satisfied that nothing was more opposed to our interests than a peace between the Abenakis and the English, I thought that I would sound the chiefs before they spoke to the English

[3] *Dummer to Vaudreuil, 19 January, 1725.* This, with many other papers relating to these matters, is in the Massachusetts Archives.

envoys, and insinuate to them everything that I had to say."[4]
This he did with such success that, instead of asking for peace,
the Indians demanded the demolition of the English forts, and
heavy damages for burning their church and killing their missionary. In short, to Vaudreuil's great satisfaction, they talked
nothing but war. The French despatch reporting this interview
has the following marginal note: "Nothing better can be done
than to foment this war, which at least retards the settlements
of the English"; and against this is written, in the hand of the
colonial minister, the word "*Approved*."[5] This was, in fact,
the policy pursued from the first, and Rale had been an instrument of it. The Jesuit La Chasse, who spoke both English and
Abenaki, had acted as interpreter, and so had had the meeting
in his power, as he could make both parties say what he
pleased. The envoys thought him more anti-English than
Vaudreuil himself, and ascribed the intractable mood of the
Indians to his devices. Under the circumstances, they made
a mistake in consenting to the interview at all. The governor,
who had treated them with civility throughout, gave them an
escort of soldiers for the homeward journey, and they and the
redeemed prisoners returned safely to Albany.

The war went on as before, but the Indians were fast growing tired of it. The Penobscots had made themselves obnoxious
by their attacks on Fort St. George, and Captain Heath marched
across country from the Kennebec to punish them.
He found their village empty. It was built, since Westbrook's
attack, at or near the site of Bangor, a little below Indian Old
Town,—the present abode of the tribe,—and consisted of
fifty wigwams, which Heath's men burned to the ground.

One of the four hostages still detained at Boston, together
with another Indian captured in the war, was allowed to visit
his people, under a promise to return. Strange to say, the
promise was kept. They came back bringing a request for peace

---

[4] *Dépêche de Vaudreuil, 7 Août,* 1725. "Comme j'ai toujours
été persuadé que rien n'est plus opposé à nos intérêts que la paix
des Abenakis avec les Anglais (la sureté de cette colonie du côté
de l'est ayant été l'unique objet de cette guerre), je songeai à
pressentir ces sauvages avant qu'ils parlassent aux Anglais et à
leur insinuer tout ce que j'avais à leur dire."—*Vaudreuil au
Ministre,* 22 *Mai,* 1725.

[5] *N. Y. Col. Docs.,* ix. 949.

from their tribesmen. On this, commissioners were sent to the St. George, where a conference was held with some of the Penobscot chiefs, and it was arranged that deputies of that people should be sent to Boston to conclude a solid peace. After long delay, four chief's appeared, fully empowered, as they said, to make peace, not for the Penobscots only, but for the other Abenaki tribes, their allies. The speeches and ceremonies being at last ended, the four deputies affixed their marks to a paper in which, for themselves and those they represented, they made submission "unto his most excellent Majesty George, by the grace of God king of Great Britain, France, and Ireland, defender of the Faith," etc., promising to "cease and forbear all acts of hostility, injuries, and discord towards all his subjects, and never confederate or combine with any other nation to their prejudice." Here was a curious anomaly. The English claimed the Abenakis as subjects of the British Crown, and at the same time treated with them as a foreign power. Each of the four deputies signed the above-mentioned paper, one with the likeness of a turtle, the next with that of a bird, the third with the untutored portrait of a beaver, and the fourth with an extraordinary scrawl, meant, it seems, for a lobster,—such being their respective totems. To these the lieutenant-governor added the seal of the province of Massachusetts, coupled with his own autograph.

In the next summer, and again a year later, other meetings were held at Casco Bay with the chiefs of the various Abenaki tribes, in which, after prodigious circumlocution, the Boston treaty was ratified, and the war ended.[6] This time the Massachusetts Assembly, taught wisdom by experience, furnished a guarantee of peace by providing for government trading-houses in the Indian country, where goods were supplied, through responsible hands, at honest prices.

The Norridgewocks, with whom the quarrel began, were completely broken. Some of the survivors joined their kindred in Canada, and others were merged in the Abenaki bands of the Penobscot, Saco, or Androscoggin. Peace reigned at last along the borders of New England; but it had cost her dear. In the year after the death of Rale, there was an incident

[6] Penhallow gives the Boston treaty. For the ratifications, see *Collections of the Maine Hist. Soc.*, iii. 377, 407.

of the conflict too noted in its day, and too strongly rooted in popular tradition, to be passed unnoticed.

Out of the heart of the White Mountains springs the river Saco, fed by the bright cascades that leap from the crags of Mount Webster, brawling among rocks and bowlders down the great defile of the Crawford Notch, winding through the forests and intervales of Conway, then circling northward by the village of Fryeburg in devious wanderings by meadows, woods, and mountains, and at last turning eastward and southward to join the sea.

On the banks of this erratic stream lived an Abenaki tribe called the Sokokis. When the first white visited the country, these Indians lived at the Falls, a few miles from the mouth of the river. They retired before the English settlers, and either joined their kindred in Maine, or migrated to St. Francis and other Abenaki settlements in Canada; but a Sokoki band called Pigwackets, or Pequawkets, still kept its place far in the interior, on the upper waters of the Saco, near Pine Hill, in the present town of Fryeburg. Except a small band of their kindred on Lake Ossipee, they were the only human tenants of a wilderness many thousand square miles in extent. In their wild and remote abode they were difficult of access, and the forest and the river were well stocked with moose, deer, bear, beaver, otter, lynx, fisher, mink, and marten. In this, their happy hunting-ground, the Pequawkets thought themselves safe; and they would have been so for some time longer if they had not taken up the quarrel of the Norridgewocks and made bloody raids against the English border, under their war-chief, Paugus.

Not far from where their wigwams stood clustered in a bend of the Saco was the small lake now called Lovewell's Pond, named for John Lovewell of Dunstable, a Massachusetts town on the New Hampshire line. Lovewell's father, a person of consideration in the village, where he owned a "garrison house," had served in Philip's War, and taken part in the famous Narragansett Swamp Fight. The younger Lovewell, now about thirty-three years of age, lived with his wife, Hannah, and two or three children on a farm of two hundred acres. The inventory of his effects, made after his death, includes five or six cattle, one mare, two steel traps with chains, a gun, two or three books, a feather-bed, and "under-bed," or mattress, along with sundry tools, pots, barrels, chests, tubs, and the like,—the equipment, in short, of a decent frontier yeoman of the time.[7] But being, like the tough veteran, his father, of a bold and adventurous disposition, he seems to have been less given to farming than to hunting and bush-fighting.

Dunstable was attacked by Indians in the autumn of 1724, and two men were carried off. Ten others went in pursuit, but fell into an ambush, and nearly all were killed. Josiah Farwell, Lovewell's brother-in-law, being, by some accounts, the only one who escaped.[8] Soon after this, a petition, styled a "Humble Memorial," was laid before the House of Representatives at Boston. It declares that in order "to kill and destroy their enemy Indians," the petitioners and forty or fifty others are ready to spend one whole year in hunting them, "provided they can meet with Encouragement suitable." The peition is signed by John Lovewell, Josiah Farwell, and Jonathan Robbins, all of Dunstable, Lovewell's name being well written, and the others after a cramped and unaccustomed fashion. The representatives accepted the proposal and voted to give each adventurer two shillings and sixpence a day,—then equal in Massachusetts currency to about one English shilling,—out of which he was to maintain himself. The men were, in addition, promised large rewards for the scalps of male Indians old enough to fight.

A company of thirty was soon raised. Lovewell was chosen captain, Farwell, lieutenant, and Robbins, ensign. They set out towards the end of November, and reappeared at Dunstable early in January, bringing one prisoner and one scalp. Towards the end of the month Lovewell set out again, this time with eighty-seven men, gathered from the villages of Dunstable, Groton, Lancaster, Haverhill, and Billerica. They ascended the frozen Merrimac, passed Lake Winnepesaukee, pushed nearly to the White Mountains, and encamped on a branch of the upper Saco. Here they killed a moose,—a timely piece of luck, for they were in danger of starvation, and Lovewell had been compelled by want of food to send back a good number of his men. The rest held their way, filing on snow-shoes

[7] See the inventory, in Kidder, *The Expeditions of Captain John Lovewell*, 93, 94.

[8] Other accounts say that eight of the ten were killed. The headstone of one of the number, Thomas Lund, has these words: "This man, with seven more that lies in this grave, was slew All in A day by the Indiens."

through the deathlike solitude that gave no sign of life except
the light track of some squirrel on the snow, and the brisk note
of the hardy little chickadee, or black-capped titmouse, so
familiar to the winter woods. Thus far the scouts had seen no
human footprint; but on the twentieth of February they found
a lately abandoned wigwam, and, following the snow-shoe
tracks that led from it, at length saw smoke rising at a distance
out of the gray forest. The party lay close till two o'clock in
the morning; then cautiously approached, found one or more
wigwams, surrounded them, and killed all the inmates, ten in
number. They were warriors from Canada on a winter raid
against the borders. Lovewell and his men, it will be seen, were
much like hunters of wolves, catamounts, or other dangerous
beasts, except that the chase of this fierce and wily human
game demanded far more hardihood and skill.

They brought home the scalps in triumph, together with the
blankets and the new guns furnished to the slain warriors by
their Canadian friends; and Lovewell began at once to gather
men for another hunt. The busy season of the farmers was at
hand, and volunteers came in less freely than before. At the
middle of April, however, he had raised a band of forty-six, of
whom he was the captain, with Farwell and Robbins as his
lieutenants. Though they were all regularly commissioned by
the governor, they were leaders rather than commanders, for
they and their men were neighbors or acquaintances on terms
of entire social equality. Two of the number require mention.
One was Seth Wyman, of Woburn, an ensign; and the other
was Jonathan Frye, of Andover, the chaplain, a youth of
twenty-one, graduated at Harvard College in 1723, and now a
student of theology. Chaplain though he was, he carried a gun,
knife, and hatchet like the others, and not one of the party
was more prompt to use them.

They began their march on April 15. A few days afterwards, one William Cummings, of Dunstable, became so disabled by the effects of a wound received from Indians some
time before, that he could not keep on with the rest, and
Lovewell sent him back in charge of a kinsman, thus reducing their number to forty-four. When they reached the west
shore of Lake Ossipee, Benjamin Kidder, of Nutfield, fell
seriously ill. To leave him defenceless in a place so dangerous
was not to be thought of; and his comrades built a small fort,
or palisaded log-cabin, near the water, where they left the sick

man in charge of the surgeon, together with Sergeant Woods and a guard of seven men. The rest, now reduced to thirty-four, continued their march through the forest northeastward towards Pequawket, while the savage heights of the White Mountains, still covered with snow, rose above the dismal, bare forests on their left. They seem to have crossed the Saco just below the site of Fryeburg, and in the night of May 7, as they lay in the woods near the northeast end of Lovewell's Pond, the men on guard heard sounds like Indians prowling about them. At daybreak the next morning, as they stood bare-headed, listening to a prayer from the young chaplain, they heard the report of a gun, and soon after discovered an Indian on the shore of the pond at a considerable distance. Apparently he was shooting ducks; but Lovewell, suspecting a device to lure them into an ambuscade, asked the men whether they were for pushing forward or falling back, and with one voice they called upon him to lead them on. They were then in a piece of open pine woods traversed by a small brook. He ordered them to lay down their packs and advance with extreme caution. They had moved forward for some time in this manner when they met an Indian coming towards them through the dense trees and bushes. He no sooner saw them than he fired at the leading men. His gun was charged with beaver-shot; but he was so near his mark that the effect was equal to that of a bullet, and he severely wounded Lovewell and one Whiting; on which Seth Wyman shot him dead, and the chaplain and another man scalped him. Lovewell, though believed to be mortally hurt, was still able to walk, and the party fell back to the place where they had left their packs. The packs had disappeared, and suddenly, with frightful yells, the whole body of the Pequawket warriors rushed from their hiding-places, firing as they came on. The survivors say that they were more than twice the number of the whites,—which is probably an exaggeration, though their conduct, so unusual with Indians, in rushing forward instead of firing from their ambush, shows a remarkable confidence in their numerical strength.[9] They no doubt expected to strike their enemies with a panic. Lovewell received another mortal wound; but he fired

[9] Penhallow puts their number at seventy, Hutchinson at eighty, Williamson at sixty-three, and Belknap at forty-one. In such cases the smallest number is generally nearest the truth.

more than once on the Indians as he lay dying. His two lieutenants, Farwell and Robbins, were also badly hurt. Eight others fell; but the rest stood their ground, and pushed the Indians so hard that they drove them back to cover with heavy loss. One man played the coward, Benjamin Hassell, of Dunstable, who ran off, escaped in the confusion, and made with his best speed for the fort at Lake Ossipee.

The situation of the party was desperate, and nothing saved them from destruction but the prompt action of their surviving officers, only one of whom, Ensign Wyman, had escaped unhurt. It was probably under his direction that the men fell back steadily to the shore of the pond, which was only a few rods distant. Here the water protected their rear, so that they could not be surrounded; and now followed one of the most obstinate and deadly bush-fights in the annals of New England. It was about ten o'clock when the fight began, and it lasted till night. The Indians had the greater agility and skill in hiding and sheltering themselves, and the whites the greater steadiness and coolness in using their guns. They fought in the shade; for the forest was dense, and all alike covered themselves as they best could behind trees, bushes, or fallen trunks, where each man crouched with eyes and mind intent, firing whenever he saw, or thought he saw, the head, limbs, or body of an enemy exposed to sight for an instant. The Indians howled like wolves, yelled like enraged cougars, and made the forest ring with their whoops; while the whites replied with shouts and cheers. At one time the Indians ceased firing and drew back among the trees and undergrowth, where, by the noise they made, they seemed to be holding a "pow-wow," or incantation to procure victory; but the keen and fearless Seth Wyman crept up among the bushes, shot the chief conjurer, and broke up the meeting. About the middle of the afternoon young Frye received a mortal wound. Unable to fight longer, he lay in his blood, praying from time to time for his comrades in a faint but audible voice.

Solomon Keyes, of Billerica, received two wounds, but fought on till a third shot struck him. He then crawled up to Wyman in the heat of the fight, and told him that he, Keyes, was a dead man, but that the Indians should not get his scalp if he could help it. Creeping along the sandy edge of the pond, he chanced to find a stranded canoe, pushed it afloat, rolled himself into it, and drifted away before the wind.

Soon after sunset the Indians drew off and left their field to their enemies, living and dead, not even stopping to scalp the fallen,—a remarkable proof of the completeness of their discomfiture. Exhausted with fatigue and hunger,—for, having lost their packs in the morning, they had no food,—the surviving white men explored the scene of the fight. Jacob Farrar lay gasping his last by the edge of the water. Robert Usher and Lieutenant Robbins were unable to move. Of the thirty-four men, nine had escaped without serious injury, eleven were badly wounded, and the rest were dead or dying, except the coward who had run off.

About midnight, an hour or more before the setting of the moon, such as had strength to walk left the ground. Robbins, as he lay helpless, asked one of them to load his gun, saying, "The Indians will come in the morning to scalp me, and I'll kill another of 'em if I can." They loaded the gun and left him.

To make one's way even by daylight through the snares and pitfalls of a New England forest is often a difficult task; to do so in the darkness of night and overshadowing boughs, among the fallen trees and the snarl of underbrush, was well-nigh impossible. Any but the most skilful woodsmen would have lost their way. The Indians, sick of fighting, did not molest the party. After struggling on for a mile or more, Farwell, Frye, and two other wounded men, Josiah Jones and Eleazer Davis, could go no farther, and, with their consent, the others left them, with a promise to send them help as soon as they should reach the fort. In the morning the men divided into several small bands, the better to elude pursuit. One of these parties was tracked for some time by the Indians, and Elias Barron, becoming separated from his companions, was never again heard of, though the case of his gun was afterwards found by the bank of the river Ossipee.

Eleven of the number at length reached the fort, and to their amazement found nobody there. The runaway, Hassell, had arrived many hours before them, and to excuse his flight told so frightful a story of the fate of his comrades that his hearers were seized with a panic, shamefully abandoned their post, and set out for the settlements, leaving a writing on a piece of birch-bark to the effect that all the rest were killed. They had left a supply of bread and pork, and while the famished eleven rested and refreshed themselves they were joined by Solomon Keyes, the man who, after being thrice wounded, had floated away in a canoe from the place of the flight. After drifting for a considerable distance, the wind blew him ashore, when, spurred by necessity and feeling himself "wonderfully strengthened," he succeeded in gaining the fort.

Meanwhile Frye, Farwell, and their two wounded companions, Davis and Jones, after waiting vainly for the expected help, found strength to struggle forward again, till the chaplain stopped and lay down, begging the others to keep on their way, and saying to Davis, "Tell my father that I expect in a few hours to be in eternity, and am not afraid to die." They left him, and, says the old narrative, "he has not been heard of since." He had kept the journal of the expedition, which was lost with him.

Farwell died of exhaustion. The remaining two lost their way and became separated. After wandering eleven days, Davis reached the fort at Lake Ossipee, and, finding food there, came into Berwick on the twenty-seventh. Jones, after fourteen days in the woods, arrived, half dead, at the village of Biddeford.

Some of the eleven who had first made their way to the fort, together with Keyes, who joined them there, came into Dunstable during the night of the thirteenth, and the rest followed one or two days later. Ensign Wyman, who was now the only commissioned officer left alive, and who had borne himself throughout with the utmost intrepidity, decision, and good sense, reached the same place along with three other men on the fifteenth.

The runaway, Hassell, and the guard at the fort, whom he had infected with his terror, had lost no time in making their way back to Dunstable, which they seem to have reached on the evening of the eleventh. Horsemen were sent in haste to carry the doleful news to Boston, on which the governor gave orders to Colonel Tyng of the militia, who was then at Dunstable, to gather men in the border towns, march with all speed to the place of the fight, succor the wounded if any were still alive, and attack the Indians, if he could find them. Tyng called upon Hassell to go with him as a guide; but he was ill, or pretended to be so, on which one of the men who had been in the fight and had just returned offered to go in his place.

When the party reached the scene of the battle, they saw the trees plentifully scarred with bullets, and presently found and buried the bodies of Lovewell, Robbins, and ten others. The Indians, after their usual custom, had carried off or hidden their own dead; but Tyng's men discovered three of them buried together, and one of these was recognized as the war-chief Paugus, killed by Wyman, or, according to a more than doubtful tradition, by John Chamberlain.[10] Not a living Indian was to be seen.

The Pequawkets were cowed by the rough handling they had met when they plainly expected a victory. Some of them joined their Abenaki kinsmen in Canada and remained their, while others returned after the peace to their old haunts by the Saco; but they never again raised the hatchet against the English.

Lovewell's Pond, with its sandy beach, its two green islands, and its environment of lonely forests, reverted for a while to its original owners,—the wolf, bear, lynx, and moose. In our day all is changed. Farms and dwellings possess those peaceful shores, and hard by, where, at the bend of the Saco, once stood, in picturesque squalor, the wigwams of the vanished Pequawkets, the village of Fryeburg preserves the name of the brave young chaplain, whose memory is still cherished, in spite of his uncanonical turn for scalping.[11] He had engaged himself to a young girl of a neighboring village, Susanna

[10] The tradition is that Chamberlain and Paugus went down to the small brook, now called Fight Brook, to clean their guns, hot and foul with frequent firing; that they saw each other at the same instant, and that the Indian said to the white man, in his broken English, "Me kill you quick!" at the same time hastily loading his piece; to which Chamberlain coolly replied, "Maybe not." His firelock had a large touch-hole, so that the powder could be shaken out into the pan, and the gun made to prime itself. Thus he was ready for action an instant sooner than his enemy, whom he shot dead just as Paugus pulled trigger, and sent a bullet whistling over his head. The story has no good foundation, while the popular ballad, written at the time, and very faithful to the facts, says that, the other officers being killed, the English made Wyman their captain,—

"Who shot the old chief Paugus, which did the foe defeat,
Then set his men in order and brought off the retreat."

[11] The town, however, was not named for the chaplain, but for his father's cousin, General Joseph Frye, the original grantee of the land.

Rogers, daughter of John Rogers, minister of Boxford. It has been said that Frye's parents thought her beneath him in education and position; but this is not likely, for her father belonged to what has been called the "Brahmin caste" of New England, and, like others of his family, had had, at Harvard, the best education that the country could supply. The girl herself, though only fourteen years old, could make verses, such as they were; and she wrote an elegy on the death of her lover which, bating some grammatical lapses, deserves the modest praise of being no worse than many New England rhymes of that day.

The courage of Frye and his sturdy comrades contributed greatly to the pacification which in the next year relieved the borders from the scourge of Indian War.[12]

[12] Rev. Thomas Symmes, minister of Bradford, preached a sermon on the fate of Lovewell and his men immediately after the return of the survivors, and printed it, with a much more valuable introduction, giving a careful account of the affair, on the evidence of "the Valorous Captain Wyman and some others of good Credit that were in the Engagement." Wyman had just been made a captain, in recognition of his conduct. The narrative is followed by an attestation of its truth signed by him and two others of Lovewell's band.

A considerable number of letters relating to the expedition are preserved in the Massachusetts Archives, from Benjamin Hassell, Colonel Tyng, Governor Dummer of Massachusetts, and Governor Wentworth of New Hampshire. They give the various reports received from those in the fight, and show the action taken in consequence. The Archives also contain petitions from the survivors and the families of the slain; and the legislative Journals show that the petitioners received large grants of land. Lovewell's debts contracted in raising men for his expeditions were also paid.

The papers mentioned above, with other authentic records concerning the affair, have been printed by Kidder in his *Expeditions of Captain John Lovewell,* a monograph of thorough research. The names of all Lovewell's party, and biographical notices of some of them, are also given by Mr. Kidder. Compare Penhallow, Hutchinson, Fox, *History of Dunstable,* and Bouton, *Lovewell's Great Fight.* For various suggestions touching Lovewell's Expedition, I am indebted to Mr. C. W. Lewis, who has made it the subject of minute and careful study.

A ballad which was written when the event was fresh, and was long popular in New England, deserves mention, if only for its general fidelity to the facts. The following is a sample of its eighteen stanzas:—

" 'T was ten o'clock in the morning when first the fight begun,
And fiercely did continue till the setting of the sun,
Excepting that the Indians, some hours before 't was night,
Drew off into the bushes, and ceased awhile to fight;

'But soon again returnèd in fierce and furious mood,
Shouting as in the morning, but yet not half so loud;
For, as we are informèd, so thick and fast they fell,
Scarce twenty of their number at night did get home well.

 .   .   .   .

"Our worthy Captain Lovewell among them there did die;
They killed Lieutenant Robbins, and wounded good young Frye,
Who was our English chaplain; he many Indians slew,
And some of them he scalped when bullets round him flew."

Frye, as mentioned in the text, had engaged himself to Susanna
Rogers, a young girl of the village of Boxford, who, after his
death, wrote some untutored verses to commemorate his fate.
They are entitled, *A Mournful Elegy on Mr. Jonathan Frye,* and
begin thus:

> "Assist, ye muses help my quill,
> Whilst floods of tears does down distil;
> Not from mine eyes alone, but all
> That hears the sad and doleful fall
> Of that young student, Mr. Frye,
> Who in his blooming youth did die.
> Fighting for his dear country's good,
> He lost his life and precious blood.
> His father's only son was he;
> His mother loved him tenderly;
> And all that knew him loved him well;
> For in bright parts he did excel
> Most of his age; for he was young,—
> Just entering on twenty-one;
> A comley youth, and pious too;
> This I affirm, for him I knew."

She then describes her lover's brave deeds, and sad but heroic
death, alone in a howling wilderness; condoles with the bereaved
parents, exhorts them to resignation, and touches modestly on her
own sorrow.

In more recent times the fate of Lovewell and his companions
has inspired several poetical attempts, which need not be dwelt
upon. Lovewell's Fight, as Dr. Palfrey observes, was long as famous in New England as Chevy Chase on the Scottish Border.

Chapter 12

1712
The Outagamies at Detroit

WE HAVE seen that the Peace of Utrecht was followed by a threefold conflict for ascendency in America,—the conflict for Acadia, the conflict for northern New England, and the conflict for the Great West; which last could not be said to take at once an international character, being essentially a competition for the fur-trade. Only one of the English colonies took an active part in it,—the province of New York. Alone among her sister communities she had a natural thoroughfare to the West, not comparable, however, with that of Canada, to whose people the St. Lawrence, the Great Lakes, and their tributary waters were a continual invitation to the vast interior.

Virginia and Pennsylvania were not yet serious rivals in the fur-trade; and New England, the most active of the British colonies, was barred out from it by the interposition of New York, which lay across her westward path, thus forcing her to turn her energies to the sea, where half a century later her achievements inspired the glowing panegyrics of Burke before the House of Commons.

New York, then, was for many years the only rival of Canada for the control of the West. It was a fatal error in the rulers of New France that they did not, in the seventeenth century, use more strenuous efforts to possess themselves, by purchase, exchange, or conquest, of this troublesome and dangerous neighbor. There was a time, under the reign of Charles II, when negotiation for the purchase of New York might have been successful; and if this failed, the conquest of the province, if attempted by forces equal to the importance of the object, would have been far from hopeless. With New York in French hands, the fate of the continent would probably have been changed. The British possessions would have been cut in two. New England, isolated and placed in constant jeopardy, would have vainly poured her unmanageable herds of raw militia against the disciplined veterans of Old France intrenched at the mouth of the Hudson. Canada would have gained complete control of her old enemies, the

Iroquois, who would have been wholly dependent on her for the arms and ammunition without which they could do nothing.

The Iroquois, as the French had been accustomed to call them, were known to the English as the Five Nations,—a name which during the eighteenth century the French also adopted. Soon after the Peace of Utrecht, a kindred tribe, the Tuscaroras, was joined to the original five members of the confederacy, which thenceforward was sometimes called the Six Nations, though the Tuscaroras were never very prominent in its history; and, to avoid confusion, we will keep the more familiar name of the Five Nations, which the French used to the last.

For more than two generations this league of tribes had held Canada in terror, and more than once threatened it with destruction. But now a change had come over the confederates. Count Frontenac had humbled their pride. They were crowded between the rival European nations, both of whom they distrusted. Their traditional hatred of the French would have given the English of New York a controlling influence over them if the advantage had been used with energy and tact. But a narrow and short-sighted conduct threw it away. A governor of New York, moreover, even were he keen and far-seeing as Frontenac himself, would often have been helpless. When the Five Nations were attacked by the French, he had no troops to defend them, nor could he, like a Canadian governor, call out the forces of his province by a word, to meet the exigency. The small revenues of New York were not at his disposal. Without the votes of the frugal representatives of an impoverished people, his hands were tied. Hence the Five Nations, often left unaided when they most needed help, looked upon their Dutch and English neighbors as slothful and unwarlike.

Yet their friendship was of the greatest importance to the province, in peace as well as in war, and was indispensable in the conflict that New York was waging single-handed for the control of the western fur-trade. The Five Nations, as we have seen,[1] acted as middlemen between the New York merchants and the tribes of the far interior, and through them English goods and English influence penetrated all the lake country, and reached even to the Mississippi.

[1] See Chapter 1.

These vast western regions, now swarming with laborious millions, were then scantily peopled by savage hordes, whose increase was stopped by incessant mutual slaughter. This wild population had various centres or rallying-points, usually about the French forts, which protected them from enemies and supplied their wants. Thus the Pottawattamies, Ottawas, and Hurons were gathered about Detroit, and the Illinois about Fort St. Louis, on the river Illinois, were Henri de Tonty and his old comrade, La Forest, with fifteen or twenty Frenchmen, held a nominal monopoly of the neighboring fur-trade. Another focus of Indian population was near the Green Bay of Lake Michigan, and on Fox River, which enters it. Here were grouped the Sacs, Winnebagoes, and Menominies, with the Outagamies, or Foxes, a formidable tribe, the source of endless trouble to the French.

The constant aim of the Canadian authorities was to keep these western savages at peace among themselves, while preventing their establishing relation of trade with the Five Nations, and carrying their furs to them in exchange for English goods. The position was delicate, for while a close understanding between the western tribes and the Five Nations would be injurious to French interests, a quarrel would be still more so, since the French would then be forced to side with their western allies, and so be drawn into hostilities with the Iroquois confederacy, which of all things they most wished to avoid. Peace and friendship among the western tribes; peace without friendship between these tribes and the Five Nations, —thus became maxims of French policy. The Canadian governor called the western Indians his "children," and a family quarrel among them would have been unfortunate, since the loving father must needs have become involved in it, to the detriment of his trading interests.

Yet to prevent such quarrels was difficult, partly because they had existed time out of mind, and partly because it was the interest of the English to promote them. Dutch and English traders, it is true, took their lives in their hands if they ventured among the western Indians, who were encouraged by their French father to plunder and kill them, and who on occasion rarely hesitated to do so. Hence English communication with the West was largely carried on through the Five Nations. Iroquois messengers, hired for the purpose, carried wampum belts "underground"—that is, secretly—to such of the interior tribes as were disposed to listen with favor to the words of Corlaer, as they called the governor of New York.

In spite of their shortcomings, the English had one powerful attraction for all the tribes alike. This was the abundance and excellence of their goods, which, with the exception of gunpowder, were better as well as cheaper than those offered by the French. The Indians, it is true, liked the taste of French brandy more than that of English rum; yet as their chief object in drinking was to get drunk, and as rum would supply as much intoxication as brandy at a lower price, it always found favor in their eyes. In the one case, to get thoroughly drunk often cost a beaver-skin; in the other, the same satisfaction could generally be had for a mink-skin.

Thus the French found that some of their western children were disposed to listen to English seductions, look askance at their Father Onontio, and turn their canoes, not towards Montreal, but towards Albany. Nor was this the worst; for there were some of Ontonio's wild and unruly western family too ready to lift their hatchets against their brethren and fill the wilderness with discord. Consequences followed most embarrassing to the French, and among them an incident prominent in the early annals of Detroit, that new establishment so obnoxious to the English, because it barred their way to the northern lakes, so that they were extremely anxious to rid themselves of it.

In the confused and tumultuous history of the savages of this continent one now and then sees some tribe or league of tribes possessed for a time with a spirit of conquest and havoc that made it the terror of its neighbors. Of this the foremost example is that of the Five Nations of the Iroquois, who, towards the middle of the seventeenth century, swept all before them and made vast regions a solitude. They were now comparatively quiet; but far in the Northwest, another people, inferior in number, organization, and mental capacity, but not in ferocity or courage, had begun on a smaller scale, and with less conspicuous success, to play a similar part. These were the Outagamies, or Foxes, with their allies, the Kickapoos and the Mascoutins, all living at the time within the limits of the present States of Wisconsin and Illinois,—the Outagamies near Fox River, and the others on Rock River.[2] The Outa-

[2] *Memoir on the Indians between Lake Erie and the Mississippi,* in *N. Y. Col. Docs.* ix. 885.

gamies, in particular, seem to have been seized with an access of homicidal fury. Their hand was against every man, and for twenty years and more they were the firebrands of the West, and a ceaseless peril to French interests in that region. They were, however, on good terms with the Five Nations, by means of whom, as French writers say, the Dutch and English of Albany sent them gifts and messages to incite them to kill French traders and destroy the French fort at Detroit. This is not unlikely, though the evidence on the point is far from conclusive.

Fort Ponchartrain, better known as Fort Detroit, was an enclosure of palisades, flanked by blockhouses at the corners, with an open space within to serve as a parade-ground, around which stood small wooden houses thatched with straw or meadow-grass. La Mothe-Cadillac, founder of the post, had been made governor of the new colony of Louisiana, and the Sieur Dubuisson now commanded at Detroit. There were about thirty French traders, *voyageurs*, and *coureurs de bois* in the place, but at this time no soldiers.

The village of the Pottawattamies was close to the French fort; that of the Hurons was not far distant, by the edge of the river. Their houses were those structures of bark, "very high, very long, and arched like garden arbors," which were common to all the tribes of Iroquois stock, and both villages were enclosed by strong double or triple stockades, such as Cartier had found at Hochelaga, and Champlain in the Onondaga country. Their neighbors, the Ottawas, who were on the east side of the river, had imitated, with imperfect success, their way of housing and fortifying themselves. These tribes raised considerable crops of peas, beans, and Indian corn; and except when engaged in their endless dances and games of ball, dressed, like converts of the mission villages, in red or blue cloth.[3] The Hurons were reputed the most intelligent as well as the bravest of all the western tribes, and, being incensed by various outrages, they bore against the Outagamies a deadly grudge, which was shared by the other tribes, their neighbors.

All these friendly Indians were still absent on their winter hunt, when, at the opening of spring, Dubuisson and his Frenchmen were startled by a portentous visitation. Two bands of Outagamies and Mascoutins, men, women, and

[3] *Memoir on the Indians between Lake Erie and the Mississippi.*

children, counting in all above a thousand, of whom about
three hundred were warriors, appeared on the meadows behind the fort, approached to within pistol-shot of the palisades, and encamped there. It is by no means certain that
they came with deliberate hostile intent. Had this been the
case, they would not have brought their women and children.
A paper ascribed to the engineer Léry says, moreover, that
their visit was in consequence of an invitation from the late
commandant, La Mothe-Cadillac, whose interest it was to
attract to Detroit as many Indians as possible, in order to
trade for their furs.[4] Dubuisson, however, was satisfied that
they meant mischief, especially when, in spite of all his
efforts to prevent them, they fortified themselves by cutting
down young trees and surrounding their wigwams with a
rough fence of palisades. They were rude and insolent, declared that all that country was theirs, and killed fowls and
pigeons belonging to the French, who, in the absence of their
friends, the Hurons and Ottawas, dared not even remonstrate.
Dubuisson himself was forced to submit to their insults in
silence, till a party of them came one day into the fort bent
on killing two of the French, a man and a girl, against whom
they had taken some offence. The commandant then ordered
his men to drive them out; which was done, and henceforward
he was convinced that the Outagamies and Mascoutins were
only watching their opportunity to burn the fort and butcher
its inmates. Soon after, their excitement redoubled. News
came that a band of Mascoutins, who had wintered on the
river St. Joseph, had been cut off by the Ottawas and Pottawattamies, led by an Ottawa chief named Saguina; on which
the behavior of the dangerous visitors became so threatening
that Dubuisson hastily sent a canoe to recall the Hurons and
Ottawas from their hunting-grounds, and a second to invite
the friendly Ojibwas and Mississagas to come to his aid. No
doubt there was good cause for alarm; yet if the dangerous
strangers had resolved to strike, they would have been apt
to strike at once, instead of waiting week after week, when
they knew that the friends and allies of the French might
arrive at any time. Dubuisson, however, felt that the situation was extremely critical, and he was confirmed in his

[4] This paper is printed, not very accurately, in the *Collection de
Documents relatifs à la Nouvelle France*, i. 623 (Québec, 1883).

anxiety by a friendly Outagamie, who, after the news of the massacre on the St. Joseph, told him that his tribesmen meant to burn the fort.

The church was outside the palisade, as were also several houses, one of which was stored with wheat. This the Outagamies tried to seize. The French fired on them, drove them back, and brought most of the wheat into the fort; then they demolished the church and several of the houses, which would have given cover to the assailants and enabled them to set fire to the palisade, close to which the buildings stood. The French worked at their task in the excitement of desperation, for they thought that all was lost.

The irritation of their savage neighbors so increased that an outbreak seemed imminent, when, on the thirteenth of May, the Sieur de Vincennes arrived, with seven or eight Frenchmen, from the Miami country. The reinforcement was so small that instead of proving a help it might have provoked a crisis. Vincennes brought no news of the Indian allies, who were now Dubuisson's only hope. "I did not know on what saint to call," he writes, almost in despair, when suddenly a Huron Indian came panting into the fort with the joyful news that both his people and the Ottawas were close at hand. Nor was this all. The Huron messenger announced that Makisabie, war-chief of the Pottawattamies, was then at the Huron fort, and that six hundred warriors of various tribes, deadly enemies of the Outagamies and Mascoutins, would soon arrive and destroy them all.

Here was an unlooked-for deliverance. Yet the danger was not over; for there was fear lest the Outagamies and their allies, hearing of the approaching succor, might make a desperate onslaught, burn the French fort, and kill its inmates before their friends could reach them. An interval of suspense followed, relieved at last by a French sentinel, who called to Dubuisson that a crowd of Indians was in sight. The commandant mounted to the top of a blockhouse, and, looking across the meadows behind the fort, saw a throng of savages coming out of the woods,—Pottawattamies, Sacs, Menominies, Illinois, Missouris, and other tribes yet more remote, each band distinguished by a kind of ensign. These were the six hundred warriors promised by the Huron messenger, and with them, as it proved, came the Ottawa war-chief Saguina. Having heard during the winter that the Outagamies and Mascoutins would go to Detroit in the spring, these various tribes had combined to attack the common enemy; and they now marched with great ostentation and some show of order, not to the French fort, but to the fortified village of the Hurons, who with their neighbors, the Ottawas, had arrived just before them.

The Hurons were reputed leaders among the western tribes, and they hated the Outagamies, not only by reason of bitter wrongs, but also through jealousy of the growing importance which these fierce upstarts had won by their sanguinary prowess. The Huron chiefs came to meet the motley crew of warriors, and urged them to instant action. "You must not stop to encamp," said the Huron spokesman; "we must all go this moment to the fort of our fathers, the French, and fight for them." Then, turning to the Ottawa war-chief: "Do you see that smoke, Saguina, rising from the camp of our enemies? They are burning three women of your village, and your wife is one of them." The Outagamies had, in fact, three Ottawa squaws in their clutches; but the burning was an invention of the crafty Huron. It answered its purpose, and wrought the hearers to fury. They ran with yells and whoops towards the French fort, the Hurons and Ottawas leading the way. A burst of answering yells rose from the camp of the enemy, and about forty of their warriors ran out in bravado, stripped naked and brandishing their weapons; but they soon fell back within their defences before the approaching multitude.

Just before the arrival of the six hundred allies, Dubuisson, whose orders were to keep the peace, if he could, among the western tribes, had sent Vincennes to the Huron village with a proposal that they should spare the lives of the Outagamies and Mascoutins, and rest content with driving them away; to which the Hurons returned a fierce and haughty refusal. There was danger that, if vexed or thwarted, the rabble of excited savages now gathered before the fort might turn from friends into enemies, and in some burst of wild caprice lift parricidal tomahawks against their French fathers. Dubuisson saw no choice but to humor them, put himself at their head, aid them in their vengeance, and even set them on. Therefore, when they called out for admittance, he did not venture to refuse it, but threw open the gate.

The savage crew poured in till the fort was full. The chiefs gathered for council on the parade, and the warriors crowded around, a living wall of dusky forms, befeathered heads, savage faces, lank snaky locks, and deep-set eyes that glittered with a devilish light. Their orator spoke briefly, but to the purpose. He declared that all present were ready to die for their French father, who had stood their friend against the bloody and perfidious Outagamies. Then he begged for food, tobacco, gunpowder, and bullets. Dubuisson replied with equal conciseness, thanked them for their willingness to die for him, said that he would do his best to supply their wants, and promised an immediate distribution of powder and bullets; to which the whole assembly answered with yells of joy.

The council dissolved, and the elder warriors stalked about the fort, haranguing their followers, exhorting them to fight like men and obey the orders of their father. The powder and bullets were served out, after which the whole body, white men and red, yelled the war-whoop together,—"a horrible cry, that made the earth tremble," writes Dubuisson.[5] An answering howl, furious and defiant, rose close at hand from the palisaded camp of the enemy, the firing began on both sides, and bullets and arrows filled the air.

The French and their allies outnumbered their enemies fourfold, while the Outagamie and Mascoutin warriors were encumbered with more than seven hundred women and children. Their frail defences might have been carried by assault; but the loss to the assailants must needs have been great against so brave and desperate a foe, and such a mode of attack is repugnant to the Indian genius. Instead, therefore, of storming the palisaded camp, the allies beleaguered it with vindictive patience, and wore out its defenders by a fire that ceased neither day nor night. The French raised two tall scaffolds, from which they overlooked the palisade, and sent their shot into the midst of those within, who were forced, for shelter, to dig holes in the ground four or five feet deep, and ensconce themselves there. The situation was almost hopeless, but their courage did not fail. They raised twelve red English blankets on poles as battle-flags, to show that they would fight to the death, and hung others over their palisades, calling out that they wished to see the whole earth red, like them, with blood; that they had no fathers but the English, and that the other tribes had better do as they did, and turn their backs to Onontio.

[5] "Cri horrible, dont la terre trembla."—*Dubuisson à Vaudreuil,* 15 *Juin,* 1712. This is the official report of the affair.

The great war-chief of the Pottawattamies now mounted to the top of one of the French scaffolds, and harangued the enemy to this effect: "Do you think, you wretches, that you can frighten us by hanging out those red blankets? If the earth is red with blood, it will be your own. You talk about the English. Their bad advice will be your ruin. They are enemies of religion, and that is why the Master of Life punishes both them and you. They are cowards, and can only defend themselves by poisoning people with their firewater, which kills a man the instant he drinks it. We shall soon see what you will get for listening to them."

This Homeric dialogue between the chief combatants was stopped by Dubuisson, who saw that it distracted the attention of the warriors, and so enabled the besieged to run to the adjacent river for water. The firing was resumed more fiercely than ever. Before night twelve of the Indian allies were killed in the French fort, though the enemy suffered a much greater loss. One house had been left standing outside the French palisades, and the Outagamies raised a scaffold behind its bullet-proof gable, under cover of which they fired with great effect. The French at length brought two swivels to bear upon the gable, pierced it, knocked down the scaffold, killed some of the marksmen, and scattered the rest in consternation.

Famine and thirst were worse for the besieged than the bullets and arrows of the allies. Parched, starved, and fainting, they could no longer find heart for bravado, and they called out one evening from behind their defences to ask Dubuisson if they might come to speak with him. He called together the allied chiefs, and all agreed that here was an opportunity to get out of the hands of the Outagamies the three Ottawa women whom they held prisoners. The commandant, therefore, told them that if they had anything to say to their father before dying, they might come and say it in safety.

In the morning all the red blankets had disappeared, and a white flag was waving over the hostile camp. The great Outagamie chief, Pemoussa, presently came out, carrying a smaller white flag and followed by two Indian slaves. Dubuisson sent his interpreter to protect him from insult and conduct him to the parade, where all the allied chiefs presently met to hear him.

"My father," he began, "I am a dead man. The sky is

bright for you, and dark as night for me." Then he held out a belt of wampum, and continued: "By this belt I ask you, my father, to take pity on your children, and grant us two days in which our old men may counsel together to find means of appeasing your wrath." Then, offering another belt to the assembled chiefs, "This belt is to pray you to remember that you are of our kin. If you spill our blood, do not forget that it is also your own. Try to soften the heart of our father, whom we have offended so often. These two slaves are to replace some of the blood you have lost. Grant us the two days we ask, for I cannot say more till our old men have held counsel."

To which Dubuisson answered in the name of all: "If your hearts were really changed, and you honestly accepted Onontio as your father, you would have brought back the three women who are prisoners in your hands. As you have not done so, I think that your hearts are still bad. First bring them to me, if you expect me to hear you. I have no more to say."

"I am but a child," replied the envoy. "I will go back to my village, and tell our old men what you have said."

The council then broke up, and several Frenchmen conducted the chief back to his followers.

Three other chiefs soon after appeared, bearing a flag and bringing the Ottawa squaws, one of whom was the wife of the war-chief, Saguina. Again the elders met in council on the parade, and the orator of the deputation spoke thus: "My father, here are the three pieces of flesh that you ask of us. We would not eat them, lest you should be angry. Do with them what you please, for you are the master. Now we ask that you will send away the nations that are with you, so that we may seek food for our women and children, who die of hunger every day. If you are as good a father as your other children say you are, you will not refuse us this favor."

But Dubuisson, having gained his point and recovered the squaws, spoke to them sternly, and referred them to his Indian allies for their answer. Whereupon the head chief of the Illinois, being called upon by the rest to speak in their behalf, addressed the envoys to this effect: "Listen to me, you who have troubled all the earth. We see plainly that you mean only to deceive our father. If we should leave him, as you wish, you would fall upon him and kill him. You are dogs who have always bitten him. You thought that we did not know all the messages you have had from the English, telling you to cut our father's throat, and then bring them into this our country. We will not leave him alone with you. We shall see who will be the master. Go back to your fort. We are going to fire at you again."

The envoys went back with a French escort to prevent their being murdered on the way, and then the firing began again. The Outagamies and Mascoutins gathered strength from desperation, and sent flights of fire-arrows into the fort to burn the straw-thatched houses. The flames caught in many places; but with the help of the Indians they were extinguished, though several Frenchmen were wounded, and there was great fright for a time. But the thatch was soon stripped off and the roofs covered with deer and bear skins, while mops fastened to long poles, and two large wooden canoes filled with water, were made ready for future need.

A few days after, a greater peril threatened the French. If the wild Indian has the passions of a devil, he has also the instability of a child; and this is especially true when a number of incoherent tribes or bands are joined in a common enterprise. Dubuisson's Indians became discouraged, partly at the stubborn resistance of the enemy, and partly at the scarcity of food. Some of them declared openly that they could never conquer those people; that they knew them well, and that they were braver than anybody else. In short, the French saw themselves on the point of being abandoned by their allies to a fate the most ghastly and appalling; and they urged upon the commandant the necessity of escaping to Michilimackinac before it was too late. Dubuisson appears to have met the crisis with equal resolution and address. He braced the shaken nerves of his white followers by appeals to their sense of shame, threats of the governor's wrath, and assurances that all would yet be well; then set himself to the more difficult task of holding the Indian allies to their work. He says that he scarcely ate or slept for four days and nights, during which time he was busied without ceasing in private and separate interviews with all the young war-chiefs, persuading them, flattering them, and stripping himself of all he had to make them presents. When at last he had gained them over, he called the tribes to a general council.

"What, children!" thus he addressed them, "when you are

on the very point of destroying these wicked people, do you think of shamefully running away? How could you ever hold up your heads again? All the other nations would say: 'Are these the brave warriors who deserted the French and ran like cowards?'" And he reminded them that their enemies were already half dead with famine, and that they could easily make an end of them, thereby gaining great honor among the nations, besides the thanks and favors of Onontio, the father of all.

At this the young war-chiefs whom he had gained over interrupted him and cried out, "My father, somebody has been lying to you. We are not cowards. We love you too much to abandon you, and we will stand by you till the last of your enemies is dead." The elder men caught the contagion, and cried, "Come on, let us show our father that those who have spoken ill of us are liars." Then they all raised the war-whoop, sang the war-song, danced the war-dance, and began to fire again.

Among the enemy were some Sakis, or Sacs, fighting for the Outagamies, while others of their tribe were among the allies of the French. Seeing the desperate turn of affairs, they escaped from time to time and came over to the winning side, bringing reports of the state of the beleaguered camp. They declared that sixty or eighty women and children were already dead from hunger and thirst, besides those killed by bullets and arrows; that the fire of the besiegers was so hot that the bodies could not be buried, and that the camp of the Outagamies and Mascoutins was a den of infection.

The end was near. The besieged savages called from their palisades to ask if they might send another deputation, and were told that they were free to do so. The chief, Pemoussa, soon appeared at the gate of the fort, naked, painted from head to foot with green earth, wearing belts of wampum about his waist, and others hanging from his shoulders, besides a kind of crown of wampum beads on his head. With him came seven women, meant as a peace-offering, all painted and adorned with wampum. Three other principal chiefs followed, each with a gourd rattle in his hand, to the cadence of which the whole party sang and shouted at the full stretch of their lungs an invocation to the spirits for help and pity. They were conducted to the parade, where the French and the allied chiefs were already assembled, and Pemoussa thus addressed them:—

"My father, and all the nations here present, I come to ask for life. It is no longer ours, but yours. I bring you these seven women, who are my flesh, and whom I put at your feet, to be your slaves. But do not think that I am afraid to die; it is the life of our women and children that I ask of you." He then offered six wampum belts, in token that his followers owned themselves beaten, and begged for mercy. "Tell us, I pray you,"—these were his last words,—"something that will lighten the hearts of my people when I go back to them."

Dubuisson left the answer to his allies. The appeal of the suppliant fell on hearts of stone. The whole concourse sat in fierce and sullen silence, and the envoys read their doom in the gloomy brows that surrounded them. Eight or ten of the allied savages presently came to Dubuisson, and one of them said in a low voice: "My father, we come to ask your leave to knock these four great chiefs in the head. It is they who prevent our enemies from surrendering without conditions. When they are dead, the rest will be at our mercy."

Dubuisson told them that they must be drunk to propose such a thing. "Remember," he said, "that both you and I have given our word for their safety. If I consented to what you ask, your father at Montreal would never forgive me. Besides, you can see plainly that they and their people cannot escape you."

The would-be murderers consented to bide their time, and the wretched envoys went back with their tidings of despair.

"I confess," wrote Dubuisson to the governor, a few days later, "that I was touched with compassion; but as war and pity do not agree well together, and especially as I understood that they were hired by the English to destroy us, I abandoned them to their fate."

The firing began once more, and the allied hordes howled round the camp of their victims like troops of ravenous wolves. But a surprise awaited them. Indians rarely set guards at night, and they felt sure now of their prey. It was the nineteenth day of the siege.[6] The night closed dark and rainy, and when morning came, the enemy were gone. All among them that had strength to move had glided away through the gloom with the silence of shadows, passed the camps of their sleeping enemies, and reached a point of land projecting into the river opposite the end of Isle au Cochon, and a few miles

[6] According to the paper ascribed to Léry it was only the eighth.

above the French fort. Here, knowing that they would be pursued, they barricaded themselves with trunks and branches of trees. When the astonished allies discovered their escape, they hastily followed their trail, accompanied by some of the French, led by Vincennes. In their eagerness they ran upon the barricade before seeing it, and were met by a fire that killed and wounded twenty of them. There was no alternative but to forego their revenge and abandon the field, or begin another siege. Encouraged by Dubuisson, they built their wigwams on the new scene of operations; and, being supplied by the French with axes, mattocks, and two swivels, they made a wall of logs opposite the barricade, from which they galled the defenders with a close and deadly fire. The Mississagas and Ojibwas, who had lately arrived, fished and hunted for the allies, while the French furnished them with powder, ball, tobacco, Indian corn, and kettles. The enemy fought desperately for four days, and then, in utter exhaustion, surrendered at discretion.[7]

The women and children were divided among the victorious hordes, and adopted or enslaved. To the men no quarter was given. "Our Indians amused themselves," writes Dubuisson, "with shooting four or five of them every day." Here, however, another surprise awaited the conquerors and abridged their recreation, for about a hundred of these intrepid warriors contrived to make their escape, and among them was the great war-chief Pemoussa.

The Outagamies were crippled, but not disabled, for but a part of the tribe was involved in this bloody affair. The rest were wrought to fury by the fate of their kinsmen, and for many years they remained thorns in the sides of the French.

There is a disposition to assume that events like that just recounted were a consequence of the contact of white men with red; but the primitive Indian was quite able to enact such tragedies without the help of Europeans. Before French or English influence had been felt in the interior of the continent, a great part of North America was the frequent witness of scenes still more lurid in coloring, and on a larger

---

[7] The paper ascribed to Léry says that they surrendered on a promise from Vincennes that their lives should be spared, but that the promise availed nothing.

scale of horror. In the first half of the seventeenth century the whole country, from Lake Superior to the Tennessee, and from the Alleghanies to the Mississippi, was ravaged by wars of extermination, in which tribes, large and powerful by Indian standards, perished, dwindled into feeble remnants, or were absorbed by other tribes and vanished from sight. French pioneers were sometimes involved in the carnage, but neither they nor other Europeans were answerable for it.[8]

[8] *Dubuisson à Vaudreuil, 15 Juin, 1712.* This is Dubuisson's report to the governor, which soon after the event he sent to Montreal by the hands of Vincennes. He says that the great fatigue through which he has just passed prevents him from giving every detail, and he refers Vaudreuil to the bearer for further information. The report is, however, long and circumstantial.

État de ce que M. Dubuisson a dépensé pour le service du Roy pour s'attirer les Nations et les mettre dans ses intérêts afin de résister aux Autagamis et aux Mascoutins qui étaient payés des Anglais pour détruire le poste du Fort de Ponchartrain du Détroit, 14 Octobre, 1712. Dubuisson reckons his outlay at 2,901 livres.

These documents, with the narrative ascribed to the engineer Léry, are the contemporary authorities on which the foregoing account is based.

Chapter 13

1697–1750
Louisiana

AT THE BEGINNING of the eighteenth century an event took place that was to have a great influence on the future of French America. This was the occupation by France of the mouth of the Mississippi, and the vindication of her claim to the vast and undefined regions which La Salle had called Louisiana. La Salle's schemes had come to nought, but they were revived, seven years after his death, by his lieutenant, the gallant and faithful Henri de Tonty, who urged the seizure of Louisiana for three reasons,—first, as a base of attack upon Mexico; secondly, as a dépôt for the furs and lead ore of the interior; and thirdly, as the only means of preventing the English from becoming masters of the West.[1]

Three years later, the Sieur de Rémonville, a friend of La Salle, proposed the formation of a company for the settlement of Louisiana, and called for immediate action as indispensable to anticipate the English.[2] The English were, in fact, on the point of taking possession of the mouth of the Mississippi, and were prevented only by the prompt intervention of the rival nation.

If they had succeeded, colonies would have grown up on the Gulf of Mexico after the type of those already planted along the Atlantic: voluntary immigrants would have brought to a new home their old inheritance of English freedom; would have ruled themselves by laws of their own making, through magistrates of their own choice; would have depended on their own efforts, and not on government help, in the invigorating consciousness that their destinies were in their own hands, and that they themselves, and not others, were to

[1] *Henri de Tonty à Cabart de Villermont*, 11 Septembre, 1694 (Margry, iv. 3).

[2] *Mémoire sur le Projet d'establir une nouvelle Colonie au Mississippi*, 1697 (Margry, iv. 21).

gather the fruits of their toils. Out of conditions like these would have sprung communities, not brilliant, but healthy, orderly, well rooted in the soil, and of hardy and vigorous growth.

But the principles of absolutism, and not those of a regulated liberty, were to rule in Louisiana. The new French colony was to be the child of the Crown. Cargoes of emigrants, willing or unwilling, were to be shipped by authority to the fever-stricken banks of the Mississippi,—cargoes made up in part of those whom fortune and their own defects had sunk to dependence; to whom labor was strange and odious, but who dreamed of gold mines and pearl fisheries, and wealth to be won in the New World and spent in the Old; who wore the shackles of a paternal despotism which they were told to regard as of divine institution; who were at the mercy of military rulers set over them by the King, and agreeing in nothing except in enforcing the mandates of arbitrary power and the withering maxim that the labor of the colonist was due, not to himself, but to his masters. It remains to trace briefly the results of such conditions.

The before-mentioned scheme of Rémonville for settling the Mississippi country had no result. In the next year the gallant Le Moyne d'Iberville—who has been called the Cid, or, more fitly, the Jean Bart, of Canada—offered to carry out the schemes of La Salle and plant a colony in Louisiana.[3] One thing had become clear,—France must act at once, or lose the Mississippi. Already there was a movement in London to seize upon it, under a grant to two noblemen. Iberville's offer was accepted; he was ordered to build a fort at the mouth of the great river, and leave a garrison to hold it.[4] He sailed with two frigates, the "Badine" and the "Marin," and towards the end of January, 1699, reached Pensacola. Here he found two Spanish ships, which would not let him enter the harbor. Spain, no less than England, was bent on making good her claim to the Mississippi and the Gulf of Mexico, and the two ships had come from Vera Cruz on this errand. Three hundred men had been landed, and a stockade fort was already built. Iberville left the Spaniards undisturbed and unchallenged, and felt his way westward along the coasts

---

[3] *Iberville au Ministre*, 18 *Juin*, 1698 (Margry, iv. 51).

[4] *Mémoire pour servir d'Instruction au Sieur d'Iberville* (Margry, iv. 72).

of Alabama and Mississippi, exploring and sounding as he went. At the beginning of March his boats were caught in a strong muddy current of fresh water, and he saw that he had reached the object of his search, the "fatal river" of the unfortunate La Salle. He entered it, encamped, on the night of the third, twelve leagues above its mouth, climbed a solitary tree, and could see nothing but broad flats of bushes and canebrakes.[5]

Still pushing upward against the current, he reached in eleven days a village of the Bayagoula Indians, where he found the chief attired in a blue capote, which was probably put on in honor of the white strangers, and which, as the wearer declared, had been given him by Henri de Tonty, on his descent of the Mississippi in search of La Salle, thirteen years before. Young Le Moyne de Bienville, who accompanied his brother Iberville in a canoe, brought him, some time after, a letter from Tonty which the writer had left in the hands of another chief, to be delivered to La Salle in case of his arrival, and which Bienville had bought for a hatchet. Iberville welcomed it as convincing proof that the river he had entered was in truth the Mississippi.[6] After pushing up the stream till the twenty-fourth, he returned to the ships by way of lakes Maurepas and Ponchartrain.

Iberville now repaired to the harbor of Biloxi, on the coast of the present State of Mississippi. Here he built a small stockade fort, where he left eighty men, under the Sieur de Sauvolle, to hold the country for Louis XIV.; and this done, he sailed for France. Thus the first foundations of Louisiana were laid in Mississippi.

Bienville, whom his brother had left at Biloxi as second in command, was sent by Sauvolle on an exploring expedition up the Mississippi with five men in two canoes. At the bend of the river now called English Turn,—*Tour à l'Anglais*,—below the site of New Orleans, he found an English corvette of ten

[5] *Journal d'Iberville* (Margry, iv. 131).

[6] This letter, which D'Iberville gives in his Journal, is dated "Du Village des Quinipissas, le 20 Avril, 1685." Iberville identifies the Quinipissas with the Bayagoulas. The date of the letter was evidently misread, as Tonty's journey was in 1686. See "La Salle and the Discovery of the Great West," 455, *note*. Iberville's lieutenant, Sugères, commanding the "Marin," gives the date correctly. *Journal de la Frégate le Marin*, 1698, 1699 (Margry, iv.).

guns, having, as passengers, a number of French Protestant families taken on board from the Carolinas, with the intention of settling on the Mississippi. The commander, Captain Louis Bank, declared that his vessel was one of three sent from London by a company formed jointly of Englishmen and Huguenot refugees for the purpose of founding a colony.[7] Though not quite sure that they were upon the Mississippi, they were on their way up the stream to join a party of Englishmen said to be among the Chickasaws, with whom they were trading for Indian slaves. Bienville assured Bank that he was not upon the Mississippi, but on another river belonging to King Louis, who had a strong fort there and several settlements. "The too-credulous Englishman," says a French writer, "believed these inventions and turned back."[8] First, however, a French engineer in the service of Bank contrived to have an interview with Bienville, and gave him a petition to the King of France, signed by four hundred Huguenots who had taken refuge in the Carolinas after the revocation of the Edict of Nantes. The petitioners begged that they might have leave to settle in Louisiana, with liberty of conscience, under the French Crown. In due time they got their answer. The King replied, through the minister, Ponchartrain, that he had not expelled heretics from France in order that they should set up a republic in America.[9] Thus, by the bigotry that had been the bane of Canada and of France herself, Louis XIV. threw away the opportunity of establishing a firm and healthy colony at the mouth of the Mississippi.

[7] *Journal du Voyage du Chevalier d'Iberville sur le Vaisseau du Roy la Renommée en* 1699 (Margry, iv. 395).

[8] Gayarré, *Histoire de la Louisiane* (1846), i. 69. Bénard de la Harpe, *Journal historique* (1831), 20. Coxe says, in the preface to his *Description of Carolana* (1722), that "the present proprietor of Carolana, my honour'd Father, . . . was the author of this English voyage to the Mississippi, having in the year 1698 equipp'd and fitted out Two Ships for Discovery by Sea, and also for building a Fortification and settling a Colony by land; there being in both vessels, besides Sailors and Common Men, above Thirty English and French Volunteers." Coxe adds that the expedition would have succeeded if one of the commanders had not failed to do his duty.

[9] Cayarré, *Histoire de la Louisiane* (1846), i. 69.

So threatening was the danger that England would seize the country, that Iberville had scarcely landed in France when he was sent back with a reinforcement. The colonial views of the King may be gathered from his instructions to his officer. Iberville was told to seek out diligently the best places for establishing pearl-fisheries, though it was admitted that the pearls of Louisiana were uncommonly bad. He was also to catch bison calves, make a fenced park to hold them, and tame them for the sake of their wool, which was reputed to be of value for various fabrics. Above all, he was to look for mines, the finding of which the document declares to be "la grande affaire."[10]

On the eighth of January, Iberville reached Biloxi, and soon after went up the Mississippi to that remarkable tribe of sun-worshippers, the Natchez, whose villages were on and near the site of the city that now bears their name. Some thirty miles above he found a kindred tribe, the Taensas, whose temple took fire during his visit, when, to his horror, he saw five living infants thrown into the flames by their mothers to appease the angry spirits.[11]

Retracing his course, he built a wooden redoubt near one of the mouths of the Mississippi to keep out the dreaded English.

In the next year he made a third voyage, and ordered the feeble establishment at Biloxi to be moved to the bay of Mobile. This drew a protest from the Spaniards, who rested their claims to the country on the famous bull of Pope Alexander VI. The question was referred to the two Crowns. Louis XIV., a stanch champion of the papacy when his duties as a Catholic did not clash with his interests as a king, refused submission to the bull, insisted that the Louisiana country was his, and declared that he would hold fast to it because he was bound, as a son of Holy Church, to convert the Indians and keep out the English heretics.[12] Spain was then at peace with France, and her new King, the Duc d'Anjou, grandson of Louis XIV., needed the support of his

[10] *Mémoire pour servir d'Instruction au Sieur d'Iberville* (Margry, iv. 348).

[11] *Journal du Voyage du Chevalier d'Iberville sur le Vaisseau du Roy la Renommée,* 1699, 1700.

[12] *Mémoire de la Junte de Guerre des Indes. Le Ministre de la Marine au Duc d'Harcourt* (Margry, iv. 553, 568).

powerful kinsman; hence his remonstrance against French encroachment was of the mildest.[13]

Besides Biloxi and Mobile Bay, the French formed a third establishment at Dauphin Island. The Mississippi itself, which may be called the vital organ of the colony, was thus far neglected, being occupied by no settlement and guarded only by a redoubt near one of its mouths.

Of the emigrants sent out by the court to the new land of promise, the most valuable by far were a number of Canadians who had served under Iberville at Hudson Bay. The rest were largely of the sort who are described by that officer as "beggars sent out to enrich themselves," and who expected the government to feed them while they looked for pearls and gold mines. The parternal providence of Versailles, mindful of their needs, sent them, in 1704, a gift of twenty marriageable girls, described as "nurtured in virtue and piety, and accustomed to work." Twenty-three more came in the next year from the same benignant source, besides seventy-five soldiers, five priests, and two nuns. Food, however, was not sent in proportion to the consumers; and as no crops were raised in Louisiana, famine and pestilence followed, till the starving colonists were forced to live on shell-fish picked up along the shores.

Disorder and discord filled the land of promise. Nicolas de la Salle, the *commissaire ordonnateur*, an official answering to the Canadian intendant, wrote to the minister Ponchartrain that Iberville and his brothers, Bienville and Chateauguay, were "thieves and knaves."[14] La Vente, curé of Mobile, joined in the cry against Bienville, and stirred soldiers and settlers to disaffection; but the bitterest accuser of that truly valuable officer was the worthy matron who held the unenviable post of directress of the "King's girls,"—that is, the young women sent out as wives for the colonists. It seems that she had matrimonial views for herself as well as for her charge; and she wrote to Ponchartrain that Major Boisbriant, commander of the garrison, would certainly have married her if Bienville

[13] Iberville wrote in 1701 a long memorial, in which he tried to convince the Spanish court that it was for the interest of Spain that the French should form a barrier between her colonies and those of England, which, he says, were about to seize the country as far as the Mississippi and beyond it.

[14] *Nicolas de la Salle au Ministre, 7 Septembre,* 1706.

had not interfered and dissuaded him. "It is clear," she adds, "that M. de Bienville has not the qualities necessary for governing the colony."[15]

Bienville was now chief in authority. Charges of peculation and other offences poured in against him, and at last, though nothing was proved, one De Muys was sent to succeed him, with orders to send him home a prisoner if on examination the accusations should prove to be true. De Muys died on the voyage. D'Artaguette, the new intendant, proceeded to make the inquiry, but refused to tell Bienville the nature of the charges against him, saying that he had orders not to do so. Nevertheless, when he had finished his investigation he reported to the minister that the accused was innocent; on which Nicolas de la Salle, whom he had supplanted as intendant, wrote to Ponchartrain that D'Artaguette had deceived him, being no better than Bienville himself. La Salle further declared that Barrot, the surgeon of the colony, was an ignoramus, and that he made money by selling the medicines supplied by the King to cure his Louisianian subjects. Such were the transatlantic workings of the paternalism of Versailles.

Bienville, who had been permitted to resume his authority, paints the state of the colony to his masters, and tells them that the inhabitants are dying of hunger,—not all, however, for he mentions a few exceptional cases of prosperity. These were certain thrifty colonists from Rochelle, who, says Bienville, have grown rich by keeping dram-shops, and now want to go back to France; but he has set a watch over them, thinking it just that they should be forced to stay in the colony.[16] This was to add the bars of a prison to the other attractions of the new home.

As the colonists would not work, there was an attempt to make Indian slaves work for them; but as these continually ran off, Bienville proposed to open a barter with the French West Indies, giving three red slaves for two black ones,—an exchange which he thought would be mutually advantageous, since the Indians, being upon islands, could no longer escape. The court disapproved the plan, on the ground that the West

[15] "Il est clair que M. de Bienville n'a pas les qualités nécessaires pour bien gouverner la colonie." Gayarré found this curious letter in the Archives de la Marine.

[16] *Dépêche de Bienville,* 12 *Octobre,* 1708.

Indians would give only their worst negroes in exchange, and that the only way to get good ones was to fetch them from Guinea.

Complaints against Bienville were renewed till the court sent out La Mothe-Cadillac to succeed him, with orders to examine the charges against his predecessor, whom it was his interest to condemn, in order to keep the governorship. In his new post, Cadillac displayed all his old faults; began by denouncing the country in unmeasured terms, and wrote in his usual sarcastic vein to the colonial minister: "I have seen the garden on Dauphin Island, which had been described to me as a terrestrial paradise. I saw there three seedling pear-trees, three seedling apple-trees, a little plum-tree about three feet high, with seven bad plums on it, a vine some thirty feet long, with nine bunches of grapes, some of them withered or rotten and some partly ripe, about forty plants of French melons, and a few pumpkins. This is M. d'Artaguette's terrestrial paradise, M. de Rémonville's Pomona, and M. de Mandeville's Fortunate Islands. Their stories are mere fables." Then he slanders the soil, which, he declares, will produce neither grain nor vegetables.

D'Artaguette, no longer fancying himself in Eden, draws a dismal picture of the state of the colony. There are, he writes, only ten or twelve families who cultivate the soil. The inhabitants, naturally lazy, are ruined by the extravagance of their wives. "It is necessary to send out girls and laboring-men. I am convinced that we shall easily discover mines when persons are sent us who understand that business."[17]

The colonists felt no confidence in the future of Louisiana. The King was its sole support, and if, as was likely enough, he should tire of it, their case would be deplorable. When Bienville ruled over them, they had used him as their scapegoat; but that which made the colony languish was not he, but the vicious system it was his business to enforce. The royal edicts and arbitrary commands that took the place of law proceeded from masters thousands of miles away, who knew nothing of the country, could not understand its needs, and scarcely tried to do so.

In 1711, though the mischievous phantom of gold and

[17] D'Artaguette in Gayarré, *Histoire de la Louisiane.* This valuable work consists of a series of documents, connected by a thread of narrative.

silver mines still haunted the colony, we find it reported that the people were beginning to work, and were planting tobacco. The King, however, was losing patience with a dependency that cost him endless expense and trouble, and brought little or nothing in return,—and this at a time when he had a costly and disastrous war on his hands, and was in no mood to bear supernumerary burdens. The plan of giving over a colony to a merchant, or a company of merchants, was not new. It had been tried in other French colonies with disastrous effect. Yet it was now tried again. Louisiana was farmed out for fifteen years to Antoine Crozat, a wealthy man of business. The countries made over to him extended from the British colonies on the east to New Mexico on the west, and the Rio del Norte on the south, including the entire region watered by the Mississippi, the Missouri, the Ohio, and their tributaries, as far north as the Illinois. In comparison with this immense domain, which was all included under the name of Louisiana, the present State so called is but a small patch on the American map.

To Crozat was granted a monopoly of the trade, wholesale and retail, domestic and foreign, of all these countries, besides the product of all mines, after deducting one-fourth reserved for the King. He was empowered to send one vessel a year to Guinea for a cargo of slaves. The King was to pay the governor and other Crown officers, and during the first nine years the troops also; though after that time Crozat was to maintain them till the end of his term.

In consideration of these and other privileges, the grantee was bound to send to Louisiana a specified number of settlers every year. His charter provided that the royal edicts and the *Coutume de Paris* should be the law of the colony, to be administered by a council appointed by the King.

When Louisiana was thus handed over to a speculator for a term of years, it needed no prophet to foretell that he would get all he could out of it, and put as little into it as possible. When Crozat took possession of the colony, the French court had been thirteen years at work in building it up. The result of its labors was a total population, including troops, government officials, and clergy, of 380 souls, of whom 170 were in the King's pay. Only a few of the colonists were within the limits of the present Louisiana. The rest lived in or around the feeble stockade forts at Mobile, Biloxi, Ship Island, and

Dauphin Island. This last station had been partially abandoned; but some of the colonists proposed to return to it, in order to live by fishing, and only waited, we are told, for help from the King. This incessant dependence on government relaxed the fibres of the colony and sapped its life-blood.

The King was now exchanged for Crozat and his grinding monopoly. The colonists had carried on a modest trade with the Spaniards at Pensacola in skins, fowls, Indian corn, and a few other articles, bringing back a little money in return. This, their only source of profit, was now cut off; they could sell nothing, even to one another. They were forbidden to hold meetings without permission; but some of them secretly drew up a petition to La Mothe-Cadillac, who was still the official chief of the colony, begging that the agents of Crozat should be restricted to wholesale dealings, and that the inhabitants might be allowed to trade at retail. Cadillac denounced the petition as seditious, threatened to hang the bearer of it, and deigned no other answer.

He resumed his sarcasms against the colony. "In my opinion this country is not worth a straw (*ne vaut pas un fétu*). The inhabitants are eager to be taken out of it. The soldiers are always grumbling, and with reason." As to the council, which was to be the only court of justice, he says that no such thing is possible, because there are no proper persons to compose it; and though Duclos, the new intendant, has proposed two candidates, the first of these, the Sieur de Lafresnière, learned to sign his name only four months ago, and the other, being chief surgeon of the colony, is too busy to serve.[18]

Between Bienville, the late governor, and La Mothe-Cadillac, who had supplanted him, there was a standing quarrel; and the colony was split into hostile factions, led by the two disputants. The minister at Versailles was beset by their mutual accusations, and Bienville wrote that his refusal to marry Cadillac's daughter was the cause of the spite the governor bore him.[19]

The indefatigable curé De la Vente sent to Ponchartrain a memorial, in the preamble of which he says that since Mon-

[18] *La Mothe-Cadillac au Ministre,* in Gayarré, i. 104, 105.
[19] "Que si M. de Lamothe-Cadillac lui portoit tant d'animosité, c'étoit à cause du refus qu'il avoit fait d'épouser sa fille."—*Bienville in Gayarré,* i. 116.

sieur le Ministre wishes to be informed exactly of the state of things in Louisiana, he, La Vente, has the honor, with malice to nobody, to make known the pure truth; after which he goes on to say that the inhabitants "are nearly all drunkards, gamblers, blasphemers, and enemies of everything good;" and he proceeds to illustrate the statement with many particulars.[20]

As the inhabitants were expected to work for Crozat, and not for themselves, it naturally followed that they would not work at all; and idleness produced the usual results.

The yearly shipment of girls continued; but there was difficulty in finding husbands for them. The reason was not far to seek. Duclos, the intendant, reports the arrival of an invoice of twelve of them, "so ugly that the inhabitants are in no hurry to take them."[21] The Canadians, who formed the most vigorous and valuable part of the population, much preferred Indian squaws. "It seems to me," pursues the intendant, "that in the choice of girls, good looks should be more considered than virtue." This latter requisite seems, at the time, to have found no more attention than the other, since the candidates for matrimony were drawn from the Parisian hospitals and houses of correction, from the former of which Crozat was authorized to take one hundred girls a year, "in order to increase the population." These hospitals were compulsory asylums for the poor and vagrant of both sexes, of whom the great Hôpital Général of Paris contained at one time more than six thousand.[22]

Crozat had built his chief hopes of profit on a trade, contraband or otherwise, with the Mexican ports; but the Spanish officials, faithful instruments of the exclusive policy of their government, would not permit it, and were so vigilant that he could not elude them. At the same time, to his vexation, he found that the King's officers in Louisiana, with more address

[20] *Mémoire du Curé de la Vente,* 1714.

[21] The earlier cargoes of girls seem to have been better chosen, and there was no difficulty in mating them. Serious disputes sometimes rose from the competition of rival suitors.—Dumont, *Mémoires historiques de la Louisiane,* chap. v.

[22] Prominent officials of the colony are said to have got wives from these sources. Nicolas de la Salle is reported to have had two in succession, both from the hospitals. Bénard de la Harpe, 107 (ed. 1831).

or better luck, and in contempt of his monopoly, which it was their business to protect, carried on, for their own profit, a small smuggling trade with Vera Cruz. He complained that they were always thwarting his agents and conspiring against his interests. At last, finding no resource left but an unprofitable trade with the Indians, he gave up his charter, which had been a bane to the colony and a loss to himself. Louisiana returned to the Crown, and was soon passed over to the new Mississippi Company, called also the Western Company.[23]

That charlatan of genius, the Scotchman John Law, had undertaken, with the eager support of the Regent Duke of Orleans, to deliver France from financial ruin through a prodigious system of credit, of which Louisiana, with its imaginary gold mines, was made the basis. The government used every means to keep up the stock of the Mississippi Company. It was ordered that the notes of the royal bank and all certificates of public debt should be accepted at par in payment for its shares. Powers and privileges were lavished on it. It was given the monopoly of the French slave-trade, the monopoly of tobacco, the profits of the royal mint, and the farming of the revenues of the kingdom. Ingots of gold, pretending to have come from the new Eldorado of Louisiana, were displayed in the shop-windows of Paris. The fever of speculation rose to madness, and the shares of the company were inflated to monstrous and insane proportions.

When Crozat resigned his charter, Louisiana, by the highest estimates, contained about seven hundred souls, including soldiers, but not blacks or Indians. Crozat's successors, however, say that the whole number of whites, men, women, and children, was not above four hundred.[24] When the Mississippi Company took the colony in charge, it was but a change of despots. Louisiana was a prison. But while no inhabitant could leave it without permission of the authorities, all Jews were expelled, and all Protestants excluded. The colonists could buy nothing except from the agents of the company, and sell nothing except to the same all-powerful masters, always at prices fixed by them. Foreign vessels were forbidden to enter any port of Louisiana, on pain of confiscation.

[23] *Lettres patentes en forme d' Édit portant établissement de la Compagnie d'Occident,* in Le Page du Pratz, *Histoire de la Louisiane,* i. 47.

[24] *Règlement de Régie,* 1721.

The coin in circulation was nearly all Spanish, and in less than two years the Company, by a series of decrees, made changes of about eighty per cent in its value. Freedom of conscience, freedom of speech, of trade, and of action, were alike denied. Hence voluntary immigration was not to be expected; "but," says the Duc de Saint-Simon, "the government wished to establish effective settlements in these vast countries, after the example of the English; and therefore, in order to people them, vagabonds and beggars, male and female, including many women of the town, were seized for the purpose both in Paris and throughout France."[25] Saint-Simon approves these proceedings in themselves, as tending at once to purge France and people Louisiana, but thinks the business was managed in a way to cause needless exasperation among the lower classes.

In 1720 it was ordered by royal edict that no more vagabonds or criminals should be sent to Louisiana. The edict, it seems, touched only one sex, for in the next year eighty girls were sent to the colony from the Parisian House of Correction called the Salpêtrière. There had been a more or less constant demand for wives, as appears by letters still preserved in the archives of Paris, the following extract from one of which is remarkable for the freedom with which the writer, a M. de Chassin, takes it upon him to address a minister of State in a court where punctilio reigned supreme. "You see, Monseigneur, that nothing is wanting now to make a solid settlement in Louisiana but a certain piece of furniture which one often repents having got, and with which I shall dispense, like the rest, till the Company sends us girls who have at least some show of virtue. If there happens to be any young woman of your acquaintance who wants to make the voyage for love of me, I should be much obliged to her, and would do my best to show her my gratitude."[26]

The Company, which was invested with sovereign powers, began its work by sending to Louisiana three companies of soldiers and sixty-nine colonists. Its wisest act was the removal of the governor, L'Épinay, who had supplanted La Mothe-Cadillac, and the reappointment of Bienville in his place. Bienville immediately sought out a spot for establishing a permanent station on the Mississippi. Fifty men were sent to

[25] Saint-Simon, *Mémoires* (ed. Chéruel), xvii. 461.
[26] *De Chassin au Ministre,* 1 *Juillet,* 1722, in Gayarré, i. 190.

clear the ground, and in spite of an inundation which overflowed it for a time, the feeble foundations of New Orleans were laid. Louisiana, hitherto diffused through various petty cantonments, far and near, had at last a capital, or the germ of one.

It was the sixth of September, 1717, when the charter of the Mississippi Company was entered in the registers of the Parliament of Paris; and from that time forward, before the offices of the Company in the Rue Quincampoix, crowds of crazed speculators jostled and fought from morning till night to get their names inscribed among the stockholders. Within five years after, the huge glittering bubble had burst. The shares, each one of which had seemed a fortune, found no more purchasers, and in its fall the Company dragged down with it its ally and chief creditor, the bank. All was dismay and despair, except in those who had sold out in time, and turned delusive paper into solid values. John Law, lately the idol and reputed savior of France, fled for his life, amid a howl of execration.

Yet the interests of the kingdom required that Louisiana should be sustained. The illusions that had given to the Mississippi Company a morbid and intoxicated vitality were gone, but the Company lingered on, and the government still lent it a helping hand. A French writer remarks that the few Frenchmen who were famishing on the shores of the Mississippi and the Gulf of Mexico had cost the King, since the colony began, more than 150,000 livres a year. The directors of the Company reported that they had shipped 7,020 persons to the colony, besides four hundred already there when they took possession, and that 5,420 still remained, the rest having died or escaped.[27] Besides this importation of whites, they had also brought six hundred slaves from Guinea. It is reckoned that the King, Crozat, and the Mississippi Company had spent among them about eight million livres on Louisiana, without any return.[28]

The bursting of the Mississippi bubble did not change the principles of administration in Louisiana. The settlers, always

[27] A considerable number of the whites brought to Louisiana in the name of the Company had been sent at the charge of persons to whom it had granted lands in various parts of the colony. Among these was John Law himself, who had the grant of large tracts on the Arkansas.

[28] Bénard de la Harpe, 371 (ed. 1831).

looking to France to supply their needs and protect them against their own improvidence, were in the habit of butchering for food the livestock sent them for propagation. The remedy came in the shape of a royal edict forbidding any colonist to kill, without permission of the authorities, any cow, sheep, or lamb belonging to himself, on pain of a fine of three hundred livres; or to kill any horse, cow, or bull belonging to another, on pain of death.

Authority and order were the watchwords, and disorder was the rule. The agents of power quarrelled among themselves, except when they leagued together to deceive their transatlantic masters and cover their own misdeeds. Each maligned the other, and it was scarcely possible for the King or the Company to learn the true state of affairs in their distant colony.

Accusations were renewed against Bienville, till in 1724 he was ordered to France to give account of his conduct, and the Sieur Perier was sent out to take his place. Perier had no easy task. The Natchez Indians, among whom the French had made a settlement and built a fort called Fort Rosalie, suddenly rose on their white neighbors and massacred nearly all of them.[29] Then followed a long course of Indian wars. The French believed that there was a general conspiracy among the southern tribes for their destruction,—though this was evidently an exaggeration of the danger, which, however, was serious. The Chickasaws, a brave and warlike people, living chiefly in what is now western Tennessee and Kentucky, made common cause with the Natchez, while the more numerous Choctaws, most of whose villages were in the present State of Mississippi, took part with the French. More than a thousand soldiers had been sent to Louisiana; but Perier pronounced them "so bad that they seem to have been made on purpose for the colony."[30] There were also about eight hundred militia. Perier showed little vigor, and had little success. His chief resource was to set the tribes against one another. He reports that his Indian allies had brought him a number of Natchez prisoners, and that he had caused six of them, four men and two women, to be burned alive, and had sent the rest as slaves

[29] *Lettre du Père le Petit*, in *Lettres Édifiantes; Dumont, Mémoires historiques*, chap. xxvii.

[30] "Nos soldats, qui semblent être faits exprès pour la colonie, tants ils sont mauvais."—*Dépêche de Perier*, 18 *Mars*, 1730.

to St. Domingo. The Chickasaws, aided by English traders from the Carolinas, proved formidable adversaries, and when attacked, ensconced themselves in stockade forts so strong that, as the governor complains, there was no dislodging the defenders without cannon and heavy mortars.

In this state of things the directors of the Mississippi Company, whose affairs had gone from bad to worse, declared that they could no longer bear the burden of Louisiana, and begged the King to take it off their hands. The colony was therefore transferred from the mercantile despotism of the Company to the paternal despotism of the Crown, and it profited by the change. Commercial monopoly was abolished. Trade between France and Louisiana was not only permitted, but encouraged by bounties and exemption from duties; and instead of paying to the Company two hundred per cent of profit on indispensable supplies, the colonists now got them at a reasonable price.

Perier was removed, and again Bienville was made governor. Diron d'Artaguette, who came with him as intendant, reported that the colonists were flying the country to escape starvation, and Bienville adds that during the past year they had subsisted for three months on the seed of reeds and wild grasses.[31] The white population had rather diminished than increased during the last twelve years, while the blacks, who had lately conspired to massacre all the French along the Mississippi, had multiplied to two thousand.[32] A French writer says: "There must have been a worm gnawing the root of the tree that had been transplanted into so rich a soil, to make it wither instead of growing. What it needed was the air of liberty." But the air of liberty is malaria to those who have not learned to breathe it. The English colonists throve in it because they and their forefathers had been trained in a school of self-control and self-dependence; and what would have been intoxication for others, was vital force to them.

Bienville found the colony again threatened with a general rising, or, as he calls it, a revolt, of the Indian tribes. The Carolina traders, having no advantage of water-ways, had journeyed by land with pack-horses through a thousand miles of wilderness, and with the aid of gifts had instigated the

---

[31] *Mémoire de Bienville*, 1730.

[32] For a curious account of the discovery of this negro plot, see Le Page du Pratz, iii. 304.

tribes to attack the French. The Chickasaws especially, friends of the English and arch-enemies of Louisiana, became so threatening that a crushing blow against them was thought indispensable. The forces of the colony were mustered to attempt it; the enterprise was mismanaged, and failed completely.[33] Bienville tried to explain the disaster, but his explanation was ill received at court; he was severely rebuked, reproved at the same time for permitting two families to emigrate to St. Domingo, and sharply ordered to suffer nobody to leave Louisiana without express license from Versailles. Deeply wounded, he offered his resignation, and it was accepted. Whatever his failings, he had faithfully served the colony, and gained from posterity the title of Father of Louisiana.

With the help of industrious nursing,—or, one might almost say, in spite of it,—Louisiana began at last to strike roots into the soil and show signs of growth, though feebly as compared with its sturdy rivals along the Atlantic seaboard, which had cost their King nothing, and had been treated, for the most part, with the coolest neglect. Cavelier de la Salle's dream of planting a firm settlement at the mouth of the Mississippi, and utilizing, by means of it, the resources of the vast interior, was, after half a century, in some measure realized. New France (using that name in its broadest geographical sense) had now two heads,—Canada and Louisiana; one looking upon the Gulf of St. Lawrence, and the other upon the Gulf of Mexico. Canada was not without jealousy of her younger and weaker sister, lest she might draw away, as she had begun to do at the first, some of the most active and adventurous elements of the Canadian population; lest she might prove a competitor in the fur-trade; and lest she should encroach on the Illinois and other western domains, which the elder and stronger sister claimed as her own. These fears were not unfounded; yet the vital interests of the two French colonies were the same, and each needed the help of the other in the prime and all-essential task of keeping the British colonies in check. The chiefs of Louisiana looked forward to a time when the great southern tribes,—Creeks, Cherokees, Choctaws, and even the dreaded Chickasaws,—won over by French missionaries to the Church, and therefore to France,

---

[33] *Dépêche de Bienville*, 6 *Mai*, 1740. Compare Le Page du Pratz, iii. chap. xxiv.

should be turned against the encroaching English to stop their westward progress and force them back to the borders of the Atlantic. Meanwhile the chiefs of Canada were maturing the plan—pursued with varying assiduity, but always kept in view—of connecting the two vital extremities of New France by a chain of forts to control the passes of the West, keep communications open, and set English invasion at defiance.

Chapter 14

1700–1732
The Outagamie War

THE RULERS OF Canada labored without ceasing in their perplexing task of engrossing the fur-trade of the West and controlling the western tribes to the exclusion of the English. Every day made it clearer that to these ends the western wilderness must be held by forts and trading-posts; and this policy of extension prevailed more and more in spite of the league of merchants, who wished to draw the fur-trade to Montreal,—in spite of the Jesuits, who felt that their influence over the remoter tribes would be compromised by the presence among them of officers, soldiers, and traders; and in spite of the King himself, who feared that the diffusion of the colony would breed disorder and insubordination.

Detroit, the most important of the western posts, struggled through a critical infancy in the charge of its founder, La Mothe-Cadillac, till, by a choice not very judicious, he was made governor of Louisiana. During his rule the population had slowly increased to about two hundred souls; but after he left the place it diminished to a point that seemed to threaten the feeble post with extinction. About 1722 it revived again; *voyageurs* and discharged soldiers settled about the fort, and the parish register shows six or eight births in the course of the year.[1]

Meanwhile, on the banks of the Mississippi another settlement was growing up which did not owe its birth to official patronage, and yet was destined to become the most noteworthy offspring of Canada in the West. It was known to the French as "the Illinois," from the name of the group of tribes belonging to that region. La Salle had occupied the banks of the river Illinois in 1682; but the curious Indian colony which he gathered about his fort on the rock of St. Louis dispersed after his death, till few or none were left except the Kaskas-

---

[1] Rameau, *Notes historiques sur la Colonie Canadienne du Detroit*.

kias, a sub-tribe of the Illinois. These still lived in the meadow below Fort St. Louis, where the Jesuits Marquette, Allouez, Rale, Gravier, and Marest labored in turn for their conversion, till, in 1700, they or some of them followed Marest to the Mississippi and set up their wigwams where the town of Kaskaskia now stands, near the mouth of the little river which bears the same name. Charlevoix, who was here in 1721, calls this the oldest settlement of the Illinois,[2]—though there is some reason to believe that the village of Cahokia, established as a mission by the Jesuit Pinet, sixty miles or more above Kaskaskia, and nearly opposite the present city of St. Louis, is, by a few weeks, the elder of the two. The *voyageurs, coureurs de bois,* and other roving Canadians made these young settlements their resort, took to wife converted squaws,[3] and ended with making the Illinois their home. The missions turned to parishes, the missionaries to curés, and the wigwams to those compact little Canadian houses that cause one to marvel at the ingenuity which can store so multitudinous a progeny within such narrow limits.

White women from Canada or Louisiana began to find their way to these wilderness settlements, which with every generation grew more French and less Indian. The river Mississippi was at once their friend and their enemy. It carried their produce to New Orleans, but undermined their rich alluvial shores, cut away fields and meadows, and swept them in its turbid eddies thirteen hundred miles southward, as a contribution to the mud-banks of the delta.

When the Mississippi Company came into power, the Illinois, hitherto a dependency of Canada, was annexed to Louisiana. Pierre Dugué de Boisbriant was sent to take command of it, and under his direction a fort was built on the bank of the Mississippi sixteen miles above Kaskaskia. It was named Fort Chartres, in honor of the Duc de Chartres, son of the Regent, who had himself once borne the same title. This work, built at first of wood and earth, was afterwards rebuilt of stone, and became one of the chief links in the chain of military communication between Canada and Louisiana.

[2] "Ce poste, le premier de tous par droit d'antiquité."—*Journal historique,* 403 (ed. 1744).

[3] The old parish registers of Kaskaskia are full of records of these mixed marriages. See Edward G. Mason, *Illinois in the Eighteenth Century.*

Here, with the commandant at its head, sat the council of three which ruled over the little settlement.[4] Here too was a garrison to enforce the decrees of the council, keep order among the settlers, and give them a protection which they greatly needed, since they were within striking distance of the formidable Chickasaws, the effects of whose hostility appear year after year on the parish register of deaths at Kaskaskia. Worse things were in store; for the gallant young Pierre d'Artaguette, who was appointed to the command in 1734, and who marched against the Chickasaws with a band of Frenchmen and Indians, was defeated, captured, and burned alive, astonishing his torturers by the fortitude with which he met his fate. The settlement had other foes not less dangerous. These were the Outagamies, or Foxes, between whom and the tribes of the Illinois there was a deadly feud. We have seen how, in 1712, a band of Outagamies, with their allies, the Mascoutins, appeared at Detroit and excited an alarm, which after a savage conflict, was ended with their ruin. In 1714 the Outagamies made a furious attack upon the Illinois, and killed or carried off seventy-seven of them.[5] A few years later they made another murderous onslaught in the same quarter. They were the scourge of the West, and no white man could travel between Canada and Louisiana except at the risk of his life.

In vain the French parleyed with them; threats and blandishments were useless alike. Their chiefs would promise, sometimes in good faith, to keep the peace and no more offend their father Onontio; but nearly all the tribes of the Lake country were their hereditary enemies, and some bloody revenge for ancient wrongs would excite their young warriors to a fury which the elders could not restrain. Thus, in 1722 the Saginaws, a fierce Algonquin band on the eastern borders of Michigan, killed twenty-three Outagamies; the tribesmen of the slain returned the blow, other tribes joined the fray, and the wilderness was again on fire.[6]

The Canadian authorities were sorely perplexed, for this

[4] The two other members were La Loire des Ursins, director of the Mississippi Company, and Michel Chassin, its commissary,— he who wrote the curious letter to Ponchartrain, asking for a wife, quoted in the last chapter.

[5] *Vaudreuil au Ministre*, 16 *Septembre*, 1714.

[6] *Idem*, 2 *Octobre*, 1723.

fierce inter-tribal war threatened their whole system of western trade. Meanwhile the English and Dutch of New York were sending wampum belts to the Indians of the upper lakes, inviting them to bring their furs to Albany; and Ramesay, governor of Montreal, complains that they were all disposed to do so. "Twelve of the upper tribes," says Lord Cornbury, "have come down this year to trade at Albany;" but he adds that as the Indians have had no presents for above six years, he is afraid "we shall lose them before next summer."[7] The governor of Canada himself is said to have been in collusion with the English traders for his own profit.[8] The Jesuits denied the charge, and Father Marest wrote to the governor, after the disaster to Walker's fleet on its way to attack Quebec, "The protection you have given to the missions has drawn on you and the colony the miraculous protection of God."[9]

Whether his accusers did him wrong or not, Vaudreuil felt the necessity of keeping the peace among the western Indians and suppressing the Outagamie incendiaries. In fact, nothing would satisfy him but their destruction. "They are the common enemies of all the western tribes," he writes. "They have lately murdered three Frenchmen and five Hurons at Detroit. The Hurons ask for our help against them, and we must give it, or all the tribes will despise us."[10]

He put his chief trust in Louvigny, formerly commandant at Michilimackinac. That officer proposed to muster the friendly tribes and march on the Outagamies just as their corn was ripening, fight them if they stood their ground, or if not, destroy their crops, burn their wigwams, and encamp on the spot till winter; then send out parties to harass them as they roamed the woods seeking a meagre subsistence by hunting. In this way he hoped to cripple, if not destroy them.[11]

The Outagamies lived at this time on the Fox River of Green Bay,—a stream which owes its name to them.[12] Their

[7] N. Y. Col. Docs., v. 65.

[8] Mémoire présenté au Comte de Ponchartrain par M. d'Auteuil, procureur-général du Roy, 1708.

[9] Marest à Vaudreuil, 21 Janvier, 1712.

[10] Vaudreuil et Bégon au Ministre, 15 Novembre, 1713.

[11] Vaudreuil au Ministre, 16 Septembre, 1714.

[12] "Les Renards [Outagamies] sont placez sur une rivière qui tombe dans la Baye des Puants [Green Bay]."—Registre du Conseil de la Marine, 28 Mars, 1716.

chief village seems to have been between thirty and forty miles from the mouth of the river, where it creeps through broad tracts of rushes, willows, and wild rice. In spite of their losses at Detroit in 1712, their strength was far from being broken.

During two successive summers preparations were made to attack them; but the march was delayed, once by the tardiness of the Indian allies, and again by the illness of Louvigny. At length, on the first of May, 1716, he left Montreal with two hundred and twenty-five Frenchmen, while two hundred more waited to join him at Detroit and Michilimackinac, where the Indian allies were also to meet him. To save expense in pay and outfit, the Canadians recruited for the war were allowed to take with them goods for trading with the Indians. Hence great disorder and insubordination, especially as more than forty barrels of brandy were carried in the canoes, as a part of these commericial ventures, in consequence of which we hear that when French and Indians were encamped together, "hell was thrown open."[13]

The Outagamies stood their ground. Louvigny says, with probable exaggeration, that when he made his attack their village held five hundred warriors, and no less than three thousand women,—a disparity of sexes no doubt due to the inveterate fighting habits of the tribe. The wigwams were enclosed by a strong fence, consisting of three rows of heavy oaken palisades. This method of fortification was used also by tribes farther southward. When Bienville attacked the Chickasaws, he was foiled by the solid wooden wall that resisted his cannon, being formed of trunks of trees as large as a man's body, set upright, close together, and made shot-proof by smaller trunks, planted within so as to close the interstices of the outer row.[14]

The fortified village of the Outagamies was of a somewhat different construction. The defences consisted of three rows of palisades, those of the middle row being probably planted upright, and the other two set aslant against them. Below, along the inside of the triple row, ran a sort of shallow trench or rifle-pit, where the defenders lay ensconced, firing through interstices left for the purpose between the palisades.[15]

[13] "Où il y a des François et des sauvages, c'est un enfer ouvert."—*Registre du Conseil de Marine*, 28 *Mars*, 1716.

[14] Le Page du Pratz.

[15] *Louvigny au Ministre*, 14 *Octobre*, 1716. Louvigny's account of the Outagamie defences is short, and not very clear. La Mothe-

Louvigny had brought with him two cannon and a mortar; but being light, they had little effect on the wooden wall, and as he was provided with mining tools, he resolved to attack the Outagamie stronghold by regular approaches, as if he were besieging a fortress of Vauban. Covered by the fire of three pieces of artillery and eight hundred French and Indian small-arms, he opened trenches during the night within seventy yards of the palisades, pushed a sap sixty feet nearer before morning, and on the third night burrowed to within about twenty-three yards of the wall. His plan was to undermine and blow up the palisades.

The Outagamies had made a furious resistance, in which their women took part with desperation; but dreading the threatened explosion, and unable to resist the underground approaches of their enemy, they asked for a parley, and owned themselves beaten. Louvigny demanded that they should make peace with all tribes friendly to the French, give up all prisoners, and make war on distant tribes, such as the Pawnees, in order to take captives who should supply the place of those they had killed among the allies of the French; that they should pay, in furs, the costs of the war, and give six chiefs, or sons of chiefs, as hostages for the fulfilment of these conditions.[16]

On the twelfth of October Louvigny reached Quebec in triumph, bringing with him the six hostages.

The Outagamie question was settled for a time. The tribe remained quite for some years, and in 1718 sent a deputation to Montreal and renewed their submission, which the governor accepted, though they had evaded the complete fulfilment of the conditions imposed on them. Yet peace was not secure for a moment. The Kickapoos and Mascoutins would not leave their neighbors, the Illinois, at rest; the Saginaws made raids on the Miamis; and a general war seemed imminent. "The difficulty is inconceivable of keeping these western tribes quiet," writes the governor, almost in despair.[17]

Cadillac, describing similar works at Michilimackinacs, says that the palisades of the innermost row alone were set close together, those of the two other rows being separated by spaces of six inches or more, through which the defenders fired from their loopholes. The plan seems borrowed from the Iroquois.

[16] *Dépêche de Vaudreuil, 14 Octobre,* 1716.

[17] *Vaudreuil au Conseil de Marine, 28 Octobre,* 1719.

At length the crisis came. The Illinois captured the nephew of Oushala, the principal Outagamie war-chief, and burned him alive; on which the Outagamies attacked them, drove them for refuge to the top of the rock on which La Salle's fort at St. Louis had been built, and held them there at mercy. They would have starved to death, had not the victors, dreading the anger of the French, suffered them to escape.[18] For this they took to themselves great credit, not without reason, in view of the provocation. At Versailles, however, their attack on the Illinois seemed an unpardonable offence, and the next ship from France brought a letter from the colonial minister declaring that the Outagamies must be effectually put down, and that "his Majesty will reward the officer who will reduce, or rather destroy, them."[19]

The authorities of Canada were less truculent than their masters at the court, or were better able to count the costs of another war. Longueuil, the provisional governor, persisted in measures of peace, and the Sieur de Lignery called a council of the Outagamies and their neighbors, the Sacs and Winnebagoes, at Green Bay. He told them that the Great Onontio, the King, ordered them, at their peril, to make no more attacks on the Illinois; and they dutifully promised to obey, while their great chief, Oushala, begged that a French officer might be sent to his village to help him keep his young warriors from the war-path.[20] The pacific policy of Longueuil was not approved by Desliettes, then commanding in the Illinois country; and he proposed to settle accounts with the Outagamies by exterminating them. "This is very well," observes a writer of the time; "but to try to exterminate them and fail would be disastrous."[21]

The Marquis de Beauharnois, who came out as governor of Canada in 1726, was averse to violent measures, since if an attempt to exterminate the offending tribe should be made without success, the life of every Frenchman in the West

[18] *Paroles des Renards* [Outagamies] *dans un Conseil tenu le 6 Septembre,* 1722.

[19] *Réponse du Ministre à la lettre du Marquis de Vaudreuil du 11 Octobre,* 1723.

[20] *Mémoire sur les Renards,* 27 *Avril,* 1727.

[21] *Mémoire concernant la Paix que M. de Lignery a faite avec les Chefs des Renards, Sakis* [Sacs], *et Puants* [Winnebagoes], 7 *Juin,* 1726.

would be in jeopardy.[22] Lignery thought that if the Outagamies broke the promises they had made him at Green Bay,
the forces of Canada and Louisiana should unite to crush
them. The missionary, Chardon, advised that they should be
cut off from all supplies of arms, ammunition, and merchan-
dise of any kind, and that all the well-disposed western tribes
should then be set upon them,—which, he thought, would
infallibly bring them to reason.[23]

The new governor, perplexed by the multitude of counsel-
lors, presently received a missive from the King, directing
him not to fight the Outagamies if he could help it, "since the
consequences of failure would be frightful."[24] On the other
hand, Beauharnois was told that the English had sent messages to the Lake tribes urging them to kill the French in
their country, and that the Outagamies had promised to do
so. "This," writes the governor, "compels us to make war in
earnest. It will cost sixty thousand livres."[25]

Dupuy, the intendant, had joined with Beauharnois in this
letter to the minister; but being at the time in a hot quarrel
with the governor, he soon after sent a communication of
his own to Versailles, in which he declares that the war against
the Outagamies was only a pretext of Beauharnois for spending the King's money, and enriching himself by buying up
all the furs of the countries traversed by the army.[26]

Whatever the motives of the expedition, it left Montreal in
June, under the Sieur de Lignery, followed the rugged old
route of the Ottawa, and did not reach Michilimackinac till
after midsummer. Thence, in a flotilla of birch canoes carrying about a thousand Indians and five hundred French, the
party set out for the fort at the head of Green Bay.[27] Here
they caught one Outagamie warrior and three Winnebagoes,
whom the Indian allies tortured to death. Then they paddled
their canoes up Fox River, reached a Winnebago village on
the twenty-fourth of August, followed the channel of the

[22] *Mémoire sur les Renards, 27 Avril, 1727.*
[23] *Ibid.*
[24] *Mémoire du Roy, 29 Avril, 1727.*
[25] *Beauharnois et Dupuy au Ministre, 25 Octobre, 1727.*
[26] *Mémoire de Dupuy, 1728.*
[27] Desliettes came to meet them, by way of Chicago, with five
hundred Illinois warriors and twenty Frenchmen. *La Perrière et
La Fresnière à Beauharnois, 10 Septembre, 1728.*

stream, a ribbon of lazy water twisting in a vague, perplexing way through the broad marsh of wild rice and flags, till they saw the chief village of the Outagamies on a tract of rising ground a little above the level of the bog.[28] It consisted of bark wigwams, without palisades or defences of any kind. Its only inmates were three squaws and one old man. These were all seized, and, to the horror of Père Crespel, the chaplain, were given to the Indian allies, who kept the women as slaves, and burned the old man at a slow fire.[29] Then, after burning the village and destroying the crop of maize, peas, beans, and squashes that surrounded it, the whole party returned to Michilimackinac.[30]

The expedition was not a success. Lignery had hoped to surprise the enemy; but the alert and nimble savages had escaped him. Beauharnois makes the best of the miscarriage, and writes that "the army did good work;" but says a few weeks later that something must be done to cure the contempt which the western allies of the French have conceived for them "since the last affair."[31]

Two years afer Lignery's expedition, there was another attempt to humble the Outagamies. Late in the autumn of 1730 young Coulon de Villiers, who twenty-four years later defeated Washington at Fort Necessity, appeared at Quebec with news that the Sieur de Villiers, his father, who commanded the post on the St. Joseph, had struck the Outagamies a deadly blow and killed two hundred of their warriors, besides six hundred of their women and children. The force under Villiers consisted of a body of Frenchmen gathered from various western posts, another body from the Illinois, led by the Sieurs de Saint-Ange, father and son, and twelve or thirteen hundred Indian allies from many friendly tribes.[32]

---

[28] *Guignas à Beauharnois, 29 Mai,* 1728.

[29] *Dépêche de Beauharnois, 1 Septembre,* 1728.

[30] The best account of this expedition is that of Père Emanuel Crespel. Lignery made a report which seems to be lost, as it does not appear in the Archives.

[31] *Beauharnois au Ministre, 15 Mai,* 1729; *Ibid., 21 Juillet,* 1729.

[32] *Beauharnois et Hocquart au Ministre, 2 Novembre,* 1730. An Indian tradition says that about this time there was a great battle between the Outagamies and the French, aided by their Indian allies, at the place called Little Butte des Morts, on the Fox River. According to the story, the Outagamies were nearly destroyed. Per-

The accounts of this affair are obscure and not very trustworthy. It seems that the Outagamies began the fray by an attack on the Illinois at La Salle's old station of Le Rocher, on the river Illinois. On hearing of this, the French commanders mustered their Indian allies, hastened to the spot, and found the Outagamies intrenched in a grove which they had surrounded with a stockade. They defended themselves with their usual courage, but, being hard pressed by hunger and thirst, as well as by the greatly superior numbers of their assailants, they tried to escape during a dark night, as their tribesmen had done at Detroit in 1712. The French and their allies pursued, and there was a great slaughter, in which many warriors and many more women and children were the victims.[33]

The offending tribe must now, one would think, have ceased to be dangerous; but nothing less than its destruction would content the French officials. To this end, their best resource was in their Indian allies, among whom the Outagamies had no more deadly enemy than the Hurons of Detroit, who, far from relenting in view of their disasters, were more eager than ever to wreak their ire on their unfortunate foe. Accordingly, they sent messengers to the converted Iroquois at the Mission of Two Mountains, and invited them to join in making an end of the Outagamies. The invitation was accepted, and in the autumn of 1731 forty-seven warriors from the Two Mountains appeared at Detroit. The party was soon made up. It consisted of seventy-four Hurons, forty-six Iroquois, and four Ottawas. They took the trail to the mouth of the river St. Joseph, thence around the head of Lake Michigan to the Chicago portage, and thence westward to Rock River. Here were the villages of the Kickapoos and Mascoutins, who had been allies of the Outagamies, but having lately quarrelled

---

haps this is a perverted version of the Villiers affair. (See *Wisconsin Historical Collections*, viii. 207.) Beauharnois also reports, under date of 6 May, 1730, that a party of Outagamies, returning from a buffalo hunt, were surprised by two hundred Ottawas, Ojibwas, Menominies, and Winnebagoes, who killed eighty warriors and three hundred women and children.

[33] Some particulars of this affair are given by Ferland, *Cours d'Histoire du Canada*, ii. 437; but he does not give his authority. I have found no report of it by those engaged.

with them, received the strangers as friends and gave them guides. The party now filed northward, by forests and prairies, towards the Wisconsin, to the banks of which stream the Outagamies had lately removed their villages. The warriors were all on snow-shoes, for the weather was cold and the snow deep. Some of the elders, overcome by the hardships of the way, called a council and proposed to turn back; but the juniors were for pushing on at all risks, and a young warrior declared that he would rather die than go home without killing somebody. The result was a division of the party; the elders returned to Chicago, and the younger men, forty Hurons and thirty Iroquois, kept on their way.

At last, as they neared the Wisconsin, they saw on an open prairie three Outagamies, who ran for their lives. The Hurons and Iroquois gave chase, till from the ridge of a hill they discovered the principal Outagamie village, consisting, if we may believe their own story, of forty-six wigwams, near the bank of the river. The Outagamie warriors came out to meet them, in number, as they pretended, much greater than theirs; but the Huron and Iroquois chiefs reminded their followers that they had to do with dogs who did not believe in God, on which they fired two volleys against the enemy, then dropped their guns and charged with the knife in one hand and the war-club in the other. According to their own story, which shows every sign of mendacity, they drove back the Outagamies into their village, killed seventy warriors, and captured fourteen more, without counting eighty women and children killed, and a hundred and forty taken prisoners. In short, they would have us believe that they destroyed the whole village, except ten men, who escaped entirely naked, and soon froze to death. They declared further that they sent one of their prisoners to the remaining Outagamie villages, ordering him to tell the inhabitants that they had just devoured the better part of the tribe, and meant to stay on the spot two days; that the tribesmen of the slain were free to attack them if they chose, but in that case, they would split the heads of all the women and children prisoners in their hands, make a breastwork of the dead bodies, and then finish it by piling upon it those of the assailants.[34]

Nothing is more misleading than Indian tradition, which

[34] *Relation de la Défaite des Renards par les Sauvages Hurons et Iroquois, le* 28 *Février,* 1732. (Archives de la Marine.)

is of the least possible value as evidence. It may be well, however, to mention another story, often repeated, touching these dark days of the Outagamies. It is to the effect that a French trader named Marin, whom they had incensed by levying blackmail from him, raised a party of Indians, with whose aid he surprised and defeated the unhappy tribe at the Little Butte des Morts, that they retired to the Great Butte des Morts, higher up Fox River, and that Marin here attacked them again, killing or capturing the whole. Extravagant as the story seems, it may have some foundation, though various dates, from 1725 to 1746, are assigned to the alleged exploit, and contemporary documents are silent concerning it. It is certain that the Outagamies were not destroyed, as the tribe exists to this day.[35]

In 1736 it was reported that sixty or eighty Outagamie warriors were still alive.[36] Their women, who when hard pushed would fight like furies, were relatively numerous and tolerably prolific, and their villages were full of sturdy boys, likely to be dangerous in a few years. Feeling their losses and their weakness, the survivors of the tribe incorporated themselves with their kindred and neighbors, the Sacs, Sakis, or Saukies, the two forming henceforth one tribe, afterwards known to the Americans as the Sacs and Foxes. Early in the nineteenth century they were settled on both banks of the upper Mississippi. Brave and restless like their forefathers, they were a continual menace to the American frontiersmen, and in 1832 they rose in open war, under their famous chief, Blackhawk, displaying their hereditary prowess both on foot and on horseback, and more than once defeating superior numbers of American mounted militia. In the next year that

[35] The story is told in Snelling, *Tales of the Northwest* (1830), under the title of *La Butte des Morts,* and afterwards, with variations, by the aged Augustus Grignon, in his *Recollections,* printed in the *Collections of the Wisconsin Historical Society,* iii.; also by Judge M. L. Martin and others. Grignon, like all the rest, was not born till after the time of the alleged event. The nearest approach to substantial evidence touching it is in a letter of Beauharnois, who writes in 1730 that the Sieur Dubuisson was to attack the Outagamies with fifty Frenchmen and five hundred and fifty Indians, and that Martin, commander at Green Bay, was to join him. *Beauharnois au Ministre, 25 Juin,* 1730.

[36] *Mémoire sur le Canada,* 1736.

excellent artist, Charles Bodmer, painted a group of them from life,—grim-visaged savages, armed with war-club, spear, or rifle, and wrapped in red, green, or brown blankets, their heads close shaven except the erect and bristling scalp-lock, adorned with long eagle-plumes, while both heads and faces are painted with fantastic figures in blue, white, yellow, black and vermilion.[37]

Three or four years after, a party of their chiefs and warriors was conducted through the country by order of the Washington government, in order to impress them with the number and power of the whites. At Boston they danced a war-dance on the Common in full costume, to the delight of the boy spectators, of whom I was one.

[37] Charles Bodmer was the artist who accompanied Prince Maximilian of Wied in his travels in the interior of North America.

The name Outagamie is Algonquin for a fox. Hence the French called the tribe Renards, and the Americans, Foxes. They called themselves Musquawkies, which is said to mean "red earth," and to be derived from the color of the soil near one of their villages.

Chapter 15

1697–1741
France in the Far West

THE OCCUPATION BY France of the lower Mississippi gave a strong impulse to the exploration of the West, by supplying a base for discovery, stimulating enterprise by the longing to find gold mines, open trade with New Mexico, and get a fast hold on the countries beyond the Mississippi in anticipation of Spain; and to these motives was soon added the hope of finding an overland way to the Pacific. It was the Canadians, with their indomitable spirit of adventure, who led the way in the path of discovery.

As a bold and hardy pioneer of the wilderness, the Frenchman in America has rarely found his match. His civic virtues withered under the despotism of Versailles, and his mind and conscience were kept in leading-strings by an absolute Church; but the forest and the prairie offered him an unbridled liberty, which, lawless as it was, gave scope to his energies, till these savage wastes became the field of his most noteworthy achievements.

Canada was divided between two opposing influences. On the one side were the monarchy and the hierarchy, with their principles of order, subordination, and obedience; substantially at one in purpose, since both wished to keep the colony within manageable bounds, domesticate it, and tame it to soberness, regularity, and obedience. On the other side was the spirit of liberty, or license, which was in the very air of this wilderness continent, reinforced in the chiefs of the colony by a spirit of adventure inherited from the Middle Ages, and by a spirit of trade born of present opportunities; for every official in Canada hoped to make a profit, if not a fortune, out of beaver-skins. Kindred impulses, in ruder forms, possessed the humbler colonists, drove them into the forest, and made them hardy woodsmen and skilful bush-fighters, though turbulent and lawless members of civilized society.

Time, the decline of the fur-trade, and the influence of the

Canadian Church gradually diminished this erratic spirit, and at the same time impaired the qualities that were associated with it. The Canadian became a more stable colonist and a steadier farmer; but for forest journeyings and forest warfare he was scarcely his former self. At the middle of the eighteenth century we find complaints that the race of *voyageurs* is growing scarce. The taming process was most apparent in the central and lower parts of the colony, such as the Côte de Beaupré and the opposite shore of the St. Lawrence, where the hands of the government and of the Church were strong; while at the head of the colony,—that is, about Montreal and its neighborhood,—which touched the primeval wilderness, an uncontrollable spirit of adventure still held its own. Here, at the beginning of the century, this spirit was as strong as it had ever been, and achieved a series of explorations and discoveries which revealed the plains of the Far West long before an Anglo-Saxon foot had pressed their soil.

The expedition of one Le Sueur to what is now the State of Minnesota may be taken as the starting-point of these enterprises. Le Sueur had visited the country of the Sioux as early as 1683. He returned thither in 1689 with the famous *voyageur* Nicolas Perrot.[1] Four years later, Count Frontenac sent him to the Sioux country again. The declared purpose of the mission was to keep those fierce tribes at peace with their neighbors; but the governor's enemies declared that a contraband trade in beaver was the true object, and that Frontenac's secretary was to have half the profits.[2] Le Sueur returned after two years, bringing to Montreal a Sioux chief and his squaw,—the first of the tribe ever seen there. He then went to France, and represented to the court that he had built a fort at Lake Pepin, on the upper Mississippi; that he was the only white man who knew the languages of that region; and that if the French did not speedily seize upon it, the English, who were already trading upon the Ohio, would be sure to do so. Thereupon he asked for the command of the upper Mississippi, with all its tributary waters, together with a monopoly of its fur-trade for ten years, and permission to work its mines, promising that if his petition were granted, he would secure

[1] *Journal historique de l'Établissement des Français à la Louisiane*, 43.

[2] *Champigny au Ministre*, 4 Novembre, 1693.

the country to France without expense to the King. The commission was given him. He bought an outfit and sailed for Canada, but was captured by the English on the way. After the peace he returned to France and begged for a renewal of his commission. Leave was given him to work the copper and lead mines, but not to trade in beaver-skins. He now formed a company to aid him in his enterprise, on which a cry rose in Canada that under pretence of working mines he meant to trade in beaver,—which is very likely, since to bring lead and copper in bark canoes to Montreal from the Mississippi and Lake Superior would cost far more than the metal was worth. In consequence of this clamor his commission was revoked.

Perhaps it was to compensate him for the outlays into which he had been drawn that the colonial minister presently authorized him to embark for Louisiana and pursue his enterprise with that infant colony, instead of Canada, as his base of operations. Thither, therefore, he went; and in April, 1700, set out for the Sioux country with twenty-five men, in a small vessel of the kind called a "felucca," still used in the Mediterranean. Among the party was an adventurous youth named Penecaut, a ship-carpenter by trade, who had come to Louisiana with Iberville two years before, and who has left us an account of his voyage with Le Sueur.[3]

The party slowly made their way, with sail and oar, against the muddy current of the Mississippi, till they reached the Arkansas, where they found an English trader from Carolina. On the tenth of June, spent with rowing, and half starved, they stopped to rest at a point fifteen leagues above the mouth of the Ohio. They had staved off famine with the buds and leaves of trees; but now, by good luck, one of them killed a bear, and soon after, the Jesuit Limoges arrived from the neighboring mission of the Illinois, in a canoe well stored with provisions. Thus refreshed, they passed the mouth of the Missouri on the thirteenth of July, and soon after were met by three Canadians, who brought them a letter from the Jesuit Marest, warning them that the river was infested by war-parties. In fact, they presently saw seven canoes of Sioux warriors, bound against the Illinois; and not long after, five

[3] *Relation de Penecaut.* In my possession is a contemporary manuscript of this narrative, for which I am indebted to the kindness of General J. Meredith Reade.

Canadians appeared, one of whom had been badly wounded in a recent encounter with a band of Outagamies, Sacs, and Winnebagoes bound against the Sioux. To take one another's scalps had been for ages the absorbing business and favorite recreation of all these Western tribes. At or near the expansion of the Mississippi called Lake Pepin, the voyagers found a fort called Fort Perrot, after its builder;[4] and on an island near the upper end of the lake, another similar structure, built by Le Sueur himself on his last visit to the place. These forts were mere stockades, occupied from time to time by the roving fur-traders as their occasions required.

Towards the end of September, Le Sueur and his followers reached the mouth of the St. Peter, which they ascended to Blue Earth River. Pushing a league up this stream, they found a spot well suited to their purpose, and here they built a fort, of which there was great need, for they were soon after joined by seven Canadian traders, plundered and stripped to the skin by the neighboring Sioux. Le Sueur named the new post Fort l'Huillier. It was a fence of pickets, enclosing cabins for the men. The neighboring plains were black with buffalo, of which the party killed four hundred, and cut them into quarters, which they placed to freeze on scaffolds within the enclosure. Here they spent the winter, subsisting on the frozen meat, without bread, vegetables, or salt, and, according to Penecaut, thriving marvellously, though the surrounding wilderness was buried five feet deep in snow.

Band after band of Sioux appeared, with their wolfish dogs and their sturdy and all-enduring squaws burdened with the heavy hide coverings of their teepees, or buffalo-skin tents. They professed friendship and begged for arms. Those of one band had blackened their faces in mourning for a dead chief, and calling on Le Sueur to share their sorrow, they wept over him, and wiped their tears on his hair. Another party of warriors arrived with yet deeper cause of grief, being the remnant

---

[4] Penecaut, *Journal. Procès-verbal de la Prise de Possession du Pays des Nadouessioux, etc., par Nicolas Perrot,* 1689. Fort Perrot seems to have been built in 1685, and to have stood near the outlet of the lake, probably on the west side. Perrot afterwards built another fort, called Fort St. Antoine, a little above, on the east bank. The position of these forts has been the subject of much discussion, and cannot be ascertained with precision. It appears by the *Prise de Possession,* cited above, that there was also, in 1689, a temporary French post near the mouth of the Wisconsin.

of a village half exterminated by their enemies. They, too, wept profusely over the French commander, and then sang a dismal song, with heads muffled in their buffalo-robes.[5] Le Sueur took the needful precautions against dangerous visitors, but got from them a large supply of beaver-skins in exchange for his goods.

When spring opened, he set out in search of mines, and found, not far above the fort, those beds of blue and green earth to which the stream owes its name. Of this his men dug out a large quantity, and selecting what seemed the best, stored it in their vessel as a precious commodity. With this and good store of beaver-skins, Le Sueur now began his return voyage for Louisiana, leaving a Canadian named D'Éraque and twelve men to keep the fort till he should come back to reclaim it, promising to send him a canoe-load of ammunition from the Illinois. But the canoe was wrecked, and D'Éraque, discouraged, abandoned Fort l'Huillier, and followed his commander down the Mississippi.[6]

Le Sueur, with no authority from government, had opened relations of trade with the wild Sioux of the Plains, whose westward range stretched to the Black Hills, and perhaps to the Rocky Mountains. He reached the settlements of Louisiana in safety, and sailed for France with four thousand pounds of his worthless blue earth.[7] Repairing at once to Versailles, he begged for help to continue his enterprise. His petition seems to have been granted. After long delay, he sailed again for Louisiana, fell ill on the voyage, and died soon after landing.[8]

[5] This weeping over strangers was a custom with the Sioux of that time mentioned by many early writers. La Mothe-Cadillac marvels that a people so brave and warlike should have such a fountain of tears always at command.

[6] In 1702 the geographer De l'Isle made a remarkable MS. map entitled *Carte de la Rivière du Mississippi, dressée sur les Mémoires de M. Le Sueur.*

[7] According to the geologist Featherstonhaugh, who examined the locality, this earth owes its color to a bluish-green silicate of iron.

[8] Besides the long and circumstantial *Relation de Penecaut*, an account of the earlier part of Le Sueur's voyage up the Mississippi is contained in the *Mémoire du Chevalier de Beaurain,* which, with other papers relating to this explorer, including portions of his Journal, will be found in Margry, vi. See also *Journal historique de l'Établissement des Français à la Louisiane,* 38–71.

Before 1700, the year when Le Sueur visited the St. Peter, little or nothing was known of the country west of the Mississippi, except from the report of Indians. The romances of La Hontan and Mathieu Sâgean were justly set down as impostures by all but the most credulous. In this same year we find Le Moyne d'Iberville projecting journeys to the upper Missouri, in hopes of finding a river flowing to the Western Sea. In 1703, twenty Canadians tried to find their way from the Illinois to New Mexico, in hope of opening trade with the Spaniards and discovering mines.[9] In 1704 we find it reported that more than a hundred Canadians are scattered in small parties along the Mississippi and the Missouri;[10] and in 1705 one Laurain appeared at the Illinois, declaring that he had been high up the Missouri and had visited many tribes on its borders.[11] A few months later, two Canadians told Bienville a similar story. In 1708 Nicolas de la Salle proposed an expedition of a hundred men to explore the same mysterious river; and in 1717 one Hubert laid before the Council of Marine a scheme for following the Missouri to its source, since, he says, "not only may we find the mines worked by the Spaniards, but also discover the great river that is said to rise in the mountains where the Missouri has its source, and is believed to flow to the Western Sea." And he advises that a hundred and fifty men be sent up the river in wooden canoes, since bark canoes would be dangerous, by reason of the multitude of snags.[12]

In 1714 Juchereau de Saint-Denis was sent by La Mothe-Cadillac to explore western Louisiana, and pushed up Red River to a point sixty-eight leagues, as he reckons, above Natchitoches. In the next year, journeying across country towards the Spanish settlements, with a view to trade, he was seized near the Rio Grande and carried to the city of Mexico. The Spaniards, jealous of French designs, now sent priests and soldiers to occupy several points in Texas. Juchereau, however, was well treated, and permitted to marry a Spanish girl with whom he had fallen in love on the way; but when, in the autumn of 1716, he ventured another journey to the

---

[9] *Iberville à* ——, 15 *Février,* 1703 (Margry, vi. 180).

[10] *Bienville au Ministre,* 6 *Septembre,* 1704.

[11] Beaurain *Journal historique.*

[12] Hubert, *Mémoire envoyé au Conseil de la Marine.*

Mexican borders, still hoping to be allowed to trade, he and his goods were seized by order of the Mexican viceroy, and, lest worse should befall him, he fled empty-handed, under cover of night.[13]

In March, 1719, Bénard de la Harpe left the feeble little French post at Natchitoches with six soldiers and a sergeant.[14] His errand was to explore the country, open trade if possible with the Spaniards, and establish another post high up Red River. He and his party soon came upon that vast entanglement of driftwood, or rather of uprooted forests, afterwards known as the Red River raft, which choked the stream and forced them to make their way through the inundated jungle that bordered it. As they pushed or dragged their canoes through the swamp, they saw with disgust and alarm a good number of snakes, coiled about twigs and boughs on the right and left, or sometimes over their heads. These were probably the deadly water-moccason, which in warm weather is accustomed to crawl out of its favorite element and bask itself in the sun, precisely as described by La Harpe. Their nerves were further discomposed by the splashing and plunging of alligators lately wakened from their wintry torpor. Still, they pushed painfully on, till they reached navigable water again, and at the end of the month were, as they thought, a hundred and eight leagues above Natchitoches. In four days more they reached the Nassonites.

These savages belonged to a group of stationary tribes, only one of which, the Caddoes, survives to our day as a separate community. Their enemies, the Chickasaws, Osages, Arkansas, and even the distant Illinois, waged such deadly war against them that, according to La Harpe, the unfortunate Nassonites were in the way of extinction, their numbers having fallen, within ten years, from twenty-five hundred souls to four hundred.[15]

La Harpe stopped among them to refresh his men, and build a house of cypress-wood as a beginning of the post he

[13] Penecaut, *Relation*, chaps. xvii., xviii. Le Page du Pratz, *Histoire de la Louisiane*, i. 13–22. Various documents in Margry, vi. 193–202.

[14] For an interesting contemporary map of the French establishment at Natchitoches, see Thomassy, *Géologie pratique de la Louisiane*.

[15] Bénard de la Harpe, in Margry, vi. 264.

was ordered to establish; then, having heard that a war with Spain had ruined his hopes of trade with New Mexico, he resolved to pursue his explorations.

With him went ten men, white, red, and black, with twenty-two horses bought from the Indians, for his journeyings were henceforth to be by land. The party moved in a northerly and westerly course, by hills, forests, and prairies, passed two branches of the Wichita, and on the third of September came to a river which La Harpe calls the southwest branch of the Arkansas, but which, if his observation of latitude is correct, must have been the main stream, not far from the site of Fort Mann. Here he was met by seven Indian chiefs, mounted on excellent horses saddled and bridled after the Spanish manner. They led him to where, along the plateau of the low, treeless hills that bordered the valley, he saw a string of Indian villages, extending for a league and belonging to nine several bands, the names of which can no longer be recognized, and most of which are no doubt extinct. He says that they numbered in all six thousand souls; and their dwellings were high, dome-shaped structures, built of clay mixed with reeds and straw, resting, doubtless, on a frame of bent poles.[16] With them were also some of the roving Indians of the plains, with their conical teepees of dressed buffalo-skin.

The arrival of the strangers was a great and amazing event for these savages, few of whom had ever seen a white man. On the day after their arrival the whole multitude gathered to receive them and offer them the calumet, with a profusion of songs and speeches. Then warrior after warrior recounted his exploits and boasted of the scalps he had taken. From eight in the morning till two hours after midnight the din of drums, songs, harangues, and dances continued without relenting, with a prospect of twelve hours more; and La Harpe, in desperation, withdrew to rest himself on a buffalo-robe, begging another Frenchman to take his place. His hosts left him in peace for a while; then the chiefs came to find him, painted his face blue, as a tribute of respect, put a cap of eagle-feath-

[16] Beaurain says that each of these bands spoke a language of its own. They had horses in abundance, descended from Spanish stock. Among them appear to have been the Ouacos, or Huecos, and the Wichitas,—two tribes better known as the Pawnee Picts. See Marcy, *Exploration of Red River*.

ers on his head, and laid numerous gifts at his feet. When at last the ceremony ended, some of the performers were so hoarse from incessant singing that they could hardly speak.[17]

La Harpe was told by his hosts that the Spanish settlements could be reached by ascending their river; but to do this was at present impossible. He began his backward journey, fell desperately ill of a fever, and nearly died before reaching Natchitoches.

Having recovered, he made an attempt, two years later, to explore the Arkansas in canoes, from its mouth, but accomplished little besides killing a good number of buffalo, bears, deer, and wild turkeys. He was confirmed, however, in the belief that the Comanches and the Spaniards of New Mexico might be reached by this route.

In the year of La Harpe's first exploration, one Du Tisné went up the Missouri to a point six leagues above Grand River, where stood the village of the Missouris. He wished to go farther, but they would not let him. He then returned to the Illinois, whence he set out on horseback with a few followers across what is now the State of Missouri, till he reached the village of the Osages, which stood on a hill high up the river Osage. At first he was well received; but when they found him disposed to push on to a town of their enemies, the Pawnees, forty leagues distant, they angrily refused to let him go. His firmness and hardihood prevailed, and at last they gave him leave. A ride of a few days over rich prairies brought him to the Pawnees, who, coming as he did from the hated Osages, took him for an enemy and threatened to kill him. Twice they raised the tomahawk over his head; but when the intrepid traveller dared them to strike, they began to treat him as a friend. When, however, he told them that he meant to go fifteen days' journey farther, to the Padoucas, or Comanches, their deadly enemies, they fiercely forbade him; and after planting a French flag in their village, he returned as he had come, guiding his way by compass, and reaching the Illinois in November, after extreme hardships.[18]

[17] Compare the account of La Harpe with that of the Chevalier de Beaurain; both are in Margry, vi. There is an abstract in *Journal historique.*

[18] *Relation de Bénard de la Harpe. Autre Relation du même. Du Tisné à Bienville.* Margry, vi. 309, 310, 313.

Early in 1721 two hundred mounted Spaniards, followed by a large body of Comanche warriors, came from New Mexico to attack the French at the Illinois, but were met and routed on the Missouri by tribes of that region.[19] In the next year, Bienville was told that they meant to return, punish those who had defeated them, and establish a post on the river Kansas; whereupon he ordered Boisbriant, commandant at the Illinois, to anticipate them by sending troops to build a fort at or near the same place. But the West India Company had already sent one Bourgmont on a similar errand, the object being to trade with the Spaniards in time of peace, and stop their incursions in time of war.[20] It was hoped also that, in the interest of trade, peace might be made between the Commanches and the tribes of the Missouri.[21]

Bourgmont was a man of some education, and well acquainted with these tribes, among whom he had traded for years. In pursuance of his orders he built a fort, which he named Fort Orléans, and which stood on the Missouri not far above the mouth of Grand River. Having thus accomplished one part of his mission, he addressed himself to the other, and prepared to march for the Comanche villages.

Leaving a sufficient garrison at the fort, he sent his ensign, Saint-Ange, with a party of soldiers and Canadians, in wooden canoes, to the villages of the Kansas higher up the stream, and on the third of July set out by land to join him, with a hundred and nine Missouri Indians and sixty-eight Osages in his train. A ride of five days brought him again to the banks of the Missouri, opposite a Kansas town. Saint-Ange had not yet arrived, the angry and turbid current, joined to fevers among his men, having retarded his progress. Meanwhile Bourgmont drew from the Kansas a promise that their warriors should go with him to the Comanches. Saint-Ange at last appeared, and at daybreak of the twenty-fourth the tents were struck and the pack-horses loaded. At six o'clock the party drew up in battle array on a hill above the Indian town, and then, with

[19] *Bienville au Conseil de Régence*, 20 *Juillet*, 1721.

[20] *Instructions au Sieur de Bourgmont*, 17 *Janvier*, 1722. Margry, vi. 389.

[21] The French had at this time gained a knowledge of the tribes of the Missouri as far up as the Arickaras, who were not, it seems, many days' journey below the Yellowstone, and who told them of "prodigiously high mountains,"—evidently the Rocky Mountains. *Mémoire de la Renaudière*, 1723.

drum beating and flag flying, began their march. "A fine prairie country," writes Bourgmont, "with hills and dales and clumps of trees to right and left." Sometimes the landscape quivered under the sultry sun, and sometimes thunder bellowed over their heads, and rain fell in floods on the steaming plains.

Renaudière, engineer of the party, one day stood by the side of the path and watched the whole procession as it passed him. The white men were about twenty in all. He counted about three hundred Indian warriors, with as many squaws, some five hundred children, and a prodigious number of dogs, the largest and strongest of which dragged heavy loads. The squaws also served as beasts of burden; and, says the journal, "they will carry as much as a dog will drag." Horses were less abundant among these tribes than they afterwards became, so that their work fell largely upon the women.

On the sixth day the party was within three leagues of the river Kansas, at a considerable distance above its mouth. Bourgmont had suffered from dysentery on the march, and an access of the malady made it impossible for him to go farther. It is easy to conceive the regret with which he saw himself compelled to return to Fort Orléans. The party retraced their steps, carrying their helpless commander on a litter.

First, however, he sent one Gaillard on a perilous errand. Taking with him two Comanche slaves bought for the purpose from the Kansas, Gaillard was ordered to go to the Comanche village with the message that Bourgmont had been on his way to make them a friendly visit, and, though stopped by illness, hoped soon to try again, with better success.

Early in September, Bourgmont, who had arrived safely at Fort Orléans, received news that the mission of Gaillard had completely succeeded; on which, though not wholly recovered from his illness, he set out again on his errand of peace, accompanied by his young son, besides Renaudière, a surgeon, and nine soldiers. On reaching the great village of the Kansas he found there five Comanche chiefs and warriors, whom Gaillard had induced to come thither with him. Seven chiefs of the Otoes presently appeared, in accordance with an invitation of Bourgmont; then six chiefs of the Iowas and the head chief of the Missouris. With these and the Kansas chiefs a solemn council was held around a fire before Bourgmont's tent; speeches were made, the pipe of peace was smoked, and presents were distributed.

On the eighth of October the march began, the five Comanches and the chiefs of several other tribes, including the Omahas, joining the cavalcade. Gaillard and another Frenchman named Quesnel were sent in advance to announce their approach to the Comanches, while Bourgmont and his followers moved up the north side of the river Kansas till the eleventh, when they forded it at a point twenty leagues from its mouth, and took a westward and southwestward course, sometimes threading the grassy valleys of little streams, sometimes crossing the dry upland prairie, covered with the short, tufted dull-green herbage since known as "buffalo grass." Wild turkeys clamored along every watercourse; deer were seen on all sides, buffalo were without number, sometimes in grazing droves, and sometimes dotting the endless plain as far as the eye could reach. Ruffian wolves, white and gray, eyed the travellers askance, keeping a safe distance by day, and howling about the camp all night. Of the antelope and the elk the journal makes no mention. Bourgmont chased a buffalo on horseback and shot him with a pistol—which is probably the first recorded example of that way of hunting.

The stretches of high, rolling, treeless prairie grew more vast as the travellers advanced. On the seventeenth, they found an abandoned Comanche camp. On the next day as they stopped to dine, and had just unsaddled their horses, they saw a distant smoke towards the west, on which they set the dry grass on fire as an answering signal. Half an hour later a body of wild horsemen came toward them at full speed, and among them were their two couriers, Gaillard and Quesnel, waving a French flag. The strangers were eighty Comanche warriors, with the grand chief of the tribe at their head. They dashed up to Bourgmont's bivouac and leaped from their horse, when a general shaking of hands ensued, after which white men and red seated themselves on the ground and smoked the pipe of peace. Then all rode together to the Comanche camp, three leagues distant.[22]

[22] This meeting took place a little north of the Arkansas, apparently where that river makes a northward bend, near the twenty-second degree of west longitude. The Comanche villages were several days' journey to the southwest. This tribe is always mentioned in the early French narratives as the Padoucas,—a name by which the Comanches are occasionally known to this day. See Whipple and Turner, *Reports upon Indian Tribes,* in *Explorations and Surveys for the Pacific Railroad* (Senate Doc., 1853, 1854).

Bourgmont pitched his tents at a pistol-shot from the Comanche lodges, whence a crowd of warriors presently came to visit him. They spread buffalo-robes on the ground, placed upon them the French commander, his officers, and his young sn; then lifted each, with its honored load, and carried them all, with yells of joy and gratulation, to the lodge of the Great Chief, where there was a feast of ceremony lasting till nightfall.

On the next day Bourgmont displayed to his hosts the marvellous store of gifts he had brought for them,—guns, swords, hatchets, kettles, gunpowder, bullets, red cloth, blue cloth, hand-mirrors, knives, shirts, awls, scissors, needles, hawks' bells, vermilion, beads, and other enviable commodities, of the like of which they had never dreamed. Two hundred savages gathered before the French tents, where Bourgmont, with the gifts spread on the ground before him, stood with a French flag in his hand, surrounded by his officers and the Indian chiefs of his party, and harangued the admiring auditors.

He told them that he had come to bring them a message from the King, his master, who was the Great Chief of all the nations of the earth, and whose will it was that the Comanches should live in peace with his other children,—the Missouris, Osages, Kansas, Otoes, Omahas, and Pawnees,—with whom they had long been at war; that the chiefs of these tribes were now present, ready to renounce their old enmities; that the Comanches should henceforth regard them as friends, share with them the blessing of alliance and trade with the French, and give to these last free passage through their country to trade with the Spaniards of New Mexico. Bourgmont then gave the French flag to the Great Chief, to be kept forever as a pledge of that day's compact. The chief took the flag, and promised in behalf of his people to keep peace inviolate with the Indian children of the King. Then, with unspeakable delight, he and his tribesmen took and divided the gifts.

The next two days were spent in feasts and rejoicings. "Is it true that you are men?" asked the Great Chief. "I have heard wonders of the French, but I never could have believed what I see this day." Then, taking up a handful of earth, "The Spaniards are like this; but you are like the sun." And he offered Bourgmont, in case of need, the aid of his two thousand Comanche warriors. The pleasing manners of his visitors, and their unparalleled generosity, had completely won his heart.

As the object of the expedition was accomplished, or seemed to be so, the party set out on their return. A ride of ten days brought them again to the Missouri; they descended in canoes to Fort Orléans, and sang Te Deum in honor of the peace.[23]

No farther discovery in this direction was made for the next fifteen years. Though the French had explored the Missouri as far as the site of Fort Clark and the Mandan villages, they were possesed by the idea—due, perhaps, to Indian reports concerning the great tributary river, the Yellowstone—that in its upper course the main stream bent so far southward as to form a waterway to New Mexico, with which it was the constant desire of the authorities of Louisiana to open trade. A way thither was at last made known by two brothers named Mallet, who with six companions went up the Platte to its South Fork, which they called River of the Padoucas,—a name given it on some maps down to the middle of this century. They followed the South Fork for some distance, and then, turning southward and southwestward, crossed the plains of Colorado. Here the dried dung of the buffalo was their only fuel; and it has continued to feed the camp-fire of the traveller in this treeless region within the memory of many now living. They crossed the upper Arkansas and apparently the Cimarron, passed Taos, and on the twenty-second of July reached Santa Fé, where they spent the winter. On the first of May, 1740, they began their return journey, three of them crossing the plains to the Pawnee villages, and the rest descending the Arkansas to the Mississippi.[24]

The bold exploit of the brothers Mallet attracted great attention at New Orleans, and Bienville resolved to renew it, find if possible a nearer and better way to Santa Fé, determine the nature and extent of these mysterious western re-

[23] *Relation du Voyage du Sieur de Bourgmont, Juin-Novembre, 1724,* in Margry, vi. 398. Le Page du Pratz, iii. 141.

[24] *Journal du Voyage des Frères Mallet, présenté à MM. de Bienville et Salmon.* This narrative is meagre and confused, but serves to establish the main points. *Copie du Certificat donné à Santa Fé aux sept* [huit] *Français par le Général Hurtado,* 24 *Juillet,* 1739. *Père Rébald au Père de Beaubois, sans date. Bienville et Salmon au Ministre,* 30 *Avril,* 1741, in Margry, vi. 455–468.

gions, and satisfy a lingering doubt whether they were not contiguous to China and Tartary.[25] A naval officer, Fabry de la Bruyère, was sent on this errand, with the brothers Mallet and a few soldiers and Canadians. He ascended the Canadian Fork of the Arkansas, named by him the St. André, became entangled in the shallows and quicksands of that difficult river, fell into disputes with his men, and, after protracted efforts, returned unsuccessful.[26]

While French enterprise was unveiling the remote Southwest, two indomitable Canadians were pushing still more noteworthy explorations into more northern regions of the continent.

[25] *Instructions données par Jean-Baptiste de Bienville à Fabry de la Bruyère,* 1 *Juin,* 1741. Bienville was behind his time in geographical knowledge. As early as 1724 Bénard de la Harpe knew that in ascending the Missouri or the Arkansas one was moving towards the "Western Sea,"—that is, the Pacific,—and might, perhaps, find some river flowing into it. See *Routes qu'on peut tenir pour se rendre à la Mer de l'Ouest,* in *Journal historique,* 387.

[26] *Extrait des Lettres du Sieur Fabry.*

Chapter 16

1716–1761
Search for the Pacific

IN THE DISASTROUS last years of Louis XIV. the court gave little thought to the New World; but under the regency of the Duke of Orléans interest in American affairs revived. Plans for reaching the Mer de l'Ouest, or Pacific Ocean, were laid before the Regent in 1716. It was urged that the best hope was in sending an expedition across the continent, seeing that every attempt to find a westward passage by Hudson Bay had failed. As starting-points and bases of supply for the expedition, it was proposed to established three posts, one on the north shore of Lake Superior, at the mouth of the river Kaministiguia, another at Lac des Cristineaux, now called Lake of the Woods, and the third at Lake Winnipeg,— the last being what in American phrase is called the "jumping-off place," or the point where the expedition was to leave behind the last trace of civilization. These posts were to cost the Crown nothing; since by a device common in such cases, those who built and maintained them were to be paid by a monopoly of the fur-trade in the adjacent countries. It was admitted, however, that the subsequent exploration must be at the charge of the government, and would require fifty good men, at three hundred francs a year each, besides equipment and supplies. All things considered, it was reckoned that an overland way to the Pacific might be found for about fifty thousand francs, or ten thousand dollars.[1]

The Regent approved the scheme so far as to order the preliminary step to be taken by establishing the three posts, and in this same year, Lieutenant La Noue, of the colony troops, began the work by building a stockade at the mouth of the Kaministiguia. Little more was done in furtherance of the exploration till three years later, when the celebrated Jesuit, Charlevoix, was ordered by the Duke of Orléans to

---

[1] *Mémoire fait et arresté par le Conseil de Marine*, 3 *Févier*, 1717; *Mémoire du Roy*, 26 *Juin*, 1717.

repair to America and gain all possible information concerning the Western Sea and the way to it.[2]

In the next year he went to the Upper Lakes, and questioned missionaries, officers, *voyageurs,* and Indians. The results were not satisfactory. The missionaries and the officers had nothing to tell; the voyagers and Indians knew no more than they, but invented confused and contradictory falsehoods to hide their ignorance. Charlevoix made note of everything, and reported to the Comte de Toulouse that the Pacific probably formed the western boundary of the country of the Sioux, and that some Indians told him that they had been to its shores and found white men there different from the French.

Believing that these stories were not without foundation, Charlevoix reported two plans as likely to lead to the coveted discovery. One was to ascend the Missouri, "the source of which is certainly not far from the sea, as all the Indians I have met have unanimously assured me;" and the other was to establish a mission among the Sioux, from whom, after thoroughly learning their language, the missionaries could, as he thinks, gain all the desired information.[3]

The Regent approved the plan of the mission; but the hostile disposition of the Sioux and the Outagamies prevented its execution for several years. In 1727 the scheme was revived, and the colonial minister at Versailles ordered the governor of Canada to send two missionaries to the Sioux. But the mission required money, and the King would not give it. Hence the usual expedient was adopted. A company was formed, and invested with a monopoly of the Sioux fur-trade, on condition of building a fort, mission-house, and chapel, and keeping an armed force to guard them. It was specially provided that none but pious and virtuous persons were to be allowed to join the Company, "in order," says the document, "to attract the benediction of God upon them and their

[2] *Charlevoix au Comte de Morville,* 1 *Avril,* 1723.

[3] The valuable journal of Charlevoix's western travels, written in the form of letters, was published in connection with his *Histoire de la Nouvelle France.* After his visit to the Lakes, he went to New Orleans, intending to return in the spring and continue his inquiries for the Western Sea; but being unable to do this, he went back to France at the end of 1722. The official report of his mission is contained in a letter to the Comte de Toulouse, 20 January, 1723.

business."[4] The prospects of the Company were thought good, and the governor himself was one of the shareholders. While the mission was given the most conspicuous place in the enterprise, its objects were rather secular than spiritual,—to attach the Sioux to the French interest by the double ties of religion and trade, and utilize their supposed knowledge to reach the Pacific.[5]

Father Guigans was made the head of the mission, and Boucher de la Perrière the military chief. The party left Montreal in June, and, journeying to the Mississippi by way of Michilimackinac, Green Bay, Fox River, and the Wisconsin, went up the great river to Lake Pepin, where the adventurous Nicolas Perrot had built two trading-posts more than forty years before. Even if his time-worn tenements were still standing, La Perrière had no thought of occupying them. On the north, or rather west, side of the lake his men found a point of land that seemed fit for their purpose, disembarked, cut down trees, and made a square stockade enclosing the necessary buildings. It was near the end of October before they were all well housed. A large band of Sioux presently appeared, and set up their teepees hard by. When the birthday of the governor came, the party celebrated it with a display of fireworks and vociferous shouts of *Vive le Roi, Vive Charles de Beauharnois*, while the Indians yelped in fright and amazement at the pyrotechnics, or stood pressing their hands upon their mouths in silent amazement. The French called their fort Fort Beauharnois, and invited the aid of Saint Michael the Archangel by naming the mission in his honor. All went well till April, when the water rose with the spring floods and filled fort, chapel, and houses to the depth of nearly three feet, ejecting the whole party, and forcing them to encamp on higher ground till the deluge subsided.[6]

Worse enemies than the floods soon found them out. These were the irrepressible Outagamies, who rose against the intruding French and incited the Sioux to join them. There

[4] *Traité de la Compagnie des Sioux*, 6 *Juin*, 1727.

[5] On this scheme, *Vaudreuil et Bégon au Ministre*, 4 *Octobre*, 1723; *Longueuil et Bégon au Ministre*, 31 *Octobre*, 1725; *Beauharnois et Dupuy au Ministre*, 25 *Septembre*, 1727.

[6] *Guignas à Beauharnois*, 28 *Mai*, 1728.

was no profit for the Company, and no safety for its agents. The stock-holders became discouraged, and would not support the enterprise. The fort was abandoned, till in 1731 a new arrangement was made, followed by another attempt.[7] For a time a prosperous trade was carried on; but, as commonly happened in such cases, the adventurers seem to have thought more of utilizing their monopoly than of fulfilling the terms on which they had received it. The wild Sioux of the plains, instead of being converted and turned into Frenchmen, proved such dangerous neighbors that, in 1737, Legardeur de Saint-Pierre, who then commanded the post, found himself forced to abandon it.[8] The enterprise had failed in both its aims. The Western Sea was still a mystery, and the Sioux were not friends, but enemies. Legardeur de Saint-Pierre recommended that they should be destroyed,—benevolent advice easy to give, and impossible to execute.[9]

René Gaultier de Varennes, lieutenant in the regiment of Carignan, married at Three Rivers, in 1667, the daughter of Pierre Boucher, governor of that place; the age of the bride, Demoiselle Marie Boucher, being twelve years, six months, and eighteen days. Varennes succeeded his father-in-law as governor of Three Rivers, with a salary of twelve hundred francs, to which he added the profits of a farm of forty acres; and on these modest resources, reinforced by an illicit trade in furs, he made shift to sustain the dignity of his office. His wife became the mother of numerous offspring, among whom was Pierre, born in 1685,—an active and hardy youth, who, like the rest of the poor but vigorous Canadian *noblesse*, seemed born for the forest and the fur-trade. When, however, the War of the Spanish Succession broke out, the young man crossed the sea, obtained the commission of lieutenant, and was nearly killed at the battle of Malplaquet, where he was shot through the body, received six sabre-cuts, and was left for dead on the field. He recovered, and returned to Canada, when, finding his services slighted, he again took to the woods. He had assumed the designation of La Vérendrye, and thence-

[7] *Beauharnois et Mosquart au Ministre*, 25 *Octobre*, 1729; *Idem*, 12 *Octobre*, 1731.

[8] *Relation du Sieur de Saint-Pierre*, 14 *Octobre*, 1737.

[9] "Cet officier [Saint-Pierre] a ajouté qu'il seroit avantageux de détruire cette nation."—*Mémoire de Beauharnois*, 1738.

forth his full name was Pierre Gaultier de Varennes de la Vérendrye.[10]

In 1728, he was in command of a small post on Lake Nipigon, north of Lake Superior. Here an Indian chief from the river Kaministiguia told him of a certain great lake which discharged itself by a river flowing westward. The Indian further declared that he had descended this river till he reached water that ebbed and flowed, and, terrified by the strange phenomenon, had turned back, though not till he had heard of a great salt lake, bordered with many villages. Other Indians confirmed and improved the story. "These people," said La Vérendrye to the Jesuit Degonnor, "are great liars, but now and then they tell the truth."[11] It seemed to him likely that their stories of a western river flowing to a western sea were not totally groundless, and that the true way to the Pacific was not, as had been supposed, through the country of the Sioux, but farther northward, through that of the Cristineaux and Assiniboins, or, in other words, through the region now called Manitoba. In this view he was sustained by his friend Degonnor, who had just returned from the ill-starred Sioux mission.

La Vérendrye, fired with the zeal of discovery, offered to search for the Western Sea if the King would give him one hundred men and supply canoes, arms, and provisions.[12] But, as was usual in such cases, the King would give nothing; and though the governor, Beauharnois, did all in his power to promote the enterprise, the burden and the risk were left to the adventurer himself. La Vérendrye was authorized to find a way to the Pacific at his own expense, in consideration of a monopoly of the fur-trade in the regions north and west of Lake Superior. This vast and remote country was held by tribes who were doubtful friends of the French, and perpetual enemies of each other. The risks of the trade were as great as its possible profits, and, to reap these, vast outlays must

[10] M. Benjamin Sulte has traced out the family history of the Varennes in the parish registers of Three Rivers and other trustworthy sources. See *Revue Canadienne*, x. 781, 849, 935.

[11] *Relation du Père Degonnor, Jésuite, Missionnaire des Sioux, adressée à M. le Marquis de Beauharnois.*

[12] *Relation de Degonnor; Beauharnois au Ministre,* 1 *Octobre,* 1731.

first be made: forts must be built, manned, provisioned, and stocked with goods brought through two thousand miles of difficult and perilous wilderness. There were other dangers, more insidious, and perhaps greater. The exclusive privileges granted to La Vérendrye would inevitably rouse the intensest jealousy of the Canadian merchants, and they would spare no effort to ruin him. Intrigue and calumny would be busy in his absence. If, as was likely, his patron, Beauharnois, should be recalled, the new governor might be turned against him, his privileges might be suddenly revoked, the forts he had built passed over to his rivals, and all his outlays turned to their profit, as had happened to La Salle on the recall of his patron, Frontenac. On the other hand, the country was full of the choicest furs, which the Indians had hitherto carried to the English at Hudson Bay, but which the proposed trading-posts would secure to the French. La Vérendrye's enemies pretended that he thought of nothing but beaver-skins, and slighted the discovery which he had bound himself to undertake; but his conduct proves that he was true to his engagements, and that ambition to gain honorable distinction in the service of the King had a large place among the motives that impelled him.

As his own resources were of the smallest, he took a number of associates on conditions most unfavorable to himself. Among them they raised money enough to begin the enterprise, and on the eighth of June, 1731, La Vérendrye and three of his sons, together with his nephew, La Jemeraye, the Jesuit Messager, and a party of Canadians, set out from Montreal. It was late in August before they reached the great portage of Lake Superior, which led across the height of land separating the waters of that lake from those flowing to Lake Winnipeg. The way was long and difficult. The men, who had perhaps been tampered with, mutinied, and refused to go farther.[13] Some of them, with much ado, consented at last to proceed, and, under the lead of La Jemeraye, made their way by an intricate and broken chain of lakes and streams to Rainy Lake, where they built a fort and called it Fort St. Pierre. La Vérendrye was forced to winter with the

[13] *Mémoire du Sieur de la Vérendrye du Sujet des Établissements pour parvenir à la Découverte de la Mer de l'Ouest,* in Margry, vi. 585.

rest of the party at the river Kaministiguia, not far from the great portage. Here months were lost, during which a crew of useless mutineers had to be fed and paid; and it was not till the next June that he could get them again into motion towards Lake Winnipeg.

This ominous beginning was followed by a train of disasters. His associates abandoned him; the merchants on whom he depended for supplies would not send them, and he found himself, in his own words, "destitute of everything." His nephew, La Jemeraye, died. The Jesuit Auneau, bent on returning to Michilimackinac, set out with La Vérendrye's eldest son and a party of twenty Canadians. A few days later, they were all found on an island in the Lake of the Woods, murdered and mangled by the Sioux.[14] The Assiniboins and Cristineaux, mortal foes of that fierce people, offered to join the French and avenge the butchery; but a war with the Sioux would have ruined La Vérendrye's plans of discovery, and exposed to torture and death the French traders in their country. Therefore he restrained himself and declined the proffered aid, at the risk of incurring the contempt of those who offered it.

Beauharnois twice appealed to the court to give La Vérendrye some little aid, urging that he was at the end of his resources, and that a grant of thirty thousand francs, or six thousand dollars, would enable him to find a way to the Pacific. All help was refused, but La Vérendrye was told that he might let out his forts to other traders, and so raise means to pursue the discovery.

In 1740 he went for the third time to Montreal, where, instead of aid, he found a lawsuit. "In spite," he says, "of the derangement of my affairs, the envy and jealousy of various persons impelled them to write letters to the court insinuating that I thought of nothing but making my fortune. If more than forty thousand livres of debt which I have on my shoulders are an advantage, then I can flatter myself that I am very rich. In all my misfortunes, I have the consolation of seeing that M. de Beauharnois enters into my views, recog-

[14] *Beauharnois au Ministre*, 14 *Octobre*, 1736; *Relation du Massacre au Lac des Bois, en Juin*, 1736; *Journal de la Vérendrye, joint à la lettre de M. de Beauharnois du—Octobre*, 1737.

nizes the uprightness of my intentions, and does me justice in spite of opposition."[15]

Meanwhile, under all his difficulties, he had explored a vast region hitherto unknown, diverted a great and lucrative fur-trade from the English at Hudson Bay, and secured possession of it by six fortified posts,—Fort St. Pierre, on Rainy Lake; Fort St. Charles, on the Lake of the Woods; Fort Maurepas, at the mouth of the river Winnipeg; Fort Bourbon, on the eastern side of Lake Winnipeg; Fort La Reine, on the Assiniboin; Fort Dauphin, on Lake Manitoba. Besides these he built another post, called Fort Rouge, on the site of the city of Winnipeg; and, some time after, another, at the mouth of the river Poskoiac, or Saskatchewan, neither of which, however, was long occupied. These various forts were only stockade works flanked with block-houses; but the difficulty of building and maintaining them in this remote wilderness was incalculable.[16]

He had inquired on all sides for the Pacific. The Assiniboins could tell him nothing. Nor could any information be expected from them, since their relatives and mortal enemies, the Sioux, barred their way to the West. The Cristineaux were equally ignorant; but they supplied the place of knowledge by invention, and drew maps, some of which seem to have been made with no other intention than that of amusing themselves by imposing on the inquirer. They also declared that some of their number had gone down a river called White River, or River of the West, where they found a plant that shed drops like blood, and saw serpents of prodigious size. They said further that on the lower part of this

[15] *Mémoire du Sieur de la Vérendrye au Sujet des Établissements pour parvenir à la Découverte de la Mer de l'Ouest.*

[16] *Mémoire en abrégé de la Carte représente les Établissements faits par le Sieur de la Vérendrye et ses Enfants* (Margry, vi. 616); *Carte des Nouvelles Découvertes dans l'Ouest du Canada dressée sur les Mémoires du M^r. de la Vérandrie et donnée au Dépôt de la Marine par M. de la Galissonnière,* 1750; Bellin, *Remarques sur la Carte de l'Amérique,* 1755; Bougainville, *Mémoire sur l'État de la Nouvelle France,* 1757.

Most of La Vérendrye's forts were standing during the Seven Years' War, and were known collectively as *Postes de la Mer de l'Ouest.*

river were walled towns, where dwelt white men who had knives, hatchets, and cloth, but no firearms.[17]

Both Assiniboins and Cristineaux declared that there was a distant tribe on the Missouri, called Mantannes (Mandans), who knew the way to the Western Sea, and would guide him to it. Lured by this assurance, and feeling that he had sufficiently secured his position to enable him to begin his western exploration, La Vérendrye left Fort La Reine in October, 1738, with twenty men, and pushed up the river Assiniboin till its rapids and shallows threatened his bark canoes with destruction. Then, with a band of Assiniboin Indians who had joined him, he struck across the prairie for the Mandans, his Indian companions hunting buffalo on the way. They approached the first Mandan village on the afternoon of the third of December, displaying a French flag and firing three volleys as a salute. The whole population poured out to see the marvellous visitors, who were conducted through the staring crowd to the lodge of the principal chief, —a capacious structure so thronged with the naked and greasy savages that the Frenchmen were half smothered. What was worse, they lost the bag that held all their presents for the Mandans, which was snatched away in the confusion, and hidden in one of the *caches*, called cellars by La Vérendrye, of which the place was full. The chief seemed much discomposed at this mishap, and explained it by saying that there were many rascals in the village. The loss was serious, since without the presents nothing could be done. Nor was this all; for in the morning La Vérendrye missed his interpreter, and was told that he had fallen in love with an Assiniboin girl and gone off in pursuit of her. The French were now without any means of communicating with the Mandans, from whom, however, before the disappearance of the interpreter, they had already received a variety of questionable information, chiefly touching white men cased in iron who were said to live on the river below at the distance of a whole summer's journey. As they were impervious to arrows,—so the story ran,—it was necessary to shoot their horses, after which, being too heavy to run, they were easily caught. This was probably suggested by the armor of the

[17] *Journal de la Vérendrye joint à Lettre de M. de Beauharnois du—Octobre*, 1737.

Spaniards, who had more than once made incursions as far as the lower Missouri; but the narrators drew on their imagination for various additional particulars.

The Mandans seem to have much declined in numbers during the century that followed this visit of La Vérendrye. He says that they had six villages on or near the Missouri, of which the one seen by him was the smallest, though he thinks that it contained a hundred and thirty houses.[18] As each of these large structures held a number of families, the population must have been considerable. Yet when Prince Maximilian visited the Mandans in 1833, he found only two villages, containing jointly two hundred and forty warriors and a total population of about a thousand souls. Without having seen the statements of La Vérendrye, he speaks of the population as greatly reduced by wars and the small-pox, —a disease which a few years later nearly exterminated the tribe.[19]

La Vérendrye represents the six villages as surrounded with ditches and stockades, flanked by a sort of bastion,—defences which, he says, had nothing savage in their construction. In later times the fortifications were of a much ruder kind, though Maximilian represents them as having pointed salients to serve as bastions. La Vérendrye mentions some peculiar customs of the Mandans which answer exactly to those described by more recent observers.

He had intended to winter with the tribe; but the loss of the presents and the interpreter made it useless to stay, and,

[18] *Journal de La Vérendrye,* 1738, 1739. This journal, which is ill-written and sometimes obscure, is printed in Brymner, *Report on Canadian Archives,* 1889.

[19] Le Prince Maximilien de Wied-Neuwied, *Voyage dans l'Intérieur de l'Amérique du Nord,* ii. 371, 372 (Paris, 1843). When Captains Lewis and Clark visited the Mandans in 1804, they found them in two villages, with about three hundred and fifty warriors. They report that, about forty years before, they lived in nine villages, the ruins of which the explorers saw about eighty miles below the two villages then occupied by the tribe. The Mandans had moved up the river in consequence of the persecutions of the Sioux and the small-pox, which had made great havoc among them. *Expedition of Lewis and Clark,* i. 129 (ed. Philadelphia, 1814). These nine villages seem to have been above Cannon-ball River, a tributary of the Missouri.

leaving two men in the village to learn the language, he began his return to Fort La Reine. "I was very ill," he writes, "but hoped to get better on the way. The reverse was the case, for it was the depth of winter. It would be impossible to suffer more than I did. It seemed that nothing but death could release us from such miseries." He reached Fort La Reine on the eleventh of February, 1739.

His iron constitution seems to have been severely shaken; but he had sons worthy of their father. The two men left among the Mandans appeared at Fort La Reine in September. They reported that they had been well treated, and that their hosts had parted from them with regret. They also declared that at the end of spring several Indian tribes, all well supplied with horses, had come, as was their yearly custom, to the Mandan villages to barter embroidered buffalo hides and other skins for corn and beans; that they had encamped, to the number of two hundred lodges, on the farther side of the Missouri, and that among them was a band said to have come from a distant country towards the sunset, where there were white men who lived in houses built of bricks and stones.

The two Frenchmen crossed over to the camp of these western strangers, among whom they found a chief who spoke, or professed to speak, the language of the mysterious white men, which to the two Frenchmen was unintelligible. Fortunately, he also spoke the language of the Mandans, of which the Frenchmen had learned a little during their stay, and hence were able to gather that the white men in question had beards, and that they prayed to the Master of Life in great houses, built for the purpose, holding books, the leaves of which were like husks of Indian corn, singing together and repeating *Jésus, Marie.* The chief gave many other particulars, which seemed to show that he had been in contact with Spaniards,—probably those of California; for he described their houses as standing near the great lake, of which the water rises and falls and is not fit to drink. He invited the two Frenchmen to go with him to this strange country, saying that it could be reached before winter, though a wide circuit must be made, to avoid a fierce and dangerous tribe called Snake Indians (*Gens du Serpent*).[20]

On hearing this story, La Vérendrye sent his eldest son,

---

[20] *Journal du Sieur de la Vérendrye,* 1740, in Archives de la Marine.

Pierre, to pursue the discovery with two men, ordering him to hire guides among the Mandans and make his way to the Western Sea. But no guides were to be found, and in the next summer the young man returned from his bootless errand.[21]

Undaunted by this failure, Pierre set out again in the next spring, 1742, with his younger brother, the Chevalier de la Vérendrye. Accompanied only by two Canadians, they left Fort La Reine on the twenty-ninth of April, and following, no doubt, the route of the Assiniboin and Mouse River, reached the chief village of the Mandans in about three weeks.

Here they found themselves the welcome guests of this singularly interesting tribe, ruined by the smallpox nearly half a century ago, but preserved to memory by the skilful pencil of the artist Charles Bodmer, and the brush of the painter George Catlin, both of whom saw them at a time when they were little changed in habits and manners since the visit of the brothers La Vérendrye.[22]

Thus, though the report of the two brothers is too concise and brief, we know what they saw when they entered the central area, or public square, of the village. Around stood the Mandan lodges, looking like round flattened hillocks of earth, forty or fifty feet wide. On examination they proved to be framed of strong posts and poles, covered with a thick matting of intertwined willow-branches, over which was laid a bed of well-compacted clay or earth two or three feet thick. This heavy roof was supported by strong interior posts.[23]

[21] *Mémoire du Sieur de la Vérendrye, joint à sa lettre du 31 Octobre,* 1744.

[22] Prince Maximilian spent the winter of 1832–33 near the Mandan villages. His artist, with the instinct of genius, seized the characteristics of the wild life before him, and rendered them with admirable vigor and truth. Catlin spent a considerable time among the Mandans soon after the visit of Prince Maximilian, and had unusual opportunities of studying them. He was an indifferent painter, a shallow observer, and a garrulous and windy writer; yet his enthusiastic industry is beyond praise, and his pictures are invaluable as faithful reflections of aspects of Indian life which are gone forever.

Beauharnois calls the Mandans *Blancs Barbus,* and says that they have been hitherto unknown. The name Mantannes, or Mandans, is that given them by the Assiniboins.

[23] The Minnetarees and other tribes of the Missouri built their lodges in a similar way.

The open place which the dwellings enclosed served for games, dances, and the ghastly religious or magical ceremonies practised by the tribe. Among the other structures was the sacred "medicine lodge," distinguished by three or four tall poles planted before it, each surmounted by an effigy looking much like a scarecrow, and meant as an offering to the spirits.

If the two travellers had been less sparing of words, they would doubtless have told us that as they entered the village square the flattened earthen domes that surrounded it were thronged with squaws and children,—for this was always the case on occasions of public interest,—and that they were forced to undergo a merciless series of feasts in the lodges of the chiefs. Here, seated by the sunken hearth in the middle, under the large hole in the roof that served both for window and chimney, they could study at their ease the domestic economy of their entertainers. Each lodge held a *gens,* or family connection, whose beds of raw buffalo hide, stretched on poles, were ranged around the circumference of the building, while by each stood a post on which hung shields, lances, bows, quivers, medicine-bags, and masks formed of the skin of a buffalo's head, with the horns attached to be used in the magic buffalo dance.

Every day had its sports to relieve the monotony of savage existence, the game of the stick and the rolling ring, the archery practice of boys, horse-racing on the neighboring prairie, and incessant games of chance; while every evening, in contrast to these gayeties, the long, dismal wail of women rose from the adjacent cemetery, where the dead of the village, sewn fast in buffalo hides, lay on scaffolds above the reach of wolves.

The Mandans did not know the way to the Pacific, but they told the brothers that they expected a speedy visit from a tribe or band called Horse Indians, who could guide them thither. It is impossible to identify this people with any certainty.[24] The two travellers waited for them in vain till

[24] The Cheyennes have a tradition that they were the first tribe of this region to have horses. This may perhaps justify a conjecture that the northern division of this brave and warlike people were the Horse Indians of La Vérendrye; though an Indian tradition, unless backed by well-established facts, can never be accepted as substantial evidence.

after midsummer, and then, as the season was too far advanced for longer delay, they hired two Mandans to conduct them to their customary haunts.

They set out on horseback, their scanty baggage and their stock of presents being no doubt carried by pack-animals. Their general course was west-southwest, with the Black Hills at a distance on their left, and the upper Missouri on their right. The country was a rolling prairie, well covered for the most part with grass, and watered by small alkaline streams creeping towards the Missouri with an opaque, whitish current. Except along the watercourses, there was little or no wood. "I noticed," says the Chevalier de la Vérendrye, "earths of different colors, blue, green, red, or black, white as chalk, or yellowish like ochre." This was probably in the "bad lands" of the Little Missouri, where these colored earths form a conspicuous feature in the bare and barren bluffs, carved into fantastic shapes by the storms.[25]

For twenty days the travellers saw no human being, so scanty was the population of these plains. Game, however, was abundant. Deer sprang from the tall, reedy grass of the river bottoms; buffalo tramped by in ponderous columns, or dotted the swells of the distant prairie with their grazing thousands; antelope approached, with the curiosity of their species, to gaze at the passing horsemen, then fled like the wind; and as they neared the broken uplands towards the Yellowstone, they saw troops of elk and flocks of mountain-sheep. Sometimes, for miles together, the dry plain was studded thick with the earthen mounds that marked the burrows of the curious marmots, called prairie-dogs, from their squeaking bark. Wolves, white and gray, howled about the camp at night, and their cousin, the coyote, seated in the dusk of evening upright on the grass, with nose turned to the sky, saluted them with a complication of yelpings, as if a score of petulant voices were pouring together from the throat of one small beast.

On the eleventh of August, after a march of about three weeks, the brothers reached a hill, or group of hills, apparently west of the Little Missouri, and perhaps a part of

[25] A similar phenomenon occurs farther west on the face of the perpendicular bluffs that, in one place, border the valley of the river Rosebud.

the Powder River Range. It was here that they hoped to find the Horse Indians, but nobody was to be seen. Arming themselves with patience, they built a hut, made fires to attract by the smoke any Indians roaming near, and went every day to the tops of the hills to reconnoitre. At length, on the fourteenth of September, they described a spire of smoke on the distant prairie.

One of their Mandan guides had left them and gone back to his village. The other, with one of the Frenchmen, went towards the smoke, and found a camp of Indians, whom the journal calls Les Beaux Hommes, and who were probably Crows, or Apsaroka, a tribe remarkable for stature and symmetry, who long claimed that region as their own. They treated the visitors well, and sent for the other Frenchmen to come to their lodges, where they were received with great rejoicing. The remaining Mandan, however, became frightened,—for the Beaux Hommes were enemies of his tribe,—and he soon followed his companion on his solitary march homeward.

The brothers remained twenty-one days in the camp of the Beaux Hommes, much perplexed for want of an interpreter. The tribes of the plains have in common a system of signs by which they communicate with each other, and it is likely that the brothers had learned it from the Sioux or Assiniboins, with whom they had been in familiar intercourse. By this or some other means they made their hosts understand that they wished to find the Horse Indians; and the Beau Hommes, being soothed by presents, offered some of their young men as guides. They set out on the ninth of October, following a south-southwest course.[26]

In two days they met a band of Indians, called by them the Little Foxes, and on the fifteenth and seventeenth two villages of another unrecognizable horde, named Pioya. From La Vérendrye's time to our own, this name "villages" has always been given to the encampments of the wandering people of the plains. All these nomadic communities joined

[26] *Journal du Voyage fait par le Chevalier de la Vérendrye en 1742.* The copy before me is from the original in the Dèpôt des Cartes de la Marine. A duplicate, in the Archives des Affaires Étrangères, is printed by Margry. It gives the above date as November 9 instead of October 9. The context shows the latter to be correct.

them, and they moved together southward, till they reached
at last the lodges of the long-sought Horse Indians. They
found them in the extremity of distress and terror. Their camp
resounded with howls and wailings; and not without cause,
for the Snakes, or Shoshones,—a formidable people living
farther westward,—had lately destroyed most of their tribe.
The Snakes were the terror of that country. The brothers were
told that the year before they had destroyed seventeen villages,
killing the warriors and old women, and carrying off the
young women and children as slaves.

None of the Horse Indians had ever seen the Pacific; but
they knew a people called Gens de l'Arc, or Bow Indians,
who, as they said, had traded not far from it. To the Bow
Indians, therefore, the brothers resolved to go, and by dint
of gifts and promises they persuaded their hosts to show them
the way. After marching southwestward for several days,
they saw the distant prairie covered with the pointed buffalo-
skin lodges of a great Indian camp. It was that of the Bow
Indians, who may have been one of the bands of the western
Sioux,—the predominant race in this region. Few or none of
them could ever have seen a white man, and we may imagine
their amazement at the arrival of the strangers, who, followed
by staring crowds, were conducted to the lodge of the chief.
"Thus far," says La Vérendrye, "we had been well received
in all the villages we had passed; but this was nothing compared with the courteous manners of the great chief of the
Bow Indians, who, unlike the others, was not self-interested
in the least, and who took excellent care of everything belonging to us."

The first inquiry of the travellers was for the Pacific; but
neither the chief nor his tribesmen knew anything of it,
except what they had heard from Snake prisoners taken in
war. The Frenchmen were surprised at the extent of the
camp, which consisted of many separate bands. The chief
explained that they had been summoned from far and near
for a grand war-party against that common foe of all,—
the Snakes.[27] In fact, the camp resounded with war-songs

[27] The enmity between the Sioux and the Snakes lasted to our
own time. When the writer lived among the western Sioux, one
of their chiefs organized a war-party against the Snakes, and numerous bands came to join the expedition from a distance in some
cases of three hundred miles. Quarrels broke out among them, and
the scheme was ruined.

and war-dances. "Come with us," said their host; "we are going towards the mountains, where you can see the great water that you are looking for."

At length the camp broke up. The squaws took down the lodges, and the march began over prairies dreary and brown with the withering touch of autumn. The spectacle was such as men still young have seen in these western lands, but which no man will see again. The vast plain swarmed with the moving multitude. The tribes of the Missouri and the Yellowstone had by this time abundance of horses, the best of which were used for war and hunting, and the others as beasts of burden. These last were equipped in a peculiar manner. Several of the long poles used to frame the teepees, or lodges, were secured by one end to each side of a rude saddle, while the other end trailed on the ground. Crossbars lashed to the poles just behind the horse kept them three or four feet apart, and formed a firm support, on which was laid, compactly folded, the buffalo-skin covering of the lodge. On this, again, sat a mother with her young family, sometimes stowed for safety in a large open willow basket, with the occasional addition of some domestic pet,—such as a tame raven, a puppy, or even a small bear-cub. Other horses were laden in the same manner with wooden bowls, stone hammers, and other utensils, along with stores of dried buffalo-meat packed in cases of raw-hide whitened and painted. Many of the innumerable dogs—whose manners and appearance strongly suggested their relatives the wolves, to whom, however, they bore a mortal grudge—were equipped in a similar way, with shorter poles and lighter loads. Bands of naked boys, noisy and restless, roamed the prairie, practising their bows and arrows on any small animal they might find. Gay young squaws—adorned on each cheek with a spot of ochre or red clay, and arrayed in tunics of fringed buckskin embroidered with porcupine quills—were mounted on ponies, astride like men; while lean and tattered hags— the drudges of the tribe, unkempt and hideous—scolded the lagging horses, or screeched at the disorderly dogs, with voices not unlike the yell of the great horned owl. Most of the warriors were on horse-back, armed with round white shields of bull-hide, feathered lances, war-clubs, bows, and quivers filled with stone-headed arrows; while a few of the elders, wrapped in robes of buffalo-hide, stalked along in groups with a stately air, chatting, laughing, and exchanging unseemly jokes.[28]

"We continued our march," says La Vérendrye, "sometimes south-southwest, and now and then northwest; our numbers constantly increasing by villages of different tribes which joined us." The variations of their course were probably due to the difficulties of the country, which grew more rugged as they advanced, with broken hills, tracts of dingy green sage-bushes, and bright, swift streams, edged with cottonwood and willow, hurrying northward to join the Yellowstone. At length, on the first of January, 1743, they saw what was probably the Bighorn Range of the Rocky Mountains, a hundred and twenty miles east of the Yellowstone Park.

A council of all the allied bands was now called, and the Frenchmen were asked to take part in it. The questions discussed were how to dispose of the women and children, and how to attack the enemy. Having settled their plans, the chiefs begged their white friends not to abandon them; and the younger of the two, the Chevalier, consented to join the warriors, and aid them with advice, though not with arms.

The tribes of the western plains rarely go on war-parties in winter, and this great expedition must have been the result of unusual exasperation. The object was to surprise the Snakes in the security of their winter camp, and strike a deadly blow, which would have been impossible in summer.

On the eighth of January the whole body stopped to encamp, choosing, no doubt, after the invariable winter custom of western Indians, a place sheltered from wind, and supplied with water and fuel. Here the squaws and children were to remain, while most of the warriors advanced against the enemy. By pegging the lower edge of the lodge-skin to the ground, and piling a ridge of stones and earth upon it to keep out the air, fastening with wooden skewers the flap of hide that covered the entrance, and keeping a constant fire, they could pass a winter endurable to Indians, though smoke, filth, vermin, bad air, the crowd, and the total absence of

[28] The above descriptive particulars are drawn from repeated observation of similar scenes at a time when the primitive condition of these tribes was essentially unchanged, though with the difference that the concourse of savages counted by hundreds, and not by thousands.

privacy, would make it a purgatory to any civilized white man.

The Chevalier left his brother to watch over the baggage of the party, which was stored in the lodge of the great chief, while he himself, with his two Canadians, joined the advancing warriors. They were on horseback, marching with a certain order, and sending watchmen to reconnoitre the country from the tops of the hills.[29] Their movements were so slow that it was twelve days before they reached the foot of the mountains, which, says La Vérendrye, "are for the most part well wooded, and seem very high."[30] He longed to climb their great snow-encumbered peaks, fancying that he might then see the Pacific, and never dreaming that more than eight hundred miles of mountains and forests still lay between him and his goal.

Through the whole of the present century the villages of the Snakes were at a considerable distance west of the Bighorn Range, and some of them were even on the upper waters of the Pacific slope. It is likely that they were so in 1743, in which case the war-party would not have only reached the Bighorn Mountains, but have pushed farther on to within sight of the great Wind River Range. Be this as it may, their scouts reached the chief winter camp of the Snakes, and found it abandoned, with lodges still standing, and many household possessions left behind. The enemy had discovered their approach, and fled. Instead of encouraging the allies, this news filled them with terror, for they feared that the Snake warriors might make a circuit to the rear, and fall upon the camp where they had left their women and children. The great chief spent all his eloquence in vain, nobody would listen to him; and with characteristic fickleness they gave over the enterprise, and retreated in a panic. "Our advance was made in good order; but not so our retreat," says the Chevalier's journal. "Everybody fled his own way. Our horses, though good, were very tired, and got little to eat." The Chevalier was one day riding with his friend, the great chief, when, looking behind him, he missed his two French at-

[29] At least this was done by a band of Sioux with whom the writer once traversed a part of the country ranged by these same Snakes, who had lately destroyed an entire Sioux village.

[30] The Bighorn Range, below the snow line, is in the main well timbered with pine, fir, oak, and juniper.

tendants. Hastening back in alarm, he found them far in the rear, quietly feeding their horses under the shelter of a clump of trees. He had scarcely joined them when he saw a party of fifteen hostile Indians stealthily creeping forward, covered by their bull-hide shields. He and his men let them approach, and then gave them a few shots; on which they immediately ran off, fire-arms being to them an astounding novelty.

The three Frenchmen now tried to rejoin the great chief and his band, but the task was not easy. The prairie, bare of snow and hard as flint, showed no trace of foot or hoof; and it was by rare good fortune that they succeeded, on the second day, not in overtaking the chief, but in reaching the camp where the women and children had been left. They found them all in safety; the Snakes had not attacked them, and the panic of the warriors was needless. It was the ninth of February. They were scarcely housed when a blizzard set in, and on the night of the tenth the plains were buried in snow. The great chief had not appeared. With such of his warriors as he could persuade to follow him, he had made a wide circuit to find the trail of the lost Frenchmen, but, to his great distress, had completely failed. It was not till five days after the arrival of the Chevalier and his men that the chief reached the camp, "more dead than alive," in the words of the journal. All his hardships were forgotten when he found his white friends safe, for he had given them up for lost. "His sorrow turned to joy, and he could not give us attention and caresses enough."

The camp broke up, and the allied bands dispersed. The great chief and his followers moved slowly through the snow-drifts towards the east-southeast, accompanied by the Frenchmen. Thus they kept on till the first of March, when the two brothers, learning that they were approaching the winter village of a people called Gens de la Petite Cerise, or Choke-Cherry Indians, sent one of their men, with a guide, to visit them. The man returned in ten days, bringing a message from the Choke-Cherry Indians, inviting the Frenchmen to their lodges.

The great chief of the Bow Indians, who seems to have regarded his young friends with mingled affection, respect, and wonder, was grieved at the thought of losing them, but took comfort when they promised to visit him again, provided that he would make his abode near a certain river which they pointed out. To this he readily agreed, and then, with mutual regret, they parted.[31] The Frenchmen repaired to the village of the Choke-Cherry Indians, who, like the Bow Indians, were probably a band of Sioux.[32] Hard by their lodges, which stood near the Missouri, the brothers buried a plate of lead graven with the royal arms, and raised a pile of stones in honor of the governor of Canada. They remained at this place till April; then, mounting their horses again, followed the Missouri upward to the village of the Mandans, which they reached on the eighteenth of May. After spending a week here, they joined a party of Assiniboins, journeyed with them towards Fort La Reine, and reached it on the second of July,—to the great relief of their father, who was waiting in suspense, having heard nothing of them for more than a year.

Sixty-two years later, when the vast western regions then called Louisiana had just been ceded to the United States, Captains Lewis and Clark left the Mandan villages with thirty-two men, traced the Missouri to the mountains, penetrated the wastes beyond, and made their way to the Pacific. The first stages of that remarkable exploration were anticipated by the brothers La Vérendrye. They did not find the Pacific, but they discovered the Rocky Mountains, or at least the part of them to which the name properly belongs; for the southern continuation of the great range had long been

[31] The only two tribes of this region who were a match for the Snakes were the Sioux and the Blackfeet. It is clear that the Bow Indians could not have been Blackfeet, as in that case, after the war-party broke up, they would have moved northward towards their own country, instead of east-southeast into the country of their enemies. Hence I incline to think the Bow Indians a band of Sioux, or Dakota,—a people then, as since, predominant in that country.

The banks of the Missouri, in the part which La Vérendrye would have reached in following an east-southeast course, were occupied by numerous bands or sub-tribes of Sioux, such as the Minneconjou, Yankton, Oncpapa, Brulé, and others, friends and relatives of the Bow Indians, supposing these to have been Sioux.

[32] The Sioux, Cheyennes, and other prairie tribes use the small astringent wild cherry for food. The squaws pound it, stones and all, and then dry it for winter use.

known to the Spaniards. Their bold adventure was achieved,
not at the charge of a government, but at their own cost
and that of their father,—not with a band of well-equipped
men, but with only two followers.

The fur-trading privilege which was to have been their
compensation had proved their ruin. They were still pursued
without ceasing by the jealousy of rival traders and the ire
of disappointed partners. "Here in Canada more than anywhere else," the Chevalier wrote, some years after his return,
"envy is the passion *à la mode*, and there is no escaping it."[33]
It was the story of La Salle repeated. Beauharnois, however,
still stood by them, encouraged and defended them, and
wrote in their favor to the colonial minister.[34] It was doubtless
through his efforts that the elder La Vérendrye was at last
promoted to a captaincy in the colony troops. Beauharnois
was succeeded in the government by the sagacious and able
Galissonière, and he too befriended the explorers. "It seems
to me," he wrote to the minister, "that what you have been
told touching the Sieur de la Vérendrye, to the effect that
he has been more busy with his own interests than in making
discoveries, is totally false, and, moreover, that any officers
employed in such work will always be compelled to give some
of their attention to trade, so long as the King allows them
no other means of subsistence. These discoveries are very
clostly, and more fatiguing and dangerous than open war."[35]
Two years later, the elder La Vérendrye received the cross
of the Order of St. Louis,—an honor much prized in Canada,
but which he did not long enjoy; for he died at Montreal in
the following December, when on the point of again setting
out for the West.

His intrepid sons survived, and they were not idle. One of
them, the Chevalier, had before discovered the river Saskatchewan, and ascended it as far as the forks.[36] His intention
was to follow it to the mountains, build a fort there, and
thence push westward in another search for the Pacific; but

[33] *Le Chevalier de la Vérendrye au Ministre,* 30 *Septembre,*
1750.
[34] *La Vérendrye père au Ministre,* 1 *Novembre,* 1746, in Margry, vi. 611.
[35] *La Galissonière au Ministre,* 23 *Octobre,* 1747.
[36] *Mémoire en abrégé des Établissements et Découvertes faits
par le Sieur de la Vérendrye et ses Enfants.*

a disastrous event ruined all his hopes. La Galissonière returned to France, and the Marquis de la Jonquière succeeded him, with the notorious François Bigot as intendant. Both were greedy of money,—the one to hoard, and the other to dissipate it. Clearly there was money to be got from the fur-trade of Manitoba, for La Vérendrye had made every preparation and incurred every expense. It seemed that nothing remained but to reap where he had sown. His commission to find the Pacific, with the privileges connected with it, was refused to his sons, and conferred on a stranger. La Jonquière wrote to the minister: "I have charged M. de Saint-Pierre with this business. He knows these countries better than any officer in all the colony."[37] On the contrary, he had never seen them. It is difficult not to believe that La Jonquière, Bigot, and Saint-Pierre were partners in a speculation of which all three were to share the profits.

The elder La Vérendrye, not long before his death, had sent a large quantity of goods to his trading-forts. The brothers begged leave to return thither and save their property from destruction. They declared themselves happy to serve under the orders of Saint-Pierre, and asked for the use of only a single fort of all those which their father had built at his own cost. The answer was a flat refusal. In short, they were shamefully robbed. The Chevalier writes: "M. le Marquis de la Jonquière, being pushed hard, and as I thought even touched, by my representations, told me at last that M. de Saint-Pierre wanted nothing to do with me or my brothers." "I am a ruined man," he continues. "I am more than two thousand livres in debt, and am still only a second ensign. My elder brother's grade is no better than mine. My younger brother is only a cadet. This is the fruit of all that my father, my brothers, and I have done. My other brother, whom the Sioux murdered some years ago, was not the most unfortunate among us. We must lose all that has cost us so much, unless M. de Saint-Pierre should take juster views, and prevail on the Marquis de la Jonquière to share them. To be thus shut out from the West is to be most cruelly robbed of a sort of inheritance which we had all the pains of acquiring, and of which others will get all the profit."[38]

[37] *La Jonquière au Ministre*, 27 *Février*, 1750.
[38] *Le Chevalier de la Vérendrye au Ministre*, 30 *Septembre*, 1750.

His elder brother writes in a similar strain: "We spent our youth and our property in building up establishments so advantageous to Canada; and, after all, we were doomed to see a stranger gather the fruit we had taken such pains to plant." And he complains that their goods left in the trading-posts were wasted, their provisions consumed, and the men in their pay used to do the work of others.[39]

They got no redress. Saint-Pierre, backed by the governor and the intendant, remained master of the position. The brothers sold a small piece of land, their last remaining property, to appease their most pressing creditors.[40]

Saint-Pierre set out for Manitoba on the fifth of June, 1750. Though he had lived more or less in the woods for thirty-six years, and though La Jonquière had told the minister that he knew the countries to which he was bound better than anybody else, it is clear from his own journal that he was now visiting them for the first time. They did not please him. "I was told," he says, "that the way would grow harder and more dangerous as we advanced, and I found, in fact, that one must risk life and property every moment." Finding himself and his men likely to starve, he sent some of them, under an ensign named Niverville, to the Saskatchewan. They could not reach it, and nearly perished on the way. "I myself was no more fortunate," says Saint-Pierre. "Food was so scarce that I sent some of my people into the woods among the Indians,—which did not save me from a fast so rigorous that it deranged my health and put it out of my power to do anything towards accomplishing my mission. Even if I had had strength enough, the war that broke out among the Indians would have made it impossible to proceed."

Niverville, after a winter of misery, tried to fulfil an order which he had received from his commander. When the Indians guided the two brothers La Vérendrye to the Rocky Mountains, the course they took tended so far southward that the Chevalier greatly feared it might lead to Spanish

---

[39] *Mémoire des Services de Pierre Gautier de la Vérendrye l'aisné, présenté à Mg^r. Rouillé, ministre et secrétaire d'État.*

[40] Legardeur de Saint-Pierre, in spite of his treatment of the La Vérendrye brothers, had merit as an officer. It was he who received Washington at Fort Le Bœuf in 1754. He was killed in 1755, at the battle of Lake George.

settlements; and he gave it as his opinion that the next attempt to find the Pacific should be made farther towards the north. Saint-Pierre had agreed with him, and had directed Niverville to build a fort on the Saskatchewan, three hundred leagues above its mouth. Therefore, at the end of May, 1751, Niverville sent ten men in two canoes on this errand, and they ascended the Saskatchewan to what Saint-Pierre calls the "Rock Mountain." Here they built a small stockade fort and called it Fort La Jonquière. Niverville was to have followed them; but he fell ill, and lay helpless at the mouth of the river in such a condition that he could not even write to his commander.

Saint-Pierre set out in person from Fort La Reine for Fort La Jonquière, over ice and snow, for it was late in November. Two Frenchmen from Niverville met him on the way, and reported that the Assiniboins had slaughtered an entire band of friendly Indians on whom Saint-Pierre had relied to guide him. On hearing this he gave up the enterprise, and returned to Fort La Reine. Here the Indians told him idle stories about white men and a fort in some remote place towards the west; but, he observes, "nobody could reach it without encountering an infinity of tribes more savage than it is possible to imagine."

He spent most of the winter at Fort La Reine. Here, towards the end of February, 1752, he had with him only five men, having sent out the rest in search of food. Suddenly, as he sat in his chamber, he saw the fort full of armed Assiniboins, extremely noisy and insolent. He tried in vain to quiet them, and they presently broke into the guard-house and seized the arms. A massacre would have followed, had not Saint-Pierre, who was far from wanting courage, resorted to an expedient which has more than once proved effective on such occasions. He knocked out the heads of two barrels of gunpowder, snatched a firebrand, and told the yelping crowd that he would blow up them and himself together. At this they all rushed in fright out the gate, while Saint-Pierre ran after them, and bolted it fast. There was great anxiety for the hunters, but they all came back in the evening, without having met the enemy. The men, however, were so terrified by the adventure that Saint-Pierre was compelled to abandon the fort, after recommending it to the care of another band of Assiniboins, who had professed great friendship. Four days after he was gone they burned it to the ground.

He soon came to the conclusion that farther discovery was impossible, because the English of Hudson Bay had stirred up the western tribes to oppose it. Therefore he set out for the settlements, and, reaching Quebec in the autumn of 1753, placed the journal of his futile enterprise in the hands of Duquesne, the new governor.[41]

Canada was approaching her last agony. In the death-struggle of the Seven Years' War there was no time for schemes of western discovery. The brothers La Vérendrye sank into poverty and neglect. A little before the war broke out, we find the eldest at the obscure Acadian post of Beauséjour, where he wrote to the colonial minister a statement of his services, which appears to have received no attention. After the fall of Canada, the Chevalier de la Vérendrye, he whose eyes first beheld the snowy peaks of the Rocky Mountains, perished in the wreck of the ship "Auguste," on the coast of Cape Breton, in November, 1761.[42]

[41] *Journal sommaire du Voyage de Jacques Legardeur de Saint-Pierre, chargé de la Découverte de la Mer de l'Ouest* (British Museum).

[42] The above narrative rests mainly on contemporary documents, official in character, of which the originals are preserved in the archives of the French Government. These papers have recently been printed by M. Pierre Margry, late custodian of the Archives of the Marine and Colonies at Paris, in the sixth volume of his *Découvertes et Établissements des Français dans l'Amérique Septentrionale,*—a documentary collection of great value, published at the expense of the American Government. It was M. Margry who first drew attention to the achievements of the family of La Vérendrye, by an article in the *Moniteur* in 1852. I owe to his kindness the opportunity of using the above-mentioned documents in advance of publication. I obtained copies from duplicate originals of some of the principal among them from the Dépôt des Cartes de la Marine, in 1872. These answer closely, with rare and trivial variations, to the same documents as printed from other sources by M. Margry. Some additional papers preserved in the Archives of the Marine and Colonies have also been used.

My friends, Hon. William C. Endicott, then Secretary of War, and Captain John G. Bourke, Third Cavalry, U. S. A., kindly placed in my hands a valuable collection of Government maps and surveys of the country between the Missouri and the Rocky Mountains visited by the brothers La Vérendrye; and I have received from Captain Bourke, and also from Mr. E. A. Snow, formerly of the Third Cavalry, much information concerning the same region, repeatedly traversed by them in peace and war.

Chapter 17

1700–1750
The Chain of Posts

WE HAVE SEEN that the contest between France and England in America divided itself, after the Peace of Utrecht, into three parts,—the Acadian contest; the contest for northern New England; and last, though greatest, the contest for the West. Nothing is more striking than the difference, or rather contrast, in the conduct and methods of the rival claimants to this wild but magnificent domain. Each was strong in its own qualities, and utterly wanting in the qualities that marked its opponent.

On maps of British America in the earlier part of the eighteenth century, one sees the eastern shore, from Maine to Georgia, garnished with ten or twelve colored patches, very different in shape and size, and defined, more or less distinctly, by dividing-lines which, in some cases, are prolonged westward till they touch the Mississippi, or even cross it and stretch indefinitely towards the Pacific. These patches are the British provinces, and the westward prolongation of their boundary lines represents their several claims to vast interior tracts, founded on ancient grants, but not made good by occupation, or vindicated by any exertion of power.

These English communities took little thought of the region beyond the Alleghanies. Each lived a life of its own, shut within its own limits, not dreaming of a future collective greatness to which the possession of the West would be a necessary condition. No conscious community of aims and interests held them together, nor was there any authority capable of uniting their forces and turning them to a common object. Some of the servants of the Crown had urged the necessity of joining them all under a strong central government, as the only means of making them loyal subjects and arresting the encroachments of France; but the scheme was plainly impracticable. Each province remained in jealous isolation, busied with its own work, growing in strength, in the capacity of self-rule and the spirit of independence, and stubbornly resisting all exercise of authority from without. If the English-speaking populations flowed westward, it was in obedience to natural laws, for the King did not aid the movement, the royal governors had no authority to do so, and the colonial assemblies were too much engrossed with immediate local interests. The power of these colonies was that of a rising flood slowly invading and conquering, by the unconscious force of its own growing volume, unless means be found to hold it back by dams and embankments within appointed limits.

In the French colonies all was different. Here the representatives of the Crown were men bred in an atmosphere of broad ambition and masterful and far-reaching enterprise. Achievement was demanded of them. They recognized the greatness of the prize, studied the strong and weak points of their rivals, and with a cautious forecast and a daring energy set themselves to the task of defeating them.

If the English colonies were comparatively strong in numbers, their numbers could not be brought into action; while if the French forces were small, they were vigorously commanded, and always ready at a word. It was union confronting division, energy confronting apathy, military centralization opposed to industrial democracy; and, for a time, the advantage was all on one side.

The demands of the French were sufficiently comprehensive. They repented of their enforced concessions at the Treaty of Utrecht, and in spite of that compact, maintained that, with a few local and trivial exceptions, the whole North American continent, except Mexico, was theirs of right; while their opponents seemed neither to understand the situation, nor see the greatness of the stakes at issue.

In 1720 Father Bobé, priest of the Congregation of Missions, drew up a paper in which he sets forth the claims of France with much distinctness, beginning with the declaration that "England has usurped from France nearly everything that she possesses in America," and adding that the plenipotentiaries at Utrecht did not know what they were about when they made such concessions to the enemy; that, among other blunders, they gave Port Royal to England when it belonged to France, who should "insist vigorously" on its being given back to her.

He maintains that the voyages of Verrazzano and Ribaut made France owner of the whole continent, from Florida northward; that England was an interloper in planting colonies along the Atlantic coast, and will admit as much if she is honest, since all that country is certainly a part of New France. In this modest assumption of the point at issue, he ignores John Cabot and his son Sebastian, who discovered North America more than twenty-five years before the voyage of Verrazzano, and more than sixty years before that of Ribaut.

When the English, proceeds Father Bobé, have restored Port Royal to us, which they are bound to do, though we ceded it by the treaty, a French governor should be at once set over it, with a commission to command as far as Cape Cod, which would include Boston. We should also fortify ourselves, "in a way to stop the English, who have long tried to seize on French America, of which they know the importance, and of which," he observes with much candor, "they would make a better use than the French do.[1] . . . The Atlantic coast, as far as Florida, was usurped from the French, to whom it belonged then, and to whom it belongs now." England, as he thinks, is bound in honor to give back these countries to their true owner; and it is also the part of wisdom to do so, since by grasping at too much, one often loses all. But France, out of her love of peace, will cede to England the countries along the Atlantic, from the Kennebec in New France to the Jordan[2] in Carolina, on condition that England will restore to her all that she gave up by the Treaty of Utrecht. When this is done, France, always generous, will consent to accept as boundary a line drawn from the mouth of the Kennebec, passing thence midway between Schenectady and Lake Champlain and along the ridge of the Alleghanies to the river Jordan, the country between this line and the sea to belong to England, and the rest of the continent to France.

If England does not accept this generous offer, she is to be told that the King will give to the Compagnie des Indes (Law's Mississippi Company) full authority to occupy "all the coun-

[1] "De manière qu'on puisse arrêter les Anglois, qui depuis longtems tachent de s'emparer de l'Amérique françoise, dont ils conoissent l'importance et dont ils feroient un meillieur usage que celuy qui les françois en front."

[2] So named by Vasquez de Ayllon. It was probably the broad river of South Carolina.

tries which the English have usurped from France;" and, pursues Father Bobé, "it is certain that the fear of having to do with so powerful a company will bring the English to our terms." The company that was thus to strike the British heart with terror was the same which all the tonics and stimulants of the government could not save from predestined ruin. But, concludes this ingenious writer, whether England accepts our offers or not, France ought not only to take a high tone (*parler avec hauteur*), but also to fortify diligently, and make good her right by force of arms.[3]

Three years later we have another document, this time of an official character, and still more radical in its demands. It admits that Port Royal and a part of the Nova Scotian peninsula, under the name of Acadia, were ceded to England by the treaty, and consents that she shall keep them, but requires her to restore the part of New France that she has wrongfully seized,—namely, the whole Atlantic coast from the Kennebec to Florida; since France never gave England this country, which is hers by the discovery of Verrazzano in 1524. Here, again, the voyages of the Cabots, in 1497 and 1498, are completely ignored.

"It will be seen," pursues this curious document, "that our kings have always preserved sovereignty over the countries between the thirtieth and the fiftieth degrees of north latitude. A time will come when they will be in a position to assert their rights, and then it will be seen that the dominions of a king of France cannot be usurped with impunity. What we demand now is that the English make immediate restitution." No doubt, the paper goes on to say, they will pretend to have prescriptive rights, because they have settled the country and built towns and cities in it; but this plea is of no avail, because all that country is a part of New France, and because England rightfully owns nothing in America except what we, the French, gave her by the Treaty of Utrecht, which is merely Port Royal and Acadia. She is bound in honor to give back all the vast countries she has usurped; but, continues the paper, "the King loves the English nation too much, and wishes too much to do her kindness, and is too generous to

[3] *Second Mémoire concernant les Limites des Colonies présenté en 1720 par Bobé, prêtre de la Congrégation de la Mission* (Archives Nationales).

exact such a restitution. Therefore, provided that England will give us back Port Royal, Acadia, and everything else that France gave her by the Treaty of Utrecht, the King will forego his rights, and grant to England the whole Atlantic coast from the thirty-second degree of latitude to the Kennebec, to the extent inland of twenty French leagues [about fifty miles], on condition that she will solemnly bind herself never to overstep these limits or encroach in the least on French ground."

Thus, through the beneficence of France, England, provided that she renounced all pretension to the rest of the continent, would become the rightful owner of an attenuated strip of land reaching southward from the Kennebec along the Atlantic seaboard. The document containing this magnanimous proposal was preserved in the Château St. Louis at Quebec till the middle of the eighteenth century, when, the boundary dispute having reached a crisis, and commissioners of the two powers having been appointed to settle it, a certified copy of the paper was sent to France for their instruction.[4]

Father Bobé had advised that France should not trust solely to the justice of her claims, but should back right with might and build forts on the Niagara, the Ohio, the Tennessee, and the Alabama, as well as at other commanding points, to shut out the English from the West. Of these positions, Niagara was the most important, for the possession of it would close the access to the Upper Lakes, and stop the western tribes on their way to trade at Albany. The Five Nations and the governor of New York were jealous of the French designs, which, however, were likely enough to succeed, through the prevailing apathy and divisions in the British colonies. "If those not immediately concerned," writes a member of the New York council, "only stand gazing on while the wolff is murthering other parts of the flock, it will come to every one's turn at last." The warning was well founded, but it was not heeded. Again: "It is the policy of the French to attack one colony at a time, and the others are so besotted as to sit still."[5]

---

[4] *Demandes de la France*, 1723 (Archives des Affaires Étrangères).

[5] *Colonel Heathcote to Governor Hunter*, 8 *July*, 1715. *Ibid. to Townshend*, 12 *July*, 1715.

For gaining the consent of the Five Nations to the building of a French fort at Niagara, Vaudreuil trusted chiefly to his agent among the Senecas, the bold, skilful, and indefatigable Joncaire, who was naturalized among that tribe, the strongest of the confederacy. Governor Hunter of New York sent Peter Schuyler and Philip Livingston to counteract his influence. The Five Nations, who, conscious of declining power, seemed ready at this time to be all things to all men, declared that they would prevent the French from building at Niagara, which, as they said, would "shut them up as in a prison."[6] Not long before, however, they had sent a deputation to Montreal to say that the English made objection to Joncaire's presence among them, but that they were masters of their land, and hoped that the French agent would come as often as he pleased; and they begged that the new King of France would take them under his protection.[7] Accordingly, Vaudreuil sent them a present, with a message to the effect that they might plunder such English traders as should come among them.[8]

Yet so jealous were the Iroquois of a French fort at Niagara that they sent three Seneca chiefs to see what was going on there. The chiefs found a few Frenchmen in a small block-house, or loopholed storehouse, which they had just built near Lewiston Heights. The three Senecas requested them to demolish it and go away, which the Frenchmen refused to do; on which the Senecas asked the English envoys, Schuyler and Livingston, to induce the governor of New York to destroy the obnoxious building. In short, the Five Nations wavered incessantly between their two European neighbors, and changed their minds every day. The skill and perseverance of the French emissaries so far prevailed at last that the Senecas consented to the building of a fort at the mouth of the Niagara, where Denonville had built one in 1687; and thus that important pass was made tolerably secure.

Meanwhile the English of New York, or rather Burnet, their governor, were not idle. Burnet was on ill terms with his assembly, which grudged him all help in serving the province whose interests it was supposed to represent. Burnet's plan was to build a fortified trading-house at Oswego, on Lake

6 *Journal of Schuyler and Livingston,* 1720.
7 *Vaudreuil au Conseil de Marine,* 24 *Octobre,* 1717.
8 *Vaudreuil et Bégon au Conseil de Marine,* 26 *Octobre,* 1719.

Ontario, in the belief that the western Indians, who greatly preferred English goods and English prices, would pass Niagara and bring their furs to the new post. He got leave from the Five Nations to execute his plan, bought canoes, hired men, and built a loopholed house of stone on the site of the present city of Oswego. As the Assembly would give no money, Burnet furnished it himself; and though the object was one of the greatest importance to the province, he was never fully repaid.[9] A small garrison for the new post was drawn from the four independent companies maintained in the province at the charge of the Crown.

The establishment of Oswego greatly alarmed and incensed the French, and a council of war at Quebec resolved to send two thousand men against it; but Vaudreuil's successor, the Marquis de Beauharnois, learning that the court was not prepared to provoke a war, contented himself with sending a summons to the commanding officer to abandon and demolish the place within a fortnight.[10] To this no attention was given; and as Burnet had foreseen, Oswego became the great centre of Indian trade, while Niagara, in spite of its more favorable position, was comparatively slighted by the western tribes. The chief danger rose from the obstinate prejudice of the Assembly, which, in its disputes with the Royal Governor, would give him neither men nor money to defend the new post.

The Canadian authorities, who saw in Oswego an intrusion on their domain and a constant injury and menace, could not attack it without bringing on a war, and therefore tried to persuade the Five Nations to destroy it,—an attempt which completely failed.[11] They then established a trading-post at Toronto, in the vain hope of stopping the northern tribes on

[9] "I am ashamed to confess that he built the fort at his private expense, and that a balance of above £56 remains due to his estate to this very day."—Smith, *History of New York,* 267 (ed. 1814).

[10] *Mémoire de Dupuy,* 1728. Dupuy was intendant of Canada. The King approved the conduct of Beauharnois in not using force. *Dépêche du Roy,* 14 *Mai,* 1728.

[11] When urged by the younger Longueuil to drive off the English from Oswego, the Indians replied, "Drive them off thyself" ("*Chassez-les toi-même*"). *Longueuil fils au Ministre,* 19 *Octobre,* 1728.

their way to the more profitable English market, and they built two armed vessels at Fort Frontenac to control the navigation of Lake Ontario.

Meanwhile, in another quarter the French made an advance far more threatening to the English colonies than Oswego was to their own. They had already built a stone fort at Chambly, which covered Montreal from any English attack by way of Lake Champlain. As that lake was the great highway between the rival colonies, the importance of gaining full mastery of it was evident. It was rumored in Canada that the English meant to seize and fortify the place called Scalp Point (*Pointe à la Chevelure*) by the French, and Crown Point by the English, where the lake suddenly contracts to the proportions of a river, so that a few cannon would stop the passage.

As early as 1726 the French made an attempt to establish themselves on the east side of the lake opposite Crown Point, but were deterred by the opposition of Massachusetts. This eastern shore was, however, claimed not only by Massachusetts, but by her neighbor, New Hampshire, with whom she presently fell into a dispute about the ownership, and, as a writer of the time observes, "while they were quarrelling for the bone, the French ran away with it."[12]

At length, in 1731, the French took post on the western side of the lake, and began to intrench themselves at Crown Point, which was within the bounds claimed by New York; but that province, being then engrossed, not only by her chronic dispute with her governor, but by a quarrel with her next neighbor, New Jersey, slighted the danger from the common enemy, and left the French to work their will. It was Saint-Luc de la Corne, Lieutenant du Roy at Montreal, who pointed out the necessity of fortifying this place,[13] in order to anticipate the English, who, as he imagined, were about to do so,—a danger which was probably not imminent, since the English colonies, as a whole, could not and would not unite for such a purpose, while the individual provinces were too much absorbed in their own internal affairs and their own jealousies and disputes to make the attempt. La Corne's suggestion found favor at court, and the governor of Canada was

---

[12] Mitchell, *Contest in America*, 22.
[13] *La Corne au Ministre*, 15 *Octobre*, 1730.

ordered to occupy Crown Point. The Sieur de la Fresnière was sent thither with troops and workmen, and a fort was built, and named Fort Frédéric. It contained a massive stone tower, mounted with cannon to command the lake, which is here but a musket-shot wide. Thus was established an advanced post of France,—a constant menace to New York and New England, both of which denounced it as an outrageous encroachment on British territory, but could not unite to rid themselves of it.[14]

While making this bold push against their neighbors of the South, the French did not forget the West; and towards the middle of the century they had occupied points controlling all the chief waterways between Canada and Louisiana. Niagara held the passage from Lake Ontario to Lake Erie. Detroit closed the entrance to Lake Huron, and Michilimackinac guarded the point where Lake Huron is joined by Lakes Michigan and Superior; while the fort called La Baye, at the head of Green Bay, stopped the way to the Mississippi by Marquette's old route of Fox River and the Wisconsin. Another route to the Mississippi was controlled by a post on the Maumee to watch the carrying-place between that river and the Wabash, and by another on the Wabash where Vincennes now stands. La Salle's route, by way of the Kankakee and the Illinois, was barred by a fort on the St. Joseph; and even if, in spite of these obstructions, an enemy should reach the Mississippi by any of its northern affluents, the cannon of Fort Chartres would prevent him from descending it.

These various western forts, except Fort Chartres and Fort Niagara, which were afterwards rebuilt, the one in stone and the other in earth, were stockades of no strength against cannon. Slight as they were, their establishment was costly; and as the King, to whom Canada was a yearly loss, grudged every franc spent upon it, means were contrived to make them self-supporting. Each of them was a station of the fur-trade, and the position of most of them had been determined more or less with a view to that traffic. Hence they had no slight commercial value. In some of them the Crown itself carried on trade through agents who usually secured a lion's share of the profits. Others were farmed out to merchants at a fixed

[14] On the establishment of Crown Point, *Beauharnois et Hocquart au Roy*, 10 *Octobre*, 1731; *Beauharnois et Hocquart au Ministre*, 14 *Novembre*, 1731.

sum. In others, again, the commanding officer was permitted to trade on condition of maintaining the post, paying the soldiers, and supporting a missionary; while in one case, at least, he was subjected to similar obligations, though not permitted to trade himself, but only to sell trading licenses to merchants. These methods of keeping up forts and garrisons were of course open to prodigious abuses, and roused endless jealousies and rivalries.

France had now occupied the valley of the Mississippi, and joined with loose and uncertain links her two colonies of Canada and Louisiana. But the strength of her hold on these regions of unkempt savagery bore no proportion to the vastness of her claims or the growing power of the rivals who were soon to contest them.

Chapter 18

1744, 1745
A Mad Scheme

THE PEACE OF UTRECHT left unsettled the perilous questions of boundary between the rival powers in North America, and they grew more perilous every day. Yet the quarrel was not yet quite ripe; and though the French governor, Vaudreuil, and perhaps also his successor, Beauharnois, seemed willing to precipitate it, the courts of London and Versailles still hesitated to appeal to the sword. Now, as before, it was a European, and not an American, quarrel that was to set the world on fire. The War of the Austrian Succession broke out in 1744. When Frederic of Prussia seized Silesia and began that bloody conflict, it meant that packs of howling savages would again spread fire and carnage along the New England border.

News of the declaration of war reached Louisbourg some weeks before it reached Boston, and the French military governor, Duquesnel, thought he saw an opportunity to strike an unexpected blow for the profit of France and his own great honor.

One of the French inhabitants of Louisbourg has left us a short sketch of Duquesnel, whom he calls "capricious, of an uncertain temper, inclined to drink, and when in his cups neither reasonable or civil."[1] He adds that the governor had offended nearly every officer in the garrison, and denounces him as the "chief cause of our disasters." When Duquesnel heard of the declaration of war, his first thought was to strike some blow before the English were warned. The fishing station of Canseau was a tempting prize, being a near and an inconvenient neighbor, at the southern end of the Strait of Canseau, which separates the Acadian peninsula from the island of Cape Breton, or Isle Royale, of which Louisbourg was the place of strength. Nothing was easier than to seize Canseau, which had no defence but a wooden redoubt buil

---

[1] *Lettre d'un Habitant de Louisbourg contenant une Relation exacte et circonstanciée de la Prise de l'Isle Royale par les Anglois*

by the fishermen, and occupied by eighty Englishmen thinking
no danger. Early in May, Duquesnel sent Captain Duvivier
against it, with six hundred, or, as the English say, nine hundred soldiers and sailors, escorted by two small armed vessels.
The English surrendered, on condition of being sent to Boston, and the miserable hamlet, with its wooden citadel, was
burned to the ground.

Thus far successful, the governor addressed himself to the
capture of Annapolis,—which meant the capture of all Acadia.
Duvivier was again appointed to the command. His heart
was in the work, for he was a descendant of La Tour, feudal
claimant of Acadia in the preceding century. Four officers
and ninety regular troops were given him,[2] and from three
to four hundred Micmac and Malicite Indians joined him on
the way. The Micmacs, under command, it is said, of their
missionary, Le Loutre, had already tried to surprise the English fort, but had only succeeded in killing two unarmed
stragglers in the adjacent garden.[3]

Annapolis, from the neglect and indifference of the British
ministry, was still in such a state of dilapidation that its sandy
ramparts were crumbling into the ditches, and the cows of the
garrison walked over them at their pleasure. It was held by
about a hundred effective men under Major Mascarene, a
French Protestant whose family had been driven into exile by
the persecutions that followed the revocation of the Edict of
Nantes. Shirley, governor of Massachusetts, sent him a small
reinforcement of militia; but as most of these came without
arms, and as Mascarene had few or none to give them, they
proved of doubtful value.

Duvivier and his followers, white and red, appeared before
the fort in August, made their camp behind the ridge of a hill
that overlooked it, and marched towards the rampart; but
being met by a discharge of cannon-shot, they gave up all
thoughts of an immediate assault, began a fusillade under
cover of darkness, and kept the garrison on the alert all night.

Duvivier had looked for help from the Acadians of the
neighboring village, who were French in blood, faith, and

[2] *Lettre d'un Habitant de Louisbourg.*
[3] *Mascarene to the Besiegers,* 3 *July,* 1744. Duquesnel had
written to all the missionaries "d'engager les sauvages à faire quel-
que coup important sur le fort" (Annapolis). *Duquesnel à Beauharnois,* 1 *Juin,* 1744.

inclination. They would not join him openly, fearing the consequences if his attack should fail; but they did what they could without committing themselves, and made a hundred and fifty scaling-ladders for the besiegers. Duvivier now returned to his first plan of an assault, which, if made with vigor, could hardly have failed. Before attempting it, he sent Mascarene a flag of truce to tell him that he hourly expected two powerful armed ships from Louisbourg, besides a reinforcement of two hundred and fifty regulars, with cannon, mortars, and other enginery of war. At the same time he proposed favorable terms of capitulation, not to take effect till the French war-ships should have appeared. Mascarene refused all terms, saying that when he saw the French ships, he would consider what to do, and meanwhile would defend himself as he could.

The expected ships were the "Ardent" and the "Caribou," then at Louisbourg. A French writer says that when Duquesnel directed their captains to sail for Annapolis and aid in its capture, they refused, saying that they had no orders from the court.[4] Duvivier protracted the parley with Mascarene, and waited in vain for the promised succor. At length the truce was broken off, and the garrison, who had profited by it to get rest and sleep, greeted the renewal of hostilities with three cheers.

Now followed three weeks of desultory attacks; but there was no assault, though Duvivier had boasted that he had the means of making a successful one. He waited for the ships which did not come, and kept the Acadians at work in making ladders and fire-arrows. At length, instead of aid from Louisbourg, two small vessels appeared from Boston, bringing Mascarene a reinforcement of fifty Indian rangers. This discouraged the besiegers, and towards the end of September they suddenly decamped and vanished. "The expedition was a failure," writes the *Habitant de Louisbourg*, "though one might have bet everything on its success, so small was the force that the enemy had to resist us."

This writer thinks that the seizure of Canseau and the attack of Annapolis were sources of dire calamity to the French. "Perhaps," he says, "the English would have let us alone if we had not first insulted them. It was the interest of

<hr/>

[4] *Lettre d'un Habitant de Louisbourg.*

the people of New England to live at peace with us, and they would no doubt have done so, if we had not taken it into our heads to waken them from their security. They expected that both parties would merely stand on the defensive, without taking part in this cruel war that has set Europe in a blaze."

Whatever might otherwise have been the disposition of the "Bastonnais," or New England people, the attacks on Canseau and Annapolis alarmed and exasperated them, and engendered in some heated brain a project of wild audacity. This was no less than the capture of Louisbourg, reputed the strongest fortress, French or British, in North America, with the possible exception of Quebec, which owed its chief strength to nature, and not to art.

Louisbourg was a standing menace to all the northern British colonies. It was the only French naval station on the continent, and was such a haunt of privateers that it was called the American Dunkirk. It commanded the chief entrance of Canada, and threatened to ruin the fisheries, which were nearly as vital to New England as was the fur-trade to New France. The French government had spent twenty-five years in fortifying it, and the cost of its powerful defences—constructed after the system of Vauban—was reckoned at thirty million livres.

This was the fortress which William Vaughan of Damariscotta advised Governor Shirley to attack with fifteen hundred raw New England militia.[5] Vaughan was born at Portsmouth in 1703, and graduated at Harvard College nineteen years later. His father, also a graduate of Harvard, was for a time lieutenant-governor of New Hampshire. Soon after leaving college, the younger Vaughan—a youth of restless and impetuous activity—established a fishing-station on the island of Matinicus, off the coast of Maine, and afterwards became the owner of most of the land on both sides of the little river

[5] Smollett says that the proposal came from Robert Auchmuty, judge of admiralty in Massachusetts. Hutchinson, Douglas, Belknap, and other well-informed writers ascribe the scheme to Vaughan, while Pepperrell says that it originated with Colonel John Bradstreet. In the Public Record Office there is a letter from Bradstreet, written in 1753, but without address, in which he declares that he not only planned the siege, but "was the Principal Person in conducting it,"—assertions which may pass for what they are worth, Bradstreet being much given to self-assertion.

Damariscotta, where he built a garrison-house, or wooden fort, established a considerable settlement, and carried on an extensive trade in fish and timber. He passed for a man of ability and force, but was accused of a headstrong rashness, a self-confidence that hesitated at nothing, and a harebrained contempt of every obstacle in his way. Once, having fitted out a number of small vessels at Portsmouth for his fishing at Matinicus, he named a time for sailing. It was a gusty and boisterous March day, the sea was rough, and old sailors told him that such craft could not carry sail. Vaughan would not listen, but went on board and ordered his men to follow. One vessel was wrecked at the mouth of the river; the rest, after severe buffeting, came safe, with their owner, to Matinicus.

Being interested in the fisheries, Vaughan was doubly hostile to Louisbourg,—their worst enemy. He found a willing listener in the governor, William Shirley. Shirley was an English barrister who had come to Massachusetts in 1731 to practise his profession and seek his fortune. After filling various offices with credit, he was made governor of the province in 1741, and had discharged his duties with both tact and talent. He was able, sanguine, and a sincere well-wisher to the province, though gnawed by an insatiable hunger for distinction. He thought himself a born strategist, and was possessed by a propensity for contriving military operations, which finally cost him dear. Vaughan, who knew something of Louisbourg, told him that in winter the snow-drifts were often banked so high against the rampart that it could be mounted readily, if the assailants could but time their arrival at the right moment. This was not easy, as that rocky and tempestuous coast was often made inaccessible by fogs and surf; Shirley therefore preferred a plan of his own contriving. But nothing could be done without first persuading his Assembly to consent.

On the ninth of January the General Court of Massachusetts—a convention of grave city merchants and solemn rustics from the country villages—was astonished by a message from the governor to the effect that he had a communication to make, so critical that he wished the whole body to swear secrecy. The request was novel, but being then on good terms with Shirley, the representatives consented, and took the oath. Then, to their amazement, the governor invited them to undertake forthwith the reduction of Louisbourg. The idea of an attack on that redoubtable fortress was not new. Since the autumn, proposals had been heard to petition the British ministry to make the attempt, under a promise that the colonies would give their best aid. But that Massachusetts should venture it alone, or with such doubtful help as her neighbors might give, at her own charge and risk, though already insolvent, without the approval or consent of the ministry, and without experienced officers or trained soldiers, was a startling suggestion to the sober-minded legislators of the General Court. They listened, however, with respect to the governor's reasons, and appointed a committee of the two houses to consider them. The committee deliberated for several days, and then made a report adverse to the plan, as was also the vote of the Court.

Meanwhile, in spite of the oath, the secret had escaped. It is said that a country member, more pious than discreet, prayed so loud and fervently, at his lodgings, for light to guide him on the momentous question, that his words were overheard, and the mystery of the closed doors was revealed. The news flew through the town, and soon spread through all the province.

After his defeat in the Assembly, Shirley returned, vexed and disappointed, to his house in Roxbury. A few days later, James Gibson, a Boston merchant, says that he saw him "walking slowly down King Street, with his head bowed down, as if in a deep study." "He entered my counting-room," pursues the merchant, "and abruptly said, 'Gibson, do you feel like giving up the expedition to Louisbourg?'" Gibson replied that he wished the House would reconsider their vote. "You are the very man I want!" exclaimed the governor.[6] They then drew up a petition for reconsideration, which Gibson signed, promising to get also the signatures of merchants, not only of Boston, but of Salem, Marblehead, and other towns along the coast. In this he was completely successful, as all New England merchants looked on Louisbourg as an arch-enemy.

The petition was presented, and the question came again before the Assembly. There had been much intercourse between Boston and Louisbourg, which had largely depended on New England for provisions.[7] The captured militiamen of

[6] Gibson, *Journal of the Siege of Louisbourg.*
[7] *Lettre d'un Habitant de Louisbourg.*

Canseau, who, after some delay, had been sent to Boston, according to the terms of surrender, had used their opportunities to the utmost, and could give Shirley much information concerning the fortress. It was reported that the garrison was mutinous, and that provisions were fallen short, so that the place could not hold out without supplies from France. These, however, could be cut off only by blockading the harbor with a stronger naval force than all the colonies together could supply. The Assembly had before reached the reasonable conclusion that the capture of Louisbourg was beyond the strength of Massachusetts, and that the only course was to ask the help of the mother-country.[8]

The reports of mutiny, it was urged, could not be depended on; raw militia in the open field were no match for disciplined troops behind ramparts; the expense would be enormous, and the credit of the province, already sunk low, would collapse under it; we should fail, and instead of sympathy, get nothing but ridicule. Such were the arguments of the opposition, to which there was little to answer, except that if Massachusetts waited for help from England, Louisbourg would be reinforced and the golden opportunity lost. The impetuous and irrepressible Vaughan put forth all his energy; the plan was carried by a single vote. And even this result was said to be due to the accident of a member in opposition falling and breaking a leg as he was hastening to the House.

The die was cast, and now doubt and hesitation vanished. All alike set themselves to push on the work. Shirley wrote to all the colonies, as far south as Pennsylvania, to ask for co-operation. All excused themselves except Connecticut, New Hampshire, and Rhode Island, and the whole burden fell on the four New England colonies. These, and Massachusetts above all, blazed with pious zeal; for as the enterprise was directed against Roman Catholics, it was supposed in a peculiar manner to commend itself to Heaven. There were prayers without ceasing in churches and families, and all was ardor, energy, and confidence; while the other colonies looked on with distrust, dashed with derision. When Benjamin Franklin, in Philadelphia, heard what was afoot, he wrote to his brother in Boston, "Fortified towns are hard nuts to crack, and your teeth are not accustomed to it; but some seem to think that

8 *Report of Council,* 12 *January,* 1745.

forts are as easy taken as snuff."[9] It has been said of Franklin that while he represented some of the New England qualities, he had no part in that enthusiasm of which our own time saw a crowning example when the cannon opened at Fort Sumter, and which pushes to its end without reckoning chances, counting costs, or heeding the scoffs of ill-wishers.

The prevailing hope and faith were, it is true, born largely of ignorance, aided by the contagious zeal of those who first broached the project; for as usual in such cases, a few individuals supplied the initiate force of the enterprise. Vaughan the indefatigable rode express to Portsmouth with a letter from Shirley to Benning Wentworth, governor of New Hampshire. That pompous and self-important personage admired the Massachusetts governor, who far surpassed him in talents and acquirements, and who at the same time knew how to soothe his vanity. Wentworth was ready to do his part, but his province had no money, and the King had ordered him to permit the issue of no more paper currency. The same prohibition had been laid upon Shirley; but he, with sagacious forecast, had persuaded his masters to relent so far as to permit the issue of £50,000 in what were called bills of credit to meet any pressing exigency of war. He told this to Wentworth, and succeeded in convincing him that his province might stretch her credit like Massachusetts, in case of similar military need. New Hampshire was thus enabled to raise a regiment of five hundred men out of her scanty population, with the condition that a hundred and fifty of them should be paid and fed by Massachusetts.[10]

Shirley was less fortunate in Rhode Island. The governor of that little colony called Massachusetts "our avowed enemy, always trying to defame us."[11] There was a grudge between the neighbors, due partly to notorious ill-treatment by the Massachusetts Puritans of Roger Williams, founder of Rhode Island, and partly to one of those boundary disputes which often produced ill-blood among the colonies. The representatives of Rhode Island, forgetting past differences, voted to raise a hundred and fifty men for the expedition, till, learning

[9] Sparks, *Works of Franklin*, vii. 16.

[10] Correspondence of Shirley and Wentworth, in *Belknap Papers. Provincial Papers of New Hampshire*, v.

[11] *Governor Wanton to the Agent of Rhode Island*, 20 December, 1745, in *Colony Records of Rhode Island*, v.

that the project was neither ordered nor approved by the Home Government, they prudently reconsidered their action. They voted, however, that the colony sloop "Tartar," carrying fourteen cannon and twelve swivels, should be equipped and manned for the service, and that the governor should be instructed to find and commission a captain and a lieutenant to command her.[12]

Connecticut promised five hundred and sixteen men and officers, on condition that Roger Wolcott, their commander, should have the second rank in the expedition. Shirley accordingly commissioned him as major-general. As Massachusetts was to supply above three thousand men, or more than three quarters of the whole force, she had a natural right to name a commander-in-chief.

It was not easy to choose one. The colony had been at peace for twenty years, and except some grizzled Indian fighters of the last war, and some survivors of the Carthagena expedition, nobody had seen service. Few knew well what a fortress was, and nobody knew how to attack one. Courage, energy, good sense, and popularity were the best qualities to be hoped for in the leader. Popularity was indispensable, for the soldiers were all to be volunteers, and they would not enlist under a commander whom they did not like. Shirley's choice was William Pepperrell, a merchant of Kittery. Knowing that Benning Wentworth thought himself the man for the place, he made an effort to placate him, and wrote that he would gladly have given him the chief command, but for his gouty legs. Wentworth took fire at the suggestion, forgot his gout, and declared himself ready to serve his country and assume the burden of command. The position was awkward, and Shirley was forced to reply, "On communicating your offer to two or three gentlemen in whose judgment I most confide, I found them clearly of opinion that any alteration of the present command would be attended with great risk, both with respect to our Assembly and the soldiers being entirely disgusted."[13]

The painter Smibert has left us a portrait of Pepperrell,— a good bourgeois face, not without dignity, though with no suggestion of the soldier. His spacious house at Kittery Point

[12] *Colony Records of Rhode Island*, v. (*February*, 1745).
[13] *Shirley to Wentworth*, 16 *February*, 1745.

still stands, sound and firm, though curtailed in some of its proportions. Not far distant is another noted relic of colonial times, the not less spacious mansion built by the disappointed Wentworth at Little Harbor. I write these lines at a window of this curious old house, and before me spreads the scene familiar to Pepperrell from childhood. Here the river Piscataqua widens to join the sea, holding in its gaping mouth the large island of Newcastle, with attendant groups of islets and island rocks, battered with the rack of ages, studded with dwarf savins, or half clad with patches of whortleberry bushes, sumach, and the shining wax-myrtle, green in summer, red with the touch of October. The flood tide pours strong and full around them, only to ebb away and lay bare a desolation of rocks and stones buried in a shock of brown drenched seaweed, broad tracts of glistening mud, sand-banks black with mussel-beds, and half-submerged meadows of eel-grass, with myriads of minute shell-fish clinging to its long lank tresses. Beyond all these lies the main, or northern channel, more than deep enough, even when the tide is out, to float a line-of-battle-ship. On its farther bank stands the old house of the Pepperrells, wearing even now an air of dingy respectability. Looking through its small, quaint window-panes, one could see across the water the rude dwellings of fishermen along the shore of Newcastle, and the neglected earthwork called Fort William and Mary, that feebly guarded the river's mouth. In front, the Piscataqua, curving southward, widened to meet the Atlantic between rocky headlands and foaming reefs, and in dim distance the Isles of Shoals seemed floating on the pale gray sea.

Behind the Pepperrell house was a garden, probably more useful than ornamental, and at the foot of it were the owner's wharves, with storehouses for salt-fish, naval stores, and imported goods for the country trade.

Pepperrell was the son of a Welshman[14] who migrated in early life to the Isles of Shoals, and thence to Kittery, where, by trade, ship-building, and the fisheries, he made a fortune, most of which he left to his son William. The young Pepper-

[14] "A native of Ravistock Parish, in Wales." Parsons, *Life of Pepperrell.* Mrs. Adelaide Cilley Waldron, a descendant of Pepperrell, assures me, however, that his father, the emigrant, came, not from Wales, but from Devonshire.

rell learned what little was taught at the village school, supplemented by a private tutor, whose instructions, however, did not perfect him in English grammar. In the eyes of his self-made father, education was valuable only so far as it could make a successful trader; and on this point he had reason to be satisfied, as his son passed for many years as the chief merchant in New England. He dealt in ships, timber, naval stores, fish, and miscellaneous goods brought from England; and he also greatly prospered by successful land purchases, becoming owner of the greater part of the growing towns of Saco and Scarborough. When scarcely twenty-one, he was made justice of the peace, on which he ordered from London what his biographer calls a law library, consisting of a law dictionary, Danvers' "Abridgment of the Common Law," the "Complete Solicitor," and several other books. In law as in war, his best qualities were good sense and good-will. About the time when he was made a justice, he was commissioned captain of militia, then major, then lieutenant-colonel, and at last colonel, commanding all the militia of Maine. The town of Kittery chose him to represent her in the General Courts, Maine being then a part of Massachusetts. Finally, he was made a member of the Governor's Council,—a post which he held for thirty-two years, during eighteen of which he was president of the board.

These civil dignities served him as educators better than tutor or village school; for they brought him into close contact with the chief men of the province; and in the Massachusetts of that time, so different from our own, the best education and breeding were found in the official class. At once a provincial magnate and the great man of a small rustic village, his manners are said to have answered to both positions,—certainly they were such as to make him popular. But whatever he became as a man, he learned nothing to fit him to command an army and lay siege to Louisbourg. Perhaps he felt this, and thought, with the governor of Rhode Island, that "the attempt to reduce that prodigiously strong town was too much for New England, which had not one officer of experience, nor even an engineer."[15] Moreover, he was unwilling to leave his wife, children, and business. He was of a religious

---

[15] *Governor Wanton to the Agent of Rhode Island in London,* 20 *December,* 1745.

turn of mind, and partial to the clergy, who, on their part, held him in high favor. One of them, the famous preacher, George Whitefield, was a guest at his house when he heard that Shirley had appointed him to command the expedition against Louisbourg. Whitefield had been the leading spirit in the recent religious fermentation called the Great Awakening, which, though it produced bitter quarrels among the ministers, besides other undesirable results, was imagined by many to make for righteousness. So thought the Rev. Thomas Prince, who mourned over the subsiding delirium of his flock as a sign of backsliding. "The heavenly shower was over," he sadly exclaims; "from fighting the devil they must turn to fighting the French." Pepperrell, always inclined to the clergy, and now in great perplexity and doubt, asked his guest Whitefield whether or not he had better accept the command. Whitefield gave him cold comfort, told him that the enterprise was not very promising, and that if he undertook it, he must do so "with a single eye," prepared for obloquy if he failed, and envy if he succeeded.[16]

Henry Sherburn, commissary of the New Hampshire regiment, begged Whitefield to furnish a motto for the flag. The preacher, who, zealot as he was, seemed unwilling to mix himself with so madcap a business, hesitated at first, but at length consented, and suggested the words, *Nil desperandum Christo duce*, which, being adopted, gave the enterprise the air of a crusade. It had, in fact, something of the character of one. The cause was imagined to be the cause of Heaven, crowned with celestial benediction. It had the fervent support of the ministers, not only by prayers and sermons, but, in one case, by counsels wholly temporal. A certain pastor, much esteemed for benevolence, proposed to Pepperrell, who had at last accepted the command, a plan, unknown to Vauban, for confounding the devices of the enemy. He advised that two trustworthy persons should cautiously walk together along the front of the French ramparts under cover of night, one of them carrying a mallet, with which he was to hammer the ground at short intervals. The French sentinels, it seems to have been supposed, on hearing this mysterious thumping, would be so bewildered as to give no alarm. While one of the two partners was thus employed, the other was to lay his ear

16 Parsons, *Life of Pepperrell*, 51.

to the ground, which, as the adviser thought, would return a hollow sound if the artful foe had dug a mine under it; and whenever such secret danger was detected, a mark was to be set on the spot, to warn off the soldiers.[17]

Equally zealous, after another fashion, was the Rev. Samuel Moody, popularly known as Father Moody, or Parson Moody, minister of York and senior chaplain of the expedition. Though about seventy years old, he was amazingly tough and sturdy. He still lives in the traditions of York as the spiritual despot of the settlement and the uncompromising guardian of its manners and doctrine, predominating over it like a rough little village pope. The comparison would have kindled his burning wrath, for he abhorred the Holy Father as an embodied Antichrist. Many are the stories told of him by the descendants of those who lived under his rod, and sometimes felt its weight; for he was known to have corrected offending parishioners with his cane.[18] When some one of his flock, nettled by his strictures from the pulpit, walked in dudgeon towards the church door, Moody would shout after him, "Come back, you graceless sinner, come back!" or if any ventured to the alehouse of a Saturday night, the strenuous pastor would go in after them, collar them, drag them out, and send them home with rousing admonition.[19] Few dared gainsay him, by reason both of his irritable temper and of the thick-skinned insensibility that encased him like armor of proof. And while his pachydermatous nature made him invulnerable as a rhinoceros, he had at the same time a rough and ready humor that supplied keen weapons for the warfare of words and made him a formidable antagonist. This commended him to the rude borderers, who also relished the sulphurous theology of their spiritual dictator, just as they liked the raw and fiery liquors that would have scorched more susceptible stomachs. What they did not like was the pitiless length of his prayers, which sometimes kept them afoot above two hours shivering in the polar cold of the unheated meeting-house, and which were followed by sermons of equal endurance; for the old man's lungs were of brass, and his nerves of hammered iron. Some of the sufferers ventured to remon-

[17] Belknap, *Hist. New Hampshire*, ii. 208.
[18] Tradition told me at York by Mr. N. Marshall.
[19] Lecture of Ralph Waldo Emerson, quoted by Cabot, *Memoir of Emerson*, i. 10.

strate; but this only exasperated him, till one parishioner, more worldly wise than the rest, accompanied his modest petition for mercy with the gift of a barrel of cider, after which the parson's ministrations were perceptibly less exhausting than before. He had an irrepressible conscience and a highly aggressive sense of duty, which made him an intolerable meddler in the affairs of other people, and which, joined to an underlying kindness of heart, made him so indiscreet in his charities that his wife and children were often driven to vain protest against the excesses of his almsgiving. The old Puritan fanaticism was rampant in him; and when he sailed for Louisbourg, he took with him an axe, intended, as he said, to hew down the altars of Antichrist and demolish his idols.[20]

Shirley's choice of a commander was perhaps the best that could have been made; for Pepperrell joined to an unusual popularity as little military incompetency as anybody else who could be had. Popularity, we have seen, was indispensable, and even company officers were appointed with an eye to it. Many of these were well-known men in rustic neighborhoods, who had raised companies in the hope of being commissioned to command them. Others were militia officers recruiting under orders of the governor. Thus, John Storer, major in the Maine militia, raised in a single day, it is said, a company of sixty-one, the eldest being sixty years old, and the youngest sixteen.[21] They formed about a quarter of the fencible population of the town of Wells, one of the most exposed places on the border. Volunteers offered themselves readily everywhere; though the pay was meagre, especially in Maine and Massachusetts, where in the new provincial currency it was twenty-five shillings a month,—then equal to fourteen shillings sterling, or less than sixpence a day,[22] the soldier furnishing his own clothing and bringing his own gun. A full third of

[20] Moody found sympathizers in his iconoclastic zeal. Deacon John Gray of Biddleford wrote to Pepperrell: "Oh that I could be with you and dear Parson Moody in that church [at Louisbourg] to destroy the images there set up, and hear the true Gospel of our Lord and Saviour there preached!"

[21] Bourne, *Hist. of Wells and Kennebunk*, 371.

[22] Gibson, *Journal; Records of Rhode Island*, v. Governor Wanton of that province says, with complacency, that the pay of Rhode Island was twice that of Massachusetts.

the Massachusetts contingent, or more than a thousand men, are reported to have come from the hardy population of Maine, whose entire fighting force, as shown by the muster-rolls, was then but 2,855.[23] Perhaps there was not one officer among them whose experience of war extended beyond a drill on muster day and the sham fight that closed the performance, when it generally happened that the rustic warriors were treated with rum at the charge of their captain, to put them in good humor, and so induce them to obey the word of command.

As the three provinces contributing soldiers recognized no common authority nearer than the King, Pepperrell received three several commissions as lieutenant-general,—one from the governor of Massachusetts, and the others from the governors of Connecticut and New Hampshire; while Wolcott, commander of the Connecticut forces, was commissioned as major-general by both the governor of his own province and that of Massachusetts. When the levies were complete, it was found that Massachusetts had contributed about 3,300 men, Connecticut 516, and New Hampshire 304 in her own pay, besides 150 paid by her wealthier neighbor.[24] Rhode Island had lost faith and disbanded her 150 men, but afterwards raised them again, though too late to take part in the siege.

Each of the four New England colonies had a little navy of its own, consisting of from one to three or four small armed vessels; and as privateering—which was sometimes a euphemism for piracy where Frenchmen and Spaniards were concerned—was a favorite occupation, it was possible to extemporize an additional force in case of need. For a naval commander, Shirley chose Captain Edward Tyng, who had signalized himself in the past summer by capturing a French privateer of greater strength than his own. Shirley authorized him to buy for the province the best ship he could find, equip her for fighting, and take command of her. Tyng soon found a brig to his mind, on the stocks, nearly ready for launching. She was rapidly fitted for her new destination, converted into a frigate, mounted with 24 guns, and named the "Massachu-

[23] Parsons, *Life of Pepperrell*, 54.

[24] Of the Massachusetts contingent, three hundred men were raised and maintained at the charge of the merchant James Gibson.

setts." The rest of the naval force consisted of the ship "Cæsar," of 20 guns; a vessel called the "Shirley," commanded by Captain Rous, and also carrying 20 guns; another, of the kind called a "snow," carrying 16 guns; one sloop of 12 guns, and two of 8 guns each; the "Boston Packet," of 16 guns; two sloops from Connecticut of 16 guns each; a privateer hired in Rhode Island, of 20 guns; the government sloop "Tartar," of the same colony, carrying 14 carriage guns and 12 swivels; and, finally, the sloop of 14 guns which formed the navy of New Hampshire.[25]

It was said, with apparent reason, that one or two heavy French ships-of-war—and a number of such was expected in the spring—would outmatch the whole colonial squadron, and, after mastering it, would hold all the transports at mercy; so that the troops on shore, having no means of return and no hope of succor, would be forced to surrender or starve. The danger was real and serious, and Shirley felt the necessity of help from a few British ships-of-war. Commodore Peter Warren was then with a small squadron at Antigua. Shirley sent an express boat to him with a letter stating the situation and asking his aid. Warren, who had married an American woman and who owned large tracts of land on the Mohawk, was known to be a warm friend to the provinces. It is clear that he would gladly have complied with Shirley's request; but when he laid the question before a council of officers, they were of one mind that without orders from the Admiralty he would not be justified in supporting an attempt made without the approval of the King.[26] He therefore saw no choice but to decline. Shirley, fearing that his refusal would be too discouraging, kept it secret from all but Pepperrell and General Wolcott, or, as others say, Brigadier Waldo. He had written to the Duke of Newcastle in the preceding autumn that Acadia and the fisheries were in great danger, and that ships-of-war were needed for their protection. On this, the duke had written to Warren, ordering him to sail for Boston and concert measures with Shirley "for the annoyance of the enemy, and his Majesty's service in North America."[27] Newcastle's letter reached Warren only two or three days after he had sent back

[25] The list is given by Williamson, ii. 227.
[26] *Memoirs of the Principal Transactions of the Last War*, 44.
[27] *Ibid.*, 46. *Letters of Shirley* (Public Record Office).

his refusal of Shirley's request. Thinking himself now suffi- ciently authorized to give the desired aid, he made all sail for Boston with his three ships, the "Superbe," "Mermaid," and "Launceston." On the way he met a schooner from Boston, and learned from its officers that the expedition had already sailed; on which, detaining the master as a pilot, he changed his course and made directly for Canseau,—the place of ren- dezvous of the expedition,—and at the same time sent orders by the schooner that any king's ships that might arrive at Boston should immediately join him.

Within seven weeks after Shirley issued his proclamation for volunteers, the preparations were all made, and the unique armament was afloat. Transports, such as they were, could be had in abundance; for the harbors of Salem and Marblehead were full of fishing-vessels thrown out of employment by the war. These were hired and insured by the province for the security of the owners. There was a great dearth of cannon. The few that could be had were too light, the heaviest being of twenty-two-pound calibre. New York lent ten eighteen- pounders to the expedition. But the adventurers looked to the French for their chief supply. A detached work near Louis- bourg, called the Grand, or Royal, Battery, was known to be armed with thirty heavy pieces; and these it was proposed to capture and turn against the town,—which, as Hutchinson remarks, was "like selling the skin of the bear before catching him."

It was clear that the expedition must run for luck against risks of all kinds. Those whose hopes were highest, based them on a belief in the special and direct interposition of Provi- dence; others were sanguine through ignorance and provincial self-conceit. As soon as the troops were embarked, Shirley wrote to the ministers of what was going on, telling them that, accidents apart, four thousand New England men would land on Cape Breton in April, and that, even should they fail to capture Louisbourg, he would answer for it that they would lay the town in ruins, retake Canseau, do other good service to his Majesty, and then come safe home.[28] On receiving this communication, the government resolved to aid the enter-

[28] *Shirley to Newcastle, 24 March, 1745.* The ministry was not wholly unprepared for this announcement, as Shirley had before reported to it the vote of his Assembly consenting to the expedi- tion. *Shirley to Newcastle, 1 February, 1745.*

prise if there should yet be time, and accordingly ordered several ships-of-war to sail for Louisbourg.

The sarcastic Dr. Douglas, then living at Boston, writes that the expedition had a lawyer for contriver, a merchant for general, and farmers, fishermen, and mechanics for soldiers. In fact, it had something of the character of broad farce, to which Shirley himself with all his ability and general good sense, was a chief contributor. He wrote to the Duke of Newcastle that though the officers had no experience and the men no discipline, he would take care to provide against these defects,—meaning that he would give exact directions how to take Louisbourg. Accordingly, he drew up copious instructions to that effect. These seem to have undergone a process of evolution, for several distinct drafts of them are preserved.[29] The complete and final one is among the Pepperrell Papers, copied entire in the neat, commercial hand of the general himself.[30] It seems to assume that Providence would work a continued miracle, and on every occasion supply the expedition with weather precisely suited to its wants. "It is thought," says this singular document, "that Louisbourg may be surprised if they [the French] have no advice of your coming. To effect it you must time your arrival about nine of the clock in the evening, taking care that the fleet be far enough in the offing to prevent their being seen from the town in the daytime." He then goes on to prescribe how the troops are to land, after dark, at a place called Flat Point Cove, in four divisions, three of which are to march to the back of

[29] The first draft of Shirley's instructions for taking Louisbourg is in the large manuscript volume entitled *Siege of Louisbourg,* in the library of the Massachusetts Historical Society. The document is called *Mem° for the attacking of Louisbourg this Spring by Surprise.* After giving minute instructions for every movement, it goes on to say that, as the surprise may possibly fail, it will be necessary to send two small mortars and twelve cannon carrying nine-pound balls, "so as to bombard them and endeavour to make Breaches in their walls and then to Storm them." Shirley was soon to discover the absurdity of trying to breach the walls of Louisbourg with nine-pounders.

[30] It is printed in the first volume of the *Collections of the Massachusetts Historical Society.* Shirley was so well pleased with it that he sent it to the Duke of Newcastle enclosed in his letter of 1 February, 1745 (Public Record Office).

certain hills a mile and a half west of the town, where two of the three "are to halt and keep a profound silence;" the third continuing its march "under cover of the said hills," till it comes opposite the Grand Battery, which it will attack at a concerted signal; while one of the two divisions behind the hills assaults the west gate, and the other moves up to support the attack.

While this is going on, the soldiers of the fourth division are to march with all speed along the shore till they come to a certain part of the town wall, which they are to scale; then proceed "as fast as can be" to the citadel and "secure the windows of the governor's apartments." After this follow page after page of complicated details which must have stricken the general with stupefaction. The rocks, surf, fogs, and gales of that tempestuous coast are all left out of the account; and so, too, is the nature of the country, which consists of deep marshes, rocky hills, and hollows choked with evergreen thickets. Yet a series of complex and mutually dependent operations, involving long marches through this rugged and pathless region, was to be accomplished, in the darkness of one April night, by raw soldiers who knew nothing of the country. This rare specimen of amateur soldiering is redeemed in some measure by a postscript in which the governor sets free the hands of the general, thus: "Notwithstanding the instructions you have received from me, I must leave you to act, upon unforeseen emergencies, according to your best discretion."

On the twenty-fourth of March, the fleet, consisting of about ninety transports, escorted by the provincial cruisers, sailed from Nantasket Roads, followed by prayers and benedictions, and also by toasts drunk with cheers, in bumpers of rum punch.[31]

---

[31] The following letter from John Payne of Boston to Colonel Robert Hale, of the Essex regiment, while it gives no sign of the prevailing religious feeling, illustrates the ardor of the New England people towards their rash adventure:—

BOSTON, Apr. 24, 1745.

SIR,—I hope this will find you at Louisbourg with a Bowl of Punch a Pipe and a P—k of C—ds in your hand and whatever else you desire (I had forgot to mention a Pretty French Madammoselle). We are very Impatiently expecting to hear from you, your Friend Luke has lost several Beaver Hatts already concerning the Expedition, he is so very zealous about it that he has turned Poor Boutier out of his House for saying he believed you would not Take the Place.—Damn his Blood says Luke, let him be an Englishman or a Frenchman and not pretend to be an Englishman when he is a Frenchman in his Heart. If drinking to your success would Take Cape Briton, you must be in Possession of it now, for it's a standing Toast. I think the least thing You Military Gent^n can do is to send us some arrack when you take ye Place to celebrate your Victory and not to force us to do it in Rum Punch or Luke's bad wine or sour cyder.

To Collonell Robert Hale
    at (or near) Louisbourg.

I am indebted for a copy of this curious letter to Robert Hale Bancroft, Esq., a descendant of Colonel Hale.

Chapter 19

1745
Louisbourg Besieged

ON BOARD ONE of the transports was Seth Pomeroy, gunsmith at Northampton, and now major of Willard's Massachusetts regiment. He had a turn for soldiering, and fought, ten years later, in the battle of Lake George. Again, twenty years later still, when Northampton was astir with rumors of war from Boston, he borrowed a neighbor's horse, rode a hundred miles, reached Cambridge on the morning of the battle of Bunker Hill, left his borrowed horse out of the way of harm, walked over Charlestown Neck, then swept by the fire of the ships-of-war, and reached the scene of action as the British were forming for the attack. When Israel Putnam, his comrade in the last war, saw from the rebel breastwork the old man striding, gun in hand, up the hill, he shouted, "By God, Pomeroy, you here! A cannon-shot would waken you out of your grave!"

But Pomeroy, with other landsmen, crowded in the small and malodorous fishing-vessels that were made to serve as transports, was now in the gripe of the most unheroic of maladies. "A terrible northeast storm" had fallen upon them, and, he says, "we lay rolling in the seas, with our sails furled, among prodigious waves." "Sick, day and night," writes the miserable gunsmith, "so bad that I have not words to set it forth."[1] The gale increased and the fleet was scattered, there being, as a Massachusetts private soldier writes in his diary, "a very fierse Storm of Snow, som Rain and very Dangerous weather to be so nigh ye Shore as we was; but we escaped the Rocks, and that was all."[2]

On Friday, April 5, Pomeroy's vessel entered the harbor of Canseau, about fifty miles from Louisbourg. Here was the English fishing-hamlet, the seizure of which by the French

[1] Diary of Major Seth Pomeroy. I owe the copy before me to the kindness of his descendant, Theodore Pomeroy, Esq.

[2] Diary of a Massachusetts soldier in Captain Richardson's company (Papers of Dr. Belknap).

had first provoked the expedition. The place now quietly changed hands again. Sixty-eight of the transports lay here at anchor, and the rest came dropping in from day to day, sorely buffeted, but all safe. On Sunday there was a great concourse to hear Parson Moody preach an open-air sermon from the text, "Thy people shall be willing in the day of thy power," concerning which occasion the soldier diarist observes,—"Several sorts of Busnesses was Going on, Som a Exercising, Som a Hearing Preaching." The attention of Parson Moody's listeners was, in fact, distracted by shouts of command and the awkward drill of squads of homespun soldiers on the adjacent pasture.

Captain Ammi Cutter, with two companies, was ordered to remain at Canseau and defend it from farther vicissitudes; to which end a blockhouse was also built, and mounted with eight small cannon. Some of the armed vessels had been set to cruise off Louisbourg, which they did to good purpose, and presently brought in six French prizes, with supplies for the fortress. On the other hand, they brought the ominous news that Louisbourg and the adjoining bay were so blocked with ice that landing was impossible. This was a serious misfortune, involving long delay, and perhaps ruin to the expedition, as the expected ships-of-war might arrive meanwhile from France. Indeed, they had already begun to appear. On Thursday, the eighteenth, heavy cannonading was heard far out at sea, and again on Friday "the common," says Pomeroy, "fired at a great rate till about 2 of the clock." It was the provincial cruisers attacking a French frigate, the "Renommée," of thirty-six guns. As their united force was too much for her, she kept up a running fight, outsailed them, and escaped after a chase of more than thirty hours, being, as Pomeroy quaintly observes, "a smart ship." She carried despatches to the governor of Louisbourg, and being unable to deliver them, sailed back for France to report what she had seen.

On Monday, the twenty-second, a clear, cold, windy day, a large ship, under British colors, sailed into the harbor, and proved to be the frigate "Eltham," escort to the annual mast fleet from New England. On orders from Commander Warren she had left her charge in waiting, and sailed for Canseau to join the expedition, bringing the unexpected and welcome news that Warren himself would soon follow. On the next day, to the delight of all, he appeared in the ship "Superbe," of sixty guns, accompanied by the "Launceston" and the "Mermaid," of forty guns each. Here was force enough to oppose any ships likely to come to the aid of Louisbourg; and Warren, after communicating with Pepperrell, sailed to blockade the port, along with the provincial cruisers, which, by order of Shirley, were placed under his command.

The transports lay at Canseau nearly three weeks, waiting for the ice to break up. The time was passed in drilling the raw soldiers and forming them into divisions of four and six hundred each, according to the directions of Shirley. At length, on Friday, the twenty-seventh, they heard that Gabarus Bay was free from ice, and on the morning of the twenty-ninth, with the first fair wind, they sailed out of Canseau harbor, expecting to reach Louisbourg at nine in the evening, as prescribed in the governor's receipt for taking Louisbourg "while the enemy were asleep."[3] But a lull in the wind defeated this plan; and after sailing all day, they found themselves becalmed towards night. It was not till the next morning that they could see the town,—no very imposing spectacle, for the buildings, with a few exceptions, were small, and the massive ramparts that belted them round rose to no conspicuous height.

Louisbourg stood on a tongue of land which lay between its harbor and the sea, and the end of which was prolonged eastward by reefs and shoals that partly barred the entrance to the port, leaving a navigable passage not half a mile wide. This passage was commanded by a powerful battery called the "Island Battery," being upon a small rocky island at the west side of the channel, and was also secured by another detached work called the "Grand," or "Royal Battery," which stood on the shore of the harbor, opposite the entrance, and more than a mile from the town. Thus a hostile squadron trying to force its way in would receive a flank fire from the one battery, and a front fire from the other. The strongest line of defence of the fortress was drawn across the base of the tongue of land from the harbor on one side to the sea on the other,—a distance of about twelve hundred yards. The ditch was eighty feet wide and from thirty to thirty-six feet deep; and the rampart, of earth faced with masonry, was about sixty feet thick. The glacis sloped down to a vast marsh, which formed one of the best defences of the place. The

[3] The words quoted are used by General Wolcott in his journal.

fortress, without counting its outworks, had embrasures for one hundred and forty-eight cannon; but the number in position was much less, and is variously stated. Pomeroy says that at the end of the siege a little above ninety were found, with "a great number of swivels;" others say seventy-six.[4] In the Grand and Island batteries there were sixty heavy pieces more. Against this formidable armament the assailants had brought thirty-four cannon and mortars, of much inferior weight, to be used in bombarding the fortress, should they chance to fail of carrying it by surprise, "while the enemy were asleep."[5] Apparently they distrusted the efficacy of their siege-train, though it was far stronger than Shirley had at first thought sufficient; for they brought with them good store of balls of forty-two pounds, to be used in French cannon of that calibre which they expected to capture, their own largest pieces being but twenty-two-pounders.

According to the *Habitant de Louisbourg*, the garrison consisted of five hundred and sixty regular troops, of whom several companies were Swiss, besides some thirteen or fourteen hundred militia, inhabitants partly of the town, and partly of neighboring settlements.[6] The regulars were in bad condition. About the preceding Christmas they had broken into mutiny, being discontented with their rations and exasperated with getting no extra pay for work on the fortifications. The affair was so serious that though order was restored, some of the officers lost all confidence in the soldiers; and this distrust proved most unfortunate during the siege. The governor, Chevalier Duchambon, successor of Duquesnel, who had died in the autumn, was not a man to grapple with a crisis, being deficient in decision of character, if not in capacity.

He expected an attack. "We were informed of the prepara-

---

[4] Brown, *Cape Breton*, 183. Parsons, *Life of Pepperrell*, 103. An anonymous letter, dated Louisbourg, 4 July, 1745, says that eighty-five cannon and six mortars have been found in the town.

[5] *Memoirs of the Principal Transactions of the Last War*, 40.

[6] "On fit venir cinq ou six cens Miliciens aux Habitans des environs; ce que, avec ceux de la Ville, pouvoit former treize à quatorze cens hommes."—*Lettre d'un Habitant de Louisbourg*. This writer says that three or four hundred more might have been had from Niganiche and its neighborhood, if they had been summoned in time. The number of militia just after the siege is set by English reports at 1,310. Parsons, 103.

314 / A Half-Century of Conflict

tions from the first," say the *Habitant de Louisbourg*. Some Indians, who had been to Boston, carried to Canada the news of what was going on there; but it was not believed, and excited no alarm.[7] It was not so at Louisbourg, where, says the French writer just quoted, "we lost precious moments in useless deliberations and resolutions no sooner made than broken. Nothing to the purpose was done, so that we were as much taken by surprise as if the enemy had pounced upon us unawares."

It was about the twenty-fifth of March[8] when the garrison first saw the provincial cruisers hovering off the mouth of the harbor. They continued to do so at intervals till daybreak of the thirtieth of April, when the whole fleet of transports appeared standing towards Flat Point, which projects into Gabarus Bay, three miles west of the town.[9] On this, Duchambon sent Morpain, captain of a privateer, or "corsair," to oppose the landing. He had with him eighty men, and was to be joined by forty more, already on the watch near the supposed point of disembarkation.[10] At the same time cannon were fired and alarm bells rung in Louisbourg, to call in the militia of the neighborhood.

Pepperrell managed the critical work of landing with creditable skill. The rocks and the surf were more dangerous than the enemy. Several boats, filled with men, rowed towards Flat Point; but on a signal from the flagship "Shirley," rowed back again, Morpain flattering himself that his appearance had frightened them off. Being joined by several other boats, the united party, a hundred men in all, pulled for another landing-place called Fresh-water Cove, or Anse de la Cormorandière, two miles farther up Gabarus Bay. Morpain and his party ran to meet them; but the boats were first in the race, and as soon as the New England men got ashore, they rushed upon the French, killed six of them, captured as many more, including an officer named Boularderie, and put the rest to flight, with the loss, on their own side, of two

[7] *Shirley to Newcastle*, 17 *June*, 1745, citing letters captured on board a ship from Quebec.

[8] 14 March, old style.

[9] Gabarus Bay, sometimes called "Chapeau Rouge" Bay, is a spacious outer harbor, immediately adjoining Louisbourg.

[10] *Bigot au Ministre*, 1 *Août*, 1745.

men slightly wounded.[11] Further resistance to the landing was impossible, for a swarm of boats pushed against the rough and stony beach, the men dashing through the surf, till before night about two thousand were on shore.[12] The rest, or about two thousand more, landed at their leisure on the next day.

On the second of May Vaughan led four hundred men to the hills near the town, and saluted it with three cheers,—somewhat to the discomposure of the French, though they described the unwelcome visitors as a disorderly crowd. Vaughan's next proceeding pleased them still less. He marched behind the hills, in rear of the Grand Battery, to the northeast arm of the harbor, where there were extensive magazines of naval stores. These his men set on fire, and the pitch, tar, and other combustibles made a prodigious smoke. He was returning, in the morning, with a small party of followers behind the hills, when coming opposite the Grand Battery, and observing it from the ridge, he saw neither flag on the flagstaff, nor smoke from the barrack chimneys. One of his party was a Cape Cod Indian. Vaughan bribed him with a flask of brandy which he had in his pocket,—though, as the clerical historian takes pains to assure us, he never used it himself,—and the Indian, pretending to be drunk, or, as some say, mad, staggered towards the battery to reconnoitre.[13] All was quiet. He clambered in at an embrasure, and found the place empty. The rest of the party followed, and one of them, William Tufts, of Medford, a boy of eighteen, climbed the flagstaff, holding in his teeth his red coat, which he made fast at the top, as a substitute for the British flag,—a proceeding that drew upon him a volley of unsuccessful cannon-shot from the town batteries.[14]

[11] *Pepperrell to Shirley*, 12 *May*, 1745. *Shirley to Newcastle*, 28 *October*, 1745. *Journal of the Siege*, attested by Pepperrell and four other chief officers (London, 1746).

[12] Bigot says six thousand, or two thousand more than the whole New England force, which was constantly overestimated by the French.

[13] Belknap, ii.

[14] John Langdon Sibley, in *N. E. Hist. and Gen. Register*, xxv. 377. The *Boston Gazette* of 3 June, 1771, has a notice of Tufts' recent death, with an exaggerated account of his exploit, and an appeal for aid to his destitute family.

Vaughan then sent this hasty note to Pepperrell: "May it please your Honour to be informed that by the grace of God and the courage of 13 men, I entered the Royal Battery about 9 o'clock, and am waiting for a reinforcement and a flag." Soon after, four boats, filled with men, approached from the town to reoccupy the battery,—no doubt in order to save the munitions and stores, and complete the destruction of the cannon. Vaughan and his thirteen men, standing on the open beach, under the fire of the town and the Island Battery, plied the boats with musketry, and kept them from landing, till Lieutenant-Colonel Bradstreet appeared with a reinforcement, on which the French pulled back to Louisbourg.[15]

The English supposed that the French in the battery, when the clouds of smoke drifted over them from the burning storehouses, thought that they were to be attacked in force, and abandoned their post in a panic. This was not the case. "A detachment of the enemy," writes the *Habitant de Louisbourg*, "advanced to the neighborhood of the Royal Battery." This was Vaughan's four hundred on their way to burn the storehouses. "At once we were all seized with fright," pursues this candid writer, "and on the instant it was proposed to abandon this magnificent battery, which would have been our best defence, if one had known how to use it. Various councils were held, in a tumultuous way. It would be hard to tell the reasons for such a strange proceeding. Not one shot had yet been fired at the battery, which the enemy could not take, except by making regular approaches, as if against the town itself, and by besieging it, so to speak, in form. Some persons remonstrated, but in vain; and so a battery of thirty cannon, which had cost the King immense sums, was abandoned before it was attacked."

Duchambon says that soon after the English landed, he got a letter from Thierry, the captain in command of the Royal Battery, advising that the cannon should be spiked and the works blown up. It was then, according to the governor, that the council was called, and a unanimous vote passed to follow Thierry's advice, on the ground that the defences of the battery were in bad condition, and that the four hundred men posted there could not stand against three or

[15] Vaughan's party seems to have consisted in all of sixteen men, three of whom took no part in this affair.

four thousand.[16] The engineer, Verrier, opposed the blowing up of the works, and they were therefore left untouched. Thierry and his garrison came off in boats, after spiking the cannon in a hasty way, without stopping to knock off the trunnions or burn the carriages. They threw their loose gunpowder into the well, but left behind a good number of cannon cartridges, two hundred and eighty large bombshells, and other ordinance stores, invaluable both to the enemy and to themselves. Brigadier Waldo was sent to occupy the battery with his regiment, and Major Seth Pomeroy, the gunsmith, with twenty soldier-mechanics, was set at drilling out the spiked touch-holes of the cannon. There were twenty-eight forty-two-pounders, and two eighteen-pounders.[17] Several were ready for use the next morning, and immediately opened on the town,—which, writes a soldier in his diary, "damaged the houses and made the women cry." "The enemy," says the *Habitant de Louisbourg,* "saluted us with our own cannon, and made a terrific fire, smashing everything within range."

The English occupation of the Grand Battery may be called the decisive event of the siege. There seems no doubt that the French could have averted the disaster long enough to make it of little help to the invaders. The water-front of the battery was impregnable. The rear defences consisted of a loop-holed wall of masonry, with a ditch ten feet deep and twelve feet wide, and also a covered way and glacis, which General Wolcott describes as unfinished. In this he mistook. They were not unfinished, but had been partly demolished, with a view to reconstruction. The rear wall was flanked by two towers, which, says Duchambon, were demolished; but General Wolcott declares that swivels were

---

[16] *Duchambon au Ministre,* 2 *Septembre,* 1745. This is the governor's official report. "Four hundred men," is perhaps a copyist's error, the actual number in the battery being not above two hundred.

[17] *Waldo to Shirley,* 12 *May,* 1745. Some of the French writers say twenty-eight thirty-six pounders, while all the English call them forty-twos,—which they must have been, as the forty-two-pound shot brought from Boston fitted them.

Mr. Theodore Roosevelt draws my attention to the fact that cannon were differently rated in the French and English navies of the seventeenth century, and that a French thirty-six carried a ball as large as an English forty-two, or even a little larger.

still mounted on them,[18] and he adds that "two hundred men might hold the battery against five thousand without cannon." The English landed their cannon near Flat Point; and before they could be turned against the Grand Battery, they must be dragged four miles over hills and rocks, through spongy marshes and jungles of matted evergreens. This would have required a week or more. The alternative was an escalade, in which the undisciplined assailants would no doubt have met a bloody rebuff. Thus this Grand Battery, which, says Wolcott, "is in fact a fort," might at least have been held long enough to save the munitions and stores, and effectually disable the cannon, which supplied the English with the only artillery they had, competent to the work before them. The hasty abandonment of this important post was not Duchambon's only blunder, but it was the worst of them all.

On the night after their landing, the New England men slept in the woods, wet or dry, with or without blankets, as the case might be, and in the morning set themselves to encamping with as much order as they were capable of. A brook ran down from the hills and entered the sea two miles or more from the town. The ground on each side, though rough, was high and dry, and here most of the regiments made their quarters,—Willard's, Moulton's, and Moore's on the east side, and Burr's and Pepperrell's on the west. Those on the east, in some cases, saw fit to extend themselves towards Louisbourg as far as the edge of the intervening marsh, but were soon forced back to a safer position by the cannon-balls of the fortress, which came bowling amongst them. This marsh was that green, flat sponge of mud and moss that stretched from this point to the glacis of Louisbourg.

There was great want of tents, for material to make them was scarce in New England. Old sails were often used instead, being stretched over poles,—perhaps after the fashion of a Sioux teepee. When these could not be had, the men built huts of sods, with roofs of spruce-boughs overlapping like a thatch; for at that early season, bark would not peel from the trees. The landing of guns, munitions, and stores was a formidable task, consuming many days and destroying many boats, as happened again when Amherst landed his cannon

[18] *Journal of Major-General Wolcott.*

at this same place. Large flat boats, brought from Boston, were used for the purpose, and the loads were carried ashore on the heads of the men, wading through ice-cold surf to the waist, after which, having no change of clothing, they slept on the ground through the chill and foggy nights, reckless of future rheumatisms.[19]

A worse task was before them. The cannon were to be dragged over the marsh to Green Hill, a spur of the line of rough heights that half encircled the town and harbor. Here the first battery was to be planted; and from this point other guns were to be dragged onward to more advanced stations, —a distance in all of more than two miles, thought by the French to be impassable. So, in fact, it seemed; for at the first attempt, the wheels of the cannon sank to the hubs in mud and moss, then the carriage, and finally the piece itself slowly disappeared. Lieutenant-Colonel Meserve, of the New Hampshire regiment, a ship-builder by trade, presently overcame the difficulty. By his direction sledges of timber were made, sixteen feet long and five feet wide; a cannon was placed on each of these, and it was then dragged over the marsh by a team of two hundred men, harnessed with rope-traces and breast-straps, and wading to the knees. Horses or oxen would have foundered in the mire. The way had often to be changed, as the mossy surface was soon churned into a hopeless slough along the line of march. The work could be done only at night or in thick fog, the men being completely exposed to the cannon of the town. Thirteen years after, when General Amherst besieged Louisbourg again, he dragged his cannon to the same hill over the same marsh; but having at his command, instead of four thousand militiamen, eleven thousand British regulars, with all appliances and means to boot, he made a road, with prodigious labor, through the mire, and protected it from the French shot by an epaulement, or lateral earthwork.

Pepperrell writes in ardent words of the cheerfulness of his men "under almost incredible hardships." Shoes and

[19] The author of *The Importance and Advantage of Cape Breton* says: "When the hardships they were exposed to come to be considered, the behaviour of these men will hardly gain credit. They went ashore wet, had no [dry] clothes to cover them, were exposed in this condition to cold, foggy nights, and yet cheerfully underwent these difficulties for the sake of executing a project they had voluntarily undertaken.

clothing failed, till many were in tatters and many bare-footed;[20] yet they toiled on with unconquerable spirit, and within four days had planted a battery of six guns on Green Hill, which was about a mile from the King's Bastion of Louisbourg. In another week they had dragged four twenty-two-pound cannon and ten coehorns—gravely called "cowhorns" by the bucolic Pomeroy—six or seven hundred yards farther, and planted them within easy range of the citadel. Two of the cannon burst, and were replaced by four more and a large mortar, which burst in its turn, and Shirley was begged to send another. Meanwhile a battery, chiefly of coehorns, had been planted on a hillock four hundred and forty yards from the West Gate, where it greatly annoyed the French; and on the next night an advanced battery was placed just opposite the same gate, and scarcely two hundred and fifty yards from it. This West Gate, the principal gate of Louisbourg, opened upon the tract of high, firm ground that lay on the left of the besiegers, between the marsh and the harbor, an arm of which here extended westward beyond the town, into what was called the Barachois, a salt pond formed by a projecting spit of sand. On the side of the Barachois farthest from the town was a hillock on which stood the house of an *habitant* named Martissan. Here, on the twentieth of May, a fifth battery was planted, consisting of two of the French forty-two-pounders taken in the Grand Battery, to which three others were afterwards added. Each of these heavy pieces was dragged to its destination by a team of three hundred men over rough and rocky ground swept by the French artillery. This fifth battery, called the Northwest, or Titcomb's, proved most destructive to the fortress.[21]

All these operations were accomplished with the utmost ardor and energy, but with a scorn of rule and precedent that astonished and bewildered the French. The raw New England men went their own way, laughed at trenches and zigzags, and persisted in trusting their lives to the night and the fog. Several writers say that the English engineer Bastide tried to teach them discretion; but this could hardly be, for Bastide, whose station was Annapolis, did not reach Louisbourg till the fifth of June, when the batteries were finished, and

[20] *Pepperrell to Newcastle, 28 June, 1745.*

[21] *Journal of the Siege,* appended to Shirley's report to Newcastle; *Duchambon au Ministre, 2 Septembre, 1745; Lettre d'un Habitant; Pomeroy, etc.*

the siege was nearly ended. A recent French writer makes the curious assertion that it was one of the ministers, or army chaplains, who took upon him the vain task of instruction in the art of war on this occasion.[22]

This ignorant and self-satisfied recklessness might have cost the besiegers dear if the French, instead of being perplexed and startled at the novelty of their proceedings, had taken advantage of it; but Duchambon and some of his officers, remembering the mutiny of the past winter, feared to make sorties, lest the soldiers might desert or take part with the enemy. The danger of this appears to have been small. Warren speaks with wonder in his letters of the rarity of desertions, of which there appear to have been but three during the siege,—one being that of a half-idiot, from whom no information could be got. A bolder commander would not have stood idle while his own cannon were planted by the enemy to batter down his walls; and whatever the risks of a sortie, the risks of not making one were greater. "Both troops and militia eagerly demanded it, and I believe it would have succeeded," writes the intendant, Bigot.[23] The attempt was actually made more than once in a half-hearted way,— notably on the eighth of May, when the French attacked the most advanced battery, and were repulsed, with little loss on either side.

The *Habitant de Louisbourg* says: "The enemy did not attack us with any regularity, and made no intrenchments to cover themselves." This last is not exact. Not being wholly demented, they made intrenchments, such as they were,—at least, at the advanced battery;[24] as they would otherwise have been swept out of existence, being under the concentred fire of several French batteries, two of which were within the range of a musket-shot.

The scarcity of good gunners was one of the chief difficulties of the besiegers. As privateering, and piracy also, against Frenchmen and Spaniards was a favorite pursuit in New England, there were men in Pepperrell's army who knew how to handle cannon; but their number was insufficient, and the general sent a note to Warren, begging that he would

[22] Ferland, *Cours d'Histoire du Canada*, ii. 477. "L'ennemi ne nous attaquoit point dans les formes, et ne pratiquoit point aucun retranchement pour se couvrir."—*Habitant de Louisbourg*.

[23] *Bigot au Ministre*, 1 *Août*, 1745.

[24] *Diary of Joseph Sherburn, Captain at the Advanced Battery*.

lend him a few experienced gunners to teach their trade to the raw hands at the batteries. Three or four were sent, and they found apt pupils.

Pepperrell placed the advanced battery in charge of Captain Joseph[25] Sherburn, telling him to enlist as many gunners as he could. On the next day Sherburn reported that he had found six, one of whom seems to have been sent by Warren. With these and a number of raw men he repaired to his perilous station, where "I found," he says, "a very poor intrenchment. Our best shelter from the French fire, which was very hot, was hogsheads filled with earth." He and his men made the West Gate their chief mark; but before they could get a fair sight of it, they were forced to shoot down the fish-flakes, or stages for drying cod, that obstructed the view. Some of their party were soon killed,—Captain Pierce by a cannon-ball, Thomas Ash by a "bumb," and others by musketry. In the night they improved their defences, and mounted on them three more guns, one of eighteen-pound calibre, and the others of forty-two,—French pieces dragged from the Grand Battery, a mile and three quarters round the Barachois.

The cannon could be loaded only under a constant fire of musketry, which the enemy briskly returned. The French practice was excellent. A soldier who in bravado mounted the rampart and stood there for a moment was shot dead with five bullets. The men on both sides called to each other in scraps of bad French or broken English; while the French drank ironical healths to the New England men, and gave them bantering invitations to breakfast.

Sherburn continues his diary. "Sunday morning. Began our fire with as much fury as possible, and the French returned it as warmly from the Citidale [citadel], West Gate, and North East Battery with Cannon, Mortars, and continual showers of musket balls; but by 11 o'clock we had beat them all from their guns." He goes on to say that at noon his men were forced to stop firing from want of powder, that he went with his gunners to get some, and that while they were gone, somebody, said to be Mr. Vaughan, brought a supply, on which the men loaded the forty-two pounders in a bungling way, and fired them. One was dismounted, and the other

---

[25] He signs his name Jos. Sherburn; but in a list of the officers of the New Hampshire Regiment it appears in full as Joseph.

burst; a barrel and a half-barrel of powder blew up, killed two men, and injured two more. Again: "Wednesday. Hot fire on both sides, till the French were beat from all their guns. May 29th went to 2 Gun [Titcomb's] Battery to give the gunners some directions; then returned to my own station, where I spent the rest of the day with pleasure, seeing our Shott Tumble down their walls and Flagg Staff."

The following is the intendant Bigot's account of the effect of the New England fire: "The enemy established their batteries to such effect that they soon destroyed the greater part of the town, broke the right flank of the King's Bastion, ruined the Dauphin Battery with its spur, and made a breach at the Porte Dauphine [West Gate], the neighboring wall, and the sort of redan adjacent."[26] Duchambon says in addition that the cannon of the right flank of the King's Bastion could not be served, by reason of the continual fire of the enemy, which broke the embrasures to pieces; that when he had them repaired, they were broken to pieces (*démantibulés*) again,—and nobody could keep his ground behind the wall of the quay, which was shot through and through and completely riddled.[27] The town was ploughed with cannon-balls, the streets were raked from end to end, nearly all the houses damaged, and the people driven for refuge into the stifling casemates. The results were creditable to novices in gunnery.

The repeated accidents from the bursting of cannon were no doubt largely due to unskilful loading and the practice of double-shotting, to which the over-zealous artillerists are said to have often resorted.[28]

It is said, in proof of the orderly conduct of the men, that not one of them was punished during all the siege; but this shows the mild and conciliating character of the general quite as much as any peculiar merit of the soldiers. The state

[26] *Bigot au Ministre*, 1 *Août*, 1745.

[27] *Duchambon au Ministre*, 2 *Septembre*, 1745.

[28] "Another forty-two pound gun burst at the Grand Battery. All the guns are in danger of going the same way, by double-shotting them, unless under better regulation than at present."—*Waldo to Pepperrell*, 20 *May*, 1745.

Waldo had written four days before: "Captain Hale, of my regiment, is dangerously hurt by the bursting of another gun. He was our mainstay for gunnery since Captain Rhode's misfortune" (also caused by the bursting of a cannon). *Waldo to Pepperrell*, 16 *May*, 1745.

of things in and about the camp was compared by the caustic Dr. Douglas to "a Cambridge Commencement," which academic festival was then attended by much rough frolic and boisterous horseplay among the disorderly crowds, white and black, bond and free, who swarmed among the booths on Cambridge Common. The careful and scrupulous Belknap, who knew many who took part in the siege, says: "Those who were on the spot have frequently, in my hearing, laughed at the recital of their own irregularities, and expressed their admiration when they reflected on the almost miraculous preservation of the army from destruction." While the cannon bellowed in the front, frolic and confusion reigned at the camp, where the men raced, wrestled, pitched quoits, fired at marks,—though there was no ammunition to spare,—and ran after the French cannon-balls, which were carried to the batteries, to be returned to those who sent them. Nor were calmer recreations wanting. "Some of our men went a fishing, about 2 miles off," writes Lieutenant Benjamin Cleaves in his diary: "caught 6 Troutts." And, on the same day, "Our men went to catch Lobsters: caught 30." In view of this truant disposition, it is not surprising that the besiegers now and then lost their scalps at the hands of prowling Indians who infested the neighborhood. Yet through all these gambols ran an undertow of enthusiasm, born in brains still fevered from the "Great Awakening." The New England soldier, a growth of sectarian hotbeds, fancied that he was doing the work of God. The army was Israel, and the French were Canaanitish idolaters. Red-hot Calvinism, acting through generations, had modified the transplanted Englishman; and the descendant of the Puritans was never so well pleased as when teaching their duty to other people, whether by pen, voice, or bombshells. The ragged artillerymen, battering the walls of papistical Louisbourg, flattered themselves with the notion that they were champions of gospel truth.

Barefoot and tattered, they toiled on with indomitable pluck and cheerfulness, doing the work which oxen could not do, with no comfort but their daily dram of New England rum, as they plodded through the marsh and over rocks, dragging the ponderous guns through fog and darkness. Their spirit could not save them from the effects of excessive fatigue and exposure. They were ravaged with diarrhœa and fever, till fifteen hundred men were at one time on the sick-list, and at another, Pepperrell reported that of the four thousand only about twenty-one hundred were fit for duty.[29] Nearly all at last recovered, for the weather was unusually good; yet the number fit for service was absurdly small. Pepperrell begged for reinforcements, but got none till the siege was ended.

It was not his nature to rule with a stiff hand,—and this, perhaps, was fortunate. Order and discipline, the sinews of an army, were out of the question; and it remained to do as well as might be without them, keep men and officers in good-humor, and avoid all that could dash their ardor. For this, at least, the merchant-general was well fitted. His popularity had helped to raise the army, and perhaps it helped now to make it efficient. His position was no bed of roses. Worries, small and great, pursued him without end. He made friends of his officers, kept a bountiful table at his tent, and labored to soothe their disputes and jealousies, and satisfy their complaints. So generous were his contributions to the common cause that according to a British officer who speaks highly of his services, he gave to it, in one form or another, £10,000 out of his own pocket.[30]

His letter-books reveal a swarm of petty annoyances, which may have tried his strength and patience as much as more serious cares. The soldiers complained that they were left without clothing, shoes, or rum; and when he implored the Committee of War to send them, Osborne, the chairman, replied with explanations why it could not be done. Letters came from wives and fathers entreating that husbands and sons who had gone to the war should be sent back. At the end of the siege a captain "humble begs leave for to go home," because he lives in a very dangerous country, and his wife and children are "in a declining way" without him. Then two entire companies raised on the frontier offered the same petition on similar grounds. Sometimes Pepperrell was beset with prayers for favors and promotion; sometimes with complaints from one corps or another that an undue share of work had been imposed on it. One Morris, of Cambridge, writes a moving petition that his slave "Cuffee," who had joined the army, should be restored to him, his lawful master. One John Alford sends the general a number of copies of the Rever. Mr. Prentice's late sermon, for distribution, assur-

---

[29] *Pepperrell to Warren,* 28 *May,* 1745.
[30] *Letter from an Officer of Marines* appended to *A particular Account of the Taking of Cape Breton* (London, 1745).

ing him that "it will please your whole army of volunteers, as he has shown them the way to gain by their gallantry the hearts and affections of the Ladys." The end of the siege brought countless letters of congratulation, which, whether lay or clerical, never failed to remind him, in set phrases, that he was but an instrument in the hands of Providence.

One of his most persistent correspondents was his son-in-law, Nathaniel Sparhawk, a thrifty merchant, with a constant eye to business, who generally began his long-winded epistles with a bulletin concerning the health of "Mother Pepperrell," and rarely ended them without charging his father-in-law with some commission, such as buying for him the cargo of a French prize, if he could get it cheap. Or thus: "If you would procure for me a hogshead of the best Clarett, and a hogshead of the best white wine, at a reasonable rate, it would be very grateful to me." After pestering him with a few other commissions, he tells him that "Andrew and Bettsy [children of Pepperrell] send their proper compliments," and signs himself, with the starched flourish of provincial breeding, "With all possible Respect, Honoured Sir, Your Obedient Son and Servant."[31] Pepperrell was much annoyed by the conduct of the masters of the transports, of whom he wrote: "The unaccountable irregular behaviour of these fellows is the greatest fatigue I meet with"; but it may be doubted whether his son-in-law did not prove an equally efficient persecutor.

[31] *Sparhawk to Pepperrell,—June,* 1745. This is but one of many letters from Sparhawk.

Chapter 20

1745
Louisbourg Taken

FREQUENT COUNCILS of war were held in solemn form at headquarters. On the seventh of May a summons to surrender was sent to Duchambon, who replied that he would answer with his cannon. Two days after, we find in the record of the council the following startling entry: "Advised unanimously that the Town of Louisbourg be attacked by storm this Night." Vaughan was a member of the board, and perhaps his impetuous rashness had turned the heads of his colleagues. To storm the fortress at that time would have been a desperate attempt for the best-trained and best-led troops. There was as yet no breach in the walls, nor the beginning of one; and the French were so confident in the strength of their fortifications that they boasted that women alone could defend them. Nine in ten of the men had no bayonets,[1] many had no shoes, and it is said that the scaling-ladders they had brought from Boston were ten feet too short.[2] Perhaps it was unfortunate for the French that the army was more prudent than its leaders; and another council being called on the same day, it was "Advised, That, inasmuch as there appears a great Dissatisfaction in many of the officers and Soldiers at the designed attack of the Town by Storm this Night, the said Attack be deferred for the present."[3]

Another plan was adopted, hardly less critical, though it found favor with the army. This was the assault of the Island Battery, which closed the entrance of the harbor to the British squadron, and kept it open to ships from France. Nobody knew precisely how to find the two landing-places of this formidable work, which were narrow gaps between rocks lashed with almost constant surf; but Vaughan would see no difficulties, and wrote to Pepperrell that if he would give him the command and leave him to manage the attack in his

---

[1] *Shirley to Newcastle, 7 June,* 1745.
[2] Douglas, *Summary,* i. 347.
[3] *Record of the Council of War, 9 May,* 1745.

own way, he would engage to send the French flag to headquarters within forty-eight hours.[4] On the next day he seems
to have thought the command assured to him, and writes from
the Grand Battery that the carpenters are at work mending
whale-boats and making paddles, asking at the same time for
plenty of pistols and one hundred hand-grenades, with men
who know how to use them.[5] The weather proved bad, and
the attempt was deferred. This happened several times, till
Warren grew impatient, and offered to support the attack with
two hundred sailors.

At length, on the twenty-third, the volunteers for the perilous enterprise mustered at the Grand Battery, whence the
boats were to set out. Brigadier Waldo, who still commanded
there, saw them with concern and anxiety, as they came dropping in, in small squads, without officers, noisy, disorderly,
and, in some cases, more or less drunk. "I doubt," he told the
general, "whether straggling fellows, three, four, or seven out
of a company, ought to go on such a service."[6] A bright moon
and northern lights again put off the attack. The volunteers
remained at the Grand Battery, waiting for better luck. "They
seem to be impatient for action," writes Waldo. "If there were
a more regular appearance, it would give me greater satisfaction."[7] On the twenty-sixth their wish for action was fully
gratified. The night was still and dark, and the boats put out
from the battery towards twelve o'clock, with about three
hundred men on board.[8] These were to be joined by a hundred
or a hundred and fifty more from Gorham's regiment, then
stationed at Lighthouse Point. The commander was not
Vaughan, but one Brooks,—the choice of the men themselves,
as were also his subordinates.[9] They moved slowly, the boats
being propelled, not by oars, but by paddles, which, if skil-

[4] *Vaughan to Pepperrell, 11 May, 1745.*

[5] *Vaughan to Pepperrell, 12 May, 1745.*

[6] *Waldo to Pepperrell, 23 May, 1745.*

[7] *Ibid., 26 May, 1745.*

[8] "There is scarce three hundred men on this atact [attack], so
there will be a sufficient number of Whail boats."—*Waldo to Pepperrell, 26 May, 10½ p. m.*

[9] The list of a company of forty-two "subscribers to go voluntarily upon an attack against the Island Battery" is preserved. It
includes a negro called "Ruben." The captain, chosen by the men,
was Daniel Bacon. The fact that neither this name nor that of
Brooks, the chief commander, is to be found in the list of commissioned officers of Pepperrell's little army (see Parsons, *Life of*

fully used, would make no noise. The wind presently rose; and when they found a landing-place, the surf was lashing the rocks with even more than usual fury. There was room for but three boats at once between the breakers on each hand. They pushed in, and the men scrambled ashore with what speed they might.

The Island Battery was a strong work, walled in on all sides, garrisoned by a hundred and eighty men, and armed with thirty cannon, seven swivels, and two mortars.[10] It was now a little after midnight. Captain d'Aillebout, the commandant, was on the watch, pacing the battery platform; but he seems to have seen nothing unusual till about a hundred and fifty men had got on shore, when they had the folly to announce their presence by three cheers. Then, in the words of General Wolcott, the battery "blazed with cannon, swivels, and small-arms." The crowd of boats, dimly visible through the darkness, as they lay just off the landing, waiting their turn to go in, were at once the target for volleys of grape-shot, langrage-shot, and musket-balls, of which the men on shore had also their share. These succeeded, however, in planting twelve scaling-ladders against the wall.[11] It is said that some of them climbed into the place, and the improbable story is told that Brooks, their commander, was hauling down the French flag when a Swiss grenadier cut him down with a cutlass.[12] Many of the boats were shattered or sunk, while those in the rear, seeing the state of things, appear to have sheered off. The affair was soon reduced to an exchange of shots between the garrison and the men who had landed, and who, standing on the open ground without the walls, were not wholly invisible, while the French, behind their ramparts, were completely hidden. "The fire of the English," says Bigot, "was extremely obstinate, but without effect, as they could not see to take aim." They kept it up till daybreak, or about two hours and a

---

Pepperrell, Appendix) suggests the conclusion that the "subscribers" were permitted to choose officers from their own ranks. This list, however, is not quite complete.

[10] *Journal of the Siege*, appended to Shirley's report.

[11] *Duchambon au Ministre*, 2 *Septembre*, 1745. *Bigot au Ministre*, 1 *Août*, 1745.

[12] The exploit of the boy William Tufts in climbing the French flagstaff and hanging his red coat at the top as a substitute for the British flag, has also been said to have taken place on this occasion. It was, as before mentioned, at the Grand Battery.

half; and then, seeing themselves at the mercy of the French, surrendered to the number of one hundred and nineteen, including the wounded, three or more of whom died almost immediately. By the most trustworthy accounts the English loss in killed, drowned, and captured was one hundred and eighty-nine; or, in the words of Pepperrell, "nearly half our party."[13] Disorder, precipitation, and weak leadership ruined what hopes the attempt ever had.

As this was the only French success during the siege, Duchambon makes the most of it. He reports that the battery was attacked by a thousand men, supported by eight hundred more, who were afraid to show themselves; and, farther, that there were thirty-five boats, all of which were destroyed or sunk,[14]—though he afterwards says that two of them got away with thirty men, being all that were left of the thousand. Bigot, more moderate, puts the number of assailants at five hundred, of whom he says that all perished, except the one hundred and nineteen who were captured.[15]

At daybreak Louisbourg rang with shouts of triumph. It was plain that a disorderly militia could not capture the Island Battery. Yet captured or silenced it must be; and orders were given to plant a battery against it at Lighthouse Point, on the eastern side of the harbor's mouth, at the distance of a short half-mile. The neighboring shore was rocky and almost inaccessible. Cannon and mortars were carried in boats to the nearest landing-place, hauled up a steep cliff, and dragged a mile and a quarter to the chosen spot, where they were planted under the orders of Colonel Gridley, who thirty years after directed the earthworks on Bunker Hill. The new battery soon opened fire with deadly effect.

The French, much encouraged by their late success, were plunged again into despondency by a disaster which had happened a week before the affair of the Island Battery, but did not come to their knowledge till some time after. On the nineteenth of May a fierce cannonade was heard from the harbor, and a large French ship-of-war was seen hotly engaged with

[13] Douglas makes it a little less. "We lost in this mad frolic sixty men killed and drowned, and one hundred and sixteen prisoners." —*Summary*, i. 353.

[14] "Toutes les barques furent brisées ou coulées à fond; le feu fut continuel depuis environ minuit jusqu'à trois heures du matin." —*Duchambon au Ministre*, 2 *Septembre*, 1745.

[15] *Bigot au Ministre*, 1 *Août*, 1745.

several vessels of the squadron. She was the "Vigilant," carrying 64 guns and 560 men, and commanded by the Marquis de la Maisonfort. She had come from France with munitions and stores, when on approaching Louisbourg she met one of the English cruisers,—some say the "Mermaid," of 40 guns, and others the "Shirley," of 20. Being no match for her, the British or provincial frigate kept up a running fight and led her towards the English fleet. The "Vigilant" soon found herself beset by several other vessels, and after a gallant resistance and the loss of eighty men, struck her colors. Nothing could be more timely for the New England army, whose ammunition and provisions had sunk perilously low. The French prize now supplied their needs, and drew from the *Habitant de Louisbourg* the mournful comment, "We were victims devoted to appease the wrath of Heaven, which turned our own arms into weapons for our enemies."

Nor was this the last time when the defenders of Louisbourg supplied the instruments of their own destruction; for ten cannon were presently unearthed at low tide from the flats near the careening wharf in the northeast arm of the harbor, where they had been hidden by the French some time before. Most of them proved sound; and being mounted at Lighthouse Point, they were turned against their late owners at the Island Battery.

When Gorham's regiment first took post at Lighthouse Point, Duchambon thought the movement so threatening that he forgot his former doubts, and ordered a sortie against it, under the Sieur de Beaubassin. Beaubassin landed, with a hundred men, at a place called Lorembec, and advanced to surprise the English detachment; but was discovered by an outpost of forty men, who attacked and routed his party.[16] Being then joined by eighty Indians, Beaubassin had several other skirmishes with English scouting-parties, till, pushed by superior numbers, and their leader severely wounded, his men regained Louisbourg by sea, escaping with difficulty from the guard-boats of the squadron. The Sieur de la Vallière, with a considerable party of men, tried to burn Pepperrell's storehouses, near Flat Point Cove; but ten or twelve of his followers were captured, and nearly all the rest wounded. Various other petty encounters took place between English scouting-parties

16 *Journal of the Siege,* appended to Shirley's report. Pomeroy, *Journal.*

and roving bands of French and Indians, always ending, according to Pepperrell, in the discomfiture of the latter. To this, however, there was at least one exception. Twenty English were waylaid and surrounded near Petit Lorembec by forty or fifty Indians, accompanied by two or three Frenchmen. Most of the English were shot down, several escaped, and the rest surrendered on promise of life; upon which the Indians, in cold blood, shot or speared some of them, and atrociously tortured others.

This suggested to Warren a device which had two objects, —to prevent such outrages in future, and to make known to the French that the ship "Vigilant," the mainstay of their hopes, was in English hands. The treatment of the captives was told to the Marquis de la Maisonfort, late captain of the "Vigilant," now a prisoner on board the ship he had commanded, and he was requested to lay the facts before Duchambon. This he did with great readiness, in a letter containing these words. "It is well that you should be informed that the captains and officers of this squadron treat us, not as their prisoners, but as their good friends, and take particular pains that my officers and crew should want for nothing; therefore it seems to me just to treat them in like manner, and to punish those who do otherwise and offer any insult to the prisoners who may fall into your hands."

Captain M'Donald, of the marines, carried this letter to Duchambon under a flag-of-truce. Though familiar with the French language, he spoke to the governor through an interpreter, so that the French officers present, who hitherto had only known that a large ship had been taken, expressed to each other without reserve their discouragement and dismay when they learned that the prize was no other than the "Vigilant." Duchambon replied to La Maisonfort's letter that the Indians alone were answerable for the cruelties in question, and that he would forbid such conduct for the future.[17]

The besiegers were now threatened by a new danger. We have seen that in the last summer the Sieur Duvivier had attacked Annapolis. Undaunted by ill-luck, he had gone to France to beg for help to attack it again; two thousand men were promised him, and in anticipation of their arrival the governor of Canada sent a body of French and Indians, under

[17] *De la Maisonfort à Duchambon*, 18 *Juin* (new style), 1745. *Duchambon à De la Maisonfort*, 19 *Juin* (new style), 1745.

the noted partisan Marin, to meet and co-operate with them. Marin was ordered to wait as Les Mines till he heard of the arrival of the troops from France; but he grew impatient, and resolved to attack Annapolis without them. Accordingly, he laid siege to it with the six or seven hundred whites and Indians of his party, aided by the so-called Acadian neutrals. Mascarene, the governor, kept them at bay till the twenty-fourth of May, when to his surprise, they all disappeared. Duchambon had sent them an order to make all haste to the aid of Louisbourg. As the report of this reached the besiegers, multiplying Marin's force fourfold, they expected to be attacked by numbers more than equal to those of their own effective men. This wrought a wholesome reform. Order was established in the camp, which was now fenced with palisades and watched by sentinels and scouting-parties.

Another tribulation fell upon the general. Shirley had enjoined it upon him to keep in perfect harmony with the naval commander, and the injunction was in accord with Pepperrell's conciliating temper. Warren was no less earnest than he for the success of the enterprise, lent him ammunition in time of need, and offered every aid in his power, while Papperrell in letters to Shirley and Newcastle praised his colleague without stint. But in habits and character the two men differed widely. Warren was in prime of life, and the ardor of youth still burned in him. He was impatient at the slow movement of the siege. Prisoners told him of a squadron expected from Brest, of which the "Vigilant" was the forerunner; and he feared that even if it could not defeat him, it might elude the blockade, and with the help of the continual fogs, get into Louisbourg in spite of him, thus making its capture impossible. Therefore he called a council of his captains on board his flagship, the "Superbe," and proposed a plan for taking the place without further delay. On the same day he laid it before Pepperrell. It was to the effect that all the King's ships and provincial cruisers should enter the harbor, after taking on board sixteen hundred of Pepperrell's men, and attack the town from the water side, while what was left of the army should assault it by land.[18] To accept the proposal would have been to pass over the command to Warren, only about twenty-one hundred

---

[18] *Report of a Consultation of Officers on board his Majesty's ship "Superbe,"* enclosed in a letter of *Warren to Pepperrell,* 24 May, 1745.

of the New England men being fit for service at the time, while of these the general informs Warren that "six hundred are gone in quest of two bodies of French and Indians, who, we are informed, are gathering, one to the eastward, and the other to the westward."[19]

To this Warren replies, with some appearance of pique, "I am very sorry that no one plan of mine, though approved by all my captains, has been so fortunate as to meet your approbation or have any weight with you." And to show his title to consideration, he gives an extract from a letter written to him by Shirley, in which that inveterate flatterer hints his regret that, by reason of other employments, Warren could not take command of the whole expedition,—"which I doubt not," says the governor, "would be a most happy event for his Majesty's service."[20]

Pepperrell kept his temper under this thrust, and wrote to the commodore with invincible courtesy: "Am extremely sorry the fogs prevent me from the pleasure of waiting on you on board your ship," adding that six hundred men should be furnished from the army and the transports to man the "Vigilant," which was now the most powerful ship in the squadron. In short, he showed every disposition to meet Warren halfway. But the commodore was beginning to feel some doubts as to the expediency of the bold action he had proposed, and informed Pepperrell that his pilots thought it impossible to go into the harbor until the Island Battery was silenced. In fact, there was danger that if the ships got in while that battery was still alive and active, they would never get out again, but be kept there as in a trap, under the fire from the town ramparts.

Gridley's artillery at Lighthouse Point had been doing its best, dropping bombshells with such precision into the Island Battery that the French soldiers were sometimes seen running into the sea to escape the explosions. Many of the Island guns were dismounted, and the place was fast becoming untenable. At the same time the English batteries on the land side were pushing their work of destruction with relentless industry, and walls and bastions crumbled under their fire. The French labored with energy under cover of night to repair the mischief; closed the shattered West Gate with a wall of stone and

[19] *Pepperrell to Warren, 28 May, 1745.*
[20] *Warren to Pepperrell, 29 May, 1745.*

earth twenty feet thick, made an epaulement to protect what
was left of the formidable Circular Battery,—all but three of
whose sixteen guns had been dismounted,—stopped the throat
of the Dauphin's Bastion with a barricade of stone, and built
a cavalier, or raised battery, on the King's Bastion,—where,
however, the English fire soon ruined it. Against that near and
peculiarly dangerous neighbor, the advanced battery, or, as
they called it, the *Batterie de Francœur*, they planted three
heavy cannon to take it in flank. "These," says Duchambon,
"produced a marvellous effect, dismounted one of the cannon
of the Bastonnais, and damaged all their embrasures,—which,"
concludes the governor, "did not prevent them from keeping
up a constant fire; and they repaired by night the mischief we
did them by day."[21]

Pepperrell and Warren at length came to an understanding
as to a joint attack by land and water. The Island Battery
was by this time crippled, and the town batteries that commanded the interior of the harbor were nearly destroyed. It
was agreed that Warren, whose squadron was now increased
by recent arrivals to eleven ships, besides the provincial
cruisers, should enter the harbor with the first fair wind, cannonade the town and attack it in boats, while Pepperrell
stormed it from the land side. Warren was to hoist a Dutch
flag under his pennant, at his main-top-gallant mast-head, as a
signal that he was about to sail in; and Pepperrell was to answer by three columns of smoke, marching at the same time
towards the walls with drums beating and colors flying.[22]

The French saw with dismay a large quantity of fascines
carried to the foot of the glacis, ready to fill the ditch, and their
scouts came in with reports that more than a thousand scaling-
ladders were lying behind the ridge of the nearest hill. Toil,
loss of sleep, and the stifling air of the casemates, in which they
were forced to take refuge, had sapped the strength of the besieged. The town was a ruin; only one house was untouched
by shot or shell. "We could have borne all this," writes the
intendant Bigot; "but the scarcity of powder, the loss of the
'Vigilant,' the presence of the squadron, and the absence of
any news from Marin, who had been ordered to join us with
his Canadians and Indians, spread terror among troops and
inhabitants. The townspeople said that they did not want

[21] *Duchambon au Ministre*, 2 *Septembre*, 1745.
[22] *Warren to Pepperrell*, 11 *June*, 1745. *Pepperrell to Warren*,
13 *June*, 1745.

to be put to the sword, and were not strong enough to resist a general assault."[23] On the fifteenth of June they brought a petition to Duchambon, begging him to capitulate.[24]

On that day Captain Sherburn, at the advanced battery, wrote in his diary: "By 12 o'clock we had got all our platforms laid, embrazures mended, guns in order, shot in place, cartridges ready, dined, gunners quartered, matches lighted to return their last favours, when we heard their drums beat a parley; and soon appeared a flag of truce, which I received midway between our battery and their walls, conducted the officer to Green Hill, and delivered him to Colonel Richman [Richmond]."

La Perelle, the French officer, delivered a note from Duchambon, directed to both Pepperrell and Warren, and asking for a suspension of arms to enable him to draw up proposals for capitulation.[25] Warren chanced to be on shore when the note came; and the two commanders answered jointly that it had come in good time, as they had just resolved on a general attack, and that they would give the governor till eight o'clock of the next morning to make his proposals.[26]

They came in due time, but were of such a nature that Pepperrell refused to listen to them, and sent back Bonaventure, the officer who brought them, with counter-proposals. These were the terms which Duchambon had rejected on the seventh of May, with added conditions; as, among others, that no officer, soldier, or inhabitant of Louisbourg should bear arms against the King of England or any of his allies for the space of a year. Duchambon stipulated, as the condition of his acceptance, that his troops should march out of the fortress with their arms and colors.[27] To this both the English commanders consented, Warren observing to Pepperrell "the uncertainty of our affairs, that depend so much on wind and weather, makes it necessary not to stickle at trifles."[28] The articles were signed on both sides, and on the seventeenth the

[23] *Bigot au Ministre*, 1 *Août*, 1745.

[24] *Duchambon au Ministre*, 2 *Septembre*, 1745.

[25] *Duchambon à Pepperrell et Warren*, 26 *Juin* (new style), 1745.

[26] *Warren and Pepperrell to Duchambon*, 15 *June*, 1745.

[27] *Duchambon à Warren et Pepperrell*, 27 *Juin* (new style), 1745.

[28] *Pepperrell to Warren*, 16 *June*, 1745. *Warren to Pepperrell*, 16 *June*, 1745.

ships sailed peacefully into the harbor, while Pepperrell with a part of his ragged army entered the south gate of the town. "Never was a place more mal'd [mauled] with cannon and shells," he writes to Shirley; "neither have I red in History of any troops behaving with greater courage. We gave them about nine thousand cannon-balls and six hundred bombs."[29] Thus this unique military performance ended in complete and astonishing success.

According to English accounts, the French had lost about three hundred men during the siege; but their real loss seems to have been not much above a third of that number. On the side of the besiegers, the deaths from all causes were only a hundred and thirty, about thirty of which were from disease. The French used their muskets to good purpose; but their mortar practice was bad, and close as was the advanced battery to their walls, they often failed to hit it, while the ground on both sides of it looked like a ploughed field, from the bursting of their shells. Their surrender was largely determined by want of ammunition, as, according to one account, the French had but thirty-seven barrels of gunpowder left,[30]—in which particular the besiegers fared little better.[31]

The New England men had been full of confidence in the result of the proposed assault, and a French writer says that the timely capitulation saved Louisbourg from a terrible catastrophe;[32] yet, ill-armed and disorderly as the besiegers were, it may be doubted whether the quiet ending of the siege was not as fortunate for them as for their foes. The discouragement of the French was increased by greatly exaggerated ideas of the force of the "Bastonnais." The *Habitant de Louisbourg* places the land-force alone at eight or nine thousand men, and Duchambon reports to the minister D'Argenson that he was attacked in all by thirteen thousand. His mortifying position was a sharp temptation to exaggerate; but his conduct can only

[29] *Pepperrell to Shirley*, 18 *June* (old style), 1745. *Ibid.*, 4 *July*, 1745.

[30] *Habitant de Louisbourg*.

[31] Pepperrell more than once complains of a total want of both powder and balls. Warren writes to him on May 29: "It is very lucky that we could spare you some powder; I am told you had not a grain left."

[32] "C'est par une protection visible de la Providence que nous avons prévenu une journée qui nous auroit été si funeste."—*Lettre d'un Habitant de Louisbourg*.

be explained by a belief that the force of his enemy was far greater than it was in fact.

Warren thought that the proposed assault would succeed, and wrote to Pepperrell that he hoped they would "soon keep a good house together, and give the Ladys of Louisbourg a Gallant Ball."[33] During his visit to the camp on the day when the flag of truce came out, he made a speech to the New England soldiers, exhorting them to behave like true Englishmen; at which they cheered lustily. Making a visit to the Grand Battery on the same day, he won high favor with the regiment stationed there by the gift of a hogshead of rum to drink his health.

Whether Warren's "gallant ball" ever took place in Louisbourg does not clearly appear. Pepperrell, on his part, celebrated the victory by a dinner to the commodore and his officers. As the redoubtable Parson Moody was the general's chaplain and the oldest man in the army, he expected to ask a blessing at the board, and was, in fact, invited to do so,—to the great concern of those who knew his habitual prolixity, and dreaded its effect on the guest. At the same time, not one of them dared rasp his irritable temper by any suggestion of brevity; and hence they came in terror to the feast, expecting an invocation of a good half-hour, ended by open revolt of the hungry Britons; when, to their surprise and relief, Moody said: "Good Lord, we have so much to thank thee for, that time will be too short, and we must leave it for eternity. Bless our food and fellowship upon this joyful occasion, for the sake of Christ our Lord, Amen." And with that he sat down.[34]

It is said that he had been seen in the French church hewing at the altar and images with the axe that he had brought for that purpose; and perhaps this iconoclastic performance had eased the high pressure of his zeal.[35]

Amazing as their triumph was, Pepperrell's soldiers were not satisfied with the capitulation, and one of them utters his disapproval in his diary thus: "Sabbath Day, ye 16th June. They came to Termes for us to enter ye Sitty to morrow, and Poore Termes they Bee too."

The occasion of discontent was the security of property assured to the inhabitants, "by which means," says that dull

[33] *Warren to Pepperrell,* 10 *June,* 1745.

[34] *Collections of Mass. Hist. Society,* i. 49.

[35] A descendant of Moody, at the village of York, told me that he was found in the church busy in the work of demolition.

chronicler, Niles, "the poor soldiers lost all their hopes and just demerit [desert] of plunder promised them." In the meagreness of their pay they thought themselves entitled to the plunder of Louisbourg, which they imagined to be a seat of wealth and luxury. Nathaniel Sparhawk, Pepperrell's thrifty son-in-law, shared this illusion, and begged the general to get for him (at a low price) a handsome service of silver plate. When the volunteers exchanged their wet and dreary camp for what they expected to be the comfortable quarters of the town, they were disgusted to see the houses still occupied by the owners, and to find themselves forced to stand guard at the doors, to protect them.[36] "A great Noys and hubbub a mongst ye Solders a bout ye Plunder; Som Cursing, som a Swarein," writes one of the digusted victors.

They were not, and perhaps could not be, long kept in order; and when, in accordance with the capitulation, the inhabitants had been sent on board vessels for transportation to France, discipline gave way, and General Wolcott records that, while Moody was preaching on a Sunday in the garrison-chapel, there was "excessive stealing in every part of the town." Little, however, was left to steal.

But if the army found but meagre gleanings, the navy reaped a rich harvest. French ships, instead of being barred out of the harbor, were now lured to enter it. The French flag was kept flying over the town, and in this way prizes were entrapped to the estimated value of a million sterling, half of which went to the Crown, and the rest to the British officers and crews, the army getting no share whatever.

Now rose the vexed question of the relative part borne by the colonies and the Crown, the army and the navy, in the capture of Louisbourg; and here it may be well to observe the impressions of a French witness of the siege. "It was an enterprise less of the English nation and its King than of the inhabitants of New England alone. This singular people have their own laws and administration, and their governor plays the sovereign. Admiral [Commodore] Warren had no authority over the troops sent by the Governor of Boston, and he was only a spectator. . . . Nobody would have said that their sea and land forces were of the same nation and under the same prince. No nation but the English is capable of such eccentrici-

---

[36] "Thursday, ye 21st. Ye French keep possession yet, and we are forsed to stand at their Dores to gard them."—*Diary of a Soldier, anonymous.*

ties (*bizarreries*),—which, nevertheless, are a part of the precious liberty of which they show themselves so jealous."[37]

The French writer is correct when he says that the land and sea forces were under separate commands, and it is equally true that but for the conciliating temper of Pepperrell, harmony could not have been preserved between the two chiefs; but when he calls Warren a mere spectator, he does glaring injustice to that gallant officer, whose activity and that of his captains was incessant, and whose services were invaluable. They maintained, with slight lapses, an almost impossible blockade, without which the siege must have failed. Two or three small vessels got into the harbor; but the capture of the "Vigilant," more than any other event of the siege, discouraged the French and prepared them for surrender.

Several English writers speak of Warren and the navy as the captors of Louisbourg, and all New England writers give the chief honor to Pepperrell and the army. Neither army nor navy would have been successful without the other. Warren and his officers, in a council of war, had determined that so long as the Island Battery and the water batteries of the town remained in an efficient state, the ships could not enter the harbor; and Warren had personally expressed the same opinion.[38] He did not mean to enter till all the batteries which had made the attempt impracticable, including the Circular Battery, which was the most formidable of all, had been silenced or crippled by the army, and by the army alone. The whole work of the siege fell upon the land forces; and though it had been proposed to send a body of marines on shore, this was not done.[39] Three or four gunners, "to put your men in

[37] *Lettre d'un Habitant de Louisbourg.*

[38] *Report of Consultation on board the "Superbe,"* 7 June, 1745. "Commodore Warren did say publickly that before the Circular Battery was reduced he would not venture in here with three times ye sea force he had with him, and, through divine assistance, we tore that [battery] and this city almost to pieces."—*Pepperrell to Shirley,* 4 July, 1745.

[39] Warren had no men to spare. He says: "If it should be thought necessary to join your troops with any men from our ships, it should only be done for some sudden attack that may be executed in one day or night."—*Warren to Pepperrell,* 11 May, 1745. No such occasion arose.

the way of loading cannon,"[40] was Warren's contribution to the operations of the siege; though the fear of attack by the ships, jointly with the land force, no doubt hastened the surrender. Beauharnois, governor of Canada, ascribes the defeat to the extreme activity with which the New England men pushed their attacks.

The *Habitant de Louisbourg* says that each of the two commanders was eager that the keys of the fortress should be delivered to him, and not to his colleague; that before the surrender, Warren sent an officer to persuade the French that it would be for their advantage to make their submission to him rather than to Pepperrell; and that it was in fact so made. Wolcott, on the other hand, with the best means of learning the truth, says in his diary that Pepperrell received the keys at the South Gate. The report that it was the British commodore, and not their own general, to whom Louisbourg surrendered, made a prodigious stir among the inhabitants of New England, who had the touchiness common to small and ambitious peoples; and as they had begun the enterprise and borne most of its burdens and dangers, they thought themselves entitled to the chief credit of it. Pepperrell was blamed as lukewarm for the honor of his country because he did not demand the keys and reject the capitulation if they were refused. After all this ebullition it appeared that the keys were in his hands, for when, soon after the siege, Shirley came to Louisbourg, Pepperrell formally presented them to him, in presence of the soldiers.

Warren no doubt thought that he had a right to precedence, as being an officer of the King in regular standing, while Pepperrell was but a civilian, clothed with temporary rank by the appointment of a provincial governor. Warren was an impetuous sailor accustomed to command, and Pepperrell was a merchant accustomed to manage and persuade. The differences appears in their correspondence during the siege. Warren is

[40] *Ibid.*, 13 *May*, 1745. On the nineteenth of May, 1746, Warren made a parting speech to the New England men at Louisbourg, in which he tells them that it was they who conquered the country, and expresses the hope that should the French try to recover it, "the same Spirit that induced you to make this Conquest will prompt you to protect it." See the speech in *Beamish-Murdock*, ii. 100–102.

sometimes brusque and almost peremptory; Pepperrell is forbearing and considerate to the last degree. He liked Warren, and, to the last, continued to praise him highly in letters to Shirley and other provincial governors;[41] while Warren, on occasion of Shirley's arrival at Louisbourg, made a speech highly complimentary to both the general and his soldiers.

The news that Louisbourg was taken, reached Boston at one o'clock in the morning of the third of July by a vessel sent express. A din of bells and cannon proclaimed it to the slumbering townsmen, and before the sun rose, the streets were filled with shouting crowds. At night every window shone with lamps, and the town was ablaze with fireworks and bonfires. The next Thursday was appointed a day of general thanksgiving for a victory believed to be the direct work of Providence. New York and Philadelphia also hailed the great news with illuminations, ringing bells, and firing of cannon.

In England the tidings were received with astonishment and a joy that was dashed with reflections on the strength and mettle of colonists supposed already to aspire to independence. Pepperrell was made a baronet, and Warren an admiral. The merchant soldier was commissioned colonel in the British army; a regiment was given him, to be raised in America and maintained by the King, while a similar recognition was granted to the lawyer Shirley.[42]

A question vital to Massachusetts worried her in the midst of her triumph. She had been bankrupt for many years, and of the large volume of her outstanding obligations, a part was not worth eight pence in the pound. Added to her load of debt, she had spent £183,649 sterling on the Louisbourg expedition. That which Smollett calls "the most important achievement of the war" would never have taken place but for her, and Old England, and not New, was to reap the profit; for Louisbourg, conquered by arms, was to be restored by diplo-

[41] See extracts in Parsons, 105, 106. The *Habitant de Louisbourg* extols Warren, but is not partial to Pepperrell, whom he calls, incorrectly, "the son of a Boston shoemaker."

[42] To Rous, captain of a provincial cruiser, whom Warren had commended for conduct and courage, was given the command of a ship in the royal navy.

"Tell your Council and Assembly, in his Majesty's name," writes Newcastle to Shirley, "that their conduct will always entitle them, in a particular manner, to his royal favor and protection."—*Newcastle to Shirley, 10 August, 1745.*

macy. If the money she had spent for the mother-country were not repaid, her ruin was certain. William Bollan, English by birth and a son-in-law of Shirley, was sent out to urge the just claim of the province, and after long and vigorous solicitation, he succeeded. The full amount, in sterling value, was paid to Massachusetts, and the expenditures of New Hampshire, Connecticut, and Rhode Island were also reimbursed.[43] The people of Boston saw twenty-seven of those long unwieldy trucks which many elders of the place still remember as used in their youth, rumbling up King Street to the treasury, loaded with two hundred and seventeen chests of Spanish dollars, and a hundred barrels of copper coin. A pound sterling was worth eleven pounds of the old-tenor currency of Massachusetts, and thirty shillings of the new-tenor. Those beneficent trucks carried enough to buy in at a stroke nine-tenths of the old-tenor notes of the province,—nominally worth above two millions. A stringent tax, laid on by the Assembly, paid the remaining tenth, and Massachusetts was restored to financial health.[44]

[43] £183,649 to Massachusetts; £16,355 to New Hampshire; £28,863 to Connecticut; £6,332 to Rhode Island.

[44] Palfrey, *New England*, v. 101–109; Shirley, *Report to the Board of Trade. Bollan to Secretary Willard*, in *Coll. Mass. Hist. Soc.*, i. 53; Hutchinson, *Hist. Mass.*, ii. 391–395. *Letters of Bollan* in Massachusetts Archives.

It was through the exertions of the much-abused Thomas Hutchinson, Speaker of the Assembly and historian of Massachusetts, that the money was used for the laudable purpose of extinguishing the old debt.

Shirley did his utmost to support Bollan in his efforts to obtain compensation, and after highly praising the zeal and loyalty of the people of his province, he writes to Newcastle: "Justice, as well as the affection which I bear to 'em, constrains me to beseech your Grace to recommend their Case to his Majesty's paternal Care & Tenderness in the Strongest manner."—*Shirley to Newcastle, 6 November, 1745.*

The English documents on the siege of Louisbourg are many and voluminous. The Pepperrell Papers and the Belknap Papers, both in the library of the Massachusetts Historical Society, afford a vast number of contemporary letters and documents on the subject. The large volume entitled *Siege of Louisbourg*, in the same repository, contains many more, including a number of autograph diaries of soldiers and others. To these are to be added the journals of General Wolcott, James Gibson, Benjamin Cleaves, Seth Pomeroy, and several others, in print or manuscript, among which is especially to be noted the journal appended to Shirley's *Letter to the Duke of Newcastle* of October 28, 1745, and bearing the names of Pepperrell, Brigadier Waldo, Colonel Moore, and Lieutenant-Colonels Lothrop and Gridley, who attest its accuracy. Many papers have also been drawn from the Public Record Office of London.

Accounts of this affair have hitherto rested, with but slight exceptions, on English sources alone. The archives of France have furnished useful material to the foregoing narrative, notably the long report of the governor, Duchambon, to the minister of war, and the letter of the intendant, Bigot, to the same personage, within about six weeks after the surrender. But the most curious French evidence respecting the siege is the *Lettre d'un Habitant de Louisbourg contenant une Relation exacte & circonstanciée de la Prise de l'Isle-Royale par les Anglois. A Québec, chez Guillaume le Sincère, à l'Image de la Vérité,* 1745. This little work, of eighty-one printed pages, is extremely rare. I could study it only by having a *literatim* transcript made from the copy in the Bibliothèque Nationale, as it was not in the British Museum. It bears the signature B. L. N., and is dated *à . . . ce* 28 *Août,* 1745. The imprint of Québec, etc., is certainly a mask, the book having no doubt been printed in France. It severely criticises Duchambon, and makes him mainly answerable for the disaster.

For French views of the siege of Louisbourg, *see* Appendix B.

Chapter 21

1745–1747
Duc D'Anville

THE TROOPS and inhabitants of Louisbourg were all embarked for France, and the town was at last in full possession of the victors. The serious-minded among them—and there were few who did not bear the stamp of hereditary Puritanism—now saw a fresh proof that they were the peculiar care of an approving Providence. While they were in camp the weather had been favorable; but they were scarcely housed when a cold, persistent rain poured down in floods that would have drenched their flimsy tents and turned their huts of turf into mud-heaps, robbing the sick of every hope of recovery. Even now they got little comfort from the shattered tenements of Louisbourg. The siege had left the town in so filthy a condition that the wells were infected and the water was poisoned.

The soldiers clamored for discharge, having enlisted to serve only till the end of the expedition; and Shirley insisted that faith must be kept with them, or no more would enlist.[1] Pepperrell, much to the dissatisfaction of Warren, sent home about seven hundred men, some of whom were on the sick list, while the rest had families in distress and danger on the exposed frontier. At the same time he begged hard for reinforcements, expecting a visit from the French and a desperate attempt to recover Louisbourg. He and Warren governed the place jointly, under martial law, and they both passed half their time in holding courts-martial; for disorder reigned among the disgusted militia, and no less among the crowd of hungry speculators, who flocked like vultures to the conquered town to buy the cargoes of captured ships, or seek for other prey. The Massachusetts soldiers, whose pay was the smallest, and who had counted on being at their homes by the end of July, were the most turbulent; but all alike were on the brink of mutiny. Excited by their ringleaders, they one day marched in a body to the parade and threw down

---

[1] *Shirley to Newcastle, 27 September, 1745.*

345

their arms, but probably soon picked them up again, as in most cases the guns were hunting-pieces belonging to those who carried them. Pepperrell begged Shirley to come to Louisbourg and bring the mutineers back to duty. Accordingly, on the sixteenth of August he arrived in a ship-of-war, accompanied by Mrs. Shirley and Mrs. Warren, wife of the commodore. The soldiers duly fell into line to receive him. As it was not his habit to hide his own merits, he tells the Duke of Newcastle that nobody but he could have quieted the malcontents,—which is probably true, as nobody else had power to raise their pay. He made them a speech, promised them forty shillings in Massachusetts new-tenor currency a month, instead of twenty-five, and ended with ordering for each man half a pint of rum to drink the King's health. Though potations so generous might be thought to promise effects not wholly sedative, the mutineers were brought to reason, and some even consented to remain in garrison till the next June.[2]

Small reinforcements came from New England to hold the place till the arrival of troops from Gibraltar, promised by the ministry. The two regiments raised in the colonies, and commanded by Shirley and Pepperrell, were also intended to form a part of the garrison; but difficulty was found in filling the ranks, because, says Shirley, some commissions have been given to Englishmen, and men will not enlist here except under American officers.

Nothing could be more dismal than the condition of Louisbourg, as reflected in the diaries of soldiers and others who spent there the winter that followed its capture. Among these diaries is that of the worthy Benjamin Crafts, private in Hale's Essex regiment, who to the entry of each day adds a pious invocation, sincere in its way, no doubt, though hackneyed, and sometimes in strange company. Thus, after noting down Shirley's gift of half a pint of rum to every man to drink the King's health, he adds immediately: "The Lord Look upon us and enable us to trust in him & may he prepare us for his holy Day." On "September ye 1, being Sabath," we find the following record: "I am much out of order. This forenoon heard Mr. Stephen Williams preach from ye 18 Luke 9 verse in the afternoon from ye 8 of Ecles: 8 verse: Blessed be the Lord that has given us to enjoy another Sabath and

---

[2] *Shirley to Newcastle*, 4 December, 1745.

opertunity to hear his Word Dispensed." On the next day, "being Monday," he continues, "Last night I was taken very Bad: the Lord be pleased to strengthen my inner man that I may put my whole Trust in him. May we all be prepared for his holy will. Rcd part of plunder, 9 small tooth combs." Crafts died in the spring, of the prevailing distemper, after doing good service in the commissary department of his regiment.

Stephen Williams, the preacher whose sermons had comforted Crafts in his trouble, was a son of Rev. John Williams, captured by the Indians at Deerfield in 1704, and was now minister of Long Meadow, Massachusetts. He had joined the anti-papal crusade as one of its chaplains, and passed for a man of ability,—a point on which those who read his diary will probably have doubts. The lot of the army chaplains was of the hardest. A pestilence had fallen upon Louisbourg, and turned the fortress into a hospital. "After we got into the town," says the sarcastic Dr. Douglas, whose pleasure it is to put everything in its worst light, "a sordid indolence or sloth, for want of discipline, induced putrid fevers and dysenteries, which at length in August became contagious, and the people died like rotten sheep." From fourteen to twenty-seven were buried every day in the cemetery behind the town, outside the Maurepas Gate, by the old lime-kiln on Rochefort Point; and the forgotten bones of above five hundred New England men lie there to this day under the coarse, neglected grass. The chaplain's diary is little but a dismal record of sickness, death, sermons, funerals, and prayers with the dying ten times a day. "Prayed at Hospital;—Prayed at Citadel;—Preached at Grand Batery;—Visited Capt. [illegible], very sick;—One of Capt.——'s company dyd.—Am but poorly myself, but able to keep about." Now and then there is a momentary change of note, as when he writes: "July 29th. One of ye Captains of ye men of war caind a soldier who struck ye capt. again. A great tumult. Swords were drawn; no life lost, but great uneasiness is caused." Or when he sets down the "say" of some Briton, apparently a naval officer, "that he had tho't ye New England men were Cowards—but now he tho't yt if they had a pick axe & spade, they w'd dig ye way to Hell & storm it."[3]

---

[3] The autograph diary of Rev. Stephen Williams is in my possession. The handwriting is detestable.

Williams was sorely smitten with homesickness, but he sturdily kept his post, in spite of grievous yearnings for family and flock. The pestilence slowly abated, till at length the burying-parties that passed the Maurepas Gate counted only three or four a day. At the end of January five hundred and sixty-one men had died, eleven hundred were on the sick list, and about one thousand fit for duty.[4] The promised regiments from Gibraltar had not come. Could the French have struck then, Louisbourg might have changed hands again. The Gibraltar regiments had arrived so late upon that rude coast that they turned southward to the milder shores of Virginia, spent the winter there, and did not appear at Louisbourg till April. They brought with them a commission for Warren as governor of the fortress. He made a speech of thanks to the New England garrison, now reduced to less than nineteen hundred men, sick and well, and they sailed at last for home, Louisbourg being now thought safe from any attempt of France.

To the zealous and energetic Shirley the capture of the fortress was but a beginning of greater triumphs. Scarcely had the New England militia sailed from Boston on their desperate venture, when he wrote to the Duke of Newcastle that should the expedition succeed, all New England would be on fire to attack Canada, and the other colonies would take part with them, if ordered to do so by the ministry.[5] And, some months later, after Louisbourg was taken, he urged the policy of striking while the iron was hot, and invading Canada at once. The colonists, he said, were ready, and it would be easier to raise ten thousand men for such an attack than one thousand to lie idle in garrison at Louisbourg or anywhere else. France and England, he thinks, cannot live on the same continent. If we were rid of the French, he continues, England would soon control America, which would make her first among the nations; and he ventures what now seems the modest prediction that in one or two centuries the British colonies would rival France in population. Even now, he is sure that they would raise twenty thousand men to capture Canada, if the King required it of them, and Warren

<hr>

[4] On May 10, 1746, Shirley writes to Newcastle that eight hundred and ninety men had died during the winter. The sufferings of the garrison from cold were extreme.

[5] *Shirley to Newcastle, 4 April, 1745.*

would be an acceptable commander for the naval part of the expedition; "but," concludes the governor, "I will take no step without orders from his Majesty."[6]

The Duke of Newcastle was now at the head of the Government. Smollett and Horace Walpole have made his absurdities familiar, in anecdotes which, true or not, do no injustice to his character; yet he had talents that were great in their way, though their way was a mean one. They were talents, not of the statesman, but of the political manager, and their object was to win office and keep it.

Newcastle, whatever his motives, listened to the counsels of Shirley, and directed him to consult with Warren as to the proposed attack on Canada. At the same time he sent a circular letter to the governors of the provinces from New England to North Carolina, directing them, should the invasion be ordered, to call upon their assemblies for as many men as they would grant.[7] Shirley's views were cordially supported by Warren, and the levies were made accordingly, though not in proportion to the strength of the several colonies; for those south of New York felt little interest in the plan. Shirley was told to "dispose Massachusetts to do its part;" but neither he nor his province needed prompting. Taking his cue from the Roman senator, he exclaimed to his Assembly, *"Delenda est Canada;"* and the Assembly responded by voting to raise thirty-five hundred men, and offering a bounty equivalent to £4 sterling to each volunteer, besides a blanket for every one, and a bed for every two. New Hampshire contributed five hundred men, Rhode Island three hundred, Connecticut one thousand, New York sixteen hundred, New Jersey five hundred, Maryland three hundred, and Virginia one hundred. The Pennsylvania Assembly, controlled by Quaker noncombatants, would give no soldiers; but, by a popular movement, the province furnished four hundred men, without the help of its representatives.[8]

As usual in the English attempts against Canada, the campaign was to be a double one. The main body of troops,

· [6] *Ibid.*, 29 October, 1745.

[7] *Newcastle to the Provincial Governors,* 14 March, 1746; *Shirley to Newcastle,* 31 May, 1746; *Proclamation of Shirley,* 2 June, 1746.

[8] Hutchinson, ii. 381, *note.* Compare *Memoirs of the Principal Transactions of the Last War.*

composed of British regulars and New England militia, was to sail up the St. Lawrence and attack Quebec, while the levies of New York and the provinces farther south, aided, it was hoped, by the warriors of the Iroquois, were to advance on Montreal by way of Lake Champlain.

Newcastle promised eight battalions of British troops under Lieutenant-General Saint-Clair. They were to meet the New England men at Louisbourg, and all were then to sail together for Quebec, under the escort of a squadron commanded by Warren. Shirley also was to go to Louisbourg, and arrange the plan of the campaign with the general and the admiral. Thus, without loss of time, the captured fortress was to be made a base of operations against its late owners.

Canada was wild with alarm at reports of English preparation. There were about fifty English prisoners in barracks at Quebec, and every device was tried to get information from them; but being chiefly rustics caught on the frontiers by Indian war-parties, they had little news to give, and often refused to give even this. One of them, who had been taken long before and gained over by the French,[9] was used as an agent to extract information from his countrymen, and was called *"notre homme de confiance."* At the same time the prisoners were freely supplied with writing materials, and their letters to their friends being then opened, it appeared that they were all in expectation of speedy deliverance.[10]

In July a report came from Acadia that from forty to fifty thousand men were to attack Canada; and on the first of August a prisoner lately taken at Saratoga declared that there were thirty-two war-ships at Boston ready to sail against Quebec, and that thirteen thousand men were to march at once from Albany against Montreal. "If all these stories are true," writes the Canadian journalist, "all the English on this continent must be in arms."

Preparations for defence were pushed with feverish energy. Fireships were made ready at Quebec, and fire-rafts at Isle-aux-Coudres; provisions were gathered, and ammunition was distributed; reconnoitring parties were sent to watch the gulf

[9] "Un ancien prisonnier affidé que l'on a mis dans nos interests."
[10] *Extrait en forme de Journal de ce qui s'est passé dans la Colonie depuis . . . le 1 Décembre, 1745, jusqu'au 9 Novembre, 1746, signé Beauharnois et Hocquart.*

and the river; and bands of Canadians and Indians lately sent to Acadia were ordered to hasten back.

Thanks to the Duke of Newcastle, all these alarms were needless. The Massachusetts levies were ready within six weeks, and Shirley, eager and impatient, waited in vain for the squadron from England and the promised eight battalions of regulars. They did not come; and in August he wrote to Newcastle that it would now be impossible to reach Quebec before October, which would be too late.[11] The eight battalions had been sent to Portsmouth for embarkation, ordered on board the transports, then ordered ashore again, and finally sent on an abortive expedition against the coast of France. There were those who thought that this had been their destination from the first, and that the proposed attack on Canada was only a pretence to deceive the enemy. It was not till the next spring that Newcastle tried to explain the miscarriage to Shirley. He wrote that the troops had been detained by head-winds till General Saint-Clair and Admiral Lestock thought it too late; to which he added that the demands of the European war made the Canadian expedition impracticable, and that Shirley was to stand on the defensive and attempt no further conquests. As for the provincial soldiers, who this time were in the pay of the Crown, he says that they were "very expensive," and orders the governor to get rid of them "as cheap as possible."[12] Thus, not for the first time, the hopes of the colonies were brought to nought by the failure of the British ministers to keep their promises.

When, in the autumn of 1746, Shirley said that for the present Canada was to be let alone, he bethought him of a less decisive conquest, and proposed to employ the provincial troops for an attack on Crown Point, which formed a halfway station between Albany and Montreal, and was the constant rendezvous of war-parties against New York, New Hampshire, and Massachusetts, whose discords and jealousies had prevented them from combining to attack it. The Dutch of Albany, too, had strong commercial reasons for not coming to blows with the Canadians. Of late, however, Massachusetts and New York had suffered so much from this inconvenient neighbor that it was possible to unite them against it; and as

[11] *Shirley to Newcastle, 22 August, 1746.*
[12] *Newcastle to Shirley, 30 May, 1747.*

Clinton, governor of New York, was scarcely less earnest to get possession of Crown Point than was Shirley himself, a plan of operations was soon settled. By the middle of October fifteen hundred Massachusetts troops were on their way to join the New York levies, and then advance upon the obnoxious post.[13]

Even this modest enterprise was destined to fail. Astounding tidings reached New England, and startled her like a thunder-clap from dreams of conquest. It was reported that a great French fleet and army were on their way to retake Louisbourg, reconquer Acadia, burn Boston, and lay waste the other seaboard towns. The Massachusetts troops marching for Crown Point were recalled, and the country militia were mustered in arms. In a few days the narrow, crooked streets of the Puritan capital were crowded with more than eight thousand armed rustics from the farms and villages of Middlesex, Essex, Norfolk, and Worcester, and Connecticut promised six thousand more as soon as the hostile fleet should appear. The defences of Castle William were enlarged and strengthened, and cannon were planted on the islands at the mouth of the harbor; hulks were sunk in the channel, and a boom was laid across it under the guns of the castle.[14] The alarm was compared to that which filled England on the approach of the Spanish Armada.[15]

Canada heard the news of the coming armament with an exultation that was dashed with misgiving as weeks and months passed and the fleet did not appear. At length in September a vessel put in to an Acadian harbor with the report that she had met the ships in mid-ocean, and that they counted a hundred and fifty sail. Some weeks later the governor and intendant of Canada wrote that on the fourteenth of October they received a letter from Chibucto with "the agreeable news" that the Duc d'Anville and his fleet had arrived there about three weeks before. Had they known more, they would have rejoiced less.

That her great American fortress should have been

---

[13] *Memoirs of the Principal Transactions of the Last War.*

[14] *Shirley to Newcastle, 29 September,* 1746. Shirley says that though the French may bombard the town, he does not think they could make a landing, as he shall have fifteen thousand good men within call to oppose them.

[15] Hutchinson, ii. 382.

snatched from her by a despised militia was more than France could bear; and in the midst of a burdensome war she made a crowning effort to retrieve her honor and pay the debt with usury. It was computed that nearly half the French navy was gathered at Brest under command of the Duc d'Anville. By one account his force consisted of eleven ships-of-the-line, twenty frigates, and thirty-four transports and fireships, or sixty-five in all. Another list gives a total of sixty-six, of which ten were ships-of-the-line, twenty-two were frigates and fireships, and thirty-four were transports.[16] These last carried the regiment of Ponthieu, with other veteran troops, to the number in all of three thousand on hundred and fifty. The fleet was to be joined at Chibucto, now Halifax, by four heavy ships-of-war lately sent to the West Indies under M. de Conflans.

From Brest D'Anville sailed for some reason to Rochelle, and here the ships were kept so long by head-winds that it was the twentieth of June before they could put to sea. From the first the omens were sinister. The admiral was beset with questions as to the destination of the fleet, which was known to him alone; and when, for the sake of peace, he told it to his officers, their discontent redoubled. The Bay of Biscay was rough and boisterous, and spars, sails, and bowsprits were carried away. After they had been a week at sea, some of the ships, being dull sailers, lagged behind, and the rest were forced to shorten sail and wait for them. In the longitude of the Azores there was a dead calm, and the whole fleet lay idle for days. Then came a squall, with lightning. Several ships were struck. On one of them six men were killed, and on the seventy-gun ship "Mars" a box of musket and cannon cartridges blew up, killed ten men, and wounded twenty-one. A store-ship which proved to be sinking was abandoned and burned. Then a pestilence broke out, and in some of the ships there were more sick than in health.

On the fourteenth of September they neared the coast of Nova Scotia, and were in dread of the dangerous shoals of Sable Island, the position of which they did not exactly know. They groped their way in fogs till a fearful storm, with thunder and lightning, fell upon them. The journalist of the voyage, a captain in the regiment of Ponthieu, says, with the

[16] This list is in the journal of a captured French officer called by Shirley M. Rebateau.

exaggeration common in such cases, that the waves ran as high as the masts; and such was their violence that a transport, dashing against the ship "Amazone," immediately went down, with all on board. The crew of the "Prince d'Orange," half blinded by wind and spray, saw the great ship "Caribou," without bowsprit or main-topmast, driving towards them before the gale, and held their breath in expectation of the shock as she swept close alongside and vanished in the storm.[17] The tempest raged all night, and the fleet became so scattered that there was no more danger of collision. In the morning the journalist could see but five sail; but as the day advanced the rest began to reappear, and at three o'clock he counted thirty-one from the deck of the "Prince d'Orange." The gale was subsiding, but its effects were seen in hencoops, casks, and chests floating on the surges and telling the fate of one or more of the fleet. The "Argonaut" was rolling helpless, without masts or rudder; the "Caribou" had thrown overboard all the starboard guns of her upper deck; and the vice-admiral's ship, the "Trident," was in scarcely better condition.

On the twenty-third they were wrapped in thick fog and lay firing guns, ringing bells, and beating drums to prevent collisions. When the weather cleared, they looked in vain for the admiral's ship, the "Northumberland."[18] She was not lost, however, but with two other ships was far ahead of the fleet and near Chibucto, though in great perplexity, having no pilot who knew the coast. She soon after had the good fortune to capture a small English vessel with a man on board well acquainted with Chibucto harbor. D'Anville offered him his liberty and a hundred louis if he would pilot the ship in. To this he agreed; but when he rejoined his fellow-prisoners they called him a traitor to his country, on which he retracted his promise. D'Anville was sorely perplexed; but Duperrier, captain of the "Northumberland," less considerate of the prisoner's feelings, told him that unless he kept his word he should be thrown into the sea, with a pair of cannon-balls made fast to his feet. At this his scruples gave way, and before

[17] *Journal historique du Voyage de la Flotte commandée par M. le Duc d'Enville*. The writer was on board the "Prince d'Orange," and describes what he saw (Archives du Séminaire de Québec; printed in *Le Canada Français*).

[18] The "Northumberland" was an English prize captured by Captains Serier and Conflans in 1744.

night the "Northumberland" was safe in Chibucto Bay. D'Anville had hoped to find here the four ships of Conflans, which were to have met him from the West Indies at this, the appointed rendezvous; but he saw only a solitary transport of his own fleet. Hills covered with forests stood lonely and savage round what is now the harbor of Halifax. Conflans and his four ships had arrived early in the month, and finding nobody, though it was nearly three months since D'Anville left Rochelle, he cruised among the fogs for a while, and then sailed for France a few days before the admiral's arrival.

D'Anville was ignorant of the fate of his fleet; but he knew that the two ships which had reached Chibucto with him were full of sick men, that their provisions were nearly spent, and that there was every reason to believe such of the fleet as the storm might have spared to be in no better case. An officer of the expedition describes D'Anville as a man "made to command and worthy to be loved," and says that he had borne the disasters of the voyage with the utmost fortitude and serenity.[19] Yet suspense and distress wrought fatally upon him, and at two o'clock in the morning of the twenty-seventh he died,—of apoplexy, by the best accounts; though it was whispered among the crews that he had ended his troubles by poison.[20]

At six o'clock in the afternoon of the same day D'Estournel, the vice-admiral, with such ships as remained with him, entered the harbor and learned what had happened. He saw with dismay that he was doomed to bear the burden of command over a ruined enterprise and a shattered fleet. The long voyage had consumed the provisions, and in some of the ships the crews were starving. The pestilence grew worse, and men were dying in numbers every day. On the twenty-eighth, D'Anville was buried without ceremony on a small island in the harbor. The officers met in council, and the papers of the dead commander were examined. Among them was a letter from the King in which he urged the recapture of Louisbourg as the first object of the expedition; but this was thought impracticable, and the council resolved to turn against Annapolis all the force that was left. It is said that D'Estournel

[19] *Journal historique du Voyage.*

[20] *Declaration of H. Kannan and D. Deas, 23 October, 1746. Deposition of Joseph Foster, 24 October, 1746, sworn to before Jacob Wendell, J. P.* These were prisoners in the ships at Chibucto.

opposed the attempt, insisting that it was hopeless, and that there was no alternative but to return to France. The debate was long and hot, and the decision was against him.[21] The council dissolved, and he was seen to enter his cabin in evident distress and agitation. An unusual sound was presently heard, followed by groans. His door was fastened by two bolts, put on the evening before by his order. It was burst open, and the unfortunate commander was found lying in a pool of blood, transfixed with his own sword. Enraged and mortified, he had thrown himself upon it in a fit of desperation. The surgeon drew out the blade, but it was only on the urgent persuasion of two Jesuits that the dying man would permit the wound to be dressed. He then ordered all the captains to the side of his berth, and said, "Gentlemen, I beg pardon of God and the King for what I have done, and I protest to the King that my only object was to prevent my enemies from saying that I had not executed his orders;" and he named M. de la Jonquière to command in his place. In fact, La Jonquière's rank entitled him to do so. He was afterwards well known as governor of Canada, and was reputed a brave and able sea-officer.

La Jonquière remained at Chibucto till late in October. Messengers were sent to the Acadian settlements to ask for provisions, of which there was desperate need; and as payment was promised in good metal, and not in paper, the Acadians brought in a considerable supply. The men were encamped on shore, yet the pestilence continued its ravages. Two English prisoners were told that between twenty-three and twenty-four hundred men had been buried by sea or land since the fleet left France; and another declares that eleven hundred and thirty-five burials took place while he was at Chibucto.[22] The survivors used the clothing of the dead as gifts to the neighboring Indians, who in consequence were attacked with such virulence by the disease that of the band at Cape Sable three fourths are said to have perished. The English, meanwhile, learned something of the condition

[21] This is said by all the writers except the author of the *Journal historique,* who merely states that the council decided to attack Annapolis, and to detach some soldiers to the aid of Quebec. This last vote was reconsidered.

[22] *Declaration of Kannan and Deas. Deposition of Joseph Foster.*

of their enemies. Towards the end of September Captain Sylvanus Cobb, in a sloop from Boston, boldly entered Chibucto Harbor, took note of the ships lying there, and, though pursued, ran out to sea and carried the results of his observations to Louisbourg.[23] A more thorough reconnoissance was afterwards made by a vessel from Louisbourg bringing French prisoners for exchange under a flag of truce; and it soon became evident that the British colonies had now nothing to fear.

La Jonquière still clung to the hope of a successful stroke at Annapolis, till in October an Acadian brought him the report that the garrison of that place had received a reinforcement of twelve hundred men. The reinforcement consisted in reality of three small companies of militia sent from Boston by Shirley. La Jonquière called a secret council, and the result seems to have been adverse to any further attempt. The journalist reports that only a thousand men were left in fighting condition, and that even of these some were dying every day.

La Jonquière, however, would not yet despair. The troops were re-embarked; five hospital ships were devoted to the sick; the "Parfait," a fifty-gun ship no longer serviceable, was burned, as were several smaller vessels, and on the fourth of October what was left of the fleet sailed out of Chibucto Harbor and steered for Annapolis, piloted by Acadians. The flag of truce from Louisbourg was compelled for a time to bear them company, and Joseph Foster of Beverly, an exchanged prisoner on board of her, deposed that as the fleet held its way, he saw "a great number of dead persons" dropped into the sea every day. Ill-luck still pursued the French. A storm off Cape Sable dispersed the ships, two of which some days later made their way to Annapolis Basin in expectation of finding some of their companions there. They found instead the British fifty-gun ship "Chester" and the Massachusetts frigate "Shirley" anchored before the fort, on which the two Frenchmen retired as they had come; and so ended the last aggressive movement on the part of the great armament.

The journalist reports that on the night of the twenty-seventh there was a council of officers on board the "Northumberland," at which it was resolved that no choice was left but

[23] *Report of Captain Cobb*, in *Shirley to Newcastle*, 13 *October*, 1746.

to return to France with the ships that still kept together. On the fourth of November there was another storm, and when it subsided, the "Prince d'Orange" found herself with but nine companions, all of which were transports. These had on board eleven companies of soldiers, of whom their senior officer reports that only ninety-one were in health. The pestilence made such ravages among the crews that four or five corpses were thrown into the sea every day, and there was fear that the vessels would be left helpless in mid-ocean for want of sailors to work them.[24] At last, on the seventh of December, after narrowly escaping an English squadron, they reached Port Louis in Brittany, where several ships of the fleet had arrived before them. Among these was the frigate "La Palme." "Yesterday," says the journalist, "I supped with M. Destrahoudal, who commands his frigate; and he told me things which from anybody else would have been incredible. This is his story, exactly as I had it from him." And he goes on to the following effect.

After the storm of the fourteenth of September, provisions being almost spent, it was thought that there was no hope for "La Palme" and her crew but in giving up the enterprise and making all sail at once for home, since France now had no port of refuge on the western continent nearer than Quebec. Rations were reduced to three ounces of biscuit and three of salt meat a day; and after a time half of this pittance was cut off. There was diligent hunting for rats in the hold; and when this game failed, the crew, crazed with famine, demanded of their captain that five English prisoners who were on board should be butchered to appease the frenzy of their hunger. The captain consulted his officers, and they were of opinion that if he did not give his consent, the crew would work their will without it. The ship's butcher was accordingly ordered to bind one of the prisoners, carry him to the bottom of the hold, put him to death, and distribute his flesh to the men in portions of three ounces each. The captain, walking the deck in great agitation all night, found a pretext for deferring the deed till morning, when a watchman sent aloft at daylight cried, "A sail!" The providential stranger was a Portuguese ship; and as Portugal was neutral in the war, she let the frigate approach to within hailing distance. The Portuguese captain soon came alongside in a boat, "accompanied,"

24 *Journal historique.*

in the words of the narrator, "by five sheep." These were eagerly welcomed by the starving crew as agreeable substitutes for the five Englishmen; and, being forthwith slaughtered, were parcelled out among the men, who would not wait till the flesh was cooked, but devoured it raw. Provisions enough were obtained from the Portuguese to keep the frigate's company alive till they reached Port Louis.

There are no sufficient means of judging how far the disasters of D'Anville's fleet were due to a neglect of sanitary precautions or to deficient seamanship. Certain it is that there were many in self-righteous New England who would have held it impious to doubt that God had summoned the pestilence and the storm to fight the battles of his modern Israel.

Undaunted by disastrous failure, the French court equipped another fleet, not equal to that of D'Anville, yet still formidable, and placed it under La Jonquière, for the conquest of Acadia and Louisbourg. La Jonquière sailed from Rochelle on the tenth of May, 1747, and on the fourteenth was met by an English fleet stronger than his own and commanded by Admirals Anson and Warren. A fight ensued, in which, after brave resistance, the French were totally defeated. Six ships-of-war, including the flag-ship, were captured, with a host of prisoners, among whom was La Jonquière himself.[25]

---

[25] *Relation du Combat rendu le 14 Mai* (new style), *par l'Escadre du Roy commandée par M. de la Jonquière, in Le Canada Français, Supplément de Documents inédits,* 33. *Newcastle to Shirley,* 30 May, 1747.

Chapter 22

1745-1747
Acadian Conflicts

SINCE THE CAPTURE of Louisbourg, France had held constantly in view, as an object of prime importance, the recovery of her lost colony of Acadia. This was one of the chief aims of D'Anville's expedition, and of that of La Jonquière in the next year. And to make assurance still more sure, a large body of Canadians, under M. de Ramesay, had been sent to Acadia to co-operate with D'Anville's force; but the greater part of them had been recalled to aid in defending Quebec against the expected attack of the English. They returned when the news came that D'Anville was at Chibucto, and Ramesay, with a part of his command, advanced upon Port Royal, or Annapolis, in order to support the fleet in its promised attack on that place. He encamped at a little distance from the English fort, till he heard of the disasters that had ruined the fleet,[1] and then fell back to Chignecto, on the neck of the Acadian peninsula, where he made his quarters, with a force which, including Micmac, Malicite, and Penobscot Indians, amounted, at one time, to about sixteen hundred men.

If France was bent on recovering Acadia, Shirley was no less resolved to keep it, if he could. In his belief, it was the key of the British American colonies, and again and again he urged the Duke of Newcastle to protect it. But Newcastle seems scarcely to have known where Acadia was, being ignorant of most things except the art of managing the House of Commons, and careless of all things that could not help his party and himself. Hence Shirley's hyperboles, though never without a basis of truth, were lost upon him. Once, it is true, he sent three hundred men to Annapolis; but one hundred and eighty of them died on the voyage, or lay helpless in Boston hospitals, and the rest could better have been spared, some being recruits from English jails, and others Irish Catholics,

---

[1] *Journal de Beaujeu*, in *Le Canada Français, Documents*, 53.

several of whom deserted to the French, with information of the state of the garrison.

The defence of Acadia was left to Shirley and his Assembly, who in time of need sent companies of militia and rangers to Annapolis, and thus on several occasions saved it from returning to France. Shirley was the most watchful and strenuous defender of British interests on the continent; and in the present crisis British and colonial interests were one. He held that if Acadia were lost, the peace and safety of all the other colonies would be in peril; and in spite of the immense efforts made by the French court to recover it, he felt that the chief danger of the province was not from without, but from within. "If a thousand French troops should land in Nova Scotia," he writes to Newcastle, "all the people would rise to join them, besides all the Indians."[2] So, too, thought the French officials in America. The governor and intendant of Canada wrote to the colonial minister: "The inhabitants, with few exceptions, wish to return under the French dominion, and will not hesitate to take up arms as soon as they see themselves free to do so; that is, as soon as we become masters of Port Royal, or they have powder and other munitions of war, and are backed by troops for their protection against the resentment of the English."[3] Up to this time, however, though they had aided Duvivier in his attack on Annapolis so far as was possible without seeming to do so, they had not openly taken arms, and their refusal to fight for the besiegers is one among several causes to which Mascarene ascribes the success of his defence. While the greater part remained attached to France, some leaned to the English, who bought their produce and paid them in ready coin. Money was rare with the Acadians, who loved it, and were so addicted to hoarding it that the French authorities were led to speculate as to what might be the object of these careful savings.[4]

Though the Acadians loved France, they were not always ready to sacrifice their interests to her. They would not supply Ramesay's force with provisions in exchange for his promissory notes, but demanded hard cash.[5] This he had not to give,

[2] *Shirley to Newcastle, 29 October,* 1745.
[3] *Beauharnois et Hocquart au Ministre, 12 Septembre,* 1745.
[4] *Ibid.*
[5] *Ibid.*

and was near being compelled to abandon his position in consequence. At the same time, in consideration of specie payment, the inhabitants brought in fuel for the English garrison at Louisbourg, and worked at repairing the rotten *chevaux de frise* of Annapolis.[6]

Mascarene, commandant at that place, being of French descent, was disposed at first to sympathize with the Acadians and treat them with a lenity that to the members of his council seemed neither fitting nor prudent. He wrote to Shirley: "The French inhabitants are certainly in a very perilous situation, those who pretend to be their friends and old masters having let loose a parcel of banditti to plunder them; whilst, on the other hand, they see themselves threatened with ruin if they fail in their allegiance to the British Government."[7]

This unhappy people were in fact between two fires. France claimed them on one side, and England on the other, and each demanded their adhesion, without regard to their feelings or their welfare. The banditti of whom Mascarene speaks were the Micmac Indians, who were completely under the control of their missionary, Le Loutre, and were used by him to terrify the inhabitants into renouncing their English allegiance and actively supporting the French cause. By the Treaty of Utrecht France had transferred Acadia to Great Britain, and the inhabitants had afterwards taken an oath of fidelity to King George. Thus they were British subjects; but as their oath had been accompanied by a promise, or at least a clear understanding, that they should not be required to take arms against Frenchmen or Indians, they had become known as the "Neutral French." This name tended to perplex them, and in their ignorance and simplicity they hardly knew to which side they owed allegiance. Their illiteracy was extreme. Few of them could sign their names, and a contemporary well acquainted with them declares that he knew but a single Acadian who could read and write.[8] This was probably the notary, Le Blanc, whose compositions are crude and illiterate. Ignorant of books and isolated in a wild and remote corner of the world, the Acadians knew nothing of affairs, and were totally

---

[6] *Admiral Knowles à* —— 1746. Mascarene in *Le Canada Français, Documents,* 82.

[7] Mascarene, in *Le Canada Français, Documents,* 81.

[8] Moïse des Derniers, in *Le Canada Français,* i. 118.

incompetent to meet the crisis that was soon to come upon them. In activity and enterprise they were far behind the Canadians, who looked on them as inferiors. Their pleasures were those of the humblest and simplest peasants; they were contented with their lot, and asked only to be let alone. Their intercourse was unceremonious to such a point that they never addressed each other, or, it is said, even strangers, as *monsieur*. They had the social equality which can exist only in the humblest conditions of society, and presented the phenomenon of a primitive little democracy, hatched under the wing of an absolute monarchy. Each was as good as his neighbor; they had no natural leaders, nor any to advise or guide them, except the missionary priest, who in every case was expected by his superiors to influence them in the interest of France, and who, in fact, constantly did so. While one observer represents them as living in a state of primeval innocence, another describes both men and women as extremely foul of speech; from which he draws inferences unfavorable to their domestic morals,[9] which, nevertheless, were commendable. As is usual with a well-fed and unambitious peasantry, they were very prolific, and are said to have doubled their number every sixteen years. In 1748 they counted in the peninsula of Nova Scotia between twelve and thirteen thousand souls.[10] The English rule had been of the lightest, —so light that it could scarcely be felt; and this was not surprising, since the only instruments for enforcing it over a population wholly French were some two hundred disorderly soldiers in the crumbling little fort of Annapolis; and the province was left, perforce, to take care of itself.

The appearance of D'Anville's fleet caused great excitement among the Acadians, who thought that they were about to pass again under the Crown of France. Fifty of them went on board the French ships at Chibucto to pilot them to the attack of Annapolis, and to their dismay found that no attack was to be made. When Ramesay, with his Canadians and Indians, took post at Chignecto and built a fort at Baye Verte, on the neck of the peninsula of Nova Scotia, the English power in that part of the colony seemed at an

[9] *Journal de Franquet*, Part II.

[10] *Description de l'Acadie, avec le Nom des Paroisses et le Nombre des Habitants*, 1748.

end. The inhabitants cut off all communication with Annapolis, and detained the officers whom Mascarene sent for intelligence.

From the first outbreak of the war it was evident that the French built their hopes of recovering Acadia largely on a rising of the Acadians against the English rule, and that they spared no efforts to excite such a rising. Early in 1745 a violent and cruel precaution against this danger was suggested. William Shirreff, provincial secretary, gave it as his opinion that the Acadians ought to be removed, being a standing menace to the colony.[11] This is the first proposal of such a nature that I find. Some months later, Shirley writes that, on a false report of the capture of Annapolis by the French, the Acadians sang *Te Deum*, and that every sign indicates that there will be an attempt in the spring to capture Annapolis, with their help.[12] Again, Shirley informs Newcastle that the French will get possession of Acadia unless the most dangerous of the inhabitants are removed, and English settlers put in their place.[13] He adds that there are not two hundred and twenty soldiers at Annapolis to defend the province against the whole body of Acadians and Indians, and he tells the minister that unless the expedition against Canada should end in the conquest of that country, the removal of some of the Acadians will be a necessity. He means those of Chignecto, who were kept in a threatening attitude by the presence of Ramesay and his Canadians, and who, as he thinks, had forfeited their lands by treasonable conduct. Shirley believes that families from New England might be induced to take their place, and that these, if settled under suitable regulations, would form a military frontier to the province of Nova Scotia "strong enough to keep the Canadians out," and hold the Acadians to their allegiance.[14] The Duke of Bedford thinks the plan a good one, but objects to the expense.[15] Commodore Knowles, then governor of Louisbourg, who, being

[11] *Shirreff to K. Gould, agent of Philips's Regiment, March,* 1745.

[12] *Shirley to Newcastle,* 14 *December,* 1745.

[13] *Ibid.,* 10 *May,* 1746.

[14] *Ibid.,* 8 *July,* 1747.

[15] *Bedford to Newcastle,* 11 *September,* 1747.

threatened with consumption and convinced that the climate was killing him, vented his feelings in strictures against everything and everybody, was of opinion that the Acadians, having broken their neutrality, ought to be expelled at once, and expresses the amiable hope that should his Majesty adopt this plan, he will charge him with executing it.[16]

Shirley's energetic nature inclined him to trenchant measures, and he had nothing of modern humanitarianism; but he was not inhuman, and he shrank from the cruelty of forcing whole communities into exile. While Knowles and others called for wholesale expatriation, he still held that it was possible to turn the greater part of the Acadians into safe subjects of the British Crown;[17] and to this end he advised the planting of a fortified town where Halifax now stands, and securing by forts and garrisons the neck of the Acadian peninsula, where the population was most numerous and most disaffected. The garrisons, he thought, would not only impose respect, but would furnish the Acadians with what they wanted most,—ready markets for their produce,—and thus bind them to the British by strong ties of interest. Newcastle thought the plan good, but wrote that its execution must be deferred to a future day. Three years later it was partly carried into effect by the foundation of Halifax; but at that time the disaffection of the Acadians had so increased, and the hope of regaining the province for France had risen so high, that this partial and tardy assertion of British authority only spurred the French agents to redoubled efforts to draw the inhabitants from the allegiance they had sworn to the Crown of England.

[16] *Knowles to Newcastle, 8 November,* 1746.

[17] Shirley says that the indiscriminate removal of the Acadians would be "unjust" and "too rigorous." Knowles had proposed to put Catholic Jacobites from the Scotch Highlands into their place. Shirley thinks this inexpedient, but believes that Protestants from Germany and Ulster might safely be trusted. The best plan of all, in his opinion, is that of "treating the Acadians as subjects, confining their punishment to the most guilty and dangerous among 'em, and keeping the rest in the country and endeavoring to make them useful members of society under his Majesty's Government." *Shirley to Newcastle,* 21 *November,* 1746. If the Newcastle Government had vigorously carried his recommendations into effect, the removal of the Acadians in 1755 would not have taken place.

Shirley had also other plans in view for turning the Acadians into good British subjects. He proposed, as a measure of prime necessity, to exclude French priests from the province. The free exercise of their religion had been insured to the inhabitants by the Treaty of Utrecht, and on this point the English authorities had given no just cause of complaint. A priest had occasionally been warned, suspended, or removed; but without a single exception, so far as appears, this was in consequence of conduct which tended to excite disaffection, and which would have incurred equal or greater penalties in the case of a layman.[18] The sentence was directed, not against the priest, but against the political agitator. Shirley's plan of excluding French priests from the province would not have violated the provisions of the treaty, provided that the inhabitants were supplied with other priests, not French subjects, and therefore not politically dangerous; but though such a measure was several times proposed by the provincial authorities, the exasperating apathy of the Newcastle Government gave no hope that it could be accomplished.

The influences most dangerous to British rule did not proceed from love of France or sympathy of race, but from the power of religion over a simple and ignorant people, trained in profound love and awe of their Church and its ministers, who were used by the representatives of Louis XV as agents to alienate the Acadians from England.

The most strenuous of these clerical agitators was Abbé Le Loutre, missionary to the Micmacs, and after 1753 vicar-general of Acadia. He was a fiery and enterprising zealot,

[18] There was afterwards sharp correspondence between Shirley and the governor of Canada touching the Acadian priests. Thus, Shirley writes: "I can't avoid now, Sir, expressing great surprise at the other parts of your letter, whereby you take upon you to call Mr. Mascarene to account for expelling the missionary from Minas for being guilty of such treasonable practices within His Majesty's government as merited a much severer Punishment." *Shirley à Galissonière, 9 Mai, 1749.*

Shirley writes to Newcastle that the Acadians "are greatly under the influence of their priests, who continually receive their directions from the Bishop of Quebec, and are the instruments by which the governor of Canada makes all his attempts for the reduction of the province to the French Crown." *Shirley to Newcastle, 20 October, 1747.* He proceeds to give facts in proof of his assertion.

inclined by temperament to methods of violence, detesting the English, and restrained neither by pity nor scruple from using threats of damnation and the Micmac tomahawk to frighten the Acadians into doing his bidding. The worst charge against him, that of exciting the Indians of his mission to murder Captain Howe, an English officer, has not been proved; but it would not have been brought against him by his own countrymen if his character and past conduct had gained him their esteem.

The other Acadian priests were far from sharing Le Loutre's violence; but their influence was always directed to alienating the inhabitants from their allegiance to King George. Hence Shirley regarded the conversion of the Acadians to Protestantism as a political measure of the first importance, and proposed the establishment of schools in the province to that end. Thus far his recommendations are perfectly legitimate; but when he adds that rewards ought to be given to Acadians who renounce their faith, few will venture to defend him.

Newcastle would trouble himself with none of his schemes, and Acadia was left to drift with the tide, as before. "I shall finish my troubleing your Grace upon the affairs of Nova Scotia with this letter," writes the persevering Shirley. And he proceeds to ask, "as a proper Scheme for better securing the Subjection of the French inhabitants and Indians there," that the governor and Council at Annapolis have special authority and direction from the King to arrest and examine such Acadians as shall be "most obnoxious and dangerous to his Majesty's Government;" and if found guilty of treasonable correspondence with the enemy, to dispose of them and their estates in such manner as his Majesty shall order, at the same time promising indemnity to the rest for past offences, upon their taking or renewing the oath of allegiance.[19]

To this it does not appear that Newcastle made any answer except to direct Shirley, eight or nine months later, to tell the Acadians that, so long as they were peaceable subjects, they should be protected in property and religion.[20] Thus left

[19] *Shirley to Newcastle, 15 August,* 1746.

[20] *Newcastle to Shirley, 30 May,* 1747. Shirley had some time before directed Mascarene to tell the Acadians that while they behave peaceably and do not correspond with the enemy, their property will be safe, but that such as turn traitors will be treated accordingly. *Shirley to Mascarene, 16 September,* 1746.

to struggle unaided with a most difficult problem, entirely out-side of his functions as governor of Massachusetts, Shirley did what he could. The most pressing danger, as he thought, rose from the presence of Ramesay and his Canadians at Chignecto; for that officer spared no pains to induce the Acadians to join him in another attempt against Annapolis, telling them that if they did not drive out the English, the English would drive them out. He was now at Mines, trying to raise the inhabitants in arms for France. Shirley thought it necessary to counteract him, and force him and his Canadians back to the isthmus whence they had come; but as the ministry would give no soldiers, he was compelled to draw them from New England. The defense of Acadia was the business of the home government, and not of the colonies; but as they were deeply interested in the preservation of the endangered province, Massachusetts gave five hundred men in response to Shirley's call, and Rhode Island and New Hampshire added, between them, as many more. Less than half of these levies reached Acadia. It was the stormy season. The Rhode Island vessels were wrecked near Martha's Vine-yard. A New Hampshire transport sloop was intercepted by a French armed vessel, and ran back to Portsmouth. Four hun-dred and seventy men from Massachusetts, under Colonel Arthur Noble, were all who reached Annapolis, whence they sailed for Mines, accompanied by a few soldiers of the gar-rison. Storms, drifting ice, and the furious tides of the Bay of Fundy made their progress so difficult and uncertain that Noble resolved to finish the journey by land; and on the fourth of December he disembarked near the place now called French Cross, at the foot of the North Mountain,—a lofty barrier of rock and forest extending along the southern shore of the Bay of Fundy. Without a path and without guides, the party climbed the snow-encumbered heights and toiled to-wards their destination, each man carrying provisions for fourteen days in his haversack. After sleeping eight nights without shelter among the snowdrifts, they reached the Aca-dian village of Grand Pré, the chief settlement of the district of Mines. Ramesay and his Canadians were gone. On learning the approach of an English force, he had tried to persuade the Acadians that they were to be driven from their homes, and that their only hope was in joining with him to meet force by force; but they trusted Shirley's recent assurance of protec-tion, and replied that they would not break their oath of fidelity to King George. On this, Ramesay retreated to his old station at Chignecto, and Noble and his men occupied Grand Pré without opposition.

The village consisted of small, low wooden houses, scattered at intervals for the distance of a mile and a half, and therefore ill fitted for defence. The English had the frame of a block-house, or, as some say, of two blockhouses, ready to be set up on their arrival; but as the ground was hard frozen, it was difficult to make a foundation, and the frames were therefore stored in outbuildings of the village, with the intention of raising them in the spring. The vessels which had brought them, together with stores, ammunition, five small cannon, and a good supply of snow-shoes, had just arrived at the landing-place,—and here, with incredible fatuity, were allowed to remain, with most of their indispensable contents still on board. The men, meanwhile, were quartered in the Acadian houses.

Noble's position was critical, but he was assured that he could not be reached from Chignecto in such a bitter season; and this he was too ready to believe, though he himself had just made a march, which, if not so long, was quite as arduous. Yet he did not neglect every precaution, but kept out scouting-parties to range the surrounding country, while the rest of his men took their ease in the Acadian houses, living on the provisions of the villagers, for which payment was afterwards made. Some of the inhabitants, who had openly favored Ramesay and his followers, fled to the woods, in fear of the consequences; but the greater part remained quietly in the village.

At the head of the Bay of Fundy its waters form a fork, consisting of Chignecto Bay on the one hand, and Mines Basin on the other. At the head of Chignecto Bay was the Acadian settlement of Chignecto, or Beaubassin, in the houses of which Ramesay had quartered his Canadians. Here the neck of the Acadian peninsula is at its narrowest, the distance across to Baye Verte, where Ramesay had built a fort, being little more than twelve miles. Thus he controlled the isthmus,—from which, however, Noble hoped to dislodge him in the spring.

In the afternoon of the eighth of January an Acadian who had been sent to Mines by the missionary Germain, came to Beaubassin with the news that two hundred and twenty English were at Grand Pré, and that more were expected.[21]

[21] Beaujeu, *Journal de la Campagne du Détachement de Canada à l'Acadie,* in *Le Canada Français,* ii. *Documents,* 16.

Ramesay instantly formed a plan of extraordinary hardihood, and resolved, by a rapid march and a night attack, to surprise the new-comers. His party was greatly reduced by disease, and to recruit it he wrote to La Corne, Récollet missionary at Miramichi, to join him with his Indians; writing at the same time to Maillard, former colleague of Le Loutre at the mission of Shubenacadie, and to Girard, priest of Cobequid, to muster Indians, collect provisions, and gather information concerning the English. Meanwhile his Canadians busied themselves with making snow-shoes and dog-sledges for the march.

Ramesay could not command the expedition in person, as an accident to one of his knees had disabled him from marching. This was less to be regretted, in view of the quality of his officers, for he had with him the flower of the warlike Canadian *noblesse*,—Coulon de Villiers, who, seven years later, defeated Washington at Fort Necessity; Beaujeu, the future hero of the Monongahela, in appearance a carpet knight, in reality a bold and determined warrior; the Chevalier de la Corne, a model of bodily and mental hardihood; Saint-Pierre, Lanaudière, Saint-Ours, Desligneris, Courtemanche, Repentigny, Boishébert, Gaspé, Colombière, Marin, Lusignan,—all adepts in the warfare of surprise and sudden onslaught in which the Canadians excelled.

Coulon de Villiers commanded in Ramesay's place; and on the twenty-first of January he and the other officers led their men across the isthmus from Beaubassin to Baye Verte, where they all encamped in the woods, and where they were joined by a party of Indians and some Acadians from Beaubassin and Isle St. Jean.[22] Provisions, ammunition, and other requisites were distributed, and at noon of the twenty-third they broke up their camp, marched three leagues, and bivouacked towards evening. On the next morning they marched again at daybreak. There was sharp cold, with a storm of snow,—not the large, moist, lazy flakes that fall peacefully and harmlessly, but those small crystalline particles that drive spitefully before the wind, and prick the cheek like needles. It was the kind of snow-storm called in Canada *la poudrerie*. They had hoped to make a long day's march; but feet and faces were freezing, and they were forced to stop, at noon, under such

[22] *Mascarene to Shirley*, 8 *February*, 1746 (1747, new style).

shelter as the thick woods of pine, spruce, and fir could supply. In the morning they marched again, following the border of the sea, their dog-teams dragging provisions and baggage over the broken ice of creeks and inlets, which they sometimes avoided by hewing paths through the forest. After a day of extreme fatigue they stopped at the small bay where the town of Wallace now stands. Beaujeu says: "While we were digging out the snow to make our huts, there came two Acadians with letters from MM. Maillard and Girard." The two priests sent a mixture of good and evil news. On one hand the English were more numerous than had been reported; on the other, they had not set up the blockhouses they had brought with them. Some Acadians of the neighboring settlement joined the party at this camp, as also did a few Indians.

On the next morning, January 27, the adventurers stopped at the village of Tatmagouche, where they were again joined by a number of Acadians. After mending their broken sledges they resumed their march, and at five in the afternoon reached a place called Bacouel, at the beginning of the portage that led some twenty-five miles across the country to Cobequid, now Truro, at the head of Mines Basin. Here they were met by Girard, priest of Cobequid, from whom Coulon exacted a promise to meet him again at that village in two days. Girard gave the promise unwillingly, fearing, says Beaujeu, to embroil himself with the English authorities. He reported that the force at Grand Pré counted at least four hundred and fifty, or, as some said, more than five hundred. This startling news ran through the camp; but the men were not daunted. "The more there are," they said, "the more we shall kill."

The party spent the twenty-eighth in mending their damaged sledges, and in the afternoon they were joined by more Acadians and Indians. Thus reinforced, they marched again, and towards evening reached a village on the outskirts of Cobequid. Here the missionary Maillard joined them,—to the great satisfaction of Coulon, who relied on him and his brother priest Girard to procure supplies of provisions. Maillard promised to go himself to Grand Pré with the Indians of his mission.

The party rested for a day, and set out again on the first of February, stopped at Maillard's house in Cobequid for the provisions he had collected for them, and then pushed on towards the river Shubenacadie, which runs from the south into

Cobequid Bay, the head of Mines Basin. When they reached the river they found it impassable from floating ice, which forced them to seek a passage at some distance above. Coulon was resolved, however, that at any risk a detachment should cross at once, to stop the roads to Grand Pré, and prevent the English from being warned of his approach; for though the Acadians inclined to the French, and were eager to serve them when the risk was not too great, there were some of them who, from interest or fear, were ready to make favor with the English by carrying them intelligence. Boishébert, with ten Canadians, put out from shore in a canoe, and were near perishing among the drifting ice; but they gained the farther shore at last, and guarded every path to Grand Pré. The main body filed on snow-shoes up the east bank of the Shubenacadie, where the forests were choked with snow and encumbered with fallen trees, over which the sledges were to be dragged, to their great detriment. On this day, the third, they made five leagues; on the next only two, which brought them within half a league of Le Loutre's Micmac mission. Not far from this place the river was easily passable on the ice, and they continued their march westward across the country to the river Kennetcook by ways so difficult that their Indian guide lost the path, and for a time led them astray. On the seventh, Boishébert and his party rejoined them, and brought a reinforcement of sixteen Indians, whom the Acadians had furnished with arms. Provisions were failing, till on the eighth, as they approached the village of Pisiquid, now Windsor, the Acadians, with great zeal, brought them a supply. They told them, too, that the English at Grand Pré were perfectly secure, suspecting no danger.

On the ninth, in spite of a cold, dry storm of snow, they reached the west branch of the river Avon. It was but seven French leagues to Grand Pré, which they hoped to reach before night; but fatigue compelled them to rest till the tenth. At noon of that day, the storm still continuing, they marched again, though they could hardly see their way for the driving snow. They soon came to a small stream, along the frozen surface of which they drew up in order, and, by command of Coulon, Beaujeu divided them all into ten parties, for simultaneous attacks on as many houses occupied by the English. Then, marching slowly, lest they should arrive too soon, they reached the river Gaspereau, which enters Mines Basin at

Grand Pré. They were now but half a league from their destination. Here they stopped an hour in the storm, shivering and half frozen, waiting for nightfall. When it grew dark they moved again, and soon came to a number of houses on the river-bank. Each of the ten parties took possession of one of these, making great fires to warm themselves and dry their guns.

It chanced that in the house where Coulon and his band sought shelter, a wedding-feast was going on. The guests were much startled at this sudden irruption of armed men; but to the Canadians and their chief the festival was a stroke of amazing good luck, for most of the guests were inhabitants of Grand Pré, who knew perfectly the houses occupied by the English, and could tell with precision where the officers were quartered. This was a point of extreme importance. The English were distributed among twenty-four houses, scattered, as before mentioned, for the distance of a mile and a half.[23] The assailants were too few to attack all these houses at once; but if those where the chief officers lodged could be surprised and captured with their inmates, the rest could make little resistance. Hence it was that Coulon had divided his followers into ten parties, each with one or more chosen officers; these officers were now called together at the house of the interrupted festivity, and the late guests having given full information as to the position of the English quarters and the military quality of their inmates, a special object of attack was assigned to the officer of each party, with Acadian guides to conduct him to it. The principal party, consisting of fifty, or, as another account says, of seventy-five men, was led by Coulon himself, with Beaujeu, Desligneris, Mercier, Léry, and Lusignan as his officers. This party was to attack a stone house near the middle of the village, where the main guard was stationed,—a building somewhat larger than the rest, and the only one at all suited for defence. The second party, of forty men, commanded by La Corne, with Rigauville, Lagny, and Villemont, was to attack a neighboring house, the quarters of Colonel Noble, his brother, Ensign Noble, and several other officers. The remaining parties, of twenty-five men each ac-

[23] *Goldthwait to Shirley*, 2 *March*, 1746 (1747). Captain Benjamin Goldthwait was second in command of the English detachment.

cording to Beaujeu, or twenty-eight according to La Corne, were to make a dash, as nearly as possible at the same time, at other houses which it was thought most important to secure. All had Acadian guides, whose services in that capacity were invaluable; though Beaujeu complains that they were of no use in the attack. He says that the united force was about three hundred men, while the English Captain Goldthwait puts it, including Acadians and Indians, at from five to six hundred. That of the English was a little above five hundred in all. Every arrangement being made, and his part assigned to each officer, the whole body was drawn up in the storm, and the chaplain pronounced a general absolution. Then each of the ten parties, guided by one or more Acadians, took the path for its destination, every man on snow-shoes, with the lock of his gun well sheltered under his capote.

The largest party, under Coulon, was, as we have seen, to attack the stone house in the middle of the village; but their guide went astray, and about three in the morning they approached a small wooden house not far from their true object. A guard was posted here, as at all the English quarters. The night was dark and the snow was still falling, as it had done without ceasing for the past thirty hours. The English sentinel descried through the darkness and the storm what seemed the shadows of an advancing crowd of men. He cried, "Who goes there?" and then shouted, "To arms!" A door was flung open, and the guard appeared in the entrance. But at that moment the moving shadows vanished from before the eyes of the sentinel. The French, one and all, had thrown themselves flat in the soft, light snow, and nothing was to be seen or heard. The English thought it a false alarm, and the house was quiet again. Then Coulon and his men rose and dashed forward. Again, in a loud and startled voice, the sentinel shouted "To arms!" A great light, as of a blazing fire, shone through the open doorway, and men were seen within in hurried movement. Coulon, who was in the front, said to Beaujeu, who was close at his side, that the house was not the one they were to attack. Beaujeu replied that it was no time to change, and Coulon dashed forward again. Beaujeu aimed at the sentinel and shot him dead. There was the flash and report of muskets from the house, and Coulon dropped in the snow, severely wounded. The young cadet, Lusignan, was hit in the shoulder; but he still pushed on, when a second shot shattered his thigh. "Friends," cried the gallant youth, as he fell by the side of his commander, "don't let two dead men discourage you." The Canadians, powdered from head to foot with snow, burst into the house. Within ten minutes, all resistance was overpowered. Of twenty-four Englishmen, twenty-one were killed, and three made prisoners.[24]

Meanwhile, La Corne, with his party of forty men, had attacked the house where were quartered Colonel Noble and his brother, with Captain Howe and several other officers. Noble had lately transferred the main guard to the stone house, but had not yet removed thither himself, and the guard in the house which he occupied was small. The French burst the door with axes, and rushed in. Colonel Noble, startled from sleep, sprang from his bed, receiving two musket-balls in the body as he did so. He seems to have had pistols, for he returned the fire several times. His servant, who was in the house, testified that the French called to the colonel through a window and promised him quarter if he would surrender; but that he refused, on which they fired again, and a bullet, striking his forehead, killed him instantly. His brother, Ensign Noble, was also shot down, fighting in his shirt. Lieutenants Pickering and Lechmere lay in bed dangerously ill, and were killed there. Lieutenant Jones, after, as the narrator says, "ridding himself of some of the enemy," tried to break through the rest and escape, but was run through the heart with a bayonet. Captain Howe was severely wounded and made prisoner.

Coulon and Lusignan, disabled by their wounds, were carried back to the houses on the Gaspereau, where the French surgeon had remained. Coulon's party, now commanded by Beaujeu, having met and joined the smaller party under Lotbinière, proceeded to the aid of others who might need their help; for while they heard a great noise of musketry from far and near, and could discern bodies of men in motion here and there, they could not see whether these were friends or foes, or discern which side fortune favored. They presently met the party of Marin, composed of twenty-five Indians, who had just been repulsed with loss from the house which they had attacked. By this time there was a gleam of daylight, and as they plodded wearily over the snowdrifts, they no longer

[24] Beaujeu, *Journal.*

groped in darkness. The two parties of Colombière and
Boishébert soon joined them, with the agreeable news that
each had captured a house; and the united force now proceeded to make a successful attack on two buildings where
the English had stored the frames of their blockhouses. Here
the assailants captured ten prisoners. It was now broad day,
but they could not see through the falling snow whether the
enterprise, as a whole, had prospered or failed. Therefore
Beaujeu sent Marin to find La Corne, who, in the absence of
Coulon, held the chief command. Marin was gone two hours.
At length he returned, and reported that the English in the
houses which had not been attacked, together with such others
as had not been killed or captured, had drawn together at
the stone house in the middle of the village, that La Corne
was blockading them there, and that he ordered Beaujeu and
his party to join him at once. When Beaujeu reached the place
he found La Corne posted at the house where Noble had
been killed, and which was within easy musket-shot of the
stone house occupied by the English, against whom a spatter-
ing fire was kept up by the French from the cover of neighboring buildings. Those in the stone house returned the fire;
but no great harm was done on either side, till the English,
now commanded by Captain Goldthwait, attempted to recapture the house where La Corne and his party were posted.
Two companies made a sally; but they had among them only
eighteen pairs of snow-shoes, the rest having been left on
board the two vessels which had brought the stores of the detachment from Annapolis, and which now lay moored hard
by, in the power of the enemy, at or near the mouth of the
Gaspereau. Hence the sallying party floundered helpless
among the drifts, plunging so deep in the dry snow that they
could not use their guns and could scarcely move, while
bullets showered upon them from La Corne's men in the
house, and others hovering about them on snow-shoes. The
attempt was hopeless, and after some loss the two companies
fell back. The firing continued, as before, till noon, or, according to Beaujeu, till three in the afternoon, when a French
officer, carrying a flag of truce, came out of La Corne's house.
The occasion of the overture was this.

Captain Howe, who, as before mentioned, had been badly
wounded at the capture of this house, was still there, a prisoner, without surgical aid, the French surgeon being at the

houses on the Gaspereau, in charge of Coulon and other wounded men. "Though," says Beaujeu, "M. Howe was a firm man, he begged the Chevalier La Corne not to let him bleed to death for want of aid, but permit him to send for an English surgeon." To this La Corne, after consulting with his officers, consented, and Marin went to the English with a white flag and a note from Howe explaining the situation. The surgeon was sent, and Howe's wound was dressed, Marin remaining as a hostage. A suspension of arms took place till the surgeon's return; after which it was prolonged till nine o'clock of the next morning, at the instance, according to French accounts, of the English, and, according to English accounts, of the French. In either case, the truce was welcome to both sides. The English, who were in the stone house to the number of nearly three hundred and fifty, crowded to suffocation, had five small cannon, two of which were four-pounders, and three were swivels; but these were probably not in position, as it does not appear that any use was made of them. There was no ammunition except what the men had in their powder-horns and bullet-pouches, the main stock having been left, with other necessaries, on board the schooner and sloop now in the hands of the French. It was found, on examination, that they had ammunition for eight shots each, and provisions for one day. Water was only to be had by bringing it from a neighboring brook. As there were snow-shoes for only about one man in twenty, sorties were out of the question; and the house was commanded by high ground on three sides.

Though their number was still considerable, their position was growing desperate. Thus it happened that when the truce expired, Goldthwait, the English commander, with another officer, who seems to have been Captain Preble, came with a white flag to the house where La Corne was posted, and proposed terms of capitulation, Howe, who spoke French, acting as interpreter. La Corne made proposals on his side, and as neither party was anxious to continue the fray, they soon came to an understanding.

It was agreed that within forty-eight hours the English should march for Annapolis with the honors of war; that the prisoners taken by the French should remain in their hands; that the Indians, who had been the only plunderers, should keep the plunder they had taken; that the English sick and wounded should be left, till their recovery, at the neighboring settlement of Rivière-aux-Canards, protected by a French guard, and that the English engaged in the affair at Grand Pré should not bear arms during the next six months within the district about the head of the Bay of Fundy, including Chignecto, Grand Pré, and the neighboring settlements.

Captain Howe was released on parole, with the condition that he should send back in exchange one Lacroix, a French prisoner at Boston,—"which," says La Corne, "he faithfully did."

Thus ended one of the most gallant exploits in French-Canadian annals. As respects the losses on each side, the French and English accounts are irreconcilable; nor are the statements of either party consistent with themselves. Mascarene reports to Shirley that seventy English were killed, and above sixty captured; though he afterwards reduces these numbers, having, as he says, received farther information. On the French side he says that four officers and about forty men were killed, and that many wounded were carried off in carts durng the fight. Beaujeu, on the other hand, sets the English loss at one hundred and thirty killed, fifteen wounded, and fifty captured; and the French loss at seven killed and fifteen wounded. As for the numbers engaged, the statements are scarcely less divergent. It seems clear, however, that when Coulon began his march from Baye Verte, his party consisted of about three hundred Canadians and Indians, without reckoning some Acadians who had joined him on the way to Grand Pré, counting a hundred and fifty according to Shirley, —which appears to be much too large an estimate. The English, by their own showing, numbered five hundred, or five hundred and twenty-five. Of eleven houses attacked, ten were surprised and carried, with the help of the darkness and storm and the skilful management of the assailants.

"No sooner was the capitulation signed," says Beaujeu, "than we became in appearance the best of friends." La Corne directed military honors to be rendered to the remains of the brothers Noble; and in all points the Canadians, both officers and men, treated the English with kindness and courtesy. "The English commandant," again says Beaujeu, "invited us all to dine with him and his officers, so that we might have the pleasure of making acquaintance over a bowl of punch." The repast being served after such a fashion as circumstances permitted, victors and vanquished sat down together; when, says Beaujeu, "we received on the part of our hosts many compliments on our polite manners and our skill in making war." And the compliments were well deserved.

At eight o'clock on the morning of the fourteenth of February the English filed out of the stone house, and with arms shouldered, drums beating, and colors flying, marched between two ranks of the French, and took the road for Annapolis. The English sick and wounded were sent to the settlement of Rivière-aux-Canards, where, protected by a French guard and attended by an English surgeon, they were to remain till able to reach the British fort.

La Corne called a council of war, and in view of the scarcity of food and other reasons it was resolved to return to Beaubassin. Many of the French had fallen ill. Some of the sick and wounded were left at Grand Pré, others at Cobequid, and the Acadians were required to supply means of carrying the rest. Coulon's party left Grand Pré on the twenty-third of February, and on the eighth of March reached Beaubassin.[25]

[25] The dates are of the new style, which the French had adopted, while the English still clung to the old style.

By far the best account of this French victory at Mines is that of Beaujeu, in his *Journal de la Campagne du Détachement de Canada à l'Acadie et aux Mines en 1746–47*. It is preserved in the Archives de la Marine et des Colonies, and is printed in the documentary supplement of *Le Canada Français*, Vol. II. It supplies the means of correcting many errors and much confusion in some recent accounts of the affair. The report of Chevalier de la Corne, also printed in *Le Canada Français*, though much shorter, is necessary to a clear understanding of the matter. Letters of Lusignan fils to the minister Maurepas, 10 October, 1747, of Bishop Pontbriand (to Maurepas?), 10 July, 1747, and of Lusignan père to Maurepas, 10 October, 1747, give some additional incidents. The principal document on the English side is the report of Captain Benjamin Goldthwait, who succeeded Noble in command. A copy of the original, in the Public Record Office, is before me. The substance of it is correctly given in *The Boston Post Boy* of 2 March, 1747, and in *N. E. Hist. Gen. Reg.* x. 108. Various letters from Mascarene and Shirley (Public Record Office) contain accounts derived from returned officers and soldiers. The *Notice of Colonel Arthur Noble,* by William Goold (*Collections Maine Historical Soc.,* 1881), may also be consulted.

Ramesay did not fail to use the success at Grand Pré to influence the minds of the Acadians. He sent a circular letter to the inhabitants of the various districts, and especially to those of Mines, in which he told them that their country had been reconquered by the arms of the King of France, to whom he commanded them to be faithful subjects, holding no intercourse with the English under any pretence whatever, on pain of the severest punishment. "If," he concludes, "we have withdrawn our soldiers from among you, it is for reasons known to us alone, and with a view to your advantage."[26]

Unfortunately for the effect of this message, Shirley had no sooner heard of the disaster at Grand Pré than he sent a body of Massachusetts soldiers to reoccupy the place.[27] This they did in April. The Acadians thus found themselves, as usual, between two dangers; and unable to see which horn of the dilemma was the worse, they tried to avoid both by conciliating French and English alike, and assuring each of their devoted attachement. They sent a pathetic letter to Ramesay, telling him that their hearts were always French, and begging him at the same time to remember that they were a poor, helpless people, burdened with large families, and in danger of expulsion and ruin if they offended their masters, the English.[28] They wrote at the same time to Mascarene at Annapolis, sending him, to explain the situation, a copy of Ramesay's threatening letter to them;[29] begging him to consider that they could not without danger dispense with answering it; at the same time they protested their entire fidelity to King George.[30]

[26] Ramesay aux Députés et Habitants des Mines, 31 Mars, 1747. At the end is written "A true copy, with the misspellings: signed W. Shirley."

[27] Shirley to Newcastle, 24 August, 1747.

[28] "Ainsis Monsieur nous vous prions de regarder notre bon Coeur etien meme Temps notre Impuissance pauvre Peuple chargez la plus part de familles nombreuse point de Recours sil falois evacuer a quoy nous sommes menacez tous les jours qui nous tien dans une Crainte perpetuelle en nous voyant a la proximitet de nos maitre depuis un sy grand nombre dannes" (printed *literatim*).—*Deputés des Mines à Ramesay*, 24 Mai, 1747.

[29] This probably explains the bad spelling of the letter, the copy before me having been made from the Acadian transcript sent to Mascarene, and now in the Public Record Office.

[30] Les Habitants à l'honorable gouverneur au for d'anapolisse royal [sic], Mai (?), 1747.

Ramesay, not satisfied with the results of his first letter, wrote again to the Acadians, ordering them, in the name of the governor-general of New France, to take up arms against the English, and enclosing for their instruction an extract from a letter of the French governor. "These," says Ramesay, "are his words: 'We consider ourself as master of Beaubassin and Mines, since we have driven off the English. Therefore there is no difficulty in forcing the Acadians to take arms for us; to which end we declare to them that they are discharged from the oath that they formerly took to the English, by which they are bound no longer, as has been decided by the authorities of Canada and Monseigneur our Bishop.' "[31]

"In view of the above," continues Ramesay, "we order all the inhabitants of Memeramcook to come to this place [Beaubassin] as soon as they see the signal-fires lighted, or discover the approach of the enemy; and this on pain of death, confiscation of all their goods, burning of their houses, and the punishment due to rebels against the King."[32]

The position of the Acadians was deplorable. By the Treaty of Utrecht, France had transferred them to the British Crown; yet French officers denounced them as rebels and threatened them with death if they did not fight at their bidding against England; and English officers threatened them with expulsion from the country if they broke their oath of allegiance to

_____

On the 27th of June the inhabitants of Cobequid wrote again to Mascarene: "Monsieur nous prenons la Liberte de vous recrire celle icy pour vous assurer de nos tres humble Respect et d'un entiere Sou-mission a vos Ordres" (*literatim*).

[31] "Nous nous regardons aujourdhuy Maistre de Beaubassin et des Mines puisque nous en avons Chassé les Anglois; ainsi il ny a aucune difficulté de forcer les Accadiens à prendre les armes pour nous, et de les y Contraindre; leur declarons à cet effêt qu'ils sont decharg é [*sic*] du Serment preté, cy devant, à l'Anglois, auquel ils ne sont plus obligé [*sic*] comme il y a été decidé par nos puissances de Canada et de Monseigneur notre Evesque" (*literatim*).

[32] *Ramesay aux Habitants de Chignecto, etc.*, 25 *Mai*, 1747.

A few months later, the deputies of Rivière-aux-Canards wrote to Shirley, thanking him for kindness which they said was undeserved, promising to do their duty thence forth, but begging him to excuse them from giving up persons who had acted "contraire aux Interêsts de leur devoire," representing the difficulty of their position, and protesting "une Soumission parfaite et en touts Respects." The letter is signed by four deputies, of whom one writes his name, and three sign with crosses.

King George. It was the duty of the British ministry to occupy the province with a force sufficient to protect the inhabitants against French terrorism, and leave no doubt that the King of England was master of Acadia in fact as well as in name. This alone could have averted the danger of Acadian revolt, and the harsh measures to which it afterwards gave rise. The ministry sent no aid, but left to Shirley and Massachusetts the task of keeping the province for King George. Shirley and Massachusetts did what they could; but they could not do all that the emergency demanded.

Shirley courageously spoke his mind to the ministry, on whose favor he was dependent. "The fluctuating state of the inhabitants of Acadia," he wrote to Newcastle, "seems, my lord, naturally to arise from their finding a want of due protection from his Majesty's Government."[33]

[33] *Shirley to Newcastle, 29 April,* 1747.
On Shirley's relations with the Acadians, *see* Appendix C.

Chapter 23

1740–1747
War and Politics

From the East we turn to the West, for the province of New York passed for the West at that day. Here a vital question was what would be the attitude of the Five Nations of the Iroquois towards the rival European colonies, their neighbors. The Treaty of Utrecht called them British subjects. What the word "subjects" meant, they themselves hardly knew. The English told them that it meant children; the French that it meant dogs and slaves. Events had tamed the fierce confederates; and now, though, like all savages, unstable as children, they leaned in their soberer moments to a position of neutrality between their European neighbors, watching with jealous eyes against the encroachments of both. The French would gladly have enlisted them and their tomahawks in the war; but seeing little hope of this, were generally content if they could prevent them from siding with the English, who on their part regarded them as their Indians, and were satisfied with nothing less than active alliance.

When Shirley's plan for the invasion of Canada was afoot, Clinton, governor of New York, with much ado succeeded in convening the deputies of the confederacy at Albany, and by dint of speeches and presents induced them to sing the war-song and take up the hatchet for England. The Iroquois were disgusted when the scheme came to nought, their warlike ardor cooled, and they conceived a low opinion of English prowess.

The condition of New York as respects military efficiency was deplorable. She was divided against herself, and, as usual in such cases, party passion was stronger than the demands of war. The province was in the midst of one of those disputes with the representative of the Crown, which, in one degree or another, crippled or paralyzed the military activity of nearly all the British colonies. Twenty years or more earlier, when Massachusetts was at blows with the Indians on her borders, she suffered from the same disorders; but her governor and Assembly were of one mind as to urging on the war, and quarrelled only on the questions in what way and under what command it should be waged. But in New York there was a strong party that opposed the war, being interested in the contraband trade long carried on with Canada. Clinton, the governor, had, too, an enemy in the person of the chief justice, James de Lancey, with whom he had had an after-dinner dispute, ending in a threat on the part of De Lancey that he would make the governor's seat uncomfortable. To marked abilities, better education, and more knowledge of the world than was often found in the provinces, ready wit, and conspicuous social position, the chief justice joined a restless ambition and the arts of a demagogue.

He made good his threat, headed the opposition to the governor, and proved his most formidable antagonist. If either Clinton or Shirley had had the independent authority of a Canadian governor, the conduct of the war would have been widely different. Clinton was hampered at every turn. The Assembly held him at advantage; for it was they, and not the King, who paid his salary, and they could withhold or retrench it when he displeased them. The people sympathized with their representatives and backed them in opposition,—at least, when not under the stress of imminent danger.

A body of provincials, in the pay of the King, had been mustered at Albany for the proposed Canada expedition; and after that plan was abandoned, Clinton wished to use them for protecting the northern frontier and capturing that standing menace to the province, Crown Point. The Assembly, bent on crossing him at any price, refused to provide for transporting supplies farther than Albany. As the furnishing of provisions and transportation depended on that body, they could stop the movement of troops and defeat the governor's military plans at their pleasure. In vain he told them, "If you deny me the necessary supplies, all my endeavors must become fruitless; I must wash my own hands, and leave at your doors the blood of the innocent people."[1]

He urged upon them the necessity of building forts on the two carrying-places between the Hudson and Lakes George

---

[1] *Extract from the Governor's Message,* in Smith, *History of New York,* ii. 124 (1830).

and Champlain, thus blocking the path of war-parties from Canada. They would do nothing, insisting that the neighboring colonies, to whom the forts would also be useful, ought to help in building them; and when it was found that these colonies were ready to do their part, the Assembly still refused. Passionate opposition to the royal governor seemed to blind them to the interests of the province. Nor was the fault all on their side; for the governor, though he generally showed more self-control and moderation than could have been expected, sometimes lost temper and betrayed scorn for his opponents, many of whom were but the instruments of leaders urged by personal animosities and small but intense ambitions. They accused him of treating them with contempt, and of embezzling public money; while he retorted by charging them with encroaching on the royal prerogative and treating the representative of the King with indecency. Under such conditions an efficient conduct of the war was out of the question.

Once, when the frontier was seriously threatened, Clinton, as commander-in-chief, called out the militia to defend it; but they refused to obey, on the ground that no Act of the Assembly required them to do so.[2]

Clinton sent home bitter complaints to Newcastle and the Lords of Trade. "They [the Assembly] are selfish, jealous of the power of the Crown, and of such levelling principles that they are constantly attacking its prerogative. . . . I find that neither dissolutions nor fair means can produce from them such Effects as will tend to a publick good or their own preservation. They will neither act for themselves nor assist their neighbors. . . . Few but hirelings have a seat in the Assembly, who protract time for the sake of their wages, at a great expence to the Province, without contributing anything material for its welfare, credit, or safety." And he declares that unless Parliament takes them in hand he can do nothing for the service of the King or the good of the province,[3] for they want to usurp the whole administration, both civil and military.[4]

[2] *Clinton to the Lords of Trade,* 10 *November,* 1747.

[3] *Ibid.,* 30 *November,* 1745.

[4] *Remarks on the Representation of the Assembly of New York, May,* 1747, in *N. Y. Col. Docs.,* vi. 365. On the disputes of the governor and Assembly see also Smith, *History of New York,* ii.

At Saratoga there was a small settlement of Dutch farmers, with a stockade fort for their protection. This was the farthest outpost of the colony, and the only defence of Albany in the direction of Canada. It was occupied by a sergeant, a corporal, and ten soldiers, who testified before a court of inquiry that it was in such condition that in rainy weather neither they nor their ammuntion could be kept dry. As neither the Assembly nor the merchants of Albany would make it tenable, the garrison was withdrawn before winter by order of the governor.[5]

Scarcely was this done when five hundred French and Indians, under the partisan Marin, surprised the settlement in the night of the twenty-eighth of November, burned fort, houses, mills, and stables, killed thirty persons, and carried off about a hundred prisoners.[6] Albany was left uncovered, and the Assembly voted £150 in provincial currency to rebuild the ruined fort. A feeble palisade work was accordingly set up, but it was neglected like its predecessor. Colonel Peter Schuyler was stationed there with his regiment in 1747, but was forced to abandon his post for want of supplies. Clinton then directed Colonel Roberts, commanding at Albany, to examine the fort, and if he found it indefensible, to burn it,— which he did, much to the astonishment of a French war-party, who visited the place soon after, and found nothing but ashes.[7]

The burning of Saratoga, first by the French and then by its own masters, made a deep impression on the Five Nations, and a few years later they taunted their white neighbors with these shortcomings in no measured terms. "You burned your

---

(1830), and Stone, *Life and Times of Sir William Johnson*, i. *N. Y. Colonial Documents*, vi., contains many papers on the subject, chiefly on the governor's side.

[5] *Examinations at a Court of Inquiry at Albany*, 11 *December*, 1745, in *N. Y. Col. Docs.*, vi. 374.

[6] The best account of this affair is in the journal of a French officer in Schuyler, *Colonial New York*, ii. 115. The dates, being in new style, differ by eleven days from those of the English accounts. The Dutch hamlet of Saratoga, surprised by Marin, was near the mouth of the Fish Kill, on the west side of the Hudson. There was also a small fort on the east side, a little below the mouth of the Batten Kill.

[7] Schuyler, *Colonial New York*, ii. 121.

own fort at Seraghtoga and ran away from it, which was a shame and a scandal to you."[8] Uninitiated as they were in party politics and faction quarrels, they could see nothing in this and other military lapses but proof of a want of martial spirit, if not of cowardice. Hence the difficulty of gaining their active alliance against the French was redoubled. Fortunately for the province, the adverse influence was in some measure counteracted by the character and conduct of one man. Up to this time the French had far surpassed the rival nation in the possession of men ready and able to deal with the Indians and mould them to their will. Eminent among such was Joncaire, French emissary among the Senecas in western New York, who, with admirable skill, held back that powerful member of the Iroquois league from siding with the English. But now, among the Mohawks of eastern New York, Joncaire found his match in the person of William Johnson, a vigorous and intelligent young Irishman, nephew of Admiral Warren, and his agent in the management of his estates on the Mohawk. Johnson soon became intimate with his Indian neighbors, spoke their language, joined in their games and dances, sometimes borrowed their dress and their paint, and whooped, yelped, and stamped like one of themselves. A white man thus playing the Indian usually gains nothing in the esteem of those he imitates; but, as before in the case of the redoubtable Count Frontenac, Johnson's adoption of their ways increased their liking for him and did not diminish their respect. The Mohawks adopted him into their tribe and made him a war-chief. Clinton saw his value; and as the Albany commissioners hitherto charged with Indian affairs had proved wholly inefficient, he transferred their functions to Johnson; whence arose more heartburnings. The favor of the governor cost the new functionary the support of the Assembly, who refused the indispensable presents to the Indians, and thus vastly increased the difficulty of his task. Yet the Five Nations promised to take up the hatchet against the French, and their orator said, in a conference at Albany, "Should any French priests now dare to come among us, we know no use for them but to roast them."[9] Johnson's present difficulties, however,

---

[8] *Report of a Council with the Indians at Albany,* 28 June, 1754.
[9] *Answer of the Six [Five] Nations to His Excellency the Governor at Albany,* 23 August, 1746.

sprang more from Dutch and English traders than from French priests, and he begs that an Act may be passed against the selling of liquor to the Indians, "as it is impossible to do anything with them while there is such a plenty to be had all round the neighborhood, being forever drunk." And he complains especially of one Clement, who sells liquor within twenty yards of Johnson's house, and immediately gets from the Indians all the bounty money they receive for scalps, "which leaves them as poor as ratts," and therefore refractory and unmanageable. Johnson says further: "There is another grand villain, George Clock, who lives by Conajoharie Castle, and robs the Indians of all their cloaths, etc." The chiefs complained, "upon which I wrote him twice to give over that custom of selling liquor to the Indians; the answer was he gave the bearer, I might hang myself."[10] Indian affairs, it will be seen, were no better regulated then than now.

Meanwhile the French Indians were ravaging the frontiers and burning farmhouses to within sight of Albany. The Assembly offered rewards for the scalps of the marauders, but were slow in sending money to pay them,—to the great discontent of the Mohawks, who, however, at Johnson's instigation, sent out various war-parties, two of which, accompanied by a few whites, made raids as far as the island of Montreal, and somewhat checked the incursions of the mission Indians by giving them work near home. The check was but momentary. Heathen Indians from the West joined the Canadian converts, and the frontiers of New York and New England, from the Mohawk to beyond the Kennebec, were stung through all their length by innumerable nocturnal surprises and petty attacks. The details of this murderous though ineffective partisan war would fill volumes, if they were worth recording. One or two examples will show the nature of all.

In the valley of the little river Ashuelot, a New Hampshire affluent of the Connecticut, was a rude border-settlement which later years transformed into a town noted in rural New England for kindly hospitality, culture without pretence, and good-breeding without conventionality.[11] In 1746 the place

[10] *Johnson to Clinton,* 7 *May,* 1747.

[11] Keene, originally called Upper Ashuelot. On the same stream, a few miles below, was a similar settlement, called Lower Ashuelot,—the germ of the present Swanzey. This, too, suffered greatly from Indian attacks.

was in all the rawness and ugliness of a backwoods hamlet. The rough fields, lately won from the virgin forest, showed here and there, among the stumps, a few log-cabins, roofed with slabs of pine, spruce, or hemlock. Near by was a wooden fort, made, no doubt, after the common frontier pattern, of a stockade fence ten or twelve feet high, enclosing cabins to shelter the settlers in case of alarm, and furnished at the corners with what were called flankers, which were boxes of thick plank large enough to hold two or more men, raised above the ground on posts, and pierced with loopholes, so that each face of the stockade could be swept by a flank fire. One corner of this fort at Ashuelot was, however, guarded by a solid blockhouse, or, as it was commonly called, a "mount."

On the twenty-third of April a band of sixty, or, by another account, a hundred Indians, approached the settlement before daybreak, and hid in the neighboring thickets to cut off the men in the fort as they came out to their morning work. One of the men, Ephraim Dorman, chanced to go out earlier than the rest. The Indians did not fire on him, but, not to give an alarm, tried to capture or kill him without noise. Several of them suddenly showed themselves, on which he threw down his gun in pretended submission. One of them came up to him with hatchet raised; but the nimble and sturdy borderer suddenly struck him with his fist a blow in the head that knocked him flat, then snatched up his own gun, and, as some say, the blanket of the half-stunned savage also, sprang off, reached the fort unhurt, and gave the alarm. Some of the families of the place were living in the fort; but the bolder or more careless still remained in their farmhouses, and if nothing were done for their relief, their fate was sealed. Therefore the men sallied in a body, and a sharp fight ensued, giving the frightened settlers time to take refuge within the stockade. It was not too soon, for the work of havoc had already begun. Six houses and a barn were on fire, and twenty-three cattle had been killed. The Indians fought fiercely, killed John Bullard, and captured Nathan Blake, but at last retreated; and after they were gone, the charred remains of several of them were found among the ruins of one of the burned cabins, where they had probably been thrown to prevent their being scalped.

Before Dorman had given the alarm, and old woman, Mrs. McKenney, went from the fort to milk her cow in a neighboring barn. As she was returning, with her full milk-pail, a naked Indian was seen to spring from a clump of bushes, plunge a long knife into her back, and dart away without stopping to take the gray scalp of his victim. She tried feebly to reach the fort; but from age, corpulence, and a mortal wound she moved but slowly, and when a few steps from the gate, fell and died.

Ten days after, a party of Indians hid themselves at night by this same fort, and sent one of their number to gain admission under pretence of friendship, intending, no doubt, to rush in when the gate should be opened; but the man on guard detected the trick, and instead of opening the gate, fired through it, mortally wounding the Indian, on which his confederates made off. Again, at the same place, Deacon Josiah Foster, who had taken refuge in the fort, ventured out on a July morning to drive his cows to pasture. A gunshot was heard; and the men who went out to learn the cause, found the deacon lying in the wood-road, dead and scalped. An ambushed Indian had killed him and vanished. Such petty attacks were without number.

There is a French paper, called a record of "military movements," which gives a list of war-parties sent from Montreal against the English border between the twenty-ninth of March, 1746, and the twenty-first of June in the same year. They number thirty-five distinct bands, nearly all composed of mission Indians living in or near the settled parts of Canada, —Abenakis, Iroquois of the Lake of Two Mountains and of Sault St. Louis (Caughnawaga), Algonquins of the Ottawa, and others, in parties rarely of more than thirty, and often of no more than six, yet enough for waylaying travellers or killing women in kitchens or cow-sheds, and solitary laborers in the fields. This record is accompanied by a list of wild Western Indians who came down to Montreal in the summer of 1746 to share in these "military movements."[12]

No part of the country suffered more than the western borders of Massachusetts and New Hampshire, and here were seen too plainly the evils of the prevailing want of concert among the British colonies. Massachusetts claimed extensive tracts north of her present northern boundary, and in the

[12] *Extrait sur les différents Mouvements Militaires qui se sont faits à Montréal à l'occasion de la Guerre, 1745, 1746.* There is a translation in *N. Y. Col. Docs.*

belief that her claim would hold good, had built a small wooden fort, called Fort Dummer, on the Connecticut, for the protection of settlers. New Hampshire disputed the title, and the question, being referred to the Crown, was decided in her favor. On this, Massachusetts withdrew the garrison of Fort Dummer and left New Hampshire to defend her own. This the Assembly of that province refused to do, on the ground that the fort was fifty miles from any settlement made by New Hampshire people, and was therefore useless to them, though of great value to Massachusetts as a cover to Northfield and other of her settlements lower down the Connecticut, to protect[13] which was no business of New Hampshire. But some years before, in 1740, three brothers, Samuel, David, and Stephen Farnsworth, natives of Groton, Massachusetts, had begun a new settlement on the Connecticut about forty-five miles north of the Massachusetts line and on ground which was soon to be assigned to New Hampshire. They were followed by five or six others. They acted on the belief that their settlement was within the jurisdiction of Massachusetts, and that she could and would protect them. The place was one of extreme exposure, not only from its isolation, far from help, but because it was on the banks of a wild and lonely river, the customary highway of war-parties on their descent from Canada. Number Four—for so the new settlement was called, because it was the fourth in a range of townships recently marked out along the Connecticut, but, with one or two exceptions, wholly unoccupied as yet—was a rude little outpost of civilization, buried in forests that spread unbroken to the banks of the St. Lawrence, while its nearest English neighbor was nearly thirty miles away. As may be supposed, it grew slowly, and in 1744 it had but nine or ten families. In the preceding year, when war seemed imminent, and it was clear that neither Massachusetts nor New Hampshire would lend a helping hand, the settlers of Number Four, seeing that their only resource was in themselves, called a meeting to consider the situation and determine what should be done. The meeting was held at the house, or log-cabin, of John Spafford, Jr., and being duly called to order, the following resolutions were adopted: that a fort be built at the charge of the proprie-

[13] *Journal of the Assembly of New Hampshire,* quoted in Saunderson, *History of Charlestown, N. H.,* 20.

tors of the said township of Number Four; that John Hastings, John Spafford, and John Avery be a committee to direct the building; that each carpenter be allowed nine shillings, old tenor, a day, each laborer seven shillings, and each pair of oxen three shillings and sixpence; that the proprietors of the township be taxed in the sum of three hundred pounds, old tenor, for building the fort; that John Spafford, Phineas Stevens, and John Hastings be assessors to assess the same, and Samuel Farnsworth collector to collect it.[14] And to the end that their fort should be a good and creditable one, they are said to have engaged the services of John Stoddard, accounted the foremost man of western Massachusetts, Superintendent of Defence, Colonel of Militia, Judge of Probate, Chief Justice of the Court of Common Pleas, a reputed authority in the construction of backwoods fortifications, and the admired owner of the only gold watch in Northampton.

Timber was abundant and could be had for the asking; for the frontiersman usually regarded a tree less as a valuable possession than as a natural enemy, to be got rid of by fair means or foul. The only cost was the labor. The fort rose rapidly. It was a square enclosing about three quarters of an acre, each side measuring a hundred and eighty feet. The wall was not of palisades, as was more usual, but of squared logs laid one upon another, and interlocked at the corners after the fashion of a log-cabin. Within were several houses, which had been built close together, for mutual protection, before the fort was begun, and which belonged to Stevens, Spafford, and other settlers. Apparently they were small log-cabins; for they were valued at only from eight to thirty-five pounds each, in old tenor currency wofully attenuated by depreciation; and these sums being paid to the owners out of the three hundred pounds collected for building the fort, the cabins became public property. Either they were built in a straight line, or they were moved to form one, for when the fort was finished, they all backed against the outer wall, so that their low roofs served to fire from. The usual flankers completed the work, and the settlers of Number Four were so well pleased with it that they proudly declared their fort a better one than Fort Dummer, its nearest neighbor, which had been built by public authority at the charge of the province.

[14] Extracts from the Town Record, in Saunderson, *History of Charlestown, N. W. (Number Four)*, 17, 18.

But a fort must have a garrison, and the ten or twelve men of Number Four would hardly be a sufficient one. Sooner or later an attack was certain; for the place was a backwoods Castle Dangerous, lying in the path of war-parties from Canada, whether coming down the Connecticut from Lake Memphremagog, or up Otter Creek from Lake Champlain, then over the mountains to Black River, and so down that stream, which would bring them directly to Number Four. New Hampshire would do nothing for them, and their only hope was a Massachusetts, of which most of them were natives, and which had good reasons for helping them to hold their ground, as a cover to its own settlements below. The governor and Assembly of Massachusetts did, in fact, send small parties of armed men from time to time to defend the endangered outpost, and the succor was timely; for though, during the first year of the war, Number Four was left in peace, yet from the nineteenth of April to the Nineteenth of June, 1746, it was attacked by Indians five times, with some loss of scalps, and more of cattle, horses, and hogs. On the last occasion there was a hot fight in the woods, ending in the retreat of the Indians, said to have numbered a hundred and fifty, into a swamp, leaving behind them guns, blankets, hatchets, spears, and other things, valued at forty pounds, old tenor,—which, says the chronicle, "was reckoned a great booty for such beggarly enemies."[15]

But Massachusetts grew tired of defending lands that had been adjudged to New Hampshire, and as the season drew towards an end, Number Four was left again to its own keeping. The settlers saw no choice but to abandon a place which they were too few to defend, and accordingly withdrew to the older settlements, after burying such of their effects as would bear it, and leaving others to their fate. Six men, a dog, and a cat remained to keep the fort. Towards midwinter the human part of the garrison also withdrew, and the two uncongenial quadrupeds were left alone.

When the authorities of Massachusetts saw that a place so useful to bear the brunt of attack was left to certain destruction, they repented of their late withdrawal, and sent Captain Phineas Stevens, with thirty men, to reoccupy it. Stevens, a

[15] Saunderson, *History of Charlestown, N. H.* 29. Doolittle, *Narrative of Mischief done by the Indian Enemy,*—a contemporary chronicle.

native of Sudbury, Massachusetts, one of the earliest settlers of Number Four, and one of its chief proprietors, was a bold, intelligent, and determined man, well fitted for the work before him. He and his band reached the fort on the twenty-seventh of March, 1747, and their arrival gave peculiar pleasure to its tenants, the dog and cat, the former of whom met them with lively demonstrations of joy. The pair had apparently lived in harmony, and found means of subsistence, as they are reported to have been in tolerable condition.

Stevens had brought with him a number of other dogs,—animals found useful for detecting the presence of Indians and tracking them to their lurking-places. A week or more after the arrival of the party, these canine allies showed great uneasiness and barked without ceasing; on which Stevens ordered a strict watch to be kept, and great precaution to be used in opening the gate of the fort. It was time, for the surrounding forest concealed what the New England chroniclers call an "army," commanded by General Debeline. It scarcely need be said that Canada had no General Debeline, and that no such name is to be found in Canadian annals. The "army" was a large war-party of both French and Indians, and a French record shows that its commander was Boucher de Niverville, ensign in the colony troops.[16]

The behavior of the dogs was as yet the only sign of danger, when, about nine o'clock on the morning of the seventh of April, one of Stevens's men took it upon him to go out and find what was amiss. Accompanied by two or three of the dogs, he advanced, gun in hand, into the clearing, peering at every stump, lest an Indian should lurk behind it. When about twenty rods from the gate, he saw a large log, or trunk of a fallen tree, not far before him, and approached it cautiously, setting on the dogs, or, as Stevens whimsically phrases it, "saying *Choboy!*" to them. They ran forward barking, on which several heads appeared above the log, and several guns were fired at him. He was slightly wounded, but escaped to the fort. Then, all around, the air rang with war-whoops, and a storm of bullets flew from the tangle of bushes that edged the clearing, and rapped spitefully, but harmlessly, against

[16] *Extrait en forme de Journal de ce qui s'est passé d'intéressant dans la Colonie à l'occasion des Mouvements de Guerre, etc.,* 1746, 1747.

the wooden wall. At a little distance on the windward side was a log-house, to which, with adjacent fences, the assailants presently set fire, in the hope that, as the wind was strong, the flames would catch the fort. When Stevens saw what they were doing, he set himself to thwart them; and while some of his men kept them at bay with their guns, the rest fell to work digging a number of short trenches under the wall, on the side towards the fire. As each trench was six or seven feet deep, a man could stand in it outside the wall, sheltered from bullets, and dash buckets of water, passed to him from within, against the scorching timbers. Eleven such trenches were dug, and eleven men were stationed in them, so that the whole exposed front of the wall was kept wet.[17] Thus, though clouds of smoke drifted over the fort, and burning cinders showered upon it, no harm was done, and the enemy was forced to other devices. They found a wagon, which they protected from water and bullets by a shield of planks,—for there was a saw-mill hard by,—and loaded it with dry fagots, thinking to set them on fire and push the blazing machine against a dry part of the fort wall; but the task proved too dangerous, "for," says Stevens, "instead of performing what they threatened and seemed to be immediately going to undertake, they called to us and desired a cessation of arms till sunrise the next morning, which was granted, at which time they said they would come to a parley." In fact, the French commander, with about sixty of his men, came in the morning with a flag of truce, which he stuck in the ground at a musket-shot from the fort, and, in the words of Stevens, "said, if we would send three men to him, he would send as many to us." Stevens agreed to this, on which two Frenchmen and an Indian came to the fort, and three soldiers went out in return. The two Frenchmen demanded, on the part of their commander, that the garrison should surrender, under a promise of life, and

[17] "Those who were not employed in firing at the enemy were employed in digging trenches under the bottom of the fort. We dug no less than eleven of them, so deep that a man could go and stand upright on the outside and not endanger himself; so that when these trenches were finished, we could wet all the outside of the fort, which we did, and kept it wet all night. We drew some hundreds of barrels of water; and to undergo all this hard service there were but thirty men."—*Stevens to Colonel W. Williams, April, 1747.*

be carried prisoners to Quebec; and they farther required that Stevens should give his answer to the French officer in person.

Wisely or unwisely, Stevens went out at the gate, and was at once joined by Niverville, attended, no doubt, by an interpreter. "Upon meeting the Monsieur," says the English captain, "he did not wait for me to give him an answer," but said, in a manner sufficiently peremptory, that he had seven hundred men with him, and that if his terms were refused, he would storm the fort, "run over it," burn it to the ground, and if resistance were offered, put all in it to the sword; adding that he would have it or die, and that Stevens might fight or not as he pleased, for it was all one to him. His terms being refused, he said, as Stevens reports, "Well, go back to your fort and see if your men dare fight any more, and give me an answer quickly; for my men want to be fighting." Stevens now acted as if he had been the moderator of a town-meeting. "I went into the fort and called the men together, and informed them what the general said, and then put it to vote whether they would fight or resign; and they voted to a man to stand it out, and also declared that they would fight as long as they had life."[18]

Answer was made accordingly, but Niverville's promise to storm the fort and "run over it" was not kept. Stevens says that his enemies had not the courage to do this, or even to bring up their "fortification," meaning their fire-wagon with its shield of planks. In fact, an open assault upon a fortified place was a thing unknown in this border warfare, whether waged by Indians alone, or by French and Indians together. The assailants only raised the war-whoop again, and fired, as before, from behind stumps, logs, and bushes. This amusement they kept up from two o'clock till night, when they grew bolder, approached nearer, and shot flights of fire-arrows into the fort, which, water being abundant, were harmless as their bullets. At daylight they gave over this exercise, called out, "Good-morning!" to the garrison, and asked for a suspension of arms for two hours. This being agreed to, another flag of truce presently appeared, carried by two Indians, who planted it in the ground within a stone's throw of the fort, and asked that two men should be sent out to confer with them. This was done, and the men soon came back with a proposal that

[18] *Stevens to Colonel William Williams, April,* 1747.

Stevens should sell provisions to his besiegers, under a promise on their part that they would give him no farther trouble. He answered that he would not sell them provisions for money, but would exchange them for prisoners, and give five bushels of Indian corn for every hostage placed in his hands as security for the release of an English captive in Canada. To this their only answer was firing a few shots against the fort, after which they all disappeared, and were seen no more. The garrison had scarcely eaten or slept for three days. "I believe men were never known to hold out with better resolution," writes Stevens; and "though there were some thousands of guns shot at us, we had but two men slightly wounded, John Brown and Joseph Ely."[19]

Niverville and his party, disappointed and hungry, now made a tour among the scattered farms and hamlets of the country below, which, incapable of resisting such an inroad, were abandoned at their approach. Thus they took an easy revenge for their rebuff at Number Four, and in a march of thirty or forty leagues, burned five small deserted forts or stockaded houses, "three meeting-houses, several fine barns, about one hundred dwellings, mostly of two stories, furnished even to chests of drawers, and killed five to six hundred sheep and hogs, and about thirty horned cattle. This devastation is well worth a few prisoners or scalps."[20] It is curious to find such exploits mentioned with complacency, as evidence of prowess.

The successful defence of the most exposed place on the frontier was welcome news throughout New England, and Commodore Charles Knowles, who was then at Boston, sent Stevens a silver-hilted sword in recognition of his conduct. The settlers of Number Four, who soon returned to their back-woods home, were so well pleased with this compliment to one of their fellows that they gave to the settlement the batpismal name of the Commodore, and the town that has succeeded the hamlet of Number Four is Charlestown to this day.[21]

[19] Stevens to Colonel W. Williams, April, 1747.

[20] N. Y. Col. Docs., x. 97.

[21] Just after the withdrawal of the French and Indians, Stevens wrote two letters giving an account of the affair, one to Governor Shirley, and the other to Colonel William Williams, who seems to have been his immediate military superior. At most points they

are substantially the same; but that to Williams contains some passages not found in the other. The letter to Shirley is printed in Saunderson, *History of Charlestown, N. H.,* 34–37, and that to Williams in *Collections of the New Hampshire Historical Society,* iv. 109–113. Stevens also kept a diary, which was long in possession of his descendants. One of these, Mr. B. F. Stevens, kindly made a search for it, at my request, and learned that it had been unfortunately destroyed by fire, in 1856. Doolittle, in his *Narrative of Mischief,* and Moyt, in his *Antiquarian Researches,* give other accounts. The French notices of the affair are few and short, as usual in cases of failure. For the principal one, see *N. Y. Col. Docs.,* x. 97. It is here said that Stevens asked for a parley, in order to capitulate; but all the English accounts say that the French made the first advances.

Chapter 24

1745–1748
Fort Massachusetts

SINCE THE LAST WAR, the settlements of Massachusetts had pushed westward and begun to invade the beautiful region of mountains and valleys that now forms Berkshire. Villages, or rudiments of villages, had grown up on the Housatonic, and an establishment had been attempted at Pontoosuc, now Pittsfield, on the extreme western limits of the province. The position of these new settlements was critical, for the enemy could reach them with little difficulty by way of Lake Champlain and Wood Creek. The Massachusetts government was not unmindful of them, and when war again broke out, three wooden forts were built for their protection, forming a line of defence westward from Northfield on the northern frontier of the province. One of these forts was in the present town of Heath, and was called Fort Shirley; another, named Fort Pelham, was in the present town of Rowe; while the third, Fort Massachusetts, was farther westward, in what is now the town of Adams, then known as East Hoosac. Two hundred men from the militia were taken into pay to hold these posts and patrol the intervening forests. Other defensive works were made here and there, sometimes by the votes of town meetings, and sometimes by individuals, at their own cost. These works consisted of a fence of palisades enclosing a farmhouse, or sometimes of a blockhouse of timber or heavy planks. Thus, at Northfield, Deacon Ebenezer Alexander, a veteran of sixty who had served at Louisbourg, built a "mount," or blockhouse, on the knoll behind his house, and carried a stockade from it to enclose the dwelling, shed, and barn, the whole at the cost of thirty-six pounds, one shilling, and sixpence, in Massachusetts currency,[1] which the town

[1] Temple and Sheldon, *History of Northfield*, 237, give the items from the original account. This is one of the best of the innumerable town histories of New England.

repaid him, his fortifications being of public utility as a place of refuge for families in case of attack. Northfield was a place notoriously dangerous, and military methods were in vogue there in season and out of season. Thus, by a vote of the town, the people were called to the Sunday sermon by beat of drum, and Eleazer Holton was elected to sound the call in consideration of one pound and ten shillings a year, the drum being hired of Ensign Field, its fortunate possessor, for the farther sum of three shillings. This was in the earlier days of Northfield. In 1734 the Sunday drum-beat was stopped, and the worshippers were summoned by the less obstreperous method of "hanging out a flagg," for the faithful discharge of which function Daniel Wright received in 1744 one pound and five shillings.[2]

The various fortifications, public and private, were garrisoned, sometimes by the owner and his neighbors, sometimes by men in pay of the Provincial Assembly. As was to be expected from a legislative body undertaking warlike operations, the work of defence was but indifferently conducted. John Stoddard, the village magnate of Northampton, was charged, among the rest of his multifarious employments, with the locating and construction of forts; Captain Ephraim Williams was assigned to the general command on the western frontier, with headquarters at Fort Shirley and afterwards at Fort Massachusetts; and Major Israel Williams, of Hatfield, was made commissary.

At Northfield dwelt the Rev. Benjamin Doolittle, minister, apothecary, physician, and surgeon of the village; for he had studied medicine no less than theology. His parishioners thought that his cure of bodies encroached on his cure of souls, and requested him to confine his attention to his spiritual charge; to which he replied that he could not afford it, his salary as minister being seventy-five pounds in irredeemable Massachusetts paper, while his medical and surgical practice brought him full four hundred a year. He offered to comply with the wishes of his flock if they would add that amount to his salary,—which they were not prepared to do, and the minister continued his heterogeneous labors as before.

As the position of his house on the village street seems to have been regarded as strategic, the town voted to fortify it with a blockhouse and a stockade, for the benefit both of the occupant and of all the villagers. This was accordingly done, at the cost of eighteen pounds, seven shillings, and sixpence for the blockhouse, and a farther charge for the stockade; and thenceforth Mr. Doolittle could write his sermons and mix his doses in peace. To his other callings he added that of historiographer. When, after a ministry of thirty-six years, the thrifty pastor was busied one day with hammer and nails in mending the fence of his yard, he suddenly dropped dead from a stroke of heart-disease,—to the grief of all Northfield; and his papers being searched, a record was found in his handwriting of the inroads of the enemy that had happened in his time on or near the Massachusetts border. Being rightly thought worthy of publication, it was printed at Boston in a dingy pamphlet, now extremely rare, and much prized by antiquarians.[3]

Appended to it are the remarks of the author on the conduct of the war. He complains that plans are changed so often that none of them take effect; that terms of enlistment are so short that the commissary can hardly serve out provisions to the men before their time is expired; that neither bread, meat, shoes, nor blankets are kept on hand for an emergency, so that the enemy escape while the soldiers are getting ready to pursue them; that the pay of a drafted man is so small that twice as much would not hire a laborer to take care of his farm in his absence; and that untried and unfit persons are commissioned as officers: in all of which strictures there is no doubt much truth.

Mr. Doolittle's rueful narrative treats mainly of miscel-

[3] *A short Narrative of Mischief done by the French and Indian Enemy, on the Western Frontiers of the Province of the Massachusetts Bay; from the Beginning of the French War, proclaimed by the King of France, March 15th, 1743-4; and by the King of Great Britain, March 29th, 1744, to August 2nd, 1748. Drawn up by the Rev. Mr. Doolittle, of Northfield, in the County of Hampshire; and found among his Manuscripts after his Death. And at the Desire of some is now Published, with some small Additions to render it more perfect. Boston; Printed and sold by S. Kneeland, in Queen Street. MDCCL.*

The facts above given concerning Mr. Doolittle are drawn from the excellent *History of Northfield* by Temple and Sheldon, and the introduction to the *Particular History of the Five Years' French and Indian War*, by S. G. Drake.

laneous murders and scalpings, interesting only to the sufferers and their friends; but he also chronicles briefly a formidable inroad that still holds a place in New England history.

It may be remembered that Shirley had devised a plan for capturing Fort Frédéric, or Crown Point, built by the French at the narrows of Lake Champlain, and commanding ready access for war-parties to New York and New England.

The approach of D'Anville's fleet had defeated the plan; but rumors of it had reached Canada, and excited great alarm. Large bodies of men were ordered to Lake Champlain to protect the threatened fort. The two brothers De Muy were already on the lake with a numerous party of Canadians and Indians, both Christian and heathen, and Rigand de Vaudreuil, town-major of Three Rivers, was ordered to follow with a still larger force, repel any English attack, or, if none should be made, take the offensive and strike a blow at the English frontier. On the third of August, Rigaud[4] left Montreal with a fleet of canoes carrying what he calls his army, and on the twelfth he encamped on the east side of the lake, at the mouth of Otter Creek. There was rain, thunder, and a violent wind all night; but the storm ceased at daybreak, and, embarking again, they soon saw the octagonal stone tower of Fort Frédéric.

The party set up their tents and wigwams near the fort, and on the morning of the sixteenth the elder De Muy arrived with a band of Indians. They had just returned from an incursion towards Albany, and reported that all was quiet in those parts, and that Fort Frédéric was in no danger. Now, to their great satisfaction, Rigaud and his band saw themselves free to take the offensive. The question was, where to strike. The Indians held council after council, made speech after speech, and agreed on nothing. Rigaud gave them a wampum-belt, and told them that he meant to attack Corlaer,—that is, Schenectady; at which they seemed well pleased, and sang war-songs all night. In the morning they changed their minds, and begged him to call the whole army to a council for debating the question. It appeared that some of them, especially the Iroquois converts of Caughnawaga, disapproved of attacking

---

[4] French writers always call him Rigaud, to distinguish him from his brother, Pierre Rigaud de Vaudreuil-Cavagnal, afterwards governor of Canada, who is usually mentioned as Vaudreuil.

Schenectady, because some of their Mohawk relatives were always making visits there, and might be inadvertently killed by the wild western Indians of Rigaud's party. Now all was doubt again, for as Indians are unstable as water, it was no easy task to hold them to any plan of action.

The Abenakis proposed a solution of the difficulty. They knew the New England border well, for many of them had lived upon it before the war, on terms of friendly intercourse with the settlers. They now drew upon the floor of the council-room a rough map of the country, on which was seen a certain river, and on its upper waters a fort which they recommended as a proper object of attack. The river was that eastern tributary of the Hudson which the French called the Kaskékouké, the Dutch the Schaticook, and the English the Hoosac. The fort was Fort Massachusetts, the most westerly of the three posts lately built to guard the frontier. "My father," said the Abenaki spokesman to Rigaud, "it will be easy to take this fort, and make great havoc on the lands of the English. Deign to listen to your children and follow our advice."[5] One Cadenaret, an Abenaki chief, had been killed near Fort Massachusetts in the last spring, and his tribesmen were keen to revenge him. Seeing his Indians pleased with the proposal to march for the Hoosac, Rigaud gladly accepted it; on which whoops, yelps, and war-songs filled the air. Hardly, however, was the party on its way when the Indians changed their minds again, and wanted to attack Saratoga; but Rigaud told them that they had made their choice and must abide by it, to which they assented, and gave him no farther trouble.

On the twentieth of August they all embarked and paddled southward, passed the lonely promontory where Fort Ticonderoga was afterwards built, and held their course till the lake dwindled to a mere canal creeping through the weedy marsh then called the Drowned Lands. Here, nine summers later, passed the flotilla of Baron Dieskau, bound to defeat and ruin by the shores of Lake George. Rigaud stopped at a place known as East Bay, at the mouth of a stream that joins Wood Creek, just north of the present town of Whitehall. Here he left the younger De Muy, with thirty men, to guard

---

[5] *Journal de la Campagne de Rigaud de Vaudreuil en* 1746 . . . *présenté à Monseigneur le Comte de Maurepas, Ministre et Secrétaire d'État* (written by Rigaud).

the canoes. The rest of the party, guided by a brother of the slain Cadenaret, filed southward on foot along the base of Skene Mountain, that overlooks Whitehall. They counted about seven hundred men, of whom five hundred were French, and a little above two hundred were Indians.[6] Some other French reports put the whole number at eleven hundred, or even twelve hundred,[7] while several English accounts make it eight hundred or nine hundred. The Frenchmen of the party included both regulars and Canadians, with six regular officers and ten cadets, eighteen militia officers, two chaplains,—one for the whites and one for the Indians,—and a surgeon.[8]

After a march of four days, they encamped on the twenty-sixth by a stream which ran into the Hudson, and was no doubt the Batten Kill, known to the French as *la rivière de Saratogue*. Being nearly opposite Saratoga, where there was then a garrison, they changed their course, on the twenty-seventh, from south to southeast, the better to avoid scouting-parties, which might discover their trail and defeat their plan of surprise. Early on the next day they reached the Hoosac, far above its mouth; and now their march was easier, "for," says Rigaud, "we got out of the woods and followed a large road that led up the river." In fact, there seem to have been two roads, one on each side of the Hoosac; for the French were formed into two brigades, one of which, under the Sieur de la Valterie, filed along the right bank of the stream, and the other, under the Sieur de Sabrevois, along the left; while the Indians marched on the front, flanks, and rear. They passed deserted houses and farms belonging to Dutch settlers from the Hudson; for the Hoosac, in this part of its course, was in the province of New York.[9] They did not stop to burn barns and houses, but they killed poultry, hogs, a cow, and a horse, to supply themselves with meat. Before night they had

[6] "Le 19, ayant fait passer l'armée en Revue qui se trouva de 700 hommes, scavoir 500 françois environ et 200 quelques sauvages."—*Journal de Rigaud*.

[7] See *N. Y. Col. Docs.*, x. 103, 132.

[8] *Ibid.*, x. 35.

[9] These Dutch settlements on the Hoosac were made under what was called the "Hoosac Patent," granted by Governor Dongan of New York in 1688. The settlements were not begun till nearly forty years after the grant was made. For evidence on this point I am indebted to Professor A. L. Perry, of Williams College.

passed the New York line, and they made their camp in or near the valley where Williamstown and Williams College now stand. Here they were joined by the Sieurs Beaubassin and La Force, who had gone forward, with eight Indians, to reconnoitre. Beaubassin had watched Fort Massachusetts from a distance, and had seen a man go up into the watch-tower, but could discover no other sign of alarm. Apparently, the fugitive Dutch farmers had not taken pains to warn the English garrison of the coming danger, for there was a coolness between the neighbors.

Before breaking up camp in the morning, Rigaud called the Indian chiefs together and said to them: "My children, the time is near when we must get other meat than fresh pork, and we will all eat it together." "Meat," in Indian parlance, meant prisoners; and as these were valuable by reason of the ransoms paid for them, and as the Indians had suspected that the French meant to keep them all, they were well pleased with this figurative assurance of Rigaud that they should have their share.[10]

The chaplain said mass, and the party marched in a brisk rain up the Williamstown valley, till after advancing about ten miles they encamped again. Fort Massachusetts was only three or four miles distant. Rigaud held a talk with the Abenaki chiefs who had acted as guides, and it was agreed that the party should stop in the woods near the fort, make scaling-ladders, battering-rams to burst the gates, and other things needful for a grand assault, to take place before daylight; but their plan came to nought through the impetuosity of the young Indians and Canadians, who were so excited at the first glimpse of the watch-tower of the fort that they dashed forward, as Rigaud says, "like lions." Hence one might fairly expect to see the fort assaulted at once; but by the maxims of forest war this would have been reprehensible rashness, and nothing of the kind was attempted. The assailants spread to right and left, squatted behind stumps, and opened a distant and harmless fire, accompanied with unearthly yells and howlings.

[10] "Mes enfans, leur dis-je, le temps approche où il faut faire d'autre viande que le porc frais; au reste, nous la mangerons tous ensemble; se mot les flatta dans la crainte qu'ils avoient qu'après la prise du fort nous ne nous réservâmes tous les prisonniers."— *Journal de Rigaud.*

Fort Massachusetts was a wooden enclosure formed, like the fort at Number Four, of beams laid one upon another, and interlocked at the angles. This wooden wall seems to have rested, not immediately upon the ground, but upon a foundation of stone, designated by Mr. Norton, the chaplain, as the "underpinning,"—a name usually given in New England to foundations of the kind. At the northwest corner was a blockhouse,[11] crowned with the watch-tower, the sight of which had prematurely kindled the martial fire of the Canadians and Indians. This wooden structure, at the apex of the blockhouse, served as a lookout, and also supplied means of throwing water to extinguish fire-arrows shot upon the roof. There were other buildings in the enclosure, especially a large log-house on the south side, which seems to have overlooked the outer wall, and was no doubt loop-holed for musketry. On the east side there was a well, furnished probably with one of those long well-sweeps universal in primitive New England. The garrison, when complete, consisted of fifty-one men under Captain Ephraim Williams, who has left his name to Williamstown and Williams College, of the latter of which he was the founder. He was born at Newton, near Boston; was a man vigorous in body and mind; better acquainted with the world than most of his countrymen, having followed the seas in his youth, and visited England, Spain, and Holland; frank and agreeable in manners, well fitted for such a command, and respected and loved by his men.[12] When the proposed invasion of Canada was preparing, he and some of his men went to take part in it, and had not yet returned. The fort was left in charge of a sergeant, John Hawks, of Deerfield, with men too few for the extent of the works, and a supply of ammunition nearly exhausted. Canada being then put on the defensive, the frontier forts were thought safe for a time. On the Saturday before Rigaud's arrival, Hawks had sent Thomas Williams, the surgeon, brother of the absent captain, to Deer-

[11] The term "blockhouse" was loosely used, and was even sometimes applied to an entire fort when constructed of hewn logs, and not of palisades. The true blockhouse of the New England frontier was a solid wooden structure about twenty feet high, with a projecting upper story and loopholes above and below.

[12] See the notice of Williams in *Mass. Hist. Coll.*, viii. 47. He was killed in the bloody skirmish that preceded the Battle of Lake George in 1755. "Montcalm and Wolfe," chap. ix.

field, with a detachment of fourteen men, to get a supply of powder and lead. This detachment reduced the entire force, including Hawks himself and Norton, the chaplain, to twenty-two men, half of whom were disabled with dysentery, from which few of the rest were wholly free.[13] There were also in the fort three women and five children.[14]

The site of Fort Massachusetts is now a meadow by the banks of the Hoosac. Then it was a rough clearing, encumbered with the stumps and refuse of the primeval forest, whose living hosts stood grimly around it, and spread, untouched by the axe, up the sides of the neighboring Saddleback Mountain. The position of the fort was bad, being commanded by high ground, from which, as the chaplain tells us, "the enemy could shoot over the north side into the middle of the parade,"—for which serious defect, John Stoddard, of Northampton, legist, capitalist, colonel of militia, and "Superintendent of Defence," was probably answerable. These frontier forts were, however, often placed on low ground with a view to an abundant supply of water, fire being the most dreaded enemy in Indian warfare.[15]

[13] "Lord's day and Monday . . . the sickness was very distressing. . . . Eleven of our men were sick, and scarcely one of us in perfect health; almost every man was troubled with the griping and flux."—Norton, *The Redeemed Captive.*

[14] Rigaud erroneously makes the garrison a little larger. "La garnison se trouve de 24 hommes, entre lesquels il y avoit un ministre, 3 femmes, et 5 enfans." The names and residence of all the men in the fort when the attack began are preserved. Hawks made his report to the provincial government under the title "*An Account of the Company in his Majesty's Service under the command of Serg*^t. *John Hawks . . . at Fort Massachusetts, August* 20 [31, new style], 1746." The roll is attested on oath "Before William Williams, *Just. Pacis.*" The number of men is 22, including Hawks and Norton. Each man brought his own gun. I am indebted to the kindness of Professor A. L. Perry for a copy of Hawk's report, which is addressed to "the Honble. Spencer Phipps, Esq., Lieut. Govr. and Commander in Chief [and] the Honble his Majesty's Council and House of Representatives in General Court assembled."

[15] When I visited the place as a college student, no trace of the fort was to be seen except a hollow, which may have been the remains of a cellar, and a thriving growth of horse-radish,—a relic of the garrison garden. My friend, Dr. D. D. Slade, has given an

Sergeant Hawks, the provisional commander, was, according to tradition, a tall man with sunburnt features, erect, spare, very sinewy and strong, and of a bold and resolute temper. He had need to be so, for counting every man in the fort, lay and clerical, sick and well, he was beset by more than thirty times his own number; or, counting only his effective men, by more than sixty times,—and this at the lowest report of the attacking force. As there was nothing but a log fence between him and his enemy, it was clear that they could hew or burn a way through it, or climb over it with no surprising effort of valor. Rigaud, as we have seen, had planned a general assault under cover of night, but had been thwarted by the precipitancy of the young Indians and Canadians. These now showed no inclination to depart from the cautious maxims of forest warfare. They made a terrific noise, but when they came within gunshot of the fort, it was by darting from stump to stump with a quick zigzag movement that made them more difficult to hit than birds on the wing. The best moment for a shot was when they reached a stump, and stopped for an instant to duck and hide behind it. By seizing this fleeting opportunity, Hawks himself put a bullet into the breast of an Abenaki chief from St. Francis,—"which ended his days," says the chaplain. In view of the nimbleness of the assailants, a charge of buckshot was found more to the purpose than a bullet. Besides the slain Abenaki, Rigaud reports sixteen Indians and Frenchmen wounded,[16]—which, under the circumstances, was good execution for ten farmers and a minister; for Chaplain Norton loaded and fired with the rest. Rigaud himself was one of the wounded, having been hit in the arm and sent to the rear, as he stood giving orders on the rocky hill about forty rods from the fort. Probably it was a chance shot, since, though rifles were invented long before, they were not yet in general use, and the yeoman garrison were armed with nothing but their own smooth-bore hunting-pieces, not to be trusted at long range. The supply of ammunition had sunk so low that Hawks was forced to give the discouraging order not to fire except when necessary to keep the enemy in check, or when the chance of hitting him should be unusually

interesting account of the spot in the *Magazine of American History* for October, 1888.

[16] "L'Ennemi me tua un abenakis et me blessa 16 hommes, tant Iroquois qu'Abenaquis, nipissings et françois."—*Journal de Rigaud*.

good. Such of the sick men as were strong enough aided the defence by casting bullets and buckshot.

The outrageous noise lasted till towards nine in the evening, when the assailants greeted the fort with a general war-whoop, and repeated it three or four times; then a line of sentinels was placed around it to prevent messengers from carrying the alarm to Albany or Deerfield. The evening was dark and cloudy. The lights of a camp could be seen by the river towards the southeast, and those of another near the swamp towards the west. There was a sound of axes, as if the enemy were making scaling-ladders for a night assault; but it was found that they were cutting fagots to burn the wall. Hawks ordered every tub and bucket to be filled with water, in preparation for the crisis. Two men, John Aldrich and Jonathan Bridgman, had been wounded, thus farther reducing the strength of the defenders. The chaplain says: "Of those that were in health, some were ordered to keep the watch, and some lay down and endeavored to get some rest, lying down in our clothes with our arms by us. . . . We got little or no rest; the enemy frequently raised us by their hideous outcries, as though they were about to attack us. The latter part of the night I kept the watch."

Rigaud spent the night in preparing for a decisive attack, "being resolved to open trenches two hours before sunrise, and push them to the foot of the palisade, so as to place fagots against it, set them on fire, and deliver the fort a prey to the fury of the flames."[17] It began to rain, and he determined to wait till morning. That the commander of seven hundred French and Indians should resort to such elaborate devices to subdue a sergeant, seven militiamen, and a minister,—for this was now the effective strength of the besieged,—was no small compliment to the spirit of the defence.

The firing was renewed in the morning, but there was no attempt to open trenches by daylight. Two men were sent up into the watch-tower, and about eleven o'clock one of them, Thomas Knowlton, was shot through the head. The number

---

[17] "Je passay la nuit à conduire l'ouvrage auquel j'avois destiné le jour précédent, résolu à faire ouvrir la tranchée deux heures avant le lever du soleil, et de la pousser jusqu'au pied de la palissade, pour y placer les fascines, y appliquer l'artifice, et livrer le fort en proye à la fureur du feu."—*Journal de Rigaud*. He mistakes in calling the log wall of the fort a palisade.

of effectives was thus reduced to eight, including the chaplain. Up to this time the French and English witnesses are in tolerable accord; but now there is conflict of evidence. Rigaud says that when he was about to carry his plan of attack into execution, he saw a white flag hung out, and sent the elder De Muy, with Montigny and D'Auteuil, to hear what the English commandant—whose humble rank he nowhere mentions—had to say. On the other hand, Norton, the chaplain, says that about noon the French "desired to parley," and that "we agreed to it." He says farther that the sergeant, with himself and one or two others, met Rigaud outside the gate, and that the French commander promised "good quarter" to the besieged if they would surrender, with the alternative of an assault if they would not. This account is sustained by Hawks, who says that at twelve o'clock an Indian came forward with a flag of truce, and that he, Hawks, with two or three others, went to meet Rigaud, who then offered honorable terms of capitulation.[18] The sergeant promised an answer within two hours; and going back to the fort with his companions, examined their means of defence. He found that they had left but three or four pounds of gunpowder, and about as much lead. Hawks called a council of his effective men. Norton prayed for divine aid and guidance, and then they fell to considering the situation. "Had we all been in health, or had there been only those eight of us that were in health, I believe every man would willingly have stood it out to the last. For my part, I should," writes the manful chaplain. But besides the sick and wounded, there were three women and five children, who, if the fort were taken by assault, would no doubt be butchered by the Indians, but who might be saved by a capitulation. Hawks therefore resolved to make the best terms he could. He had defended his post against prodigious odds for twenty-eight hours. Rigaud promised that all in the fort should be treated with humanity as prisoners of war, and exchanged at the first opportunity. He also promised that none of them should be given to the Indians, though he had lately assured his savage allies that they should have their share of the prisoners.

[18] *Journal of Sergeant Hawks,* cited by William L. Stone, *Life and Times of Sir William Johnson,* i. 227. What seems conclusive is that the French permitted Norton to nail to a post of the fort a short account of its capture, in which it is plainly stated that the first advances were made by Rigaud.

At three o'clock the principal French officers were admitted into the fort, and the French flag was raised over it. The Indians and Canadians were excluded; on which some of the Indians pulled out several of the stones that formed the foundation of the wall, crawled through, opened the gates, and let in the whole crew. They raised a yell when they saw the blood of Thomas Knowlton trickling from the watch-tower where he had been shot, then rushed up to where the corpse lay, brought it down, scalped it, and cut off the head and arms. The fort was then plundered, set on fire, and burned to the ground.

The prisoners were led to the French camp; and here the chaplain was presently accosted by one Doty, Rigaud's interpreter, who begged him to persuade some of the prisoners to go with the Indians. Norton replied that it had been agreed that they should all remain with the French; and that to give up any of them to the Indians would be a breach of the capitulation. Doty then appealed to the men themselves, who all insisted on being left with the French, according to the terms stipulated. Some of them, however, were given to the Indians, who, after Rigaud's promise to them, could have been pacified in no other way. His fault was in making a stipulation that he could not keep. Hawks and Norton, with all the women and children, remained in the French camp.

Hearing that men were expected from Deerfield to take the places of the sick, Rigaud sent sixty Indians to cut them off. They lay in wait for the English reinforcement, which consisted of nineteen men, gave them a close fire, shot down fifteen of them, and captured the rest.[19] This or another party of Rigaud's Indians pushed as far as Deerfield and tried to waylay the farmers as they went to their work on a Monday morning. The Indians hid in a growth of alder-bushes along the edge of a meadow where men were making hay, accompanied by some children. One Ebenezer Hawks, shooting partridges, came so near the ambushed warriors that they could not resist the temptation of killing and scalping him. This alarmed the haymakers and the children, who ran for their lives towards a mill on a brook that entered Deerfield River, fiercely pursued by about fifty Indians, who caught and

[19] One French account says that the Indians failed to meet the English party. *N. Y. Col. Docs.* x. 35.

scalped a boy named Amsden. Three men, Allen, Sadler, and Gillet, got under the bank of the river and fired on the pursuers. Allen and Gillet were soon killed, but Sadler escaped unhurt to an island. Three children of Allen—Eunice, Samuel, and Caleb—were also chased by the Indians, who knocked down Eunice with a tomahawk, but were in too much haste to stop and scalp her, and she lived to a good old age. Her brother Samuel was caught and dragged off, but Caleb ran into a field of tall maize, and escaped.

The firing was heard in the village, and a few armed men, under Lieutenant Clesson, hastened to the rescue; but when they reached the spot the Indians were gone, carrying the boy Samuel Allen with them, and leaving two of their own number dead. Clesson, with such men as he had, followed their trail up Deerfield River, but could not overtake the light-footed savages.

Meanwhile, the prisoners at Fort Massachusetts spent the first night, well guarded, in the French and Indian camps. In the morning, Norton, accompanied by a Frenchman and several Indians, was permitted to nail to one of the charred posts of the fort a note to tell what had happened to him and his companions.[20] The victors then marched back as they had come, along the Hoosac road. They moved slowly, encumbered as they were by the sick and wounded. Rigaud gave the Indians presents, to induce them to treat their prisoners with humanity. Norton was in charge of De Muy, and after walking four miles sat down with him to rest in Williamstown valley. There was a yell from the Indians in the rear. "I trembled," writes Norton, "thinking they had murdered some of our people, but was filled with admiration when I saw all our prisoners come up with us, and John Aldrich carried on the back of his Indian master." Aldrich had been shot in the foot

[20] The note was as follows: "August 20 [31, new style], 1746. These are to inform you that yesterday, about 9 of the clock, we were besieged by, as they say, seven hundred French and Indians. They have wounded two men and killed one Knowlton. The General de Vaudreuil desired capitulations, and we were so distressed that we complied with his terms. We are the French's prisoners, and have it under the general's hand that every man, woman, and child shall be exchanged for French prisoners."

and could not walk. "We set out again, and had gone but a little way before we came up with Josiah Reed." Reed was extremely ill, and could go no farther. Norton thought that the Indians would kill him, instead of which one of them carried him on his back. They were said to have killed him soon after, but there is good reason to think that he died of disease. "I saw John Perry's wife," pursues the chaplain; "she complained that she was almost ready to give out." The Indians threatened her, but Hawks spoke in her behalf to Rigaud, who remonstrated with them, and they afterwards treated her well. The wife of another Soldier, John Smead, was near her time, and had lingered behind. The French showed her great kindness. "Some of them made a seat for her to sit upon, and brought her to the camp, where, about ten o'clock, she was gracioulsy delivered of a daughter, and was remarkably well. . . . Friday: this morning I baptized John Smead's child. He called its name *Captivity*." The French made a litter of poles, spread over it a deerskin and a bear-skin, on which they placed the mother and child, and so carried them forward. Three days after, there was a heavy rain, and the mother was completely drenched, but suffered no harm, though "Miriam, the wife of Moses Scott, hereby catched a grievous cold." John Perry was relieved of his pack, so that he might help his wife and carry her when her strength failed. Several horses were found at the farms along the way, and the sick Benjamin Simons and the wounded John Aldrich were allowed to use two of them. Rarely, indeed, in these dismal border-raids were prisoners treated so humanely; and the credit seems chiefly due to the efforts of Rigaud and his officers. The hardships of the march were shared by the victors, some of whom were sorely wounded; and four Indians died within a few days.

"I divided my army between the two sides of the Kaské-kouké" (Hoosac), says Rigaud, "and ordered them to do what I had not permitted to be done before we reached Fort Massachusetts. Every house was set on fire, and numbers of domestic animals of all sorts were killed. French and Indians vied with each other in pillage, and I made them enter the [valleys of all the] little streams that flow into the Kaské-kouké and lay waste everything there. . . . Wherever we went we made the same havoc, laid waste both sides of the river, through twelve leagues of fertile country, burned houses, barns, stables, and even a meeting-house,—in all, above two hundred establishments,—killed all the cattle, and ruined all the crops. Such, Monseigneur, was the damage I did our enemies during the eight or nine days I was in their country."[21] As the Dutch settlers had escaped, there was no resistance.

The French and their allies left the Hoosac at the point where they had reached it, and retraced their steps northward through the forest, where there was an old Indian trial. Recrossing the Batten Kill, or "River of Saratoga," and some branches of Wood Creek, they reached the place where they had left their canoes, and found them safe. Rigaud says: "I gave leave to the Indians, at their request, to continue their fighting and ravaging, in small parties, towards Albany, Schenectady, Deerfield, Saratoga, or wherever they pleased, and I even gave them a few officers and cadets to lead them." These small ventures were more or less successful, and produced, in due time, a good return of scalps.

The main body, now afloat again, sailed and paddled northward till they reached Crown Point. Rigaud rejoiced at finding a haven of refuge, for his wounded arm was greatly inflamed: "and it was time I should reach a place of repose." He and his men encamped by the fort and remained there for some time. An epidemic, apparently like that at Fort Massachusetts, had broken out among them, and great numbers were seriously ill.

Norton was lodged in a French house on the east side of the lake, at what is now called Chimney Point; and one day his guardian, De Muy, either thinking to impress him with the strength of the place, or with an amusing confidence in the minister's incapacity for making inconvenient military observations, invited him to visit the fort. He accepted the invitation, crossed over with the courteous officer, and reports the ramparts to have been twenty feet thick, about twenty feet high, and mounted with above twenty cannon. The octagonal tower which overlooked the ramparts, and answered in some sort to the donjon of a feudal castle, was a bomb-proof structure in vaulted masonry, of the slaty black limestone of the neighborhood, three stories in height, and armed with nine

[21] *Journal de Rigaud.*

or ten cannon, besides a great number of patereroes,—a kind of pivot-gun much like a swivel.[22]

In due time the prisoners reached Montreal, whence they were sent to Quebec; and in the course of the next year those who remained alive were exchanged and returned to New England.[23] Mrs. Smead and her infant daughter "Captivity" died in Canada, and, by a singular fatality, her husband had scarcely returned home when he was waylaid and killed by Indians. Fort Massachusetts was soon rebuilt by the province, and held its own thenceforth till the war was over. Sergeant Hawks became a lieutenant-colonel, and took a creditable part in the last French war.

For two years after the incursion of Rigaud the New England borders were scourged with partisan warfare, bloody, monotonous, and futile, with no event that needs recording, and no result beyond a momentary check to the progress of settlement. At length, in July, 1748, news came that the chief contending powers in Europe had come to terms of agreement, and in the next October the Peace of Aix-la-Chapelle was signed. Both nations were tired of the weary and barren conflict, with its enormous cost and its vast entail of debt. It was agreed that conquests should be mutually restored. The chief conquest of England was Louisbourg, with the island of Cape Breton,—won for her by the farmers and fishermen of New England. When the preliminaries of peace were under discussion, Louis XV. had demanded the restitution of the lost fortress; and George II. is said to have replied that it was not his to give, having been captured by the people of Boston.[24] But his sense of justice was forced to yield to diplomatic necessity, for Louisbourg was the indispensable price of peace. To the indignation of the northern provinces, it was restored to its former owners. "The British ministers," says

[22] Kalm also describes the fort and its tower. Little trace of either now remains. Amherst demolished them in 1759, when he built the larger fort, of which the ruins still stand on the higher ground behind the site of its predecessor.

[23] Of the twenty-two men in the fort when attacked, one, Knowlton, was killed by a bullet; one, Reed, died after the surrender; ten died in Canada, and ten returned home. *Report of Sergeant Hawks.*

[24] *N. Y. Col. Docs.,* x. 147.

Smollett, "gave up the important island of Cape Breton in exchange for a petty factory in the East Indies" (Madras), and the King deigned to send two English noblemen to the French court as security for the bargain.

Peace returned to the tormented borders; the settlements advanced again, and the colonists found a short breathing space against the great conclusive struggle of the Seven Years' War.

Appendix

ALL THE FOLLOWING correspondence is from the Public Record Office: America and West Indies.

SHIRLEY TO NEWCASTLE, 14 DEC., 1745.
(*Extract.*)

". . . Having lately procur'd from Fort Major Phillips of Annapolis Royal the late Lieutenant Governor Armstrong's Original Instrument mention'd in my late State of the Province of Nova Scotia to be given by him to the French Inhabitants of that Province, by virtue of which and of another of the same tenour given 'em by him in 1730, they claim an Exemption from bearing Arms is defence of his Majesty's Government, I inclose your Grace a Copy of it. Mr. Phillips in his letter inclosing this Instrument to me observes that the 'Inhabitants of Nova Scotia at the first news of Louisbourg's being surrendred were in great Consternation and at Minas in particular they appear'd in Tears in the Publick Places, where nine months before they had assisted in singing Te Deum, on a false report that Annapolis Royal was surrendred to Monsieur Duvivier.' He goes on to say that a report was spread there that Monsieur Duvivier was arriv'd at Canada with rigging for two Men of War, and the Renommée a French thirty gun Ship with two Prizes at Quebec. And all the Nova Scotia Priests were gone to Canada for Instructions; and give out that there are 2000 Canadeans at Chignecto waiting ready for another attempt against his Majesty's Garrison. To which I would beg leave to subjoin that it seems to me far from being improbable that the French will Attempt the reduction of Nova Scotia early in the Spring, by gaining which they will have a fine provision Country to assemble 8 or 10,000 fighting men and all the tribes of Indians ready to join in an attempt against Louisbourg at a few days Warning as I observ'd to your Grace in a late Letter; But if they should not attempt Louisbourg they would irresistably break up all the Eastern Settlements of this Province and I doubt not the whole Province of New Hampshire it self, which would make 'em masters of all Mast Country and Naval Stores and of a rich Soil for Corn as well as Cattle and this would also enable 'em to make deep impressions on all the Western frontier of this Province, New York and Connecticut, and, how far they might penetrate is not Certain but so far at least as might make it very difficult to dislodge 'em and give 'em such an hold of the Continent as to make 'em think in time of pushing with the assistance of the Indians for the Mastery of it, which is richly worth contending for with all their might as it would in their hands lay the surest foundation for an Universal Monarchy by Sea and Land that ever a people had. This train of Consequences from the Enemies being Masters of Nova Scotia may seem remote, my Lord, but they are not impossible, and it may be very difficult for the French to regain Louisbourg at least without being Masters of Nova Scotia, and that seems under the present Circumstances of the Garrison where no recruits are yet Arriv'd from England and the Inhabitants of the Country Surrounding it are Enemies in their hearts no difficult acquisition and to be made with a small Train of Artillery in three weeks at farthest. I would submit it to your Grace's consideration whether the Garrison should not be reinforc'd as soon as may be. And the Inhabitants should not be forthwith put upon a good foot of Subjection and fidelity. Thus in obedience to your Grace's Direction I have troubled you with my whole sentiments concerning the Province of Nova Scotia which as I can't think it probable that the French will sleep the next year after the blow we have given 'em at Louisbourg (which, if they don't recover it soon by retaking Cape Breton or getting Nova Scotia will prove their Death wound in North America) seems to be most likely to be attack'd by 'em of any place in these parts, and I hope your Grace will excuse my Repetition of the Danger of it.

> "I am with the most Dutiful Regards,
> "My Lord Duke,
> "Your Grace's most Obed^t.
> "and most Devoted Servant
> "W. SHIRLEY."

SHIRLEY TO NEWCASTLE, 11 FEB. 1746.
(*Extract.*)

"MY LORD DUKE.

"Since my last to your Grace I have received the Inclos'd packett from Mr. Mascarene Containing a Representation of the State of Nova Scotia from himself and his Majesty's Council of that Province with a copy of a Letter from him to me, Showing the reasons of his late Conduct towards the French Inhabitants; Your Grace will perceive that this representation is drawn up in Stronger Terms against the Inhabitants than mine; I could wish the Gentlemen had been more Explicit in what they would Recommend as the most adviseable Method of Securing his Majesty's Government within the Province and against the French Inhabitants—But as that is not done except in Short hints, And Mr. Little, to whom both Mr. Mascarene and Mr. Secretary Shirreff referr me for a Larger Account of the Sentiments of the Gentlemen of the Garrison concerning these Matters, Offers his Service to go with my dispatches to England and return directly with any Orders his Majesty may be pleased to give thereupon, I have sent him to wait upon your Grace, and it is possible that when he is upon the Spot ready to Answer any Questions, it may be of Service—Having before troubled your Grace So Largely upon this head, I will beg leave to referr to my former Letters, Mr. Little Mr. Agent Kilby and Mr. Bollan, which two last can, I believe, give Considerable Light on the affair; And shall only add that the Spring before last the Garrison was very narrowly Saved from the Enemy by the Arrival of the New England Auxiliaries, and the last Spring, by the Expedition against Cape Breton, that the preservation of it this Spring will be of the Utmost Importance to his Majesty's Service in America, and that nothing will more effectually Secure that than putting the Inhabitants upon a proper foot of Subjection, in the most Speedy Manner, to prevent their Revolt, which Cannot be done without his Majesty's Special directions for that purpose; for the procuring of which, I find Mr. Mascarene, and his whole Council have a dependance upon me; the Language of their Several Letters being that they *Commit themselves to my Care;* and will take no step without my Advice or approbation, which has been the Case for above these last two years, And I mention to your Grace in Excuse for my being So importunate in the Affairs of another Government, which the Gentlemen of the Garrison lay me Under a Necessity of being; And I am further Urg'd to this by the late Accounts, wch. Mr. Mascarene and the other Gentlemen have sent me of the Appearance of four hundred Indians well Cloathed, Arm'd, and Supply'd with Stores from Canada near St. Johns River, Seventeen French Officers being Seen among 'em, and another Body of French in the Neighbourhood of the Province, and Reports that Mr. Duvivier in the Parfaite Man of Warr, and another Ship of Force were at Qubec with Stores, and another was seen to put into St. Johns Island; That the Priests who went to Canada for Instructions are returned with Supplies and large promises to the Indians (before well dispos'd and upon the point of putting themselves under Our protection on the taking of Louisbourg) and Encouragements for the Inhabitants to depend upon a powerfull force against the Fort at Annapolis Royal this Spring. These alarms indeed have been Something Allay'd by Letters from the Deputies of Minas and other Districts to Mr. Mascarene, which for my own part I have no great dependance upon.

"But it seems plain upon the whole, that the French are making the Utmost Efforts to retain the Indians of those parts in their Interest, and gaining over the Inhabitants of Nova Scotia, So that the Taking of Speedy measures for Securing these last and gaining over the former which will depend upon that, as the preservation of Nova Scotia does upon both, is a Matter of the Highest Consequence.

"Upon this Occasion it seems necessary for me to apprise your Grace, that Mr. Mascarene and his Council have not So good an harmony Subsisting between them as could be wish'd, and that all the Officers have of late differ'd in Sentiments with him particularly upon the Behaviour of the French Inhabitants, Concerning whom he indeed has himself alter'd his Opinion in Some measure; But I think there may be Still danger of too much tenderness towards 'em on his part, and perhaps rigour on theirs in carrying any Orders of his Majesty's into Execution; So that by their Jarring, the Execution of the Orders may possibly be Obstructed, if they are left to themselves

"Wherefore if their Chief Governour's Age and health,

and other Circumstances would have permitted him to have been Upon the Spott, and Assisted in this Service, it would I believe have been for the Advantage of it, for him to have made 'em a short Visit at least this year, And if it could have been repeated for the two or three proceeding years it would have been still more so. . . ."

SHIRLEY TO NEWCASTLE, 10TH MAY, 1746.
(*Extract.*)

". . . I think it my indispensable duty to suggest again to Your Grace my Fears that the Enemy will soon find an opportunity of snatching Accadie by some Sudden Stroke from his Majesty's Government unless the danger is re-mov'd out of the Heart of it there by a Removal of the most dangerous of the french Inhabitants from thence, & transplanting English Families there in their room, which I think very practicable from hence, having lately found means of transplanting upwards, I believe, of an hundred Families from the Province to Louisbourg towards the Settlement of it, which yet I dont esteem of such Importance to be immediately done as the Settlement of Nova Scotia with faithful Subjects.

"In the meanwhile 'till this can be happily effected & the Indians in those parts secur'd in the English Interest, I have propos'd to Mr. Warren that a Detachment of 100 Men should be sent from Louisbourg to reinforce the garrison at Annapolis Royal, since the late Miscarriage of 182 out of 302 of the Recruits designed for Annapolis in their Passage from England to the garrison there. Ninety-six of the Remainder of 'em, which came in here, I with difficulty have got recovered in his Majesty's Castle William & at the Hospital in Boston, & sent a month ago to Annapolis where I hear they are safely arriv'd, and twenty more who are in a fair way of being serviceable, I shall send from the Hospital within three days But the Garrison will still be weak as Mr. Mascarene has dismiss'd most of the New England Auxiliaries, and they have not, I am informed, 220 effective private Men left besides their Artificers & Workmen: I have also recommended to Mr. Warren the frequent Sending of a Ship of War to look into the Bason of Annapolis & make the Garrison there a short Visit in order to prevent a

Surprise & by his Opinion in Concurrence with Sir Willm Pepperrell's, Mr. Mascarene's & my own a Sloop has been hir'd & employ'd for about these last four Months to attend upon that garrison, & carry Intelligence between Annapolis Royal, Louisbourg & Boston concerning the State of it & the Enemy's Motions which we conceiv'd necessary to be done for its Security, and hope your Grace will not disapprove of.

"What Mr. Frontenac observed some years ago to Mr Pontchartrain concerning the french King's recovering of Accadie & making himself absolute Master of the great Bank [of Newfoundland] as in the inclos'd Extract of his Letter, seems so seasonable to be consider'd at this time, that I would beg leave to observe to your Grace upon it, that his Maj^ty's holding the Possession of Annapolis Royal & Newfoundland (already conceded to his Crown by the Treaty of Utrecht) with his late Acquisition of Cape Breton, will put the whole Cod Fishery more in his Power than Mr Frontenac's Scheme could have put it into the French Kings, and that besides what Mr Frontenac calls a Commerce more advantageous than the Conquest of the Indies, and computes the Returns of at twenty Millions (I suppose french Livres) per annum, it would furnish his Majesty with as good a Nursery of Seamen for the Royal Navy as the Colliery in England does, not to mention the great consumption of British Manufactures which must be occasioned in carrying the Fishery on;—that the holding of Annapolis Royal in particular will be establishing to his Majesty the Mastery of the Northern Part of this Continent against the French, Secure to him inexhaustible Nurseries of Masts, Yards, Bowsprits & other Stores for his Navy, & Timber for Ship building within his Northern Colonies independent of any foreign State to be purchased with British Manufacturers & transported in British Vessels—that the Inhabitants of the Northern Colonies would in time make such an Addition of Subjects to the Crown of Great Britain as would make their number Superior to that of any Prince's upon the Continent of Europe; and in the meanwhile the Vent of Woolen & other British Manufactures, & all Kinds of European Commodities imported into the Colonies from Great Britain must increase in proportion to the Increase of their Inhabitants: by all which means the main Sources of Wealth, & a larger Extent of Power by Sea

& Land than any State in Christendom at present enjoys,
seems capable of being secur'd to his Maj^{ty's} Dominions;
But which will in the End otherwise be in all human Probability the Lot of the french Dominions; And I would in
particular observe to your Grace the most practicable Step
the Enemy can attempt making towards their obtaining that
seems clearly to be their rendring themselves Masters of
Nova Scotia, the Consequences of wch would give 'em so
strong an hold upon this Continent as would make it
difficult to dislodge 'em & put it very much in their Power
to harrass & annoy his Maj^{tys} Colonies both by Land & Sea,
in such manner as to weaken 'em extremely, if not by degrees finally subdue 'em.

> "I am with the most dutiful Regards,
> "My Lord Duke,
> "Your Grace's most devoted
> "and obedient Servant
> "W. SHIRLEY."

SHIRLEY TO NEWCASTLE, 31 MAY, 1746.
(*Extract.*)

". . . I would beg Leave to observe to your Grace, y^t the
Danger to his Majesty's garrison arises chiefly from within
the heart of the government itself, the Inhabitants & neighboring Indians whose Numbers are sufficient of themselves
with a small assistance from Canada & the help of a proper
Train of Artillery, slipt up the Bay in small Vessels (w^{ch}
would give 'em great Encouragement to take up Arms ag^t
the garrison) to reduce it. However while the Attempt
against Canada is depending, that will certainly go far towards holding the Inhabitants of Nova Scotia in suspense,
till the success of it is known; & I hope by next Spring they
may either be put upon a better foot of Subjection, or the
most dangerous among 'em removed. . . ."

SHIRLEY TO NEWCASTLE, 18 JUNE, 1746.
(*Extract.*)

". . . I may assure your Grace y^t. one of the principal
motives I had to desire I might succeed General Phillips
in his Command, was the hopes I have of it's putting it in
my power to promote his Majesty's Service in his Province

of Acadie, or Nova Scotia by securing the fidelity & Allegiance of the Inhabitants there to his Majesty's Government in the best manner, and thereby preventing the French from making themselves masters of it, the Acquisition of wch. to them with the help of the Indians would likewise endanger the Loss of the Province of New Hampshire & the Mast Country to his Majesty with the Fishery of the Acadie or Cape Sable's Shoar, including that of Canso, to his Subjects here in present, & should not Canada be reduc'd, would enable the enemy to harrass & Diminish all his Majesty's Colonies & on the Continent, & have an inevitable Tendency to make themselves masters of the whole of it in time; not to mention the Continual Danger, wch. their possession of Nova Scotia would at the same time expose Cape Breton & even Newfoundland to.

"The Considerations have induc'd me to take the Liberty of submitting it to your Grace, whether it might not be for his Majesty's Service, that before the six Regiments to be employ'd ag^{t}. Canada return to England, orders may be sent that such part of 'em as shall be thought necessary to assist in removing the most obnoxious of the French Inhabitants of Nova Scotia from thence, should be employ'd in that Service, wch. would not take up much time; I am not certain whether a sufficient Strength might not be spar'd from the Garrison at Louisbourg a short time for this purpose, wch. if it could, would make the Assistance of any other Troops needless.

"And I would particularly submit it to your Grace's Consideration, whether in case of any Disappointment in the present Attempt for the reduction of Canada, the immediate removal of some at least of the French Inhabitants of Nova Scotia, & securing the province in the best manner would not be . . . adviseable and even necessary.

"If your Grace should think this deserves so much of your Attention there will be time enough for transmitting his Majesty's Commands to me upon it before the present Expedition is over.

> "I am with the most Dutifull Regard
> "My Lord Duke
> "Your Grace's most Devoted
> "& most obedient Servant
> "W. SHIRLEY."

SHIRLEY TO NEWCASTLE, 28 JULY, 1746.
(*Extract.*)

"I must acknowledge I should rather apprehend the
french Fleet (if it is design'd for North America) is order'd
to Canada; or else to Annapolis Royal, where the Enemy
may depend that upon the Appearance of such an Armament the french Inhabitants of Nova Scotia (to the Amount
of between 5 & 6000 fighting men) and a considerable
Number of Indians & some Canadeans, would immediately
join 'em, and they would have a most convenient Country
to rendezvous in within a very few days sail of Chap-
peaurouge Bay at Cape Breton, and be not far from
Canada, than that they should attempt to enter Louisbourg
Harbour with their Ships; and I am the more inclin'd to
this Opinion from the Accounts I have receiv'd lately from
Mr Mascarene, and the Officers of the Garrison at Annapolis Royal which inform me that the french Inhabitants at
Menis & Schiegneto (in Nova Scotia) have cut off all communication with the garrison for these last five Weeks, and
have stop'd the Messengers sent from thence by Mr Mascarene for Intelligence; being in Expectation of an Armament from France; And indeed it seems probable that this
will for ever be the Case; and that the Province of Nova
Scotia will never be out of Danger, whilst the french Inhabitants are suffer'd to remain in Nova Scotia upon their
present Foot of Subjection."

SHIRLEY TO NEWCASTLE, 15 AUG. 1746.
(*Extract.*)

"I shall finish my troubleing your Grace upon the Affairs
of Nova Scotia with this Letter after having once more
Submitted it to your Grace's Consideration as a proper
Scheme for better securing the Subjection of the French
Inhabitants and Indians there; that the Governor &
Council or such other Person or Persons as his Majesty
shall think fitt to join with 'em, should have a special
authority and directions from his Majesty, forthwith to
Apprehend & Examine a convenient number of such of
the Inhabitants, as shall be by them judg'd to be most
obnoxious & Dangerous to his Majesty's Government, &

upon finding 'em guilty of holding any treasonable Correspondence with the Enemy &c to dispose of them & their Estates in such manner, as his Majesty shall order by his Commissions and to promise his Majesty's Gracious Pardon & a general Indemnity to the Rest for what is past upon their taking the Oaths of Allegiance to his Majesty; And to Cause either two strong Blockhouses (or small Forts) capable of holding 100 Men each to be Built, one in Menis & the other in Schiegnecto, which may be Garrison'd out of Phillip's Regiment when Compleated, or else that at least one Blockhouse (or small Fort) should be Built at Menis capable of holding 150 men; and a trading house be kept at the Fort at Menis or some other part of the Province well Stock'd with all proper Supplies for the Indians to be sold or barter'd to 'em for Furrs &c at the most reasonable Rates, and some presents annually distributed to 'em: by which means and removing the Romish Priests out of the Province, & introducing Protestant English Schools, and French Protestant Ministers, and due encouragement given to such of the Inhabitants, as shall Conform to the Protestant Religion, and send their Children to the English Schools, the present Inhabitants might probably at least be kept in Subjection to his Majesty's Government, and from treasonable correspondencies with the Canadians; and the next Generation in a great measure become true Protestant Subjects; and the Indians there soon Reclaim'd to an entire dependance upon & subjection to his Majesty; which might also have an happy Influence upon some of the Tribes now in the French Interest.

> "Your Grace will be pleas'd to Excuse all
> "Incorrectness in this rough Sketch.
> "I am with the most Dutiful Regard,
> "My Lord Duke,
> "Your Grace's most Devoted &
> "Most Obedient Servant
> "W. SHIRLEY."

SHIRLEY TO MASCARENE, BOSTON, SEPT^R. 16, 1746.

"SIR,
"Having been inform'd that the french Inhabitants of Nova Scotia entertain some Jealousy of a Design in the

English Government to remove them with their Families from their Settlements, & transport them to France or elsewhere; I desire (if you think it may be for his Majesty's Service) that you would be pleas'd to signify to 'em, that it is probable if his Majesty had declar'd such Intention I might have heard of the same, but that I am perfectly unacquainted with any such Design, and am perswaded there is no just Ground for this Jealousy; And be pleas'd to assure 'em that I shall use my best Endeavours by a proper Representation of their Case to be laid before his Majesty, to obtain the Continuance of his Royal Favour & Protection to such of them, as shall behave dutifully, & refuse to hold any Correspondence with his Enemies; and I doubt not but that all such of 'em will be protected by his Majesty in the Possession of their Estates & Settlements in Nova Scotia.

"And I desire you would also be pleas'd to inform them that it is expected from his Maj^tys french Subjects in that Province, who have for so long time enjoyed the same Privileges with his natural born Subjects there, & have been under a much easier Government than any of the french King's Subjects are in the neighbouring Province of Canada & other Parts of the french King's Dominions, that their Interest as well as their Duty and Gratitude should bind them to a strict Fidelity & Obedience to his Majesty and His Government; But on the contrary if any of the Inhabitants of the said Province shall join with the Enemy (especially those that have been sent from Canada to seduce them from their Duty to his Majesty & Attachment to the English Interest) they must expect to be treated in the same manner as his Majesty's English Subjects would be under the like Provocations.

"I am with great regard

"Sir ,

"Your most obedient

"humble servant

"W. Shirley."

Shirley to Newcastle, Boston, September 19, 1746.

"My Lord Duke,

"I express'd some hopes in my last but one to your Grace, that I should not be oblig'd to add to my former

Accounts of the imminent danger, his Majesty's Province of Nova Soctia was in of being surpriz'd by the Enemy; But find my self under a Necessity of doing it from the Advices which I have since receiv'd from M^r. Mascarene, and the Intelligence contain'd in three Declarations upon Oath, Copies of all which are inclos'd.

"Upon the Receipt of M^r. Mascaene's Letter, the Contents of which are confirm'd to me by other authentick Accounts, it appear'd to me that there was no room to doubt but that a considerable Body of French and Indians from Canada was assembled in Nova Scotia, with Expectations of a Reinforcement from France; and if they fail'd of that this Year a Design of at least wintering in Minas or some other Part of the Country, by which means they would have an Opportunity of fortifying themselves in it, transporting their great artillery (which there was then the utmost reason to believe they had landed either at Bay Verte or Chebucto Harbour) to Annapolis, and work upon the French Inhabitants already ripe for a Revolt to join 'em in attacking his Majesty's Garrison there so early in the Spring that it would be extremely difficult if not impracticable to relieve it by any Succours either from Louisbourg or the Colonies on the Continent. Whereupon I immediately sent M^r. Mascarene an Assurance that I would send him as soon as possible 300 of the new Levies from this Province, 200 of 'em (which seems to be as many as the Garrison can hold at present besides the Troops already there) for the Reinforcement of it, and 100 of 'em to be employ'd in two Sloops up the Bay in the manner M^r. Mascarene proposes in his Letter to me, and that I would do the utmost in my Power to make the number up 2000 soon afterwards, in order to dislodge the Enemy, & prevent 'em from wintering in the Province; And in the mean time upon my advising with Rear Admiral Warren (who is still here) he immediately sent his Majesty's Ship Chester a 50 Gun Ship to Annapolis Royal for the further Countenance & Protection of the Garrison there.

"Some Days after this I receiv'd Information that a Fleet of upwards of 30 sail were discover'd about 15 Leagues to the Westward of Chibucto Harbour, which lies upon the Cape Sable Shoar (the Coast of Accadie or Nova Scotia) about 150 Leagues to the Eastward of Boston, and about

60 Leagues Westward of Louisbourg, & about 80 distant from Annapolis Royal according to Champions inclos'd Deposition, which was confirm'd by another of the same Tenour made by one Thornton sent me from Piscataqua, upon which I dispatched an arm'd Brigantine with orders to look into Chibucto Harbour, & if the Master should discover any thing to proceed directly to Louisbourg, & give Vice Admiral Townsend & Govern^r. Knowles Intelligence of it, & to send me Advice of it Express by some fishing Vessel taken up at Sea; But the Brigantine return'd in less than 24 hours with one Stanwood a Fisherman on board, whose Vessel fell in with the Fleet on the 9th. day of Septr. about 10 Leagues to the Westward of Chibucto, the particulars of which are contain'd in his inclos'd Deposition; and the day after Stanwood's falling in with this Fleet, Haskell another Master of a fishing Vessel discover'd it standing a right course for Chibucto about 8 Leagues to the westw^d. of it, & was chas'd by one of 'em according to the inclos'd Deposition; which Series of Intelligence, as no Vessel has arriv'd here yet from this Fleet (which must in all probability have happen'd had it come from England) compar'd with the Accounts in the English News Papers of the Brest Fleet's sailing, & the Intelligence gain'd from a french Prize lately taken by one of M^r. Townsend's Squadron near the Mouth of S^t. Lawrence, that she came out with the Brest Squadron & sail'd in Company with it eight days; the Account we had of two large french Ships being seen to go into Chibucto Harbour about two Months ago; the behavior of the French in Nova Scotia, & their declar'd Expectations of a large French Armament about this time, seems to make it very probable that these Ships may be part of the Brest Squadron, & that they have an immediate design upon Nova Scotia at least.—Hereupon I sent an Express Boat to Louisbourg to apprize Admiral Townsend & M^r. Knowles of it, & another to Annapolis Royal to give M^r. Mascarene Advice of it, & to let him know that I was embarking 300 Men for the Reinforcement of the Garrison under his Command (which is done & part of 'em sail'd) with a Promise of farther Succours, and to apprize him that from the publick Accounts in the English Prints we had reason to depend upon the speedy Arrival of Lieut^t. General S^t. Clair with the British Troops under his Command, & a Squadron

of his Majesty's Ships with 'em at Louisbourg; And as I have reason to think that an Apprehension generally prevails among the french Inhabitants of Nova Scotia, that they shall all of 'em soon be remov'd from their Settlements there without Distinction, which may have a bad Influence upon 'em in favour of the Enemy at this critical Time. I have wrote M^r. Mascarene a Letter (a copy of which I inclose to your Grace) which is translated into French, & printed, in order to be dispers'd among the french inhabitants, if M^r. Mascarene (to whose Discretion I have submitted it either to make Use of or suppress the printed Copies) shall be of Opinion that the Publication of it among 'em may be for his Majesty's Service.

"If the Fleet discover'd on the Cape Sable Coast should be Part of that from Brest, doubtless their visit to Nova Scotia has been encourag'd by the general Disposition of the Inhabitants, & the strength they will add to 'em for the Reduction of that Province, & afterwards for an Attempt upon Louisbourg (if they should think it adviseable to make one) as also for the defence of Canada. Should they succeed in an immediate Attempt upon Nova Scotia (which I should not be surpriz'd at) & General S^t. Clair with the Squadron expected from England should arrive in time for that purpose, I should propose attempting the immediate recovery of it out of the Enemy's hands this Year; For their holding that Province till they can fortify it and farther strengthen themselves there must be attended with very bad Consequences to his Majesty's Service, worse than may be immediately apprehended, & create no inconsiderabl Perplexities; at least it seems a clear point to me, that if the French should hold the Possession of Nova Scotia in Addition to Canada, the fate of Affairs in his Majesty's Northern Colonies will be suddenly alter'd in a surprizing manner & it will then soon be discern'd that the Mastery of the Northern Parts of this Continent, together with the Sources of Wealth & Power depending upon it, will be in a very fair way of being finally transfer'd to the Enemy.

"Upwards of two Months ago upon receiving Intelligence of the Appearance of two large French Ships being seen to go into Chibucto Harbour, M^r. Warren & I sent M^r. Townsend notice of it; But as we had not learn'd whether any Vessell had been sent from Louisbourg to look into that Harbour, I sent an arm'd Brigantine to make Discoveries there, which was hinder'd from proceeding thither as is before mention'd; & I have now sent a Schooner thither with a Person who has undertaken to go into it in a Whale boat high enough to make an exact discovery of the Enemy's strength (if any of their Ships are there) & to carry the Account to Louisbourg; But it seems possible if any of 'em have been there, that after landing some Troops and Stores at Chibucto, & getting what Intelligence they can from the Nova Scotians, their Ships may be gone to Canada; for which Place we have been inform'd that sixteen french Vessels, some of 'em Ships of War, had some time ago pass'd up the River of S^t. Laurence; & since that six other Vessels with Stores; so that it is very probable that Quebec is much better prepar'd to receive a Visit from his Majesty's Land & Sea Forces now than it was a little time ago."

SHIRLEY TO NEWCASTLE, 23 OCT. 1746.
(*Extract*.)

"It is agreed by all the Prisoners that the French have not fortify'd at Chebucto, nor sent any Troops from thence by Land to join the Canadeans; as also that M^r. Destonnel the chief D'escadre & Commandant upon the Death of the Duke D'Anville, who was of Opinion, to return to France after the Admiral's Death without attempting any thing, upon being over rul'd in a Council of War & having his Flagg struck, fell upon his Sword, & dy'd of his Wound as all of 'em say, except Sanders.

"It seems very observable from Sander's Declaration how ready a Disposition the Nova Scotians show'd to afford Refreshm^{ts}. & Pilots to the Enemy, & that they had signified to the french Ministry their readiness to join with any force they found send for the Reduction of his Majes$^{ty's}$ Garrison at Annapolis Royal. Also from the number of Engineers the French had with 'em that their Scheme was to hold & fortify Annapolis, for wch. Purpose it seems to be that the 50 brass Cannon were brought, rather than for raising Batteries against the Fort: and that from the Number of their small Arms, which they had with 'em to arm the Nova Scotians (doubtless) as well as the Indians, they had a dependance upon being join'd by them. Likewise the Apprehensions which prevail among the Nova Scotians that they are at present rather Neutrals than Subjects to the Crown of Great Britain. And I think it is not to be doubted now but that the principal Part of the french Scheme was the Reduction of Nova Scotia in the first Place.

"Upon the whole the sickly State of the French Fleet, w^c. is extremely ill mann'd, the hurry & Uneasiness they discover'd upon seeing the Contents of the Packets which fell into their hands, & precipitate departure from Chebucto, with their detaining the Flag of Truce & English Prisoners 'till they were got 30 Leagues from Chebucto, & then dismissing 'em with a Notion that their Fleet was going up the Bay of Fundy to Annapolis (instead of carrying 'em up there with 'em to prevent that's being known to us) makes it seem probable that the Enemy is making the best of their way to France or the West Indies, & was afraid of even M. Townsend's following 'em.

        "I am with the most dutiful Regard
        "My Lord Duke,
          "Your Grace's most Devoted
            "and most Obedient Servant
                "W. SHIRLEY."

SHIRLEY TO NEWCASTLE, BOSTON, 21 NOV. 1746.
(Extracts.)

"MY LORD DUKE,

"I am afraid your Grace will think, from my incessant Representations of the State of Nova Scotia, that I imagine that Province should be the sole Object of your Attention. Nothing could induce me to be so importunate with your Grace upon this Subject, but the fullest perswasion of the very great Importance of that Place to the Crown, & the British Subject, of the immediate bad Consequences of the Loss of it to his majesty's Service, & the imminent danger of its being lost, unless something is forthwith done for the effectual Security of it.

"The inclos'd Extract from M^r. Mascarene's Letter & Copy of Lieut^t. Colonel Gorham's will disclose in a great Measure to your Grace their Apprehensions, & the Condition of the Province: The number of the Enemy, are increas'd at Menis; they have again stop't all Communication between the Inhabitants & the Garrison, & are likely to keep footing there this Winter; and particularly from Col⁰. Gorham's Letter your Grace will perceive what Pains the Canadeans and Malcontents among the Inhabitants take to prevent my Letter lately dispers'd among 'em, in order to setle the Minds of the Inhabitants, (a Copy of which I have before sent your Grace) from having its proper Influence; & how the Nova Scotians are alarm'd at the Rumour of a design to remove 'em from their Settlements; And it appears to me by what I farther learn from Captain Fotheringham to whom Mʳ. Mascarene refers me in his Letter, that unless something vigorous, as that Letter intimates, is done by the Middle of April at farthest, the greatest Part of the Province at least will be in the hands of the Canadeans, and it will be too late then to attempt to reclaim the Inhabitants.

. . . .

"For the securing Nova Scotia from its present dangers I would further humbly propose it as my Opinion to be consider'd by your Grace, that if his Majesty should be pleas'd as soon as possibly might be after the Receipt of this, to cause it to be signified to the Inhabitants of Nova Scotia, that the Assurances lately given 'em by me of his Royal Protection to such of 'em as should behave dutifully and avoid all traiterous Correspondence with the Enemy at this Juncture (or to that Effect) were approv'd of by him, and should be made good to 'em, it would have a great Tendency to remove their present Apprehensions of being sent off with their Families from their Settlements in Nova Scotia, which seems to distress & perplex 'em; & effectually to prevent 'em from being drawn over to take up Arms against his Majesty, unless it should be some of the most obnoxious of 'em; which if his Majesty would be pleas'd to send over at the same time his special directions to apprehend, and proceed against, such a Proceeding against the Delinquents and gracious Declaration towards the others, would, I dare say, have a proper Effect for securing the general Fidelity of the Inhabitants, at least so far as to keep 'em from joining with the Enemy; And least the Succours now sent to Annapolis should not be a sufficient force to dislodge the Enemy this Winter, I would farther humbly propose it for your Graces' Consideration, that his Majesty's Orders should be forthwith sent to myself and the other three Governments of New England, that in case the Canadeans should not be withdrawn out of Nova Scotia, they should immediately cause the Soldiers rais'd in their respective Colonies & Provinces for his Majesty's Service in the Expedition against Canada to be transported to Annapolis Royal, as their Place of Rendezvous istead of Louisbourg, & to be employed in driving the Canadeans out of Nova Scotia, and be farther subjected to such Orders as his Majesty shall be pleas'd to signify in those Directions; and if this Order was to extend to the Governour of New York, it might not be an unnecessary Caution. I am apprehensive if such Orders are not sent, that the Attention of the several Governm^{ts}. to the Reduction of Crown Point might very much interfere with the Preservation of Nova Scotia, which is of infinitely more Consequence.

"These are the things which occur to me at present, & which I would submit to your Grace's Consideration, as what seems to require more immediate Dispatch; As to the danger of the french Fleet's early Return from the West Indies to Nova Scotia and what Strength of Ships may be necessary to protect that Province, Cape Breton, and the other Colonies against that Fleet, or any other french Armament which may be sent from Europe in the Spring to visit these Parts, I leave to Admiral Warren, who now goes to England in the Chester, and with whom, pursuant to the Directions of your Grace's two Letters to me in March & April last, I have acted in Concert upon all such Occasions as requir'd my consulting him with the greatest Satisfaction and Harmony, having had the Pleasure to find my own Sentiments agreable to his in all Matters of Consequence and a most hearty Disposition in him for his Majesty's Service, and to whom I have often talk'd over the Affairs of Nova Scotia.

. . . .

"I will avoid repeating what I have particularly mention'd to your Grace in late Letters concerning fortifying of Chebucto Harbour and building a Blockhouse or small Fort for 150 Men at Menis, with a Trading House there for the Indians, and a Blockhouse only at Canso for 100 Men, instead of new building and enlarging that at Annapolis Royal, and erecting a larger Fortification at Canso; which in my humble Opinion would greatly strengthen that Province, and together with the introducing of french Protestant Ministers, and English Schools, & some small Encouragement by Privileges to such as should conform to the Prtestant Religion, or send their Children to the English Schools, and Presents to the Indians with Supplies of all necessaries for 'em at the most reasonable Rates, in Exchange for their Furrs &c.; the Disallowance of the publick Exercise of the Roman Catholic Religion, at least after a short Term of Years, & forbidding Romish Priests under severe Penalties to come into the Country either among the Inhabitants or Indians; and if it might be consistent with his Majesty's Pleasure, a Civil Government to be in due time introduc'd among the Inhabitants; These things, I say, my Lord together with making Examples of the most obnoxious among the Inhabitants, and his Majesty's extending his Clemency and the Continuance of his Protection to the rest upon taking the proper Oath of Allegiance, seem to have the most promising Aspect for making good Subjects of the present Generation of Inhabitants, at least better than they are now and good Protestants of the next Generation of 'em; especially if there was to be a Mixture of English or other Protestants introduc'd among 'em, which the Invitation of a Civil Government to be set up among 'em would bid fair for doing; and the Trading House would create in the Indians a firm Dependance upon, and Attachment to his Majesty's Government, especially if a proper Protestant Missionary or two was supported to live among 'em at their head Quarters, as is the Method of the french Priests; by wch. means they gain so great an Ascendency over them.

"Just as I had finished the last Paragraph a Letter from Governor Knowles to Admiral Warren & myself, dated the 10th. Instant, was deliver'd to me, in which he informs me that 'he has given his Opinion in his Letters to your Grace, that it will be necessary to drive *all the French* (I suppose he means *Inhabitants*) out of Accadie (Nova Scotia) in the Spring, and that he hopes he shall have Orders to assist in doing it, if Admiral Warren does not go upon the Expedition to Quebeck, which he apprehends is rendred more difficult than it was, by such a Number of Ships being got safe up to Quebeck this Year, as no doubt they have carried all manner of warlike Stores.' And in his Letter to me of the 24th. of October he says 'if his Majesty should be pleas'd to transport the Rebels who are Objects of his Mercy, & encourage other Highland Families to come over, he thinks the Colony of Nova Scotia would soon be repeopled;' which it is possible he may have also propos'd to your Grace as in his Opinion the best Method of peopling that Colony, after the present french Inhabitants are drove off.

"As the Sentiments, which I have taken the Liberty to offer to your Grace upon this Subject, happen to be something different from M^r. Knowles's, I think it may not only be proper but my Duty to mention the Reasons of my preferring the Scheme for attempting to make the present french Inhabitants good Subjects to his Majesty, and keeping 'em in the Country, to that of driving 'em off & introducing some of the Rebels and other Highlanders in their Room.

"It seems very difficult to drive all the Inhabitants of Accadie out of so large a Province as that is, and which consists chiefly of Woods; It is most probable that many of the hardiest Men would retire (for some time at least) with their Cattle into the Woods, & form Parties with the Indians; and the remainder would doubtless retreat with their Families to Canada: Those, who are acquainted with the Indian Manner of Life & making War know that one hundred of 'em under Cover of the Woods can confine a very large Frontier within their Garrison,s even tho' they have Companies continually scouting between one Garrison and another: this is at present the Case of this Province & the other Colonies of New England & New York, tho' the People there are us'd to the Woods, & the Skulking of the Indians behind the Bushes & in Ditches with their other Wiles, & have large numbers of the Militia constantly upon Guard for their Protection; their Cattle is continually destroy'd; if any of 'em venture out into their Fields, they are frequently kill'd & scalp'd; and sometimes not only single Families or Garrisons are surpriz'd and cut off, as has happen'd lately in this Province, but even whole Villages, as was the Case of Sarahtoga in New York a few Months ago; so that those of the french Inhabitants, who should mix with the Indians in the Woods, would have it in their Power to put his Majesty's Garrison under such Circumstances as that it could not possibly subsist longer in the Country than they could do it without fresh Provisions, Wood & other Materials & Supplies from thence; from all which they would be wholly cut off, when the Inhabitants were drove away; And as to such of the Inhabitants, who should go with their Families to Canada, it must be expected that a very large Body of the Men would return arm'd next Spring with some Canadeans to join the Indians; from all which it seems justly to be apprehended that an Attempt to drive all the french Inhabitants from their Settlements, should it succeed, would in Effect be driving 5 or 6000 Men to take up Arms against his Majesty's Government there very Year during the War; make the reclaiming of the Indians of Nova Scotia impracticable, render it impossible for his Majesty's Garrison there to subsist long in the Country in time of War even with the Indians only; Besides, the Addition of about 6000 fighting Men with their Families to Canada, which would greatly strengthen the French upon this Continent, and would entail upon the Posterity of those who are thus expell'd (for several Generations at least) a Desire of recovering their former Possessions in Nova Scotia, seems to be no inconsiderable Matter, but what next to the Loss of the Country should be avoided on the Part of his Majesty, & is I dare say an Event, which the French next to their Acquisition of this Colony would desire: It is indeed now to be wish'd that General Nicholson had upon the first Reduction of the Colony to the Obedience to the Crown of Great Britain, remov'd the french Inhabitants, when they were but a few, out of the Country, as was done at Louisbourg; and that during the Interval of Peace the Colony had been planted with Protestant Subjects; But after their having remain'd so long in the Country upon the foot of British Subjects under the Sanction of the treaty of Utrecht, and making Improvements on their Lands for one or two Generations, and being grown up into such a Number of Families, to drive 'em all off their Settlements without farther Inquiry seems to be liable to many Objections. Among others it may be doubted whether under the Circumstances of these Inhabitants it would clearly appear to be a just Usage of 'em; it is true that the Notion of their Neutrality (which seems to have been entertain'd for some time by the English as well as themselves) is ill-grounded, and does not comport with the Terms of their Allegiance to his Majesty, to which such of 'em as chose to remain in the Province are bound by the treaty of Utrecht; whereby the french King yielded up the Inhabitants as well as the Soil of Accadie, and together with their Persons transferred their Allegiance to the Crown of Great Britain; But if it is consider'd that this Notion was founded upon an Act of the late Lieut^t Governour Armstrong then the residing Commander in Chief of the Province, whereby he took upon himself to grant 'em by a Writing under his Hand an Exemption from bearing Arms upon any Account whatever, on their consenting to take an Oath of Allegiance to his present Majesty, which, whether it was done by him with, or without Authority, appear'd at least to them to be authentick; it may perhaps be deem'd too rigorous a Punishment for their behavior grounded on such a Mistake, to involve the innocent with the Guilty in the Loss of their Estates, and the Expulsion of their Families out of the Country; it is not improbable but that there may be many among 'em who would even prefer his Majesty's Governm^t. to a french one, & have done nothing to deserve such a Forfeiture; Some Allowances may likewise be made for their bad Situation between the Canadeans, Indians & English, the Ravages of all which they have felt by Turns in the Course of the War; during which they seem to have been continually plac'd between two fires, the force and Menaces of the Canadeans & Indians plundering 'em of whatever they wanted, & deterring 'em in the strongest manner from having any Communiction with his Majesty's Garrison, on the one hand; and the Resentm^{ts} of the Garrison for their withholding their Intelligence & Supplies on the other, tho' at the same time it was not in a Condition to protect 'em from the Enemy; Wherefore it seems a Matter worthy of your Grace's Consideration, whether under such doubtful Circumstances the driving all the French Inhabitants of Nova Scotia off their Settlements, and thereby very greatly strengthening the Enemy upon this Continent, not only against the Garrison in present, but finally against all the British Colonies there, and depopulating one of his Majesty's Provinces for some time (how long may be uncertain) is more eligible than treating 'em as Subject, confining their Punishm^t to the most guilty & dangerous among 'em, & keeping the rest in the Country, and endeavouring to make them & their Posterity useful Members of Society under his Majesty's Government: I can't omit likewise observing to your Grace, that it would be exceeding difficult to fill up the Chasm which driving off the Inhabitants would make in the Country; During the Rupture with France it would certainly be impracticable, and I doubt whether it would not be so when Peace shall be made with France, if the Indians should continue at War with us; For what Number of Families can be propos'd to begin a Settlemᵗ. in the Country, after the Expulsion of the French Inhabitants, with safety against the Indians, & which would be continually expos'd to be destroyed by 'em, whilst they were carrying on their Settlements; They must expect no Protection against the Indians from within the Garrison, out of the Reach of their great Guns; the Company of Rangers, which live without the Walls of the Fort, would afford more of that than a thousand Garrison Soldiers would do: Whereas if the Stock of french Inhabitants was continued in the Country, an Accommodation with the Indians would be more easily brought about and preserv'd, they would be a Cover for any Number of Families that might be introduc'd among 'em whilst they were carrying on Settlements; & secure to the Garrison its necessary Supplies of fresh Provisions, Fuel, Materials for repairing the Works, & Stores of Sorts that the Country affords.

"As to repeopling the Province with some of the late Rebels and other Highland Families, it seems much to be doubted whether it might not be too hazardous to fill that Colony, wᶜʰ. should be the Barrier of all his Majesty's Colonies upon this Continent, with a Set of poor, ignorant, deluded Wretches just come out of a most unnatural Rebellion; that from their Neighbourhood to Canada would be continually expos'd to the Artifices and Attempts of french Romish Priests upon 'em who it is reasonable to think would not fail to instill the same Notions into 'em in America, which seduc'd 'em from their Allegiance in Great Britain, with a Promise of more effectual Support & Protection from the French here, than they had in the Highlands; Indeed, my Lord, this seems to be a dangerous experiment, and what might produce the worst of Consequences.

"I beg leave to submit it to your Grace's Consideration, whether the most staunch Protestants, & Families the most zealously affected to his Majesty's Government, a Number at least of such, should not rather, if possible, be transplanted there as soon as may be; I could wish four or five hundred of 'em could be induc'd to go from some Part of New England; I think from the Experience I had of the Inhabitants of this Province at least upon the late Alarm given by the french Fleet, I might safely venture to be answerable to his Majesty, that if I had suggested in my late Orders for assembling a Body of 'em under Arms in Boston from all Parts of this Province to oppose any Attempt of the Enemy, that there was a design of landing a Son of the Pretender's here, it would not have been possible to have kept any one Man, who was capable of marching hither, from appearing under Arms with the most determin'd Resolution of hazarding his Life to the utmost in defence of his Majesty's Governm^t.; And as the late Appearances of a fondness for removing from hence to Cape Breton seem to be quite vanished at present, I should not be without hopes of some families removing from these Parts to Nova Scotia upon due Encouragement; Protestants likewise from among the Swiss Cantons, & other Northern Parts in Germany, who are generally bred up in the Exercise of arms, and make sober and industrious Settlers, might be safely trusted in Accadie; Great Numbers of 'em yearly flock into Pensilvania, whereby the Inhabitants of that Province are almost incredibly increas'd within these twenty Years; And from the behavior of the Irish coming out of the Northern Parts of Ireland hither, a Number of which is setled in the Eastern Parts of this Province, I should think they too might be safely trusted in Nova Scotia; and it is certain that these poor unhappy Highlanders (I mean such of 'em as may be design'd to be transported into the Plantations) would be more safely dispos'd of among the four Governm^{ts}. of New England, or in New York & the Jerseys, where they would not be in danger either of corrupting the Inhabitants, or being again seduc'd themselves, but might make useful Subjects to his Majesty.

"I hope, my Lord, I shall be excus'd if I have gone beyond my Line in submitting these Observations to your Grace, at a time when the fate of one of his Majesty's Northern Colonies, the most important of 'em all to the Crown in many respects, as I apprehend, and which will be in the hands of the french the Key to all the other British Colonies upon this Continent, & even to Cape

Breton, And in his Majesty's Possession the Barrier of
'em against the Enemy seems to come to a Crisis."

SHIRLEY TO NEWCASTLE, BOSTON, NEW ENGLAND,
27 FEBRUARY, 1747.

"MY LORD DUKE,

"I am sorry that I am now to Acquaint your Grace with
the Advices I receiv'd last night by Express from Nova
Scotia giving me an Account that the Detachment of
Troops under the Command of Lieut. Colonel Noble,
which I Inform'd your Grace in my last of the 21st. instant
had taken possession of Minas, and had kept it near two
months, was for want of a proper Security for the Men
and Intelligence from the Inhabitants surpriz'd on the 31st.
of January last at three o'Clock in the morning by between
5 & 600 Canadeans & Indians in which Lieut. Colo. Noble
with four Officers more and about 80 men were killed, and
three Officers and about 60 Men were wounded and taken
prisoners before it was light enough for our people to get
together; they however obliged the Enemy, upwards of 20
of whom were kill'd, and about 15 wounded, to allow 'em
an honourable Capitulation, a Copy of which I inclose to
your Grace together with the Account given of this Affair
by the Officer who was Commandant of the Detachment
at the time of the Capitulation, & Extracts from Lieut.
Gouvernour Mascarene's Letter to me upon this Subject,
from whence I choose your Grace should receive the Accot.
in the same light it has been Conveyed to me in, and which
upon the best Inquiry I can make, seems to be a just one.
I also Inclose to your Grace an Extract from Col. Noble's
Letter to me dated two days before his death, giving me
an Account of the Situation of Affairs then at Minas; from
whence your Grace will perceive that even then he was in
Expectation of being Join'd by the Rhode Island Forces &
the Company from this Province, which had the Misfortune
to be Shipreck'd; and that, had they arriv'd at Annapolis,
and the New Hampshire Companies had not return'd home
without acting, the Enemy would in all probability have
been drove out of Nova Scotia, and every good purpose,
which I had propos'd, been answer'd before this time. As
it is I shall use my best Endeavours forthwith to fit out a
sufficient force by Sea to destroy Mr. Ramsay's Vessels at

Schiegnecto, and recover our own by Spring, & to send M^r. Mascarene such a Reinforcement of Troops as may still drive the Enemy out of Nova Scotia by the same time and prevent any bad Consequences from the late Accident there, which seems necessary to be done (if possible) and I shall hope to succeed in, if the neighbouring Governments of New England will assist in, which I shall urge 'em to do.

"I likewise inclose the Answer of the Inhabitants of Minas to the French Letter which I some time ago Inform'd your Grace I sent M^r. Mascarene last Fall, and a Paragraph out of one of his Letters to me upon the same matter; whereby your Grace will perceive that that Letter seems to have had an happy Effect upon the Inhabitants at a most critical Conjuncture.

"The late Secresy of the Inhabitants of Minas with regard to the Enemys Motions, and the very certain Intelligence which the Enemy gain'd of the particular Quarters of the English Officers, notwithstanding their Supplying the King's Troops with Provisions, and the Curtesy of their Behavior to 'em before this Surprize, and their professions of being sorry for it afterwards seems to shew the necessity of his Majesty's Keeping a strong Blockhouse there with a Garrison of 150 men; And the constant ill behavior of the Inhabitants of Schiegnecto seems to make another Blockhouse with a like Garrison there equally necessary, as I at first propos'd to your Grace from Louisbourg; and these two with a Fort and Garrison at Chebucto of 300 Men at least, and the continuance of a Garrison of 300 at Annapolis Royal as it is at present, with a strong Blockhouse at Canso garrison'd with 100 Men would through the constant Correspondence that might be kept up between the several Garrisons be an effectual Security to the Province against the Enemy, and oblige the Inhabitants in a little time to contribute towards the protection & Expence of the Government, and for ever frustrate any hopes the French could Entertain of making themselves Masters of it, by their constant Endeavours to Seduce the Inhabitants from their Allegiance; all which would make Nova Scotia really His Majesty's which it seems scarcely to have been yet: And I would Submit it to your Grace's Consideration whether a Company of Rangers consisting of 100 Indians, or rather two Companies, consisting of 50 each, one to be posted at the Blockhouse at Minas, and the other in Schiegnecto

would not be of the greatest Service, in Scouting thro'
every part of the Province and in the Woods upon all
Emergencies (for which the Regular Troops are by no
means fit) and particularly in preventing the French from
Introducing Men from Canada into the Province by the
Bay Vert; I think the great Service which Lieu^t Colonel
Gorham's Company of Rangers has been of to the Garrison at Annapolis Royal, is a demonstration of the Use-
fulness of such a Corps, besides that it may be a means
of bringing Indians out of the French Interest into his
Majesty's Service, and go far towards reclaiming 'em in
general; especially if (as I have before propos'd for your
Grace's Consideration) two Trading or Truck Houses were
to be maintain'd one at Minas, and the other at Chiegnecto,
for supplying the Indians with all necessaries in Exchange
for furrs, and proper presents were made to 'em in the
manner which the French use to Keep 'em in their Interest.

"And if your Grace would allow me the Freedom to offer
my Sentiments concerning what appears to me to be farther
necessary for putting this important Province of Nova
Scotia (I think I may justly call it the most important to the
Crown of any upon his Continent) in Security, I sho'd
propose one of His Majesty's Arm'd Sloops (or Snows)
with a Tender to be constantly employ'd in the Bay of
Fundy for visiting all parts of it upon every occasion, as
well as the several Harbours on the Cape Sable Coast; and
one of his Majesty's Frigates to be employ'd for the protection of the Fishery at Canso (as was always usual in time
of peace) which together with a Tender would also be of
great Service in duly attending the Bay Verte, upon every
Occasion, and likewise visiting the Coast of Accadie (or
Cape Sables) besides protecting the Fishery.

"Since writing the last Paragraph I have heard of some
other particular circumstances, which make it very sus-
picious that several of the Inhabitants at least of Minas
knew of the Enemy's Motions, & I find that it is the general
Opinion of the Officers that they did.

"I am with the most dutiful Regard,

"My Lord Duke,

"Your Grace's most devoted,

"& most humble Servant

"W. SHIRLEY"

SHIRLEY TO NEWCASTLE, BOSTON, APRIL 29TH, 1747.
(*Extract.*)

"MY LORD DUKE,

"Since finishing Governour Knowles's, & my joint Letter
to your Grace I have learn'd from one of the English Prisoners just Arriv'd from Schiegnecto in Exchange for one
of the French Prisoners sent by me from Boston, and who
was carry'd Captive from Minas, where he was taken by the
Enemy in the late Surprize, that when the Canadeans went
from Minas to Schiegnecto they march'd out of the Grand
Prè about 500, but were reduc'd to about 350 before they
reach'd Schiegnecto, by several of their party's leaving 'em
at every great Village in Minas, thro' which they pass'd
which makes it Evident that 150 of the Inhabitants of that
District had Join'd the Canadeans in their late Attack upon
the English at Grand Prè, and may Serve farther to shew
your Grace the imminent Danger of all the Inhabitants of
Minas's still Joining the Enemy, unless speedy measures are
taken for driving the Canadeans out of the Country, and
Securing the fidelity of the Inhabitants in some better manner than it is at present; and how opportunely the forces
sent last Winter from hence to Annapolis, and the Assurances I took the liberty of sending the Nova Scotians
that those, who behav'd as good Subjects, sho'd have His
Majesty's protection in their Estates, arriv'd there for saving the whole District of Minas from an open Revolt.

"This fluctuating State of the Inhabitants of Accadie
seems, my Lord, naturally to arise from their finding a
want of due protection from His Majesty's Government;
and their Apprehensions that the French will soon be
Masters of the Province, which their repeated Attempts
every year for the Reduction of His Majesty's Fort at
Annapolis Royal, and the Appearance of the late Duke
D'Anville's Squadron from France upon their Coast with
that View strongly Impress upon 'em, as does also the
Residence of the Enemy in the Province, and the Sollici-
tations of their own Priests; and to this, I believe, may be
added some Jealousy, which the Enemy and Priests are for
ever instilling into 'em, that the English want only a safe
Opportunity of driving all the French Inhabitants off their
Settlements; which tho' Mr. Mascarene assures me that his
communicating to 'em my printed Letter promising 'em

His Majesty's protection, had so far allay'd as together
with the Arrival of the late Detachment of Soldiers sent
from hence in the Winter for the Defence & protection of
the Province, to disappoint M^r. de Ramsay's Attempt upon
the Inhabitants of Minas for bringing 'em to an open
Revolt, and to make him retire from Minas to Schiegnecto,
yet as the hopes my Letter may have made 'em entertain
have not been yet Confirm'd by Assurances of His Majesty's
Royal protection directly from England I cant but think,
there is a most apparant danger of Nova Scotia's being soon
lost, if the Expedition against Canada should not proceed
this year, nor any Measures be taken, or particular Orders
be sent by His Majesty for Securing the Province against
the Enemy & strengthening his Government among the
Inhabitants, For I perceive that the General Assembly of
this Province, from whence only the Succors & Support
which His Majesty's Garrison at Annapolis Royal has
hitherto received for the Protection & Defence of Nova
Scotia, have been sent, are tir'd of having 'em drawn wholly
from their own people, and despair of its being effectual
without His Majesty's more immediate Interposition for
the protection of that province; And I look upon it as a
very happy Incident, that I had it in my power to send M^r.
Mascarene the Support, I did the last Winter, and beginning
of the Spring, out of the Levies rais'd for the Expedition
against Canada, which I insisted upon doing as they were
in His Majesty's Pay (tho' rais'd for another Service) but
should not have been able to do it (I believe) had it depended wholly upon the Consent of the Assembly, tho'
generally well dispos'd for His Majesty's Service."

NEWCASTLE TO SHIRLEY, 30 MAY, 1747.
(*Extract.*)

"As you and M^r. Warren have represented, That an
Opinion prevailed amongst the Inhabitants of Nova Scotia,
That It was intended to remove Them from their Settlements and Habitations in that Province; And as that Report
may probably have been artfully spread amongst Them in
order to induce Them to withdraw Themselves from their
Allegiance to His Majesty, and to take Part with the
Enemy; His Majesty thinks it necessary, That proper measures should be taken, to remove any such ill-grounded Sug-

gestions; and, for that Purpose, It is the King's Pleasure, That you should declare in some publick and authentick manner to His Majesty's Subjects, Inhabitants of that Province, That there is not the least Foundation for any Apprehension of that nature; But That, on the contrary, It is His Majesty's Resolution to protect, and maintain, all such of Them as shall continue in their Duty, and Allegiance to His Majesty, in the quiet & peaceable Possession of their respective Habitations, and Settlements And That They shall continue to enjoy the free Exercise of their Religion.

"His Majesty did propose to have signed a Proclamation to the purport above mentioned and to have transmitted it to you, to have been published in Nova Scotia; But as the Advices, that have been received here, of a Body of the New England Troops, which were advanced to Menis having been surprised by a Party of the French Canadeans and their Indians, and having been either cut off, or taken Prisoners; And the great Probability there is, That this Misfortune could not have happened to that Body of Troops, without the Assistance or, at least, Connivance of the Inhabitants of Nova Scotia; make it very difficult to fix the Terms of the intended Proclamation; His Majesty thinks it more advisable to leave it to you to make such a Declaration in His Name, as you shall be of Opinion, the present Circumstances of the Province may require."

SHIRLEY TO NEWCASTLE, 8 JUNE, 1747.
(*Extract.*)

"I have nothing to add to my Letters, which I have lately transmitted to your Grace, except that Mʳ. de Ramsay is still at Chiegnecto with his party in Expectation of a Reinforcement from Canada, and the Arrival of an Armament from France, and that he has not thought fit to venture again to Manis [*Mines*], but insists in his Messages to the Inhabitants there that they should look upon themselves as Subjects to the French King since the New England Troops were oblig'd to retire out of their District by Capitulation, but that this has had no Effect upon the Inhabitants, the Reinforcement, which I sent there afterwards, having taken repossession of Manis, and hoisted the King's Flagg there, and the Deputies of Manis having thereupon renew'd their Oaths of Fidelity to His Majesty at Annapolis Royal; I continue the last Reinforcement at the Garrison still for the Security of that and Manis; But it is not strong enough to drive the French from Schiegnecto, it being suspected that the Inhabitants of that District, who were ever refractory to His Majesty's Government, would not scruple to Join the Enemy in case of an attack upon 'em; And I could not think it adviseable for me to send all the Forces, which I had rais'd for the Expedition against Canada within this Government upon another Service (as I must have done to have been strong enough to force the Enemy out of Schiegnecto after the Action at Minas) when I was in daily Expectation of receiving His Majesty's Commands concerning the prosecution of the intended expedition, and besides, the Assembly, which has been at a great Expense for the raising of the men for the service of the Expedition only, strongly insisted upon my reserving 1500 of 'em to go against Crown Point, as your Grace will perceive by the inclos'd Copy of their Answer to my Message; However the several Reinforcements, which I did send to Annapolis, have preserv'd the Garrison and province from falling into the Enemys hands the last year, and not only made the Enemy quit Manis, but still Confine 'em to Schiegnecto; and had the Rhode Island & New Hampshire Troops Join'd the Massachusetts Forces at Manis, as was propos'd, and both those Governments promis'd me they should, and one of the Massachusetts Companies had not been lost in their passage, we should have been strong enough (I am perswaded) to have drove the Enemy the last Winter quite out of the Province of Nova Scotia: As it is, I doubt not, if no Armament arrives from France, we shall be able to keep 'em out of Annapolis and Manis till I receive His Majesty's Commands, which I am in daily Expectation of, and will, I hope, Enable me to take effectual Measures for getting rid of the Enemy and Securing the Province against their Attempts for the future."

SHIRLEY TO NEWCASTLE, BOSTON, 25 JUNE, 1747.
(*Extract.*)

"MY LORD DUKE,

"Since my last to your Grace, I have Accounts from Nova Scotia, that the French have rais'd a Battery of Nine

Guns on the back of Schiegnecto to oppose the landing of
Forces from Bay Verte, that they were also building a Fort
& had landed Cannon & Mortars there, which they were
now hawling by Land, and may use either for Fortifying
that District, or transport from thence to Annapolis Royal
for the Reduction of his Majesty's Garrison; There has
been likewise further Accounts from thence that the Inhabitants were in Expectation of 1000 Men from Canada,
which together with the Indians & People of Schiegnecto,
& some of Manis, it is said, would make up M^r. De
Ramsay's Party 5000, who were then to proceed against
Annapolis; and that three large French Ships of Force had
been seen in Bay Verte, vizt. two from Canada & one from
France and landed Troops & Stores. These Accounts gain
Credit the more easily as it seems not to be doubted, but
that the French have the Reduction of Nova Scotia extremely at heart, and will be continually making some
Attempt or other against it, whilst the Warr lasts; and I
am sorry to find by a Message lately sent me from the
Assembly desiring I would recall the Soldiers, I last sent
to Annapolis, that they seem out of heart about the effectual Preservation of it from the Enemy. Should the French
gain it by any sudden Stroke, I am perswaded, they would
be so strong there by the Addition of all the Inhabitants to
their other Forces, as well as the Numbers they would
draw from Canada, & by immediate Fortifications of it,
that it would require a very considerable Armament &
Number of Troops to recover it from 'em; which makes me
think it my Indispensable Duty to trouble your Grace with
so frequent a Repetition of my Apprehensions concerning
it. The enemy may indeed be now look'd upon as Masters
of Scheignecto which Place it is evident they are busy in
fortifying; & would have been so likewise of Manis by this
time, had they not been oblig'd to withdraw their Troops
from thence last Fall by the Arrival of the Detachments, I
sent there."

SHIRLEY TO NEWCASTLE, 8 JULY, 1747.
(*Extract.*)

"I shall now take the Liberty to submit to your Grace's
Consideration the most practicable Scheme, that occurs to
me at present for effectually driving & keeping the Cana-

deans out of Nova Scotia; vizt. if M^r. Knowles when the Season is too far advanc'd for the French to make an Attempt from France against Louisbourg, should detach 1000 Men out of that Garrison to be join'd by 2000 from New England at Annapolis Royal, and from thence to proceed to Schiegnecto; that Force would, I apprehend, drive the Enemy off, and easily make us Masters of all the Inhabitants of that District, who seem to have ever been so deeply engaged on the Side of the Enemy as to make 'em forfeit all pretence of right to hold their Possessions; and if the 2000 New England Men were to share among 'em that District upon Condition of their setling there with their Families in such a defensible manner as they should be directed to do, and the french Inhabitants of that District were to be transplanted into New England, and distributed among the four Governments there; That I apprehend might be a Settlement of the District of Schiegnecto strong enough to keep the Canadeans out, and to defend themselves against the Indians and the Inhabitants of the two other Districts of Nova Scotia, vizt. Menis & Annapolis, being thus lock'd up between the Settlement in Schiegnecto at one End, and his Majesty's Garrison at the other, and aw'd by the removal of the french Inhabitants of Schiegnecto from off their Lands, would be constantly held to their good behaviour, and by Intermarriages & the spreading of the English Settlement from Schiegnecto, the whole Province, or at least the greatest part of it, might in two or three Generations become English Protestants—I would add that such an Exchange of the present Inhabitants of Schiegnecto for New England Men, would make up to the four Colonies of New England the Loss of the Families propos'd to be remov'd from thence to Nova Scotia upon this Occasion hinder Canada's being strengthened by the Expulsion of the French from their Possessions, & prevent the English Settlement at Schiegnecto from being harrass'd by their continual Attempts to recover their former Lands; And the Encouragement given to the New England Men by the propos'd Distribution of the Lands among 'em would besides make the raising of 2000 Men for this Service much more practicable, & less expensive to the Crown.

"Upon the whole, my Lord, if the War continues, unless some measures are very suddenly taken for the better

Security of Nova Scotia, there seems to be great danger that that Province will not long remain his Majesty's.

> "I am with the most dutiful regard,
> "My Lord Duke,
> "Your Grace's most devoted and
> "most Obedient Servant
> "W Shirley."

Shirley to Newcastle, 24 August, 1747.

"My Lord Duke,

"The French Declaration, of which the inclos'd is a Copy, did not come to my hands till I had finished the letter, wch. accompanies it: And I send it your Grace, as it may serve to shew the Views of the French with respect to Accadie, the Dependance they have upon the Dispositions of the Inhabitants, what advantage they propos'd to themselves from the New England Levies under the Command of the late Lieutent. Col. Noble's quitting Menis by Capitulation, and the necessity there was of my sending the last Detachment of soldiers to Mr. Mascarene to take repossession of Menis, and make the Inhabitants of it renew their oath of fidelity to his Majesty; which had its desired Effect.

> "I am with the most Dutifull regard
> "My Lord Duke,
> "Your Grace's Most Devoted,
> "and Most Obedient Humble Servant
> "W Shirley."

Shirley to Newcastle, 20 Oct. 1747.
(Extract.)

"The general Inclination which, the french Inhabitants of Nova Scotia have to the french Interest, proceeds from their Ties of Consanguinity to the French of Canada, but more especially from those of their Religion, which last seems to put 'em greatly under the Influence of their Priests, who continually receive their Directions from the Bishop of Quebeck, & are the Instruments, by which the Governour of Canada makes all his Attempts for the Reduction of the Province to the french Crown, & Keeps the Indians of Nova Scotia (commonly called the Cape Sable

Indians) in their Dependence upon him; particular Instances of which may be given in the first Body of French & Indians, which attack'd the King's Garrison soon after the Declaration of the present War's being headed by a Priest of Nova Scotia; and the principal Part in giving Intelligence to the Enemy, maintaining the Correspondence between Canada and Nova Scotia, assembling Cape Sable Indians, & influencing such of the Inhabitants as had joined with or assisted the Enemy, has been manag'd by another Priest of that Province; Other Instances of this Kind might be given, as particularly the Attempt to bring the Inhabitants into Revolt soon after the late Surprize at Menis by endeavouring to influence 'em with the Authority of the Bishop of Quebeck pronouncing 'em to be free from their Oath of Allegiance to his Majesty. But I shall content myself with observing to your Grace only one piece of Policy made use of by the french Priests in Nova Scotia for preserving the whole Body of the People intirely french, and Roman Catholick's, vizt. forbidding all Inter-marriages with the English under Pain of Excommunication, (of which I am informed there has been one or two late Instances in actual Excommunication upon this Occasion) & which has had so general an Effect as to prevent the Settlement of any one English Family within the Province, from the first Reduction of it to the present time, tho' some have atempted to setle in the Country; & to Keep out Inter-marriages between the French & his Majesty's English Subjects, as that I never heard of any one Instance besides the before mentioned ones; And I would humbly submit it to your Grace's Consideration if the free Exercise of the Roman Catholick Religion and an unlimited Toleration of Roman Priests in Nova Scotia should continue to have the same Effect in that Colony for the next succeeding forty years, as it has had within these last forty; the Inhabitants there are suffer'd to remain a distinct Body of French in the Neighbourhood of Canada, with the Ties of Consanguinity & Religion between *them* & the Canadeans still growing stronger, untill they double or perhaps treble their Number (the French of Canada likewise at the same time increasing their Strength & Numbers) whether it may not prove in the End cherishing a Colony of Inhabitants of the subversion of the King's Government in it, & the strengthening of the french Interest upon the Continent.

"The Treaty of Utrecht, my Lord, by which the cession of Accadie (or Nova Scotia) with its Inhabitants was made to the Crown of Great Britain does not seem to lay his Majesty under an Obligation to allow the french Inhabitants the Exercise of the Roman Catholick Religion; and as his Majesty is as yet under no Promise to do it, I should hope that Methods might be found for weakening the Ties of Consanguinity & Religion between even the present Generation of the french inhabitants of Nova Scotia & those of Canada, by beginning new ones between his Majesty's English & french subjects there, and at the same time controuling the pernicious Power of the Romish Priests over the french Inhabitants & the Indians of that Province, which may possibly be cut off or at least obstructed by his Majesty's making a Promise to continue the french Inhabitants in the free Exercise of their Religion.

"Wherefore as his Majesty has been pleas'd to refer it to my Opinion to fix the Terms of the Declaration, which he has commanded me to make in his Name to the Inhabitants of Nova Scotia; whereby it became my Duty to avoid every thing in it, which appear'd to me to have a Tendency to disserve his Government within that Province, I have taken the Liberty to suspend promising 'em the free Exercise of the Romish Religion, tho' it is mention'd in your Grace's Letter to have been part of what was at first propos'd to have been included in his Majesty's intended Proclamation, till I could transmit my Sentiments to your Grace, and I should have his Majesty's farther Directions upon it; & have in the mean time made a Declaration of such Points, as seem'd necessary to be ascertained to the Inhabitants for quieting their Minds, & would not admit of Delay.

"I might mention to your Grace some local Reasons for my Omitting in the Declaration what I have done, but shall not presume to trouble you with any but what I thought it my indispendsable Duty to lay before your Grace.

"I am with the most dutiful Regard
"My Lord Duke,
"Your Grace's most Devoted
"and most Obedient Servant
"W SHIRLEY."

Index